HOLMAN
Old
Testament
Commentary

HOLMAN
Old Testament Commentary

Ecclesiastes, Song of Songs

GENERAL EDITOR
Max Anders

AUTHORS
David George Moore
and Daniel L. Akin

HOLMAN
REFERENCE

Nashville, Tennessee

ISBN 0–8054–9482–0
Dewey Decimal Classification: 223.8
Subject Heading: BIBLE. O.T. Ecclesiastes
BIBLE. O.T. Song of Songs

Ecclesiastes/David George Moore; Song of Songs/Daniel L. Akin
        p.   cm. — (Holman Old Testament commentary)
    Includes bibliographical references. (p.).
    ISBN
        1. Bible. O.T. —Commentaries.   I. Title.   II. Series.

—dc21

1 2 3 4 5 6   07 06 05 04 03
R

*T*o Doreen: After more than fifteen years of marriage, I am more in awe of God's wonderful work of grace in your life. Your friendship, wisdom in the ways of God, unflagging loyalty, steadfast affection for our boys, and many kindnesses make me proud to be your husband. You incarnate the "Proverbs 31 woman."

*T*o David Joseph and Christoper Daniel: Words are inadequate to convey the pride and delight Mommy and I have in raising you. Our prayer is that you would find your greatest joy in knowing Jesus.

David George Moore

*T*o Bill and Jane Cutrer whose friendship to Charlotte and me cannot be put into words and whose marriage beautifully mirrors the teaching of the Song.

Daniel L. Akin

Contents

Contents

Editorial Preface

Today's church hungers for Bible teaching, and Bible teachers hunger for resources to guide them in teaching God's Word. The Holman Old Testament Commentary provides the church with the food to feed the spiritually hungry in an easily digestible format. The result: new spiritual vitality that the church can readily use.

Bible teaching should result in new interest in the Scriptures, expanded Bible knowledge, discovery of specific scriptural principles, relevant applications, and exciting living. The unique format of the Holman Old Testament Commentary includes sections to achieve these results for every Old Testament book.

Opening quotations stimulate thinking and lead to an introductory illustration and discussion that draw individuals and study groups into the Word of God. "In a Nutshell" summarizes the content and teaching of the chapter. Verse-by-verse commentary answers the church's questions rather than raising issues scholars usually admit they cannot adequately solve. Bible principles and specific contemporary applications encourage students to move from Bible to contemporary times. A specific modern illustration then ties application vividly to present life. A brief prayer aids the student to commit his or her daily life to the principles and applications found in the Bible chapter being studied. For those still hungry for more, "Deeper Discoveries" take the student into a more personal, deeper study of the words, phrases, and themes of God's Word. Finally, a teaching outline provides transitional statements and conclusions along with an outline to assist the teacher in group Bible studies.

It is the editors' prayer that this new resource for local church Bible teaching will enrich the ministry of group, as well as individual, Bible study, and that it will lead God's people truly to be people of the Book, living out what God calls us to be.

Acknowledgments

I have incurred many debts in writing my commentary on Ecclesiastes. I gratefully acknowledge those who have offered assistance, guidance, and always love.

Max Anders, the general editor for this series, kindly invited me to contribute. His enthusiasm and conscientiousness fueled mine. Steve Bond, my editor at Broadman & Holman, responded quickly to my many inquiries. Steve's efficiency and gracious spirit relieved me of many burdens.

I am privileged to write and speak under the auspices of *Two Cities Ministries*. Many thanks to past and present board members who provide sage counsel and support: Joel Altsman, Jane Backus, Roger Berry, Tom Bognanno, Mark Cotnam, Gilbert Hooper, David Lill, Suzanne Schutze, and Trudy Smith. Many friends have financially supported the ministry. To all I owe hearty and humble thanks.

Over the years I have taught the Book of Ecclesiastes in a variety of settings. There are simply too many to recall, but a few bear special mention: the Sigma Chi House at Stanford University, Grace Covenant Church, Westlake Bible Church, Camelback Bible Church, Grace Bible Fellowship, Austin Christian Fellowship, Westlake Hills Presbyterian Church, KIXL radio, and the Veritas Forum.

Four men, Roger Berry, Warren Culwell, Darin Maurer, and Tim Taylor, have provided regular accountability, prayers, and many good laughs. My good friend of 25 years, Prof. Robert Pyne of Dallas Theological Seminary, is a consistent source of edifying and stimulating dialogue on the many issues that interest us. My dear friend Kurt Richardson "introduced" me to Scipio Africanus and always cheers me on.

Three couples, two from afar and one nearby, have provided much encouragement: John and Jane Freeman, O'Neill and Vickie McDonald, and Wylie and Alliene Vale.

My father and my sister Lisa have spurred me on with their many words of encouragement.

Barb Miaso, my secretary for ten years, has provided immeasurable help. Her competence and grace in converting thousands of pages of my pathetic scrawl to the computer is a thing of beauty.

—*David George Moore*

Holman Old Testament Commentary Contributors

Vol. 1, Genesis
ISBN 0-8054-9461-8
Kenneth O. Gangel
and Stephen J. Bramer

Vol. 2, Exodus, Leviticus, Numbers
ISBN 0-8054-9462-6
Glen Martin

Vol. 3, Deuteronomy
ISBN 0-8054-9463-4
Doug McIntosh

Vol. 4, Joshua
ISBN 0-8054-9464-2
Kenneth O. Gangel

Vol. 5, Judges, Ruth
ISBN 0-8054-9465-0
W. Gary Phillips

Vol. 6, 1 & 2 Samuel
ISBN 0-8054-9466-9
Stephen Andrews

Vol. 7, 1 & 2 Kings
ISBN 0-8054-9467-7
Gary Inrig

Vol. 8, 1 & 2 Chronicles
ISBN 0-8054-9468-5
Winfried Corduan

Vol. 9, Ezra, Nehemiah, Esther
ISBN 0-8054-9469-3
Knute Larson and Kathy Dahlen

Vol. 10, Job
ISBN 0-8054-9470-7
Steven J. Lawson

Vol. 11, Psalms 1–72
ISBN 0-8054-9471-5
Steven J. Lawson

Vol. 12, Psalms 73–150
ISBN 0-8054-9481-2
Steven J. Lawson

Vol. 13, Proverbs
ISBN 0-8054-9472-3
Max Anders

Vol. 14, Ecclesiastes, Song of Songs
ISBN 0-8054-9482-0
David George Moore and Daniel L. Akin

Vol. 15, Isaiah
ISBN 0-8054-9473-1
Trent C. Butler

Vol. 16, Jeremiah, Lamentations
ISBN 0-8054-9474-X
Fred M. Wood and Ross McLaren

Vol. 17, Ezekiel
ISBN 0-8054-9475-8
Mark F. Rooker

Vol. 18, Daniel
ISBN 0-8054-9476-6
Kenneth O. Gangel

Vol. 19, Hosea, Joel, Amos, Obadiah, Jonah, Micah
ISBN 0-8054-9477-4
Trent C. Butler

Vol. 20, Nahum, Habakkuk, Zephaniah, Haggai, Zechariah, Malachi
ISBN 0-8054-9478-2
Stephen R. Miller

Holman New Testament Commentary Contributors

Vol. 1, Matthew
ISBN 0-8054-0201-2
Stuart K. Weber

Vol. 2, Mark
ISBN 0-8054-0202-0
Rodney L. Cooper

Vol. 3, Luke
ISBN 0-8054-0203-9
Trent C. Butler

Vol. 4, John
ISBN 0-8054-0204-7
Kenneth O. Gangel

Vol. 5, Acts
ISBN 0-8054-0205-5
Kenneth O. Gangel

Vol. 6, Romans
ISBN 0-8054-0206-3
Kenneth Boa and William Kruidenier

Vol. 7, 1 & 2 Corinthians
ISBN 0-8054-0207-1
Richard L. Pratt Jr.

Vol. 8, Galatians, Ephesians, Philippians, Colossians
ISBN 0-8054-0208-X
Max Anders

Vol. 9, 1 & 2 Thessalonians, 1 & 2 Timothy, Titus, Philemon
ISBN 0-8054-0209-8
Knute Larson

Vol. 10, Hebrews, James
ISBN 0-8054-0211-X
Thomas D. Lea

Vol. 11, 1 & 2 Peter, 1, 2, 3 John, Jude
ISBN 0-8054-0210-1
David Walls and Max Anders

Vol. 12, Revelation
ISBN 0-8054-0212-8
Kendell H. Easley

Holman Old Testament Commentary

Twenty volumes designed for Bible study and teaching to enrich the local church and God's people.

Series Editor	Max Anders
Managing Editor	Steve Bond
Project Editor	Dean Richardson
Product Development Manager	Ricky D. King
Marketing Manager	Stephanie Huffman
Executive Editor	David Shepherd
Page Composition	TF Designs, Greenbrier, TN

Introduction to

Ecclesiastes

A PERSONAL NOTE ABOUT THIS STUDY

It is a great privilege to write this commentary because Ecclesiastes is one of my favorite books of the Old Testament. It has ministered to me in many wonderful ways over the past twenty years.

My enthusiasm for Ecclesiastes is not unique. Peter Kreeft said that Ecclesiastes is the book that caused him at the ripe old age of fifteen to be a philosopher (Kreeft, 7). Noted French scholar and author Jacques Ellul has said, "I have read, meditated on, and prayed over Ecclesiastes for more than fifty years. It has perhaps given me more, spoken to me more, than any other" (Ellul, 1). Ellul saw his book on Ecclesiastes as the capstone of his life's work. That's quite a statement from someone who authored over forty books.

Most remarkable may be the comments of R. C. Sproul. He says that Ecclesiastes has a fond place in his heart because it was instrumental in his conversion to Christ. Amazingly, God used the second half of Ecclesiastes 11:3, "Whether a tree falls to the south or to the north, in the place where it falls, there will it lie." Hearing this verse, Sproul says in one of his audiotapes that he saw himself "lying on the floor of the forest having fallen . . . and rotting and disintegrating."

Well-known writers have also weighed in with praise for Ecclesiastes. Melville declared, "The truest of all books is Solomon's and Ecclesiastes is the fine hammered steel of woe" (quoted in Provan, 15). Thomas Wolfe believed that "Ecclesiastes is the greatest single piece of writing I have ever known, and the wisdom expressed in it the most lasting and profound" (quoted in Kreeft, 16).

THEME

The Book of Ecclesiastes has been interpreted in a number of different ways. It is recognized by some as the most misunderstood book of the Bible (Ryken, 126). Some of these views tell us more about the interpreter than the book. Jerome believed it was a book that promoted asceticism. Luther, among others, was quite critical of this view (Luther, 4–5,31). The skeptic Voltaire even used passages from Ecclesiastes to support his philosophical views (Bridges, iv).

Indeed, the overall theme or purpose of Ecclesiastes has engendered no small number of interpretations. Some believe a more positive view is being articulated by the book (Johnston, 14–15). As one commentator (Kaiser, 15) observes, the inclusion in the epilogue of searching for "delightful words" (12:10 NASB) supports this optimistic perspective.

Others hold that those who attempt to give a more positive perspective to Ecclesiastes are not reading "statements about God in perspective" (Longman, 35). Still others hold that there are *both* positive and negative aspects of the overall argument of Eccleaiastes (Eaton, 44). One says that "three words correctly summarize the purpose of the book: comfort, disillusionment, and warning" (Leupold, 18).

There is no doubt that the book contains a good deal of sobering truths about life, but they are mentioned to contrast with other truths that demonstrate what life can be like when God intervenes. This is not a life devoid of pain, suffering, and confusion over what God is doing (Wright, "The Riddle of the Sphinx," 334). Indeed, Ecclesiastes is quite clear in stating that we can't fully know the mind of God (Whybray, *Ecclesiastes*, 29–30). Statements about the limitations of human understanding are common (see Eccl. 1:18; 3:11).

The writer is prodding us to realize that no matter how exciting our life may be, it is ultimately meaningless apart from God. Without God we are "totally ignorant and inescapably unhappy" (Pascal, 49). But he is also striving to illumine our understanding about another truth—that no matter how mundane the activities of a person's life, with God, they can be extremely meaningful. The implication of all this is dramatic indeed. Donald Trump hobnobbing in Manhattan can never have the lasting fulfillment and joy that a Christian mother changing a baby's diaper in the quiet obscurity of her home has. Joy doesn't come from what you do. It comes from your relationship to God. The fact that Ecclesiastes found "eventual incorporation into the Feast of Tabernacles" which is "essentially a joyful autumn festival" (Webb, 106) also moves us to consider this reality.

The capacity for great joy even among Christians is often stifled by our hankering for more possessions, pleasure, and power. As Christians, we may be able to disguise our ungodly quest with religious phraseology, but our desire for more often mimics the world. So Ecclesiastes offers perspective to both non-Christians and Christians alike.

Solomon uses whatever means he can to get us to see the folly of finding fulfillment apart from God. Embracing the fact that the good life is one empowered by God is not what we naturally gravitate toward. Even as Christians, we are, as the hymn writer said, "Prone to wander, Lord I feel it. Prone to leave the God I love."

One commentator aptly captures Solomon's strategy in trying to convince us about the good life:

> He questions, even ridicules, the status quo with merciless verve. Then having gotten inside jaundiced minds, he turns our cynicism on its head to point us to the only way of meaningful life. It is a masterly tour de force—a divinely inspired bait-and-switch apologetic that carries the reader from the edge of hell to the threshold of heaven (Keddie, ix).

So, in the end, I am not convinced that words like *pessimistic* or *optimistic* best describe what Ecclesiastes is all about. I prefer *realistic*. This "realistic" book offers an honest and hopeful picture of how life ought to be lived (Luther, 7), even with all the lack of clarity about what God is doing. It also encourages us to live with the future in view (see Eccl. 12:9–14).

Comparing Ecclesiastes to a garment, one scholar put it this way: "Ecclesiastes is a garment to wear when we have finished with performance and are ready for work—not with an inflated idea of what we can achieve, but with contentment and confidence, knowing that our times are in God's hands. A pair of overalls, perhaps. A garment for those who are through, once for all, with triumphalism and cant, and are willing to face life as it really is" (Webb, 109).

SIGNIFICANT PHRASES IN ECCLESIASTES

A. "Under the Sun"

The phrase "under heaven" (1:13; 2:3; 3:1) is taken by many (e.g., Whybray, *Ecclesiastes*, 37; Longman, 66) but not all commentators (Moore, *Ecclesiastes*, 11) as similar to/synonymous with "under the sun." There might be a slight difference in the two terms (Seow, 104–06).

In Ecclesiastes 8:14,16, the phrase "on earth" is used, but the idea seems to be similar to "under the sun." The basic meaning for this phrase is man's perspective on life devoid of God, though that should be balanced with the fact that God does invade life "under the sun." Ecclesiastes 5:18 is a good example of this. Other ancient cultures such as the Egyptians, Babylonians, and Phoenicians had a similar phrase (Ellul, 57).

B. "Meaningless"

Some versions of the Bible like the New American Standard Bible use both "vanity" and "futility." In the NIV, Ecclesiastes 6:4 and 11 do not use "meaningless," but the Hebrew word that translates it is there.

Meaningless is used in a variety of ways. It can mean transient or breath-like, empty, and futile. A common way of reading *hebel* is as a reminder that life is beyond comprehension (Seow, 47, 59; Murphy, lviii–lix), a mystery that doesn't lend itself to simplistic answers. *Hebel* can also connote "worthless," but we must be careful with this lest we give the impression that the created order is not to be enjoyed. We will cover this further when we look at Ecclesiastes 1.

We must keep in mind that certain biblical words can have a wide range of meanings, which then overlap with other words (Carson, 25–66). Various nuances of "vanity" need to be kept in mind. This will help us steer clear of using *hebel* in a one-dimensional or narrow way. The context will be the final arbiter on the best translation of *hebel*.

C. "Chasing After the Wind"

The use of wind in the wisdom literature of the Bible "is frequently a metaphor for things that have no abiding value or are insubstantial" (Seow, 122).

This phrase evokes all types of strong images. Trying to follow the wind is futile. We never know when the wind will change directions. We are not given any warning. Even if one could "corner" the wind, the ability to capture the wind is impossible. It simply slips through our fingers. It is the same for the person who chases after the "American dream." Just when a person thinks he has "captured" enough money and possessions to make himself happy and secure, it ends up producing anxiety, boredom, emptiness, and restlessness. But if we give up "chasing after the wind," we will find life (Matt. 16:25).

Consider the sobering remarks of Napoleon:

> I die before my time and my body shall be given back to the earth and devoured by worms. What an abysmal gulf between my deep miseries and the eternal Kingdom of Christ. I marvel that whereas the ambitious dreams of myself and of Alexander and of Caesar should have vanished into thin air, a Judean peasant—Jesus—should be able to stretch his hands across the centuries, and control the destinies of men and nations (Quoted in Morley, 296).

AUTHORSHIP AND DATE

Some argue that an anonymous preacher (Qoheleth) wrote the book. Various reasons are given to bolster this claim. One is that the Bible does not record Solomon as having repented. Also, using the word *teacher* was a literary device of ancient Jewish authors to call themselves "Solomon" in order to preserve their own anonymity and to declare their "indebtedness to their teacher and model, the ideal wise man" (Kreeft, 25). There is also some textual evidence for someone other than Solomon authoring Ecclesiastes in 1:12. In this verse the perfect tense is used which would suggest that Solomon was no longer king. This would make room for a later writer to have compiled the book. Tremper Longman offers a number of other compelling reasons for the non-Solomonic authorship of Ecclesiastes (Longman, 2–8).

There are also some good arguments for favoring Solomonic authorship. First, the notion that the Scriptures do not record Solomon as having repented can certainly be contested. Specifically, Ecclesiastes 2:1–11 could possibly be viewed as a statement of repentance. Second, the requirements of being "son of David, king in Jerusalem" (1:1) points to Solomon. Third, parallels between 1 Kings and Ecclesiastes fit the life of Solomon. For example, there are similarities in what both say about Solomon's wisdom (Eccl. 1:16; cf. 1 Kgs. 3:12) (Kaiser, 26). Fourth, in response to the grammar of Ecclesiastes 1:12 being an argument against Solomonic authorship, Kaiser wrote: "The perfect tense actually denotes a state of action that began in the past and stretches forward to the present. Only in later Hebrew is it restricted to past events. This form of the verb would be proper even if Solomon were writing" (p. 27).

Furthermore, ancient Jewish tradition held to Solomonic authorship (Bridges, viii; Wright, "The Interpretation of Ecclesiastes," 18) as did the Patristic tradition (e.g., Gregory of Nyssa, *On the Making of Man*, 395; Gregory of Nazianzen, 248).

One recent study argued that "Ecclesiastes is fully in the realm of pre-exilic language" (Fredericks, quoted in Garrett, 259). Although Duane Garrett acknowledged that this particular study has received some criticism, it certainly does not invalidate Fredericks's basic thesis (Garrett, 259).

It is striking how dismissive some modern commentators can be about the possibility of Solomonic authorship. According to one, Ecclesiastes makes no sense if it were written by Solomon (Davidson, 1, cf. 5). Another said, "The tenor of the book and the language in which it is written *render impossible* the identification with Solomon or any Hebrew" (Murphy, xxi, emphasis added).

More humility is called for when it comes to the tools of biblical scholarship. Textual criticism is "not an exact science, though many of its practitioners act as if it were" (Kreeft, 25). Its Enlightenment roots (Garrett, 254) also should alert us to the fact that there is a *philosophical* assumption that is bound up with it—the possibility of unbiased, detached, human reasoning about the Bible.

We must always keep in mind that all of us are "subjects," so it is impossible to be totally objective! In that regard Lesslie Newbigin's book, *Proper Confidence,* is an important work that all scholars would do well to consider.

Roland Murphy wisely states that precritical exegesis is important to consider because it offers alternative readings of the biblical text that modern scholars wouldn't think of (Murphy, lvi). Unfortunately, the general tendency is for modern scholars to disregard or at least downplay the impact of patristic commentary. Not surprisingly, modern scholars are many times guilty of making the text of Scripture say what *they* want it to say (Provan, 33).

The idea of editors (redactors) working on Ecclesiastes before reaching its final form is also a popular notion. Some claim that Ecclesiastes contains much contradictory material—but wouldn't redactors smooth those over? Other problems with assuming different people put Ecclesiastes together are cited by various scholars, and many of these scholars don't hold to Solomonic authorship (Eaton, 40–43; Murphy, xxxiii; Provan, 32–33; Whybray, *Ecclesiastes*, 17–18).

There is general agreement that the author's thought is fundamentally Hebraic (Whybray, *Ecclesiastes*, 28–29). Ecclesiastes is an "intensely Jewish book" (Murphy, xlii). David Hubbard's list of characteristics for this view (Eaton, 32) also provides credible evidence for the Jewish origin of the author.

This issue of authorship is complex, and there likely will be strong differences of opinion about this. For sake of literary ease, I will refer to the author of Ecclesiastes as "Solomon." Whoever wrote Ecclesiastes certainly had Solomon in mind.

Dating Ecclesiastes is also a debated area as one might suspect from the various views on authorship. For those who hold to Solomonic authorship, an earlier date naturally follows (Kaiser, 31; Bridges, viii–ix). Typically, these commentators place the dating toward the end of Solomon's life as he reflected on his life from the perspective of a repentant heart. Others find that the use of Aramaic suggests (or even conclusively proves) a postexilic date (Seow, 20–21; Crenshaw, 49). Some give dates as late as the mid part of the third century B.C. or even later (Whybray, *Ecclesiastes*, 11–12).

A good warning was given by Tremper Longman to those who believe that the language of a book is the best way to determine dating because it seems so objective.

> We do not know the history of the Hebrew language or the foreign languages that influenced it well enough to use Qohelet's language as a barometer of the book's origin. Are certain features late, or do they reflect vernacular or dialectical peculiarities in Hebrew? We can never be certain. My conclusion is that the language of the book is not a certain barometer of date (Longman, 15; cf. Eaton, 18).

The ambiguity of the evidence suggests that the wise conclusion is a healthy dose of agnosticism when it comes to dating Ecclesiastes. Holding to later or earlier dates, as is the case with holding to Solomonic authorship or not, is issue that Christians must disagree about in a charitable manner. The evidence is simply too inconclusive to make them issues of orthodoxy.

OUTLINE

The Book of Ecclesiastes is not an easy book to outline, although this has not hindered many from making an attempt to understand its structure (Kaiser, 21; Ellul, 34–35; Leupold 25–27; Wyngaarden, 157–58). Addison Wright has gone to fairly elaborate lengths to argue for a certain structural flow. His attempt has been characterized as idiosyncratic, strained, and arbitrary (Seow, 44–45; Longman, 21; Eaton, 49).

A recent work argues that Solomon organizes Ecclesiastes around observations and instructions (Webb, 86–88). This seems to have some merit. Some wonder "why any author, ancient or modern, would construct a work that is so structurally complex" (Seow, 43). For those who believe that *all* books of the Bible must contain some clearly delineated organizational structure, it is important to reconsider whether that expectation might reflect a modern value of scholarship that is being foisted on the ancient text of Scripture. One scholar provided good balance by noting that Ecclesiastes is not "utterly without structure," yet "it follows no elaborate or symmetrical scheme. Even so, its 'wandering' is not purposeless but moves steadily toward a final destination" (Garrett, 270).

The reader is also directed to the section on genre for a description of the varied literary approaches in Ecclesiastes.

CANONICITY

The acceptance of Ecclesiastes into the canon by the Jews was made on the basis of whether it "made the hands unclean." "In early Jewish thought, a book makes the hands 'unclean' if it is divinely inspired. In other words, it is so holy that special rituals accompany its being physically handled while it is read or carried" (Longman, 27).

Though disputed by early Jewish scholars as to whether Ecclesiastes actually "defiled the hands," it did by the end of the first century A.D. find acceptance in the Hebrew canon "at least according to the majority in the Jamnia academy" (Seow, 4).

Michael Eaton wrote some wise words that remind us that canonicity always involves a measure of faith.

What elicits recognition of any part of Scripture as inherently authoritative? A certain circularity is inevitable, whatever one's position. The person who is hostile to claims for authority in any religious document will bring his presuppositions to Ecclesiastes and find his doubts confirmed. Another person who comes to the Bible, perhaps to Ecclesiastes, with openness is ready to hear and find that the Preacher speaks to him as never before. Both have travelled in a circle—the latter perhaps in a spiral, for his position is higher than before (Eaton, 27).

GENRE

Although Ecclesiastes has some similarities to other Ancient Near Eastern wisdom literature, it is quite different in its ethical dimension with its focus on the fear of God (Shank, 65). Furthermore, it is a mistake simply to assign Ecclesiastes to "wisdom" literature (Longman, 17). There is prose along with poetry in Ecclesiastes. Interestingly, recent research has shown that these two categories of poetry and prose are not always the two distinct genres that we previously assumed (Longman, 23–24; Whybray, *Ecclesiastes*, 16).

Adapting what Zimmerli has said (Murphy, xxxvii), it seems that Ecclesiastes may be best viewed as composing elements true of both wisdom literature and narrative. Granted, it includes principles for wise living, but "story lines" emerge as well. Crenshaw agreed that there are several types of genre in Ecclesiastes but held that the dominant one is "reflection arising from personal observation" (Crenshaw, 28).

OTHER PERTINENT BACKGROUND

A. Allusions to Genesis

There seem to be a couple of possible allusions to Genesis 3:19 where it speaks of returning to the dust (Eccl. 3:20; 12:7). This would not be surprising since Solomon wanted to underscore the brevity and transitory nature of life. However, he "does not simply repeat the teaching of Genesis, but works with it in his own distinctive way" (Webb, 103).

Among commentators there are varying levels of confidence about whether Ecclesiastes is alluding to Genesis or not. Some have "no doubt" that passages like Ecclesiastes 3:20 and 12:7 bear "primary reference" to Genesis 3:19 (Shank, 62). Those who are less definitive in the connection still find an amazing similarity between the two books (Eaton, 46; Whybray, *Ecclesiastes*, 29).

Whether direct allusion to Genesis is being made or not, it is clear that the two books "exhibit substantial agreement about the central point of the creation motif—that life is to be celebrated as a 'good creation of God'" (Johnston, 22).

B. New Testament Usage

Although the New Testament never directly quotes Ecclesiastes, it seems that there is a possible allusion from the apostle Paul in Romans 8:20 (Longman, 39; Webb, 107; Wright, "The Interpretation of Ecclesiastes," 22).

C. Why Yahweh *Is Not Used*

Some are troubled by the fact that *Yahweh*, the covenant name for God, is not used in Ecclesiastes. Many good explanations have been offered for this. Yahweh is not used because *foundational* spiritual issues had to be resolved first (Leupold, 30–31). Still others contend that Ecclesiastes has an evangelistic thrust (reaching out to the Arameans and others) which would make using the name *Yahweh* premature (Kaiser, 32). This view would see the purpose of Ecclesiastes as somewhat similar to what Paul did on Mars Hill (Eaton, 47). Finally, it is good to remember that Elohim and Yahweh are complementary, *not* contradictory, names for God (Murphy, lxviii).

Whybray commented accordingly:

> He [the author of Ecclesiastes] took for granted not only the existence but also the omnipotence of the one God. In this belief he did not deviate in the least from the Jewish faith of his time. This God, whom he calls (ha-)Elohim but who is in fact identical with the Yahweh of the Old Testament, is the sole creator of the world and holds the fate of every human being in his hands. Whatever happens on earth is his 'work.' Man must, therefore, recognize that all human endeavours are futile apart from him, and that all moments of happiness come from him as his gifts. He is therefore to be worshiped, and Qoheleth takes it for granted that his readers will do so (Whybray, *Ecclesiastes*, 27).

D. *The Afterlife in Ecclesiastes*

Some people might be too dismissive on whether Ecclesiastes includes any teaching on the afterlife (Murphy, lxviii). Granted, there is much left unsaid about "future things," but passages in Ecclesiastes 3, 8, and 12 give some teaching on the afterlife. More will be said about this in the body of the commentary.

MAINTAINING PERSPECTIVE

Some people erroneously view God's wisdom as quaint, archaic maxims that cannot address the nitty-gritty push and shove of modern life. Nothing could be further from the truth. Marvin Wilson offers some helpful insight into the practicality of Old Testament wisdom: "To the Greek, knowledge was the main way to virtue; the path to the good life was through the intellect. But to the Hebrew, wisdom went beyond intellectual pursuit; it was practical" (Wilson, *Our Father Abraham*, 282).

Although some question whether there is a dichotomy between Hebrew and Greek ways of "knowing," it is undeniable that wisdom is viewed in the Old Testament as extremely useful.

Ecclesiastes 1

A Long Introduction to a Serious Problem (Part 1)

I. **INTRODUCTION**
Dr. Solomon's Sobering Diagnosis

II. **COMMENTARY**
A verse-by-verse explanation of the chapter.

III. **CONCLUSION**
A House Built on Sand

An overview of the principles and applications from the chapter.

IV. **LIFE APPLICATION**
A "Slough of Despond"

Melding the chapter to life.

V. **PRAYER**
Tying the chapter to life with God.

VI. **DEEPER DISCOVERIES**
Historical, geographical, and grammatical enrichment of the commentary.

VII. **TEACHING OUTLINE**
Suggested step-by-step group study of the chapter.

VIII. **ISSUES FOR DISCUSSION**
Zeroing the chapter in on daily life.

Ecclesiastes 1

Q u o t e

"*More* than at any other time in history, mankind faces a crossroads. One path leads to despair and utter hopelessness. The other, to total extinction. Let us pray we have the wisdom to choose correctly."

W o o d y   A l l e n

 I N   A   N U T S H E L L

Solomon has diagnosed that we have a deadly disease of the soul. Even though this disease is life threatening (both in this life and the life to come), most people "feel fine" and conclude tragically that they are fine.

A Long Introduction to a Serious Problem (Part 1)

I. INTRODUCTION

Dr. Solomon's Sobering Diagnosis

*Y*ou go to the doctor for your annual physical. Everything seems great. Both your blood pressure and cholesterol are low. You pass the stress test with flying colors. It looks like the consistent exercise and diet regimen have put you in good shape. You head home and silently congratulate yourself for a job well-done.

You receive a call the next morning from the nurse at the doctor's office. "Mr. Stephens, we would like you to meet us this afternoon at the office." Since your afternoon is jam-packed with appointments and phone calls, you get rather perturbed and ask what all this is about. "It's rather serious, Mr. Stephens. We would prefer to tell you in person. We would also encourage you to have your wife join us." Stunned and perplexed, you mutter that you will be there.

You arrive at the doctor's office a few minutes late. Immediately you are led into a room where your wife greets and then embraces you.

"Please sit down, Jim." Your doctor, who's been a golfing buddy for the past twenty years, never sounded more somber. "Jim, all your test results came back, and it looks as if you've got colon cancer."

Disbelief quickly followed by anger floods your heart. "How can this be? I've got low blood pressure and low cholesterol!"

Your protestations are interrupted by your doctor's counsel. "Jim, this may be life threatening. We don't know for sure at this time. But we need to do all we can to treat it."

Imagine yourself in this predicament. It would be foolish to ignore your doctor's diagnosis and go on your merry way simply because you "feel fine." The Scriptures warn us about this type of thinking. "There is a way that *seems right* to a man, but in the end it leads to death" (Prov. 14:12, emphasis added; cf. 12:15, 16:2, 30:12).

Solomon is like that doctor. He knows that we are dying (physically and spiritually) because of sin. Unfortunately, we are not of the same persuasion. Most of us balk at the serious nature of Solomon's diagnosis, so the prescription gets thrust aside. But "Dr. Solomon" is not easily deterred by his patients' obstinacy. He will take much time and effort to convince us of the lethal nature of our soul sickness.

II. COMMENTARY

A Long Introduction to a Serious Problem (Part 1)

MAIN IDEA: *Solomon makes several poignant observations about how the world works. These observations force us to face the unsettling but undeniable truth that life truly is meaningless apart from God. Our clever attempts to make life meaningful apart from God are ultimately futile.*

A Introduction (1:1–2)

SUPPORTING IDEA: *Solomon's abrupt introduction is designed to arrest the apathy of the spiritually lethargic. This happens to be all of us who are apart from the grace of God!*

1:1. The **Teacher** (Qoheleth) is a term that designates a man "who assembles a group, that is, a congregation; one whom we should call a preacher" (Leupold, 38).

1:2. Consider the abrupt nature of this introduction. Right from the start Solomon confronts us with the bleak reality that life apart from God is meaningless. Solomon does not slowly groom us into his argument. Rather, he blasts us with large doses of reality from the very beginning. Imagine someone introducing himself today in such a way. We would certainly call him intense or serious-minded. We might even be tempted to call him mad. But Solomon is not psychologically impaired. He simply wants to dump cold water on any delusion we may have that life is meaningful apart from God.

Meaningless! Meaningless! is a superlative. There is no greater way of stating the vanity of life apart from God. But the vanity applies to various activities of life done *apart* from God, not to the good world that God has created (Leupold, 41; Kaiser, 48).

Jerome said:

> But if all created things are good, as being the handiwork of a good Creator, how comes it that all things are vanity? If the earth is vanity, are the heavens vanity too?—and the angels, the thrones, the dominions, the powers, and the rest of the virtues? No; if things which are good in themselves as being the handiwork of a good Creator are called vanity, it is because they are compared with things which are better still (Jerome, 73–74).

The world, which God has created, is to be appreciated for its beauty and cared for accordingly.

Ⓑ The Vanity of Life Apart from God (1:3–11)

SUPPORTING IDEA: *Solomon proceeds to build the case that life apart from God is meaningless. He does so by reminding us of three undeniable truths: (1) our relationship to nature (1:3–8); (2) there is nothing new under the sun (1:9–10); and (3) no legacy can be left (1:11).*

1:3. Solomon invokes the phrase **under the sun.** This is simply another way of saying that life has no meaning apart from God. We will see this phrase used many times throughout the Book of Ecclesiastes.

Solomon's question that is being posed will also be answered several times. **Man,** that is, human beings, because of the generic male (Longman, 60) have no profit for their **labor** . . . again, **under the sun.** Keep in mind that Solomon focuses our attention on the uncertainty and meaninglessness of life. His depressing observations about life apart from God cause us to cry out for some better way to live. That better way will be given in due time. For now, he must convince us of how desperate and hopeless the situation is apart from God.

1:4–7. In these verses Solomon compared and contrasted man with nature to make an obvious and unsettling point. Note that the **generations come and generations go, but the earth remains forever** (v. 4). Obviously, the earth is not eternal. Only God is. This is simply a way of saying a great long while or a relatively long period of time (Leupold, 45; cf. Longman, 68).

The sun rises and the sun sets, and hurries back to where it rises (v. 5). **The wind blows to the south and turns to the north; round and round it goes, ever returning on its course** (v. 6). And lastly, we see the repetitive nature of the waters: **All streams flow into the sea, yet the sea is never full. To the place the streams come from, there they return again** (v. 7).

Here we have the opposite of what *seems* right. Isn't it human beings who have great value and worth? We see this quite clearly in texts like Psalm 8. It was only after man, both male and female, was created (Gen. 1:27) that God pronounced his work "very good" (Gen. 1:31). Humans truly are the capstone of God's creation, yet we have an uncertain and transient existence. But the material world, which is of much less value than man, has relative stability and consistency. Understandably, we cry out at the inequity of this situation. We are extremely uncomfortable with these graphic reminders of our mortality.

The Pulitzer prize-winning book, *The Denial of Death* by Ernest Becker, described this reality. We also see it poignantly described in Hebrews 2:14–15: "Since the children have flesh and blood, he [Jesus] too shared in their humanity so that by his death he might destroy him who holds the power of death—that is, the devil—*and free those who all their lives were held in slavery by their fear of death*" (emphasis added).

Solomon is demonstrating through these four elements of earth, fire, wind, and water—which were the very things the ancients thought the world was made up of (Flew, 125)—that man's uncertainty and transience dog his path at every turn. In other words, we can count on the fact that the sun will rise tomorrow, but we can't count on whether we will be alive to see it!

Gregory of Nyssa observed:

> The earth, says the wise Preacher, 'abideth for ever,' ministering to every generation, first one, then another, that is born upon it; but men, though they are so little even their own masters, that they are brought into life without knowing it by their Maker's will, and before they wish are withdrawn from it, nevertheless in their excessive vanity think that they are her lords; that they now born, now dying, rule that which remains continually (Gregory of Nyssa, *On Virginity*, 349).

Having done evangelism at various beaches, I have found dusk to be a particularly good time for sharing the gospel. The crowds are gone, and you can usually find people alone staring at the monotonous rolling in and out of the waters. What does their brief and uncertain existence mean in light of the constancy of the ocean? Nature is eerily quiet in providing any clues.

A few lines from the song "Ol' Man River" by Oscar Hammerstein II jar us to consider this truth. In the song, a black man is wondering why the "colored folks work while the white folks play." He looks to the river for perspective: "Ol' man river, dat ol' man river, He mus' know sumpin', but don't say nuthin', He jes' keeps rollin', He keeps on rollin' along."

Nature's muteness and lack of sympathy for man's transient life is captured well in a poem by Stephen Crane.

> A man said to the universe:
> "Sir, I exist."
> "However," replied the universe,
> "The fact has not created in me
> A sense of obligation"
> (as quoted in Sire, 13; cf. Lockerbie, 91–109).

1:8. The response of man to this situation comes as no surprise. It is difficult for him to find satisfaction and meaning in life apart from God. Luther aptly described the heart as "a constantly yawning chasm" (Luther, 19).

1:9–10. Solomon now moves to the second way he demonstrated that life apart from God has no meaning—that **there is nothing new under the sun**. At first glance these words may seem naïve. Saying that **there is nothing new** seems like an overstatement. Today we have many things like computers and cars which the ancients never had. So how can Solomon make the claim that **there is nothing new under the sun**? Clearly we moderns have gadgets and gizmos that the ancients didn't.

Solomon's point is to direct our attention to the fact that things like power, status, wealth, and pleasure are the same things that people have always pursued in search of the "good life." The "packaging" of these things is certainly different today—cars instead of chariots—but the quest is basically the same. There is no new pursuit that can give meaning and purpose to our lives apart from God.

After the Dallas Cowboys won the Super Bowl in 1972, Tom Brookshire, a famous American broadcaster, asked Dwayne Thomas, a star of the game, "What does it feel like to win the ultimate game?" Thomas declared, "If it's the ultimate game, why is it being played again next year?" Martin Thomas's response captures the spirit of this passage. Or as a postcard that a Christian police officer gave me stated, "Life is not just one thing after another. It's the same thing over and over and over" (Twiestmeyer).

1:11. Solomon also makes his case that life apart from God is meaningless by pointing to the futility of trying to leave a legacy. Simply having a hospital or street named after you is surely not the answer. After surveying his life, one well-known writer felt like he had "ploughed the sea" (Guinness, 244–45). We think of the famous lines from Ozymandias, "Look on my works, ye Mighty, and despair! No thing beside remains. Round the decay of that colossal wreck, boundless and bare the lone and level sands stretch far away" (Shelley, 76; cf. Keyes, 60).

The futility of this worldly pursuit is captured well by Kierkegaard: "Like worldly contempt, worldly honor is a whirlpool, a place of confused forces, an illusory moment in the flux of opinions" (Kierkegaard, 58).

C The Riddle of Life's Purpose (1:12–18)

> **SUPPORTING IDEA:** Solomon tries to discover where meaning and purpose in life can be found, but his quest only produces further frustrations.

1:12–13. Some see Solomon using two different meanings here. **Devoted** shows he literally got at the roots of a matter and **explore** depicts investigation of a matter on all sides (Kaiser, 53). Others see little support for this distinction (Longman, 79). Regardless of either view, he found that after an immense amount of effort there is only failure. It's grievous to fail when you know you have given something your best effort. For example, it's one thing to get a low grade on a test that you did not study for. It's quite another thing to get a low grade on a test that you diligently prepared for. It is no wonder Solomon called this situation an affliction. He expended great effort and came up with no answers.

1:14. All the things that are done under the sun (or apart from God) . . . **are meaningless, a chasing after the wind. Chasing after the wind** is a wonderfully descriptive phrase. Imagine a little child before a floor fan. (Martin) She feels the sensation of the wind, so she concludes that wind can be captured. The picture is humorous. The reaching and subsequent failure to grasp it is met with curiosity. Sometimes it provokes anger in a child. In the same way trying to capture meaning apart from God is like **chasing after the wind**. Not only is wind impossible to capture; it also changes its course with no sign or warning.

1:15. The attempt to find meaning in life apart from God is inherently flawed. We can't do anything to fix it. The utopian ideals of man are a farce. Political solutions like George Bush's New World Order or Bill Clinton's New Covenant will not resolve our problem. No matter how creative and persistent man's effort to have fulfillment in life apart from God, he is reminded that it is fundamentally flawed. He can't fix the "unfixable." It is God himself who has ordained it this way (see Eccl. 7:13).

1:16–18. Solomon commented that he had more wisdom than any other person in Jerusalem. Solomon asked God for wisdom and received it bountifully (1 Kgs. 3). Clearly Solomon knew a lot. First Kings 4:30–33 says that he knew 3,000 proverbs and 1,005 songs. To get some idea of how much that is, consider that the Book of Proverbs has about 900 proverbs. Solomon also knew a lot about trees, animals, birds, creeping things, and fish (1 Kgs. 4:33). His wisdom was well attested even among non-Jews like the Queen of Sheba. But for all his wisdom, Solomon couldn't solve the riddle of how to find meaning apart from God.

Madness has "connotations of a boastful arrogance that sets itself against God rather than praising God" (Provan, 70). Solomon realized the futility of his effort (v. 17). It caused great heartache (v. 18). It is this way today with some of the most thoughtful non-Christians. They can easily analyze that humanity doesn't get along well without God, yet they struggle to find an antidote. It's painful to see the problem so clearly and yet struggle for an answer.

Furthermore, consider the unique pain of Solomon. As the wisest person in the world, he knew that if he could not resolve the riddle of life, no one could (cf. vv. 12–13). No wonder he felt such despair!

The great historian, Arnold Toynbee, also had poignant words on our human predicament: "The increase in our knowledge . . . has not brought with it an understanding of the nature of the purpose (if there is a purpose) of life and consciousness themselves" (Peterson, *Evangelism for Our Generation*, 32).

The more our knowledge grows, the more despondent modern society seems to become because it cannot find any ultimate or lasting answers. The vast amount of data makes us less discerning. Consider the humorous example that New York University Professor Neil Postman gave:

The experiment is best conducted in the morning when I see a colleague who appears not to be in possession of a copy of *The New York Times*. "Did you read the *Times* this morning?" I ask. If my colleague says, "Yes," there is no experiment that day. But if the answer is "No," the experiment can proceed. "You ought to check out Section C today," I say. "There's a fascinating article about a study done at the University of Minnesota." "Really? What's it about?" is the usual reply. The choices at this point are almost endless, but there are two that produce rich results. The first: "Well, they did this study to find out what foods are best to eat for losing weight, and it turns out that a normal diet supplemented by chocolate eclairs eaten three times a day is the best approach. It seems that there's some special nutrient in the eclairs—encomial dyoxin—that actually uses up calories at an incredible rate."

The second changes the theme and, from the start, the university: "The neurophysiologists at Johns Hopkins have uncovered a connection between jogging and reduced intelligence. They tested more than twelve hundred people over a period of five years, and found that as the number of hours people jogged increased there was a statistically significant decrease in their intelligence. They don't know exactly why, but there it is."

My role in the experiment, of course, is to report something quite ridiculous—one might say, beyond belief. If I play my role with a sense of decorum and collegial intimacy, I can achieve results worth reporting: about two-thirds of the victims will believe or at least not wholly *disbelieve* what I have told them. Sometimes they say, "Really? Is that possible?" Sometimes they do a double-take and reply, "*Where'd* you say that study was done?" And sometimes they say, "You know, I've *heard* something like that." I should add that for reasons that are probably worth exploring I get the clearest cases of credulity when I use the University of Minnesota and Johns Hopkins as my sources of authority; Stanford and MIT give only fair results (Postman, *Technopoly*, 56–57).

Even all the recent talk about the importance of virtues, which is an encouraging sign, has led to an impasse among the "experts." How does one become virtuous? Not everyone believes that religion is indispensable (Fineman, 31–36; Himmelfarb, 3–20).

Like a serious-minded doctor, Solomon details our spiritual sickness. We want the cure from him. But he knows we aren't ready for that yet because we are not fully convinced of how lethal our sickness is. In the next chapter

Solomon will continue to make the case about how spiritually sick we are. At the end of chapter 2, he will start to introduce the cure.

MAIN IDEA REVIEW: *Solomon makes several poignant observations about how the world works. These observations force us to face the unsettling but undeniable truth that life truly is meaningless apart from God. Our clever attempts to make life meaningful apart from God are ultimately futile.*

III. CONCLUSION

A House Built on Sand

It is easy to fall prey to the notion that there is some way to achieve lasting fulfillment in life apart from God. We find some activity that is gratifying. We begin to excel at school, business, sports, politics, or even parenting. (Yes, raising good, upstanding children can be a substitute for God. When it is, we need to call it what it truly is—idolatry.)

Achievement at a high level is satisfying—for a time. But when reminders of mortality grab our attention, it becomes clear that we are building our "houses on sand" (see Matt. 7:26–27).

The eminent presidential biographer, Doris Kearns Goodwin, captured this truth when speaking of President Lyndon B. Johnson:

> A month before he died, he spoke to me with immense sadness in his voice. He said he was watching the American people absorbed in a new president, forgetting him, forgetting even the great civil rights laws that he had passed. He was beginning to think his quest for immortality had been in vain, that perhaps he would have been better off focusing his time and attention on his wife and his children, so then he could have had a different sort of immortality through his children and their children in turn. He could have depended on them in a way he couldn't depend on the American people. But it was too late. Four weeks later he was dead. Despite all his money and power he was completely alone when he died, his ultimate terror realized (Goodwin, Commencement Address, 1).

PRINCIPLES

- Our spiritual malady is far more serious than we could ever imagine.
- Divine revelation is required to give us an accurate picture of how lost we are.
- Humans try to achieve fulfillment apart from God in many ways.

- All human solutions are destined to disappoint and disillusion us.
- The person who doesn't embrace the covenant-keeping God of the Bible is doomed to despair.

APPLICATIONS

- Meditate "day and night" on God's evaluation of the human predicament.
- Honestly evaluate the various substitutes for God that you might be tempted to believe will bring lasting fulfillment.
- Recognize like Christian in *Pilgrim's Progress* that one must first despair of his lostness before he can truly appreciate the gospel of God's grace.

IV. LIFE APPLICATION

A "Slough of Despond"

We live during a time when it is common to soften the hard edges of the gospel. We hear much about resurrection life but little about being crucified with Christ. True Christians realize that the grace of God cannot be correctly understood apart from an awareness of their sinfulness. We must experience despair and grief over our sin before the grace of God will make sense. Joy does come in the "morning," but *mourning* must precede it. Solomon wants us to first mourn over our desperate condition. This is the message that faithful ministers like John Bunyan have preached throughout the history of the church.

Toward the beginning of *Pilgrim's Progress,* Christian falls into the "Slough of Despond."

> And he said unto me, "This miry slough is such a place as cannot be mended. It is the descent whither the scum and filth that attends conviction for sin doth continually run, and therefore is it called the Slough of Despond; for still [continually or constantly] as the sinner is awakened about his lost condition, there ariseth in his soul many fears, and doubts, and discouraging apprehensions, which all of them get together, and settle in this place. And this is the reason of the badness of this ground" (Bunyan, 23).

Christian finds out that the "Slough of Despond" is a place that can't be "mended." In other words, deep conviction over our sin can't be avoided if we are to know the grace of God's forgiveness.

V. PRAYER

Father in heaven, please keep me from the popular deception that meaning and purpose can be found in anything (or anyone!) apart from you. Amen.

VI. DEEPER DISCOVERIES

A. Understanding "Meaningless" (1:2)

As mentioned in the introduction, *meaningless* (*hebel*) can mean different things depending on the context. It is ultimately the context that we must be sensitive to if we are to translate this word correctly (Longman, 64). Here it seems that empty, futile, or breathlike (= transient) could all apply, though these latter two may be the most dominant meaning in this book (Crenshaw, 57–58; Whybray, *Ecclesiastes,* 36).

B. The Sun Hurries (1:5)

Hurries literally means "pants" and can connote either eagerness to go back or weariness. I lean toward the former meaning because of the argument about our futility compared with the created world. Commentators have their leanings based on their overall understanding of the book (Kidner, 25; Longman, 69).

C. Leaving a Legacy Is a Poor Substitute for God (1:11)

Some may take issue with this by mentioning people like Winston Churchill, Gandhi, or John F. Kennedy. Didn't they leave a legacy? Aren't they fondly remembered? There are a number of responses that can be given to these questions.

First, keep in mind that Ecclesiastes is wisdom literature, and this particular genre describes reality in the way that it *usually* occurs for most people. A few exceptions to the general rule will always occur.

Second, it is not a good bet to think that you will be in that very small minority which is the exception to the rule. Wise living would dictate otherwise.

Third, history may remember you differently than you ever imagined. Hitler is certainly remembered differently than he imagined. So are Stalin and Lenin. And the list goes on. Even Mother Theresa, for all the adulation she received, was criticized by some people. In fact, during Mother Theresa's funeral an American journalist asked a British journalist to detail the reasons why he was so critical of her ministry to the outcasts of India. It was a surreal sight to see the funeral procession and hear the various criticisms leveled against her work by this British journalist. So if Mother Theresa is not immune from harsh criticism by some, it is unwise to believe that leaving a legacy is a good way to stave off the futility of finding ultimate meaning in life apart from God.

Fourth, as the years pass, people tend to forget you. The three people I mentioned (Churchill, Gandhi, and Kennedy) are well-known figures of the twentieth century. But their popularity will fade with time. Most people aren't familiar with various luminaries of history like Charlemagne or Erasmus. Going back further, how many are familiar with the great Roman military leader, Scipio Africanus?

D. What Is Twisted Cannot Be Straightened (1:15)

Various nuances for these phrases can be found (Kidner, 30; Luther, 26–27; Eaton, 63). We are faced with grave limitations in making sense of the world and in making it a place free of difficulties.

VII. TEACHING OUTLINE

A. INTRODUCTION
1. Lead Story: Dr. Solomon's Sobering Diagnosis
2. Context: We should keep in mind that chapter and verse divisions in the Bible are not inspired. They were made as aids for studying Scripture, but they can be arbitrary at times and therefore hinder the flow of a passage. Ecclesiastes 1 forms one-half of a lengthy introduction about the futility of trying to find meaning apart from God. This introduction concludes with Ecclesiastes 2:23.
3. Transition: This chapter begins Solomon's personal pilgrimage in seeking to discover how and where it is possible to find meaning and fulfillment in life apart from God.

B. COMMENTARY
1. Introduction (1:1–2)
2. The Vanity of Life Apart from God (1:3–11)
3. The Riddle of Life's Purpose (1:12–18)

C. CONCLUSION: A HOUSE BUILT ON SAND

VIII. ISSUES FOR DISCUSSION

1. Do you see the wisdom in Solomon's giving such an abrupt introduction?
2. If there is "nothing new under the sun," why do we continue to act as if there is?
3. In what areas of life are you most tempted to "chase after the wind"?

Ecclesiastes 2

A Long Introduction to a Serious Problem (Part 2)

Quote

"*D*iversion is the first and most effective way to hide the elephant [i.e.—the big questions/issues of life]. An elephant can be hidden by mice, if there are enough of them. So our world is full of thousands of little things, which keep us diverted from the one big thing. We are kept so busy that we have no time to think."

Peter Kreeft

Ecclesiastes 2

 I N   A   N U T S H E L L

After Solomon exhausts or rather gets exhausted in attempting to have his mind unpack the riddle of life, he proceeds to turn to the appetites of the body as the possible source of his fulfillment. Solomon's thinking goes something like this: If my wisdom can't get me the "good life," maybe my commitment to satisfy my sensual pleasures can. In other words, great pain was caused by analyzing life so much (1:18), so avoiding such intense philosophizing might be the key to a happier life.

A Long Introduction to a Serious Problem (Part 2)

I. INTRODUCTION

Court Jesters and Other Diversions

We humans will use any diversion to keep from thinking about the "big issues" of life. Staring into the abyss can certainly be taxing. Tolstoy speaks about the destructive side of diversions in his novella, *The Death of Ivan Ilych*. Tolstoy's character, Ivan Ilych, is a lawyer who aspires to make something of himself. Most of the story depicts the various diversions that occupy Ilych's attention. Even when certain diversions seemed to be getting old, Ilych found new ways to keep from thinking about spiritual reality. "When nothing was left to arrange [speaking of his new house] it became rather dull and something seemed to be lacking, but they [Illych and his wife] were then making acquaintances, forming habits, and life was growing full" (Tolstoy, 117).

Our tendency toward busyness often masks a deep spiritual malady. We spend our lives "in frenzied work and frenzied play," as political philosopher Allan Bloom once said, "so as not to face the fact, not to look into the abyss" (Bloom, 143). Solomon has already taken a peep into this abyss and found it haunted. He is ready for another approach.

In this chapter Solomon describes a test of sorts that he gave himself. He will determine whether unmitigated pleasure can possibly give a person the "good life." It may be helpful to picture Solomon as a student in the classroom of life. We are students as well. Solomon has taken great notes for this particular test on a "crib sheet" of sorts. Amazingly, the teacher (God) is more than happy to have us look at Solomon's notes. Unfortunately, most of us don't believe they are any good. We don't learn from Solomon's mistakes. We must make our own.

II. COMMENTARY

A Long Introduction to a Serious Problem (Part 2)

> **MAIN IDEA:** *The things which Solomon will give himself to in order to find meaning and purpose in life are the same things that we moderns chase after. The packaging of these things may be different in our computer age, but the desire for more possessions, pleasure, and power is nothing new.*

A A Test That Always Fails (2:1–11)

> **SUPPORTING IDEA:** *Exploring the possibility that various diversions offer fulfillment now occupies Solomon's attention. He finally realizes this is also a futile pursuit not worthy of his time.*

2:1. This verse serves as sort of a preliminary summary statement for the test that Solomon gave himself. Note how many times the first person pronoun "I" is used. Solomon is not some detached theoretician. He is actively engaged in this test.

2:2. Solomon found that **laughter** as a remedy for finding meaning and purpose in life was a sign of insanity. We will also see in chapter 7 how frivolity keeps us from considering what life is all about.

Pleasure in and of itself doesn't offer anything of lasting value. Pleasure that doesn't find its source in God is transitory, so it ultimately disappoints. It leads to the "what next?" syndrome. Thomas à Kempis put it this way, "Oftentimes a man vehemently struggles for something he desires, but when he has attained it, he changes his mind. For the affections remain not firmly around the same thing, but rather drive us from one thing to another" (à Kempis, 169).

2:3. Note that Solomon **tried cheering myself with wine, and embracing folly—my mind still guiding me with wisdom.** Later on, in verse 9 of this chapter, he said that "my wisdom stayed with me" during this test. Solomon was not taking some irrational leap into pleasure. Rather, he was evaluating pleasure's benefits as he went throughout this test. He gave himself to what might be described as "informed hedonism." It has also been labelled a "controlled experiment and not . . . mere self-indulgence" (Whybray, *Ecclesiastes*, 53).

First Kings 4:22–23 adds some detail to the amount of food Solomon had at his disposal every day: "Solomon's daily provisions were thirty cors of fine flour and sixty cors of meal, ten head of stall-fed cattle, twenty of pasture-fed cattle and a hundred sheep and goats, as well as deer, gazelles, roebucks and choice fowl."

It has been estimated that this would feed ten thousand to twenty thousand people each day (Stedman, 23). This would have been like a huge "Great Gatsby" party every single day! But note that Solomon never abandoned the brutal realities of life even in the midst of describing such merriment: Is there any good for people during **the few days of their lives**? This elephant-sized question continued to haunt Solomon's thinking.

2:4–8. Solomon listed the impressive things he had at his disposal: several homes, vineyards, gardens, parks, and all kinds of fruit trees and ponds. Even Marx used Solomon's model of irrigation (Ellul, 87). Solomon had many slaves, along with more **herds and flocks than anyone in Jerusalem before me**. This statement about being the most wealthy or the greatest (see 2:9) is very important, as we will see shortly.

The idea of collected silver and gold does not mean to gather in the sense of picking something off the ground but to accumulate, treasure up, or possess in quantity (Ellul, 234). Indeed, **silver and gold** were so common during Solomon's reign that they seemed as plentiful as stones (1 Kgs. 10:27; 2 Chr. 1:15). A **harem** could be "a crude reference to women who are used for sexual pleasure only" (Longman, 92).

2:9. The statement about Solomon's greatness makes an important point. If the most powerful and wealthy man in the world could not find happiness in possessions apart from God, then the futility of pursuing such things becomes evident for the rest of us. This lesson is similar to what Solomon learned about being the wisest man in the world (see commentary on Eccl. 1:12–13,18).

2:10. If this were the final statement of Solomon's test, we might be led to believe that "money is able to buy happiness." Or, "If we are not seeking heavenly pleasures, we shall soon be hankering after those that are shadowy and elusive" (Bridges, 28, see also 30).

Again, let's consider how diversions affect all of us. Pascal commented accordingly:

> However sad a man may be, if you can persuade him to take up some diversion he will be happy while it lasts, and however happy a man may be, if he lacks diversion and has no absorbing passion or entertainment to keep boredom away, he will soon be depressed and unhappy. Without diversion there is no joy; with diversion there is no sadness. That is what constitutes the happiness of persons of rank, for they have a number of people to divert them and the ability to keep themselves in this state (Pascal, 70–71).

This is the lethal trap of wealth. Wealth can provide many diversions that give us an artificial sense of happiness and peace. But once a person thinks about the bigger issues of life such as his own existence (both the brevity and uncertainty of it), a deep sense of despair creeps in. This is why most people just don't think about these sober realities: "Being unable to cure death, wretchedness and ignorance, men have decided, in order to be happy, not to think about such things" (Pascal, 66).

2:11. When we consider what life is like apart from a relationship with God, we begin to face the harsh reality of its chaos and meaninglessness. Having the courage to ponder the big issues of life is a supernatural event—one that God must initiate. We Westerners are certainly not encouraged to think deeply about such issues. Kreeft comments accordingly:

> Of the twenty-one great civilizations that have existed on our planet, according to Toynbee's reckoning, ours, the modern West, is the first that does not have or teach its citizens any answer to the question why they exist. A euphemistic way of saying this is that our society is pluralistic and leaves us free to choose or create our own ultimate values. A more candid way of saying the same thing is that our society has nothing but its own ignorance to give us on this, the most important of all questions. As society grows, it knows more and more about less and less. It knows more about the little things and less about the big things (Kreeft, 20–21).

It was my privilege several years ago to share the gospel with a man who had been awarded the Nobel prize. Though I had never met this man before, he described how he would make some major changes in his life if it were possible to do so. Incredibly, he would not have chosen to be a university professor because he had found the competition among his colleagues so acute. In fact, he told me that his colleagues were more competitive with him *after* winning the Nobel prize because academia fosters an environment where it is good to unseat the "reigning authorities." He went on to describe how the Nobel prize meant nothing to him in comparison with his desire for more meaningful relationships.

I don't know where this man is with respect to a saving relationship with Jesus Christ (he called himself a "theist"), but he graphically portrays what Solomon described: when a person *considers* whether life can bring meaning apart from God, he finds it to be **meaningless, a chasing after the wind; nothing was gained under the sun.**

You may be saying to yourself that it would be nice to make a little more money than you presently earn or possibly to have more status in your company. Most of us in the West do not have the *need* for more. We have *want* for more! This is where the authority of Scripture is very practical. If we can learn from others like Solomon, we may be able to keep ourselves from falling prey to the same sort of folly.

Thomas à Kempis offers some sage counsel:

Let temporal things be used, but things eternal desired. You cannot be satisfied with any temporal good, because you were not created to enjoy these alone. Although you should possess all created good, yet you could not be happy therewith nor blessed; but in God, who created all things, consists your whole blessedness (à Kempis, 126–27).

Ⓑ The Relative Advantage of Street Smarts (2:12–17)

SUPPORTING IDEA: *Solomon's transition to consider whether the dutiful person is better off than the fool also proves that there is no good substitute for God.*

2:12–13. Worldly **wisdom** certainly has some *temporal* advantages over **folly**. It is preferable to understand how to cope in this perplexing world. Balancing your checkbook and changing the oil in your car are prudent activities. So are obeying the laws of the land. But worldly wisdom clearly has its limitations, as we see in verse 14.

2:14. It is good to be a contributing and ethical citizen, but this will not shield us from the inevitable. Death will have its way with all of us. One Puritan preacher stated the case in stark terms:

What has become of those men in former ages of the world that lived here, and vapored so much in their generation, who had all the earth according to their desires? What's become of Agrippa and Bernice with all their pageantry and greatness? Now they have acted their parts and are gone off the common stage of the world, and all their vanity is buried with them in one grave. What difference is there between the poor and rich when they die? They all go the same way. They lived for a little time and flourished in the things of the earth and now are gone, but have left a great deal of guiltiness behind them. Look to their example, and what's become of them? Consider that your case must be as theirs within a short while. The wheel is turning around which will bring you as low as them, so that you, before long, must be numbered among the dead. Oh, it's a mighty means to take our hearts from the things of this earth! (Burroughs, 65).

2:15. If it is true that death will overtake both the fool and the wise, what is the point of trying so hard to be good? This question occurs to many "good people" who quit trying to be good and decide to go wild by engaging in reckless and destructive behavior. Others pride themselves on continuing to be "good" and conclude erroneously that dependence on God is not necessary. The reality of death arrests both these types of "good people" from thinking that their own efforts will bring them lasting fulfillment apart from God.

2:16. This verse reminds us of what we saw earlier in Ecclesiastes 1:11. There is great sobriety in Solomon's statement that the wise and the foolish die in similar ways. Although one may be surrounded by hundreds of caring friends, all of us die on our own. Death is the great equalizer.

2:17. Solomon's conclusion is stark. He hated life because there was nothing to be gained "under the sun"—again, life apart from God. All our strivings apart from God are marked by futility. Although the message of Ecclesiastes has been bleak so far, Solomon is about to show the indispensable ingredient that brings meaning to life.

Ⓒ The Missing Ingredient (2:18–26)

SUPPORTING IDEA: *Solomon's search takes a new turn as he is confronted with the reality that God intervenes in the affairs of man.*

2:18–19. Solomon concluded that all of his efforts to achieve meaning apart from God were futile. The prospect of leaving his fortune to someone else did not lessen Solomon's concern because that person might be a fool. It was unnerving to Solomon because there were no guarantees. What Solomon had worked so hard for could be squandered by a fool.

2:20–23. Solomon's depression over the meaninglessness of life **under the sun** is reaching its nadir point. Although a person may strive and even be commited to his work, the prospect exists of leaving all that he has accomplished to a fool. One commentator said that this passage reminds him of American pioneers who gave their all, only to have others come along who didn't appreciate these efforts (Leupold, 72–73). Sleep certainly does not come easily to a person whose reputation could be tarnished by a fool.

Up to this point we have heard the bleak diagnosis of Solomon. We are glad finally to receive the prescription that can cure our soul sickness.

2:24–26. The words **better** and **than** are not in the Hebrew text (Stedman, 32). A literal rendering of this verse is, "There is nothing in man to eat and drink and tell himself that his labor is good." Or we could say it this way, "There is not a good [inherent] in man" (Kaiser, 44–45). This is a powerful statement that we humans can't create anything good on our own. We are dependent on God for any lasting goodness or fulfillment.

A person's recognition of his own spiritual poverty causes him to flee to God. As verse 24 says, **This too, I see, is from the hand of God.** This recognition itself is clearly a supernatural event.

Prosperous times have a tendency to draw us away from God. Afflictions that cause us to see how spiritually impoverished we are cause us to look elsewhere for perspective. This is why the psalmist said, "Before I was afflicted I went astray, but now I obey your word. . . . It was good for me to be afflicted so that I might learn your decrees" (Ps. 119:67,71). It is not that God delights in affliction. He delights in offering life, but he knows that we do not gravitate naturally toward the source of spiritual life (Jer. 2:13). In our arrogance, we think we can live apart from God (Ps. 2:3). So God uses affliction to get us to see where meaningful life is found.

Verse 25 is stark. It is impossible to have true joy apart from God. It is no surprise that the first introduction of God comes with the first introduction of joy. This joy, as we will see in 3:13, is "the gift of God." We can't experience joy and fulfillment by sheer dint of will.

God's joy doesn't answer every difficult or vexing question such as the problem of evil and suffering (Moore, *The Battle for Hell*, 73–75). Although Christian philosophers and theologians have done an admirable job of addressing these difficult issues, it is ultimately our trust in God that provides solace, joy, and peace.

One well-known Christian wrote eloquently about the joy found in God alone:

> Oh! that I might rest on Thee! Oh! that Thou wouldst enter into my heart, and inebriate it, that I might forget my ills, and embrace Thee, my only good? . . . And this is the happy life, to rejoice to Thee, of Thee, for Thee; this is it, and there is no other. For those who think there is another, pursue some other and not the true joy (Augustine, *Confessions*, 20, see also 180–81; cf. Augustine, *The City of God*, XVIII.XLI; Kierkegaard, 31).

Being good in God's sight means that we recognize that he is the only one who can give true meaning and fulfillment in life (v. 26). This is clearly at odds with our society's idea of goodness. God gives wisdom, knowledge, and joy. This wisdom is not the type spoken of earlier in the Book of Ecclesiastes. God's wisdom helps us to live skillfully, although his wisdom looks foolish to unbelievers (1 Cor. 1:19–25).

The issue being mentioned in the latter part of this verse is not that non-Christians always leave their wealth to Christians, although there are some amazing examples of this (Stedman, 34; cf. Prov. 13:22). We know from Scripture that there are many times when unbelievers are prospering in health and wealth while believers are languishing (Ps. 73). Rather, the issue here may point to the fact that unbelievers will ultimately leave the world with nothing and the Christian will be the inheritor of all things in the future kingdom.

In other words, this verse may be another example of Solomon's reminding us of a reality that extends beyond the grave (see Wright, *Expositor's Bible Commentary: Ecclesiastes*, 1159). Luther understood this as a statement of how the "impious" can never fully experience joy in their labors. Non-Christians must leave their work to the godly who can experience joy because they alone are empowered by God (Luther, 48).

How can we better order our priorities according to the reality of what we have just considered in chapter 2? Chapter 3 provides the answer.

> **MAIN IDEA REVIEW:** *The things which Solomon will give himself to in order to find meaning and purpose in life are the same things that we moderns chase after. The packaging of these things may be different in our computer age, but the desire for more possessions, pleasure, and power is nothing new.*

III. CONCLUSION

Unsatisfying Diversions

Many people live with the illusion that seeking pleasure as the *summum bonum* of life will yield lasting fulfillment. They are convinced that "pleasure sought is pleasure found." Ironically, the same people believe that it is virtuous to "seek truth," as long as one never subscribes to the naïve notion that truth can be found. It is no wonder then why "modern man" is aimless, restless, and bored. Anxiety is commonly used as a defining characteristic for such people. But why do those who mock absolute truth and embrace self-indulgent pleasure as the highest good have such anxiety? Solomon has told us why: No diversion can completely satisfy as a substitute for God.

PRINCIPLES

- Various diversions like hobbies, shopping, and sports are not wrong in and of themselves. But they may keep one from pondering the most important issue of life: one's relationship with God.
- The seeming happiness of some non-Christians would disappear if they seriously considered their lives.
- The greatest joy comes from knowing God.

APPLICATIONS

- Consider your most frequent diversions (television, sports, hobbies, shopping, etc.). Ask God to show you if these are impediments to growing "in the grace and knowledge of our Lord and Savior Jesus Christ" (2 Pet. 3:18).
- Write a "mission statement" for your family. For direction, the author's own mission statement is available by E-mail upon request (dgm@twocities.org).

IV. LIFE APPLICATION

"Taste and See"

There is no such thing as an innocent diversion if it takes our attention away from the things of God. Even wholesome hobbies can keep us from running our spiritual race with endurance (Heb. 12:1–2).

Our fondness for diversions often masks the fact that true joy (or pleasure, to quote John Piper) in God has not been found. "Society is a bored, gluttonous king employing a court jester to divert it after an overindulgent meal" (Peterson, *A Long Obedience in the Same Direction*, 92). It is sinful not to find joy in God (Augustine, *Confessions*, 42).

C. S. Lewis aptly described our tendency toward inferior pleasures. We are happy "like an ignorant child who wants to go on making mud pies in a slum because he cannot imagine what is meant by the offer of a holiday at the sea" (Lewis, *The Weight of Glory*, 26). The "day at the beach" seems fanciful, something that delusional religious fanatics believe in. But here is where God asks us to test the waters. We are invited to "taste and see that the LORD is good" (Ps. 34:8). In believing this promise of God we find the ultimate delight that makes all other diversions look anemic and lifeless.

V. PRAYER

Dear Lord, please keep me from the various diversions that rob consistent joy in you. May I experience the deep and abiding delight that comes from knowing you. Amen.

VI. DEEPER DISCOVERIES

A. Similar Stories in Ancient Literature (2:1)

Several commentators point out that Solomon's comments are similar to an ancient Egyptian story, "The Man Who Was Tired of Life." Similar stories don't prove that borrowing from a common oral tradition took place among biblical writers. For one thing the stories have their uniqueness. Furthermore, similarities like these shouldn't surprise us, considering the universal need people have for making sense of the world.

B. Food: A Substitute for God (2:3)

We humans are prone to stop asking the big questions about life if only our bodily pleasures are consistently met. Consider the humorous observation of Annie Dillard:

The mind wants the world to return its love, or its awareness; the mind wants to know all the world, and all eternity, and God. The mind's sidekick, however, will settle for two eggs over easy. The dear, stupid body is as easily satisfied as a spaniel. And, incredibly, the simple spaniel can lure the brawling mind to its dish. It is everlastingly funny that the proud, metaphysically ambitious, clamoring mind will hush if you give it an egg (Dillard, 24).

It is not difficult to fill up an entire lifetime with various diversions. Food and other bodily pleasures are certainly poor "substitute[s] for transcendent meaning" (Wilson, *Joy at the End of the Tether,* 28), but they can occupy the lifetime of a fool.

VII. TEACHING OUTLINE

A. INTRODUCTION
1. Lead Story: Court Jesters and Other Diversions
2. Context: Chapter 2 is a continuation of a lengthy introduction. Solomon looks in detail at whether life can have meaning apart from God.
3. Transition: A significant shift occurs in Ecclesiastes 2:1 with Solomon's attempt to find meaning in life apart from God. He goes from musings of the mind to gratifications of the body.

B. COMMENTARY
1. A Test That Always Fails (2:1–11)
2. The Relative Advantage of Street Smarts (2:12–17)
3. The Missing Ingredient (2:18–26)

C. CONCLUSION: UNSATISFYING DIVERSIONS

VIII. ISSUES FOR DISCUSSION

1. If joy is a defining characteristic of a Christian, why do so few of us have it?
2. Does it help us spiritually if we think about our mortality? Why or why not?
3. What are some signs that an "innocent hobby" has become a hindrance to a person's walk with God?

Ecclesiastes 3

Palm Pilots, Day Timers, and the Shrinking American Soul

Quote

"*When* the disciples began to seem 'busy,' Christ set a little child in their midst. The crowd that storms and blusters in the bewildered name of the century might well tempt a serious man to set just such an unfortunate sufferer in their midst. The sight of him certainly would not detain anyone that willed anything eternal; but busyness has nothing whatever to do with the Eternal."

Søren Kierkegaard

Ecclesiastes 3

I N   A   N U T S H E L L

This well-known passage of Scripture graphically portrays the sovereignty of God over all human affairs. Although human beings cannot know how God is working out his eternal purposes, there is clarity on how we ought to respond in the midst of a fallen world.

Palm Pilots, Day Timers, and the Shrinking American Soul

I. INTRODUCTION

An Obsession with Time

*W*e are obsessed with time. Time has become a commodity. The well-known saying that "time is money" expresses the prevalence of this sort of thinking. We feel that we must protect "our time." This seeking to control and neurotically manage time is justified by too many Christians.

Why do we buy into such a false notion of time? One contributor is pride. We enjoy saying that we are busy because that makes us look important (Kinsley, 82; see also Peterson, *The Contemplative Pastor*, 18). Another factor is that we want to please others. We make too many commitments because we desperately desire the approval of others. A third factor, largely overlooked by Christians, is unease over getting to know God better. Time alone with God may reveal something that needs to be changed.

Dallas Willard put his finger on the issue:

> But solitude, like all of the disciplines of the spirit, carries its risks. In solitude, we confront our own soul with its obscure forces and conflicts that escape our attention when we are interacting with others. Thus, "Solitude is a terrible trial, for it serves to crack open and burst apart the shell of our superficial securities. It opens out to us the unknown abyss that we all carry within us . . . [and] discloses the fact that these abysses are haunted (Louis Bouyer)." We can only survive solitude if we cling to Christ there. And yet what we find of him in that solitude enables us to return to society as free persons (Willard, *The Spirit of the Disciplines*, 161).

Robert Banks has shown how we have gone from understanding time by seasonal change to virtual idolatry in wanting to control every millisecond (Banks, 98–106). Neil Postman also has some pointed and probing words on this subject.

> In Mumford's great book, *Technics and Civilization,* he shows how, beginning in the fourteenth century, the clock made us into time-keep-

ers, and then time-savers, and now time-servers. In the process, we have learned irreverence toward the sun and the seasons, for in a world made up of seconds and minutes, the authority of nature is superseded. Indeed, as Mumford points out, with the invention of the clock, eternity ceased to serve as the measure and focus of human events. And thus, though few would have imagined the connection, the inexorable ticking of the clock may have had more to do with the weakening of God's supremacy than all the treatises produced by the philosophies of the Enlightenment; that is to say, the clock introduced a new form of conversation between man and God, in which God appears to have been the loser. Perhaps Moses should have included another commandment: Thou shalt not make mechanical representations of time (Postman, *Amusing Ourselves to Death,* 11–12).

We must keep in mind that more can happen in a minute if God is in it than we could achieve in a lifetime apart from him. Miracles like the parting of the Red Sea or Jesus feeding the five thousand remind us of this reality. Those of us who crave closure and hate interruptions really need to take this to heart! The interruption to our schedule may be a wonderful opportunity for ministry. Of course, there are other times when an interruption may keep us from doing God's will. We must walk closely with the Lord to be able to discern what to do and not do.

Unlike us, the ancient Hebrews were more freed up to give full sway to their humanity because *everything* had an appropriate time. They worked hard, but they did not rush like we moderns do (Wilson, *Our Father Abraham,* 139).

II. COMMENTARY

> **MAIN IDEA:** *Although this list of events is quite extensive, it is certainly not exhaustive. Many more things could be added, but it does cover a full range of human activities. The generic nature of this list allows for many applications.*

Palm Pilots, Day Timers, and the Shrinking American Soul

A God Rules over All Events (3:1–11)

> **SUPPORTING IDEA:** *There is a "time for everything" and a "season for every activity under heaven." This passage demonstrates that things must be done at the right time and in the right way for them to be good (Cassian, 508).*

3:1. There is always enough time to do God's will (Ellul, 233–34). There may not be enough time to accomplish our own selfish agendas, but there is plenty of time to do what God has ordained for us. Time presents no frustration to him. He will accomplish all that concerns us. What a liberating truth!

3:2. Beginnings and ends are depicted in this verse. There are times for births and times to plant. There are also times for death and times to uproot. The sovereignty of God over the length of our lives is taught in Scripture (Gen. 27:2; Job 14:5; Ps. 139:16). As a result, Psalm 90:12 is an appropriate application: "Teach us to number our days aright, that we may gain a heart of wisdom." Jonathan Edwards was a great example of living with this in mind. Among his dozens of resolutions, we find this one written when he was nineteen: "I frequently hear persons in old age say how they would live, if they were to live their lives over again: Resolved, that I will live just so as I can think I shall wish I had done, supposing I live for old age" (Edwards, *Works,* vol. 1, xxii).

3:3. Times for killing, healing, tearing down, and building up apply to many different things. Times for killing certainly fits Old Testament teaching on subjects like holy war and the death penalty. Other things also seem to be in view since these "words are widely used outside battle contexts" (Longman, 115).

3:4. These couplets are clearly related—weeping/mourning and laughing/dancing. There is truly freedom to weep. There are God-given times designated for it. To do otherwise during a great personal loss would betray that a person is either afraid of giving vent to God-given emotions or possibly too pragmatic.

Pragmatists want to reduce all of life to what is manageable and efficient. They guard their emotions even during times of tragedy lest "too much time gets wasted." "They are well acquainted with ambition, energy, power, and organization, but not love" (Houston, 108).

3:5. A time to **scatter stones and a time to gather them** is described by one commentator as a "standard practice in Old Testament times for conquering armies both to scatter stones on their enemies' fields to make them unproductive (2 Kgs. 3:19,25; Isa. 5:2) and to gather stones for the purpose of preparing the highway for the advance of the victorious soldiers (Isa. 62:10)" (Keddie, 31). This seems to be the most "plausible explanation" (Whybray, *Ecclesiastes,* 71).

Another commentator takes the throwing and gathering couplet to refer to stones which are harmful to the soil and stones which can be used profitably as memorials to God (Bridges, 56–57).

There are many applications that flow from **a time to embrace and a time to refrain**. In the church, we know that those who hold correct doctrine should be embraced. In this respect, we think of Paul receiving "the right hand of fellowship" from the early church leaders (Gal. 2:1–9). To refrain at times from embracing should also take place if the church is to maintain its purity (Matt. 18:15–18; 1 Cor. 5:9–13; 1 Tim. 5:19–20).

St. Augustine believed this verse applied to periods before and after Christ. Before Christ it was good to get married and have children. After Christ's coming there is no longer the same necessity to have children (Augustine, *On Marriage and Concupiscence,* 269)!

3:6. This verse also has a number of possible applications. In our relationship with God, we appreciate that he is the searching and seeking God (Matt. 18:11; Luke 15). But it is most sobering to realize that there are times when God gives people up as lost (Jer. 7:16; 11:14). **A time to keep and a time to throw away** could apply to a number of different areas of life. Even good household management is predicated upon this principle, although it shouldn't be limited to that (Murphy, 34).

3:7. A time to tear and a time to mend reminds us that the ripping of one's garment in Bible times indicated grief (2 Sam. 13:31). Sewing the cloth back together showed that the problem had passed (Kaiser, 65).

A time to be silent and a time to speak reminds us that the truly religious person knows how to control his tongue (Jas. 3:2). It takes wisdom to know when to speak and when to remain quiet (Ambrose, *Duties of the Clergy,* 2). Job's "counselors" were wise when they sat quietly with Job and empathized with him (Job 2:11–13). But Job's counselors eventually began talking about things they couldn't fully understand. There may have been something Job's friends should have said, but what they did say was not it. God's Word warns us about talking too much (Prov. 10:19) and speaking too quickly (Prov. 12:18).

Sometimes silence is golden, but there are times when silence is yellow. These are times when we must speak. Not to speak against injustice is sin. Also, to remain quiet about one's testimony is wrong (Acts 4:17–20; 2 Cor. 5:18–20; 1 Pet. 3:15). One church father applied this verse to those who clamored to be teachers but were not qualified (Clement of Rome, 59).

3:8. Love is a defining character quality of the Christian. The believer is to love his neighbor as himself (Matt. 22:39). He is even commanded to love his enemies (Matt. 5:43–44). But love is more than silly sentimentalism. In our therapeutic age, we must remember that it is not antithetical to the Christian virtue of love to show anger (see Eph. 4:26). When Jesus cleansed the temple (John 2), he did not stop being a loving God. Rather, the *manifestation* of his love took on a different look. In the same way, our willingness to hate at times is a manifestation of love. If we do not get angry at sin and its effects, do we really know the full truth about God's love?

Both times of war and peace permeate the Old Testament. This verse and 3:2–3 on killing also remind us how uncertain our lives are.

3:9. If a worker toils in his own strength, there is little profit. It is much wiser to be submissive to the seasons that God gives.

3:10–11. God is the one who orders our steps (Ps. 37:23). He has made everything appropriate in its time. Although man has a deep yearning to know God's eternal plan, he can't. It isn't that God is cruel by concealing his plan from us. It is simply that he could never adequately explain it to us in our sinful and fallen condition.

Consider a two-year-old taking quantum mechanics from a teacher of physics. The teacher is clever, witty, and enthusiastic. He even has puppets of Heisenberg and Einstein. Can he teach quantum theory in such a way that two-year-olds will learn? Hardly. The deficiency is not with the teacher. It is with the students. The material is far too lofty for minds occupied with matters such as their next meal and having their diapers changed.

Even with our glorified bodies in heaven, it will take all of eternity to appreciate God's plan. Although we will no longer be adversely affected by our fallenness in heaven, we remain finite. And a finite human being can never totally exhaust an infinite, self-existent God. That's why heaven will never get boring. God will continually reveal himself to us.

Trying to conceptualize God's greatness brings great wonder and humility.

> Here is where I got an Excedrin headache in my philosophy class. Before the world began there was nothing. But what in the world is "nothing"? Have you ever tried to think about nothing? Where can we find it? Obviously nowhere. Why? Because it is nothing and nothing doesn't exist. It can't exist, because if it did then it would be something and not nothing. Are you starting to get a headache like mine? Think about it for a second. . . . I can't tell you to think about "it" because nothing isn't an "it." I can only say "nothing isn't" (Sproul, *The Holiness of God,* 16).

Our desire to seek out the things of God is good and proper. We grow spiritually by desiring God's wisdom as a hidden treasure (Prov. 2:1–5) even though our understanding is limited.

But to value the seeking out of the things of God, a person must be vigilant to evaluate how biblical his view of time is. Consider the counsel of Richard Foster:

> A mind that is harassed and fragmented by external affairs is hardly prepared for meditation. The church Fathers often spoke of *Otium Sanctum,* "holy leisure." It refers to a sense of balance in the life, an ability to be at peace through the activities of the day, an ability to rest and take time to enjoy beauty, an ability to pace ourselves. With our ability to define people in terms of what they produce, we would do well to cultivate "holy leisure." And if we expect to succeed in the contemplative way, we must pursue "holy leisure" with a determination that is ruthless to our date books (Foster, 27).

𝐁 Response to God's Sovereign Plan (3:12–15)

SUPPORTING IDEA: *All of us are tempted to spend time speculating about what God may be doing. But God's Word teaches that there are many things that will remain unclear to us this side of heaven. Will we submit to God's wise plan even though much of it is hidden from us, or will we become bitter? This option is before us in this section.*

3:12–13. Since we cannot fully know God's eternal plan, are we to become disillusioned? Not at all! Rather, we should occupy ourselves with giving thanks, doing good, and seeing good in all our labor. This is not a mindless mantra but the outworking of a trusting and godly heart. Seeing good in our labor is the gift of God. We are reminded again that this can't be done apart from the supernatural enabling of God.

We tend to think that God is interested only in our "souls." Things like our work seem unimportant to him. But this is not true. God is redeeming all of life for the Christian—including work. The effects of the fall on work still remain, but the Christian is able to see the redemptive plan of God in all things, including work.

3:14. Not only is God's work eternal, but it lacks nothing. God's ways are indeed perfect (Jas. 1:17–20). If we get in on what God is doing, this has eternal ramifications. But we must be cautioned about how easy it is to presume that we know exactly what God is doing. Like the apostles, we may find that our ministry is different than what we imagined. In John 4:35 Jesus told his disciples to "look at the fields! They are ripe for harvest." The people whom the disciples saw when they "looked up" were Samaritans (John 4:40), not the type of harvest they envisioned!

In light of this, fearing God is a most appropriate response. God's command for us to fear him (Deut. 6:24) is not the order of some power-hungry deity. But God knows that if we don't fear him, we will give respect to someone or something else which will eventually destroy us (Pss. 115:1–8; 135:13–18; Rom. 1:21–32). The command to fear God is actually proof of his love for us (Deut. 6:24).

3:15. C. S. Lewis spoke of God's "unbounded now." God sees all of human history in one fell swoop, one eternal or unbounded *now*. This leads to a difficult question. If God sees what I will do in the future (his foreknowledge), doesn't that logically lead to future events being so determined that my choices seem artificial? In discussions like these, we must be careful to go no further than the biblical text allows. In our efforts to piece together various passages or truth of Scripture, we may actually presume to know *how* they harmonize.

Consider the example of Ezekiel 37:1–14: Ezekiel saw "bones that were very dry" (v. 2). He was asked by God, "Son of man, can these bones live?" (v.

3). Ezekiel answered, "O Sovereign LORD, you alone know" (v. 3). This was a clear affirmation of God's sovereignty in bringing salvation. But then God asked Ezekiel to prophesy (v. 4). That seemed pointless! If God alone could give life to "these bones" (v. 5), why did Ezekiel need to prophesy? But God commanded Ezekiel, and the prophet obeyed (vv. 7,10).

There is no doubt from this passage as well as the rest of Scripture that God is in control. Theologians have reminded us that the Scriptures portray our God as great and wise enough to have a world in which the choices we make are authentic, yet never a surprise to him.

Everything God does is eternally significant. When we are submissive to what he is seeking to accomplish, we find ourselves participating in the eternal as well. Remembering that we participate in rather than contribute to the work of God also has major ramifications (Henrichsen). If we believe that we are indispensable to the work of God (i.e., we make a contribution that no one else can), then we will have not only an inflated sense of our own importance, but we will also be prone to burnout. If someone says they need us, we feel we must go. But if we believe we *participate* in the work of God, we will be thankful for the ministry opportunities the Lord gives us. We will be under no delusion that we are God's gift to the human race. There is much freedom and peace in being able to say no to ministry opportunities that we don't believe are God's will for us, even when other people do.

Once while speaking to a group of vocational Christian workers, I asked, "How many of you feel that you are indispensable to the work of God?" None said they were. So far, so good. They understood the blasphemous nature of such a belief. But many went on to confess that the way they went about ministering to others showed they did believe they were indispensable to the kingdom of God.

C God's Sovereignty and Evil and Injustice (3:16–22)

SUPPORTING IDEA: *Rabbi Harold Kushner wrote a poignant account of his son's illness and death in a popular book entitled,* When Bad Things Happen to Good People. *Through Kushner's struggle to harmonize God's power and goodness, he came to a most unfortunate conclusion. God would love to intervene more often when evil and suffering are taking place on earth, Kushsner said, but he is unable to do so. His motives are good and loving, but his ability is limited. There is far too much chaos for him to address it all. Kushner's view does not seem to impair his affection for God or his motivation to pray. But why pray or adore such a limited God?*

3:16. **Under the sun** there will be injustice and wickedness. Longman pointed out that "the repetitions in this poetic line are for emphasis" (p. 127). When people do not fear God, they no longer look to an arbiter bigger than themselves. I experienced this firsthand in arresting various shoplifters, one a convicted felon. He simply pled insanity and was released.

3:17–18. Solomon consoled himself in the fact that God will judge all people (cf. Eccl. 8:8–9; 12:13–14). There is a divinely appointed time for these matters.

3:19–22. Animals have no way to escape the inevitability of death, and neither do we. This bleak situation demonstrates the futility of life apart from God. In this section, some interpreters believe Solomon was expressing his agnosticism about the afterlife. He seems to focus on what he can see (Provan, 94). Others believe that this question does not totally discount the possibility of an afterlife but that the author found "speculation" about the subject a "waste of time" (Crenshaw, 104).

This question is not necessarily a categorical denial of the afterlife, but we must be careful how optimistic an answer we expect (Garrett, 303–05). We may be trying to preserve an orthodox view that is unwarranted from the text (Longman 130–31).

The concluding verse of chapter 3 brings us back to earlier verses in this chapter. Man ought to be happy in his present activities because this is what God has ordained. The uncertainty of the future also provides motivation to enjoy life in the present. But too many of us have a wrong view of time and do not fully experience the present.

Consider the sobering words of Pascal:

> We never keep to the present. We recall the past; we anticipate the future as if we found it too slow in coming and were trying to hurry it up, or we recall the past as if to stay its too rapid flight. We are so unwise that we wander about in times that do not belong to us, and do not think of the only one that does; so vain that we dream of times that are not and blindly flee the only one that is. The fact is that the present usually hurts. We thrust it out of sight because it distresses us, and if we find it enjoyable, we are sorry to see it slip away. We try to give it the support of the future, and think how we are going to arrange things over which we have no control for a time we can never be sure of reaching.

> Let each of us examine his thoughts; he will find them wholly concerned with the past or the future. We almost never think of the present, and if we do think of it, it is only to see what light it throws on our plans for the future. The present is never our end. The past and the present are our means, the future alone our end. Thus we never actu-

ally live, but hope to live, and since we are always planning how to be happy, it is inevitable that we should never be so (Pascal, 43).

MAIN IDEA REVIEW: *Although this list of events is quite extensive, it is certainly not exhaustive. Many more things could be added, but it does cover a full range of human activities. The generic nature of this list allows for many applications.*

III. CONCLUSION

Too Little Time

Many new concepts like *multitasking* (doing several things at one time) and *timestackers* (Morrow, 73) have floated effortlessly into the vocabulary of Americans. As Christians, we always should define our world from a biblical perspective, but we don't. Instead of saying that we are people pleasers, lazy, or selfishly ambitious, we say that we simply have too many demands placed on us. Some Christians may have schedules that cause exhaustion. I am thinking of single parents, parents who have to deal with a severe illness or handicap, and other such predicaments.

But many of us are "pressed for time" because of our desire to earn others' praise or to accomplish some great feat. Instead of using euphemisms, we must recapture the moral and spiritual language of Scripture. We aren't just busy. We lack faith and so choose to sin.

PRINCIPLES

- It is possible to accomplish all that God has for us to do. But it is not possible to do God's will and accomplish our own selfish and sinful agendas at the same time.
- Describing the Industrial Age, John Ruskin said, "It is not that men are ill-fed, but that they have no pleasure in the work by which they make their bread, and therefore look to wealth as the only means of pleasure" (Ruskin, quoted in Guinness, 200).
- God is redeeming all of life for the Christian, including work. This does not mean that the Christian will be free of taxing work and grumpy bosses. It does mean that he will be able to trust that the good hand of God wants to use him for redemptive purposes that go beyond this world.
- Evil and injustice can cause us to lose heart. As Christians, we are not called upon to paper over the rough edges of life in a fallen world. Nor should we act like we know exactly what God is

doing. We are called upon to trust the Lord and stay busy with what he has called us to do.

APPLICATIONS

- Does the description of a pragmatist in Ecclesiastes 3:4 character-ize your life? If so, what changes might God have in store for your life?
- Does your schedule have a tendency to keep you preoccupied with the "cares of this world"? If so, remember that your priori-ties must change *before* you will be motivated to change your schedule.
- Do an honest inventory of your priorities (with the help and accountability of other believers) and consider whether your val-ues match those of Scripture.
- Plan a period of solitude as a part of each day.

IV. LIFE APPLICATION

Focused but Flexible

When I was ministering to college students at Stanford University, I wanted to start a Bible study in the Sigma Chi house, but I couldn't get any-thing going. After trying in vain for over a year, my "God-given opportunity disguised as a hassle" happened one day. It was a beautiful spring day, and I was anxious to get to the campus post office before the hordes of students converged on it after the last morning class period. As I made my way across the plaza, I heard a traveling evangelist on the free-speech platform. He was one of those "evangelists" who points out specific sins in the lives of people he has never met. Equally audacious was his claim of being free from sin him-self!

My spirit was provoked. I believed that God was telling me to go over and ask some questions. Here's where I reminded God that this did not "fit" into my priority of getting the packages mailed. "Sorry, God, I'm not available. Ask someone else!" But God was not through with me.

After arguing with God for about five minutes, I finally caved in. I went over and engaged this evangelist on various issues related to the gospel. A crowd of several hundred students gathered around. After our give-and-take, a student approached me about the possibility of doing a debate that evening on what true Christianity is all about. Guess who he was? The president of the Sigma Chi fraternity! After the debate several members of the Sigma Chi house asked me about the possibility of leading an evening Bible study for them.

This study was one of the highlights of my week. Many times I got home at 1:00 to 2:00 a.m. because these young men wanted to talk more. From that study at least two men went on to become medical doctors. At the beginning of the Bible study, they were not convinced abortion was wrong, but both eventually came to see that position as biblically indefensible. That's just some of the fruit that came from the Bible study.

Back to my packages that got mailed a couple days late. Was I upset that my agenda was thwarted? No way. In fact, I don't even remember what I was mailing or to whom! But what I will never forget are the godly convictions that were forged in that Bible study. So be focused on your priorities, but remain flexible to God's leading.

V. PRAYER

Help me to trust you more fully, Lord, especially where my understanding of what you are doing is limited. Amen.

VI. DEEPER DISCOVERIES

A. The Biblical View of Time (3:1–11)

I have a friend who used to schedule every fifteen minutes of his day. The absurdity of his approach was made evident to me on more than one occasion. I remember his mom asking him to take out the garbage, and he retorted that the five minutes it took did not fit into his afternoon schedule!

Some Christians point to a passage like Ephesians 5:15–16 to support the notion that every second of every day must be managed: "Be very careful, then, how you live—not as unwise but as wise, making the most of every opportunity, because the days are evil."

This passage uses the word *kairos,* not *chronos,* for time. *Chronos* is the word from which we get "chronological" or "chronometric." It deals with "clock" time. But Paul used *kairos* in Ephesians 5. *Kairos* deals with opportunity or season. We must be wise in how we treat every opportunity. The truth of this passage should cause us not to be overly anxious about every second of every day but to consider wisely and weigh the opportunities before us. It is much more of a "big-picture" perspective on time, just like we observed in Ecclesiastes 3:1–11.

B. "A Time to Love" (3:8)

It is common at marriage conferences to hear that love does not necessarily involve feelings. There is even a proof text in Ephesians 5:25 given to support such a notion. Since you can't command someone's emotions, and since Paul is commanding, "Husbands, love your wives," it seems clear that love does not necessarily include feelings or emotions. But a closer look at Scripture, and even the supporting passage for this idea—Ephesians 5:25–29—will show the problem with this teaching.

Note that 1 Corinthians 13:3 says that a person can do the ultimate *behavior* ("surrender my body to the flames") and yet still not have love. Love certainly includes certain behavior, but love is not totally described by tangible acts, even heroic ones. Let's go back to Ephesians 5.

In the verses following verse 25, we get a fuller picture of what it may look like to "love our wives." For instance, Paul says that husbands should care for their wives "as their own bodies" (v. 28). Obviously, all of us are committed (including our emotions and feelings) to our own well-being.

It also ought to be said that affections or desires are better words to use than emotions or feelings. The latter two words connote fickleness. Affections and desires remind us that we will delight in what we value or treasure. And wives certainly are a treasure!

This is one of many examples to illustrate how unbiblical views of love have crept into the church. When Ecclesiastes 3:8 says that there is "a time to love," we should think about *all* that may involve.

C. "So That They May See That They Are Like the Animals" (3:18)

Although the issue of our mortality is the primary aspect of this comparison with "beasts," it is interesting to note that the concept of beastlikeness is common in the Scriptures.

When people turn their backs on God, they become like beasts before him (Ps. 73:21–22). King Nebuchadnezzar of Babylonia is probably the most graphic example of this. Because of his pride, he literally started to take on the characteristics of a grazing animal (Dan. 4:32). Lest anyone think that this is an impossibility, *zoanthropy*, the malady of a human taking on beastlike characteristics, has been observed in modern times (Pentecost, 1342).

Furthermore, false teachers are called "brute beasts" or "unreasoning animals" (2 Pet. 2:12; Jude 10). These false teachers live their lives by instinct rather than the dictates of Scripture (2 Pet. 2:19–22).

Man's beastlikeness does not mean that the image of God in man has been obliterated. All people retain God's image, but we must keep in mind that it can be marred by persistent sin. As Millard Erickson noted:

> God's creation was for definite purposes. Man was intended to know, love, and obey God. He was to live in harmony with his fellow man, as the story of Cain and Abel indicates. And he was certainly placed here upon earth to exercise dominion over the rest of creation. But these relationships and this function presuppose

something else. Man is most fully human when he is active in these relationships and performs this function. Man qua [as] man has a nature that includes the whole of what constitutes personality: intelligence, will, emotions. *We experience full humanity only when we are properly related to God.* No matter how cultured and genteel a person may be, he is not fully human unless he has become a redeemed disciple of God. This is man's *telos,* that for which he was created (Erickson, 513–14, emphasis added).

VII. TEACHING OUTLINE

A. INTRODUCTION
1. Lead Story: An Obsession with Time
2. Context: Chapter 3 shows us how to live the kind of life that God honors.
3. Transition: In chapters 1 and 2, Solomon details what life is like apart from God. In chapter 3, he shifts to describing the way life is best lived.

B. COMMENTARY
1. God Rules over All Events (3:1–11)
2. Response to God's Sovereign Plan (3:12–15)
3. God's Sovereignty and Evil and Injustice (3:16–22)

C. CONCLUSION: TOO LITTLE TIME

VIII. ISSUES FOR DISCUSSION

1. During the second century A.D., Justin Martyr mentioned that the yokes and plows Jesus and his father Joseph made were still in use (Guinness, 202). Since it is inconceivable to imagine Jesus making a table with crooked legs (Sayers, 77), how important is it that Christians model excellence at their places of employment?
2. Sacred/secular is a false dichotomy. All of our activities are to glorify God, even the mundane like eating and drinking (1 Cor. 10:31). In light of this, is it correct to say "that the only reason we are left on planet earth is to share the gospel"?
3. Sleep is not only a "biological necessity; it can also be an act of faith" (Peterson, *Answering God,* 62). Even Penelope, with her great eagerness to see Odysseus return, realized that heaven had appointed a time for sleep (Homer, *Odyssey,* 295).

Since God has made us (and modeled for us) the work-and-rest cycle, why is it so common to hear Christians say that they wished they didn't have to sleep?

Ecclesiastes 4

Ambitious Pursuits, Corrupt Desires

Quote

"*Every* day I put love on the line. There is nothing I am less good at than love. I am far better in competition than in love. I am far better at responding to my instincts and ambitions to get ahead and make my mark than I am at figuring out how to love another. I am schooled and trained in acquisitive skills, in getting my own way. And yet, I decide, every day, to set aside what I can do best and attempt what I do very clumsily—open myself to the frustrations and failures of loving, daring to believe that failing in love is better than succeeding in pride."

Eugene H. Peterson

IN A NUTSHELL

The Bible is full of examples and exhortations on the value of developing friendships. Because it is such a realistic book, the Bible also portrays the sins that keep us from developing quality relationships. This chapter in Ecclesiastes reminds us to value friendship over worldly accomplishments.

Ambitious Pursuits, Corrupt Desires

I. INTRODUCTION

Valuing Friendships in a Competitive Culture

*I*n this chapter we will observe that good relationships are to be highly prized. In a technological age when the accomplishment of tasks in a quick and efficient manner is considered the greatest good, it is easy to see why so many of us are busy yet terribly lonely. The hard-charging atmosphere caused by driven, ambitious people leaves little time for meaningful relationships.

This came home to me during my six years in college ministry at Stanford University. It was common for students to tell me how "close" I was to certain people on campus. In point of fact, however, I was just getting to know many of these people. We were simply acquaintances. But in a highly competitive environment like Stanford, deep relationships can be hard to come by. Any friendly exchange with another person constitutes "closeness."

In a world where there is a reckless spirit of competition, it is wise to have good friends who buoy your spirits. Not having the support of committed relationships causes untold damage. This is a recurring theme in the wisdom literature of Scripture (Prov. 13:20; 18:1).

II. COMMENTARY

Ambitious Pursuits, Corrupt Desires

MAIN IDEA: *Many diversions keep us from building meaningful relationships. Some of them seem impossible to avoid. The pace of life in a technological age has too many of its hooks in us. Taking time to develop and keep loyal friendships strikes many of us as unrealistic. Solomon takes time in this chapter to address some of the internal motivations like pride and ambition that prevent or at least complicate the development of meaningful relationships.*

Injustice Coupled with No Support Brings Despair (4:1–3)

SUPPORTING IDEA: *Solomon hearkens back to the theme of injustice (cf. Eccl. 3:16). Injustice causes us to lose heart, especially if we are on the receiving end of it. Loyal friendships can bring comfort during such difficult and trying circumstances.*

4:1. Looking at **all the oppression** is a hyperbole. Only God sees all injustice. This phrase simply underscores that the author saw "the pervasiveness of oppression" (Seow, 186). Both the oppressed and oppressors had one thing in common: There was no one to comfort them. We can understand this with the oppressed, but how can this be with the oppressors? After all, they have the power. We will see later, however, that people are fickle about who they want in power (4:13–16). The precarious nature of "being in charge" provides little comfort.

4:2. The grievous nature of corruption and justice caused Solomon to see the advantage of being dead rather than alive (cf. Job 3:3).

4:3. Solomon even goes so far as to say that this situation was so painful that not existing at all was the preferable option. It was indeed a bleak picture **under the sun**.

Coping in the Midst of Trials (4:4–12)

SUPPORTING IDEA: *Solomon proceeds to describe various options that people choose in order to exist in a world that is marked by injustice, selfish ambition, and looking out for "number one."*

4:4. Some people determine that the way to "make it" in this sin-saturated world is to allow the competitive juices to flow. Competition per se is not evil, especially the type that seeks to make personal goals. But competition that seeks to overpower another or to make that person look stupid or inferior is sinful. This type of competition is common in our world. As Solomon will graphically demonstrate, this leads to heartache and loneliness.

In case we don't "feel" that we are very competitive, it is time for honest evaluation. How do we respond inwardly when someone does a better job at something we value? Do we feel "beat"? If we feel that we "lost," we know where the competitive spirit is coming from!

4:5. Some people decide to give up or never try in the midst of such a competitive environment. This is not a wise alternative. The "grotesque imagery of self-cannibalism" (Seow, 179) graphically conveys the foolishness of this option.

4:6. Other people find the balance between meaningful work and peace of mind. Contentment, they conclude, is much more valuable than the material benefits that come from being ambitious in a destructive manner. Indeed, this is the preferable option, much better than reckless competition and superior to laziness. Some successful business people have decided to simplify their lives in order to have more peace of mind and the space for meaningful relationships (Swenson).

Robert Bellah and his associates put it this way:

> Perhaps life is not a race whose only goal is being foremost. Perhaps the truth lies in what most of the world outside the modern West has always believed, namely that there are practices of life, good in themselves, that are inherently fulfilling. Perhaps work that is intrinsically rewarding is better for human beings than work that is only extrinsically rewarded. Perhaps enduring commitment to those we love and civic friendship toward our fellow citizens are preferable to restless competition and anxious self-defense. Perhaps common worship, in which we express our gratitude and wonder in the face of the mystery of being itself, is the most important thing of all. If so, we will have to change our lives and begin to remember what we have been happier to forget (Bellah, et al., 295).

4:7–8. Sadly, many people continue to be workaholics even when there is no progeny to leave their wealth to. Material prosperity coupled with the "advantages" of technology is a lethal drug that keeps many of us from reflecting on the important matters of life. One commentator noted the wasted life of one well-known fool: "Billionaire Howard Hughes ended his days a chronic recluse, haunted by his fears of disease—a living-death testimony to the impotence (or was it danger?) of material prosperity in the face of profound spiritual darkness. Isolation is often the concomitant of worldly success" (Keddie, 47).

As we get older, it becomes more difficult to avoid thinking about the big issues of life. Sadly, much damage has already taken place. I see this firsthand when I visit a retirement community in Florida where retired CEOs have plenty of money yet complain about the aging process and being estranged from family members.

President Eisenhower was once asked what he thought were the cause and cure for inflation. "That's easy," he replied. "The cause is the greed of the American people. The cure is to curb the greed of Americans" (Wilson, *Our Dance Has Turned to Death*, 94). Indeed, but greed is fueled by strong passions that do not go away easily. Among other things, we must give up the illusion that we can "have it all" (Yankelovich, 175).

4:9–12. The stereotype of the "friendless American male" tends to make us think that the problem is unique to men. But supercompetitive, driven people who don't have time for meaningful relationships are found among both genders. Solomon had learned some significant lessons about the poverty of a life that has only material wealth. Friendships are truly indispensable to a rich life.

The Scriptures warn us about those who separate themselves from others (Prov. 18:1; Heb. 10:24–25; 1 Pet. 5:8–9). First Peter 5:8–9 teaches that separating from other believers makes one vulnerable to spiritual attack. Since all of us can be deceived (Ps. 19:12; Jer. 17:9; 1 Cor. 4:1–5), we desperately need others to keep us accountable (Heb. 3:13).

Jesus sent his disciples out in twos (Luke 10:1). Anyone who has done much evangelism understands the wisdom in this. Even the apostle Paul, for all his courage and giftedness, needed people to cheer him up on various occasions (2 Cor. 7:6; cf. 2 Cor. 1:8–11).

Synergy is a popular word that suggests among other things that $1 + 1 = 3$. The effect of two people working in harmony together can be much greater than those two laboring on their own (Eccl. 4:9). Times of pain and struggle come upon all of us and it is truly tragic when there is no support.

As a minister, I have observed people who have enjoyed much support from others during times of tragedy, and I have seen individuals who have had little or no support. For those in the latter category, some honest inventory is needed. Is there a lack of support from others because one is not engaged in the lives of others? The old aphorism applies: "I went out to look for a friend and they were nowhere. I went out to be a friend and they were everywhere."

A popular buzzword in churches is "community." It's not surprising, considering the rabid individualism and competitive nature of the modern world.

Unfortunately, true community is not what people in many churches really want. What they really desire is either people meeting their needs on their terms or what some prominent sociologists have labeled "lifestyle enclaves" (Bellah, et al., 71–75). Lifestyle enclaves are artificial communities. They are groups of people with the same socioeconomic background who exist solely to satisfy their individual and collective desires. This is not the biblical meaning of community.

Some polls show that large numbers of people believe marriage, friends, and family contribute most to their happiness. This can be as high as four times more the happiness than those who credit individual pursuits such as career or hobbies (Dreyfous). It would be wise for all of us to order our schedules accordingly.

It is common for interpreters to see an allusion to travel imagery in these verses (Garrett, 308; Whybray, *Ecclesiastes*, 87). In a world marked by violence and cruelty, the support of others can be a great benefit (cf. 2 Sam. 10:11).

Ⓒ Poor Substitutes for Friendship (4:13–16)

SUPPORTING IDEA: *Some people are tempted to believe that having power over others is a good substitute for meaningful relationships. They reason that it would be wonderful to have people at their beck and call. Solomon describes the foolishness of that belief.*

4:13–14. There seems to be a *relative* advantage in having a young king over an old one who is no longer teachable. Coming out of prison possibly indicates that the young leader was a revolutionary type who had been imprisoned for opposing the "old guard" (Wright, *Expositor's Bible Commentary: Ecclesiastes,* 1,166).

4:15–16. Initially, we are excited to have someone new lead us. But the newness eventually wears off, and we become disgruntled once again with those in leadership over us. This cycle of anticipation, followed by disappointment and ultimately a desire for new blood, is characteristic of the human condition. It depicts vanity and "a chasing after the wind" (4:16).

While I was teaching in Poland during the summer of 1991, a number of Poles confided that Lech Walesa, the hero of Polish independence and solidarity, had become a great disappointment to them in his new role as president of the country. His poor grammar and lack of manners were two things that they mentioned to me.

By nature we tend to grow weary and critical of those who are in authority over us. We tend to put too much hope that some new leader will rescue us from our present plight. The restlessness that we experience in wanting someone new to lead us is not just a political phenomenon. Churches experience this kind of thing all the time. The present pastor is too old, too stuck in his ways. A change is needed—ideally a younger man with fresh ideas. But fresh ideas do tend to get stale, and young pastors do get old!

I almost experienced this firsthand while in the throes of indecision about whether God wanted me to be a senior pastor. One of the interested churches told me that they wanted a younger minister like me because their present pastor who was retiring was a nice man but "too set in his ways." I'm sure this church would have discovered that I'm equally "set in some of my ways!" In the providence of God, I had just studied this section of Ecclesiastes when I received the call inquiring about my possible interest.

MAIN IDEA REVIEW: *Many diversions keep us from building meaningful relationships. Some of them seem impossible to avoid. The pace of life in a technological age has too many of its hooks in us. Taking time to develop and keep loyal friendships strikes many of us as unrealistic. Solomon takes time in this chapter to address some of the internal motivations like pride and ambition that prevent or at least complicate the development of meaningful relationships.*

III. CONCLUSION

The Problem with Selfish Ambition

Reckless or selfish ambition is a common temptation for many prominent and not-so-prominent people. Consider the words of President Lyndon Johnson: "Ambition is an uncomfortable companion many times. He creates a discontent with present surroundings and achievements; he is never satisfied but always pressing forward to better things in the future" (Goodwin, *Lyndon Johnson*, 51).

Ambition in itself is not wrong. Paul made it his ambition to preach the gospel in new places (Rom. 15:17–20). But it is selfish ambition (Jas. 3:14), as President John Adams so memorably put it, that we must have a "habitual contempt" of (McCullough, *John Adams*, 19). We are wise if we repent daily of our lust for power. We are wiser still if we replace it with a consistent commitment to people. Loyal friends will bring us joy and happiness through the many vicissitudes of this world.

PRINCIPLES

- It is tempting to value status, power, and wealth and to forget the importance of friendships.
- Contentment comes from resting in God's plan and provision.
- In the midst of a hostile world, friendships are a God-given means of support and encouragement.

APPLICATIONS

- Guard against the trap of workaholism.
- Contentment comes by trusting God's definition of success. Bathe your mind in the scriptural language of success. Start by reading Isaiah 2 and Jeremiah 45.
- Remember that the riches of friendship are superior to the riches of the world.

IV. LIFE APPLICATION

The Power of Relationships

Two of the three Cappodocian Fathers, Basil the Great and Gregory of Nazianzen, were described as having "one soul dwelling in two bodies" (Chan, 176). In Scripture we see loyal friendships like David and Jonathan, Paul and Timothy. Borrowing Paul's terminology, we too can have "kindred spirits," but we must be willing to look out for the interests of others before our own (Phil. 2:1–8). It was a supernatural thing to do in Paul's day. It is no less so today.

If we grow in our understanding of what God values, we will see the wisdom of relating to other brothers and sisters in the Lord. May we not be fooled by the reckless ambition that permeates our culture!

V. PRAYER

Dear God, you have created us as social beings. May we see more clearly that friendships are to be prized above worldly ambition and achievement. Amen.

VI. DEEPER DISCOVERIES

A. "Two Handfuls with Toil and Chasing After the Wind" (4:6)

It is not wrong to value a hard day's work. But it can be destructive spiritually (and physically) to feel the compulsion to work constantly. When he created the world, God made the "night" and called it "good" (Gen. 1:18). More commentary on God separating the light from darkness can be found in Psalm 104:19–23. The darkness is "appointed" for nocturnal animals (v. 20 NASB). We humans are to do our work "until evening" (v. 23).

We may be tempted to think that the lightbulb has supplanted the practicality of these verses. For those of us who stay up late, or possibly complain that "it would be great if we didn't have to sleep," we ought to reconsider whether we truly believe that God is always working on our behalf, even while we sleep (Ps. 127:2).

B. "A Cord of Three Strands" (4:12)

The history of biblical interpretation on this verse demonstrates that it is not uncommon to find commentators who believed this third cord to be Jesus. Even some modern commentators give credence to this idea (Eaton, 92–93). The temptation to take a text such as this and go beyond what it means is something all of us must guard against. Understandably, we may desire to emphasize an important theological point. For example, some go so far as to say that the "cord of three" is the Trinity (Davidson, 31).

Christians do have Jesus to "bond them together." But the desire to underscore an important theological point must always be submitted to a careful study of the scriptural text.

VII. TEACHING OUTLINE

A. INTRODUCTION

1. Lead Story: Valuing Friendships in a Competitive Culture
2. Context: Chapter 4 reminds us that friends are a wonderful blessing in a world marked by selfishness, injustice, and greed.
3. Transition: We can find comfort and support in this world if we take advantage of a God-given priority—people—instead of power and possessions.

B. COMMENTARY

1. Injustice Coupled with No Support Brings Despair (4:1–3)
2. Coping in the Midst of Trials (4:4–12)
3. Poor Substitutes for Friendship (4:13–16)

C. CONCLUSION: THE PROBLEM WITH SELFISH AMBITION

VIII. ISSUES FOR DISCUSSION

1. Can you identify several friends who would be available at a moment's notice if you experienced some personal tragedy? If not, consider how much of a premium you have put on developing good friends.
2. Read Craig Blomberg's book, *Neither Poverty nor Riches*. Preferably read this with a couple of other friends for better discussion and accountability.
3. Imagine being on your deathbed. Are you satisfied with how much time you invested in family and friends? If not, what can you do to keep from having major regrets at the end of your life?

Ecclesiastes 5

Speak, for Thy Servant Is Listening

Q u o t e

"On the whole, I do not find Christians, outside of the cata-

combs, sufficiently sensible of conditions. Does anyone have

the foggiest idea what sort of power we so blithely invoke? Or,

as I suspect, does not one believe a word of it? The churches are

children playing on the floor with their chemistry sets, mixing

up a batch of TNT to kill a Sunday morning. It is madness to

wear ladies' straw hats and velvet hats to church; we should all be

wearing crash helmets. Ushers should issue life preservers and

signal flares; they should lash us to our pews. For the sleeping

god may wake someday and take offense, or the waking god may

draw us out to where we can never return."

Annie Dillard

I N   A   N U T S H E L L

Many times our prayers reveal that we believe God needs to hear from us more than we need to hear from him. Clearly, this is unwise. In this chapter Solomon teaches us the importance of proper worship. This involves a willingness to be silent before a holy God.

Speak, for Thy Servant Is Listening

I. INTRODUCTION

Quick to Hear and Slow to Speak

*W*hen we approach God in prayer, are we alert to the importance of waiting silently for him to speak, or are we eager to cite a litany of personal needs that God must answer? Peter, James, and John had to learn this important lesson on the Mount of Transfiguration (Matt. 17:1–13, esp. v. 5).

It is not that God is uninterested in our needs. We know that he is. It is imperative, though, that we remember the proper relationship when speaking with God. He is the Creator; we are the creatures. The degree to which we remember this crucial truth is the degree to which we will come to God in reverence and awe. As Habakkuk 2:20 reminds us, "The LORD is in his holy temple; let all the earth be silent before him."

II. COMMENTARY

Speak, for Thy Servant Is Listening

> **MAIN IDEA:** *Many things can distract us from worshiping God. Solomon speaks openly about a few of the major hindrances. Distractions like the "love of money" keep us from the greatest treasure of all—an intimate relationship with the living God.*

Improper Versus Proper Worship (5:1–7)

> **SUPPORTING IDEA:** *When it comes to the worship of God, we want to fill quiet spaces with meaningless chatter. This not only reflects spiritual immaturity; it also demonstrates the sin in our hearts.*

5:1. The possibility of presumptuous and foolish worship is described in this opening verse. The fool's sacrifice is a habit that is hard to break because he is ignorant of the fact that he is doing evil. Religious sincerity not anchored in truth is lethal. Our inclination to self-deception is taught in both testaments of God's Word (2 Sam. 12:1–13; Ps. 19:12; 1 Cor. 4:1–5; Heb. 3:13). Without regular intake of the Bible, Spirit-led prayer, and the accountability of others, we are doomed to keep repeating our foolish prayers.

If we don't come to God with a willingness to hear from him first, we are doing something far more sinful than we could ever imagine. We should "not talk to God as boldly and carelessly as we do to one another, not speak what comes uppermost" (Henry, 1006).

5:2. In this verse we see the Creator/creature distinction that is essential to God-honoring prayers. Hasty words and impulsive thoughts have disastrous consequences. An example from the history of Israel should prove helpful.

In Numbers 11, the Israelites wanted meat to eat because they were tired of manna. They fondly recalled the food they had eaten in Egypt (vv. 5–6). The Lord decided to grant his grumbling people what they thought they needed (v. 18). The food that the people of God so desperately wanted would become loathsome to them (v. 20). The very thing that the people of God *felt* would bring life actually brought death and God's judgment (v. 33).

Because of our tendency to speak hasty words and use impulsive speech, it is wise to let our words be few (cf. Ps. 46:10; Matt. 6:7). The phrase **do not be quick with your mouth** can be misunderstood. This warning is given in a context that has a specific point to make: Don't be so quick to list personal requests when talking to God.

This warning doesn't prohibit lengthy prayers or even repetitive prayers. There is clearly biblical support for those types of prayers. The words of Charles Bridges are instructive in this regard: "Solomon speaketh not against all length in prayer (for Christ prayed whole nights), not against all repetition, when it proceedeth from zeal, love, and holy fervency—as that of Daniel (9:16–19), but of that, which is a 'vain ingeminating [reiterating] of the same things without faith or wisdom'" (Bridges, 102).

We need to keep in mind that Matthew 6:7 prohibits *meaningless* repetition, not *meaningful* repetition. Depending on a person's motives, the Lord's Prayer could fall into either of these categories.

5:3. Some interpreters take the mention of dreams here as an indication of daydreams (Kidner, 53; cf. Garrett, 311), which is well served by the context. I lean toward the idea that Solomon is describing the reality that dreams come at night as a result of much worry (cf. Eccl. 5:12). **Many cares** or great anxiety caused the dreams.

5:4. God delights in those people who keep their word because he is the original "promise keeper" (Num. 23:19; 2 Cor. 1:20). The importance of the spoken and kept word is not something he takes lightly. Those who are devastated by the severity of this verse will want to remember that "promise breakers" like Peter can be restored (Matt. 16:21–23; 26:33–35; cf. John 21:3–17)!

5:5. This verse is quite clear and is further illustrated by both positive and negative examples in the Bible. We think of Jephthah's presumptuous vow about his daughter (Judg. 11:30–31), Ananias and Sapphira's pride-filled vow (Acts 5:1–4), and Jonah's desperate vow (Jonah 2:9). We also remember one of the most God-glorifying vows recorded in Scripture—the one Hannah made about her son Samuel (1 Sam. 1:11).

As Proverbs 20:25 exhorts, "It is a trap for a man to dedicate something rashly and only later to consider his vows." We must be careful about how quickly we make vows.

5:6. Our speech is powerful (Jas. 3:5–6) and can cause great evil (Prov. 10:19; 12:18). Much destruction comes from not heeding this clear and powerful teaching.

5:7. There is nothing substantive or long-lasting about dreams. The morning comes and the dream is forgotten. Many words are also empty and don't amount to anything of real value. But the person who fears God (a common theme in Ecclesiastes) is on solid ground (1 John 2:17; Ps. 34:9).

𝐁 Distraction 1: Observing Injustice (5:8–9)

SUPPORTING IDEA: *Injustice can cause a person to question the goodness of God. It certainly can be disruptive to the quiet adoration of almighty God. Solomon has already mentioned the topic of injustice (see Eccl. 3:16–18). It is important enough to revisit.*

5:8–9. We are not to **be surprised** when we observe injustice. Solomon anticipates the deep disillusionment that can come from false expectations. Refusing to admit that our world is full of pain, suffering, and injustice is to place one's head in the proverbial sand.

Solomon warns that injustice can be an impediment to worshiping God "in spirit and in truth" (John 4:24). We must never lose sight of the fact that man, not God, is the author of evil (see Eccl. 7:29), and that true communion with God gives a *better perspective* on injustice than anything. Asaph learned this critical lesson (Ps. 73), and so must we. We can rest in God's power and goodness even though we may not understand fully what he is doing.

The common philosophical idea that we must choose between God as good and God as all-powerful is a false dichotomy put forth by those who rely too much on human reasoning as the way to resolve questions about God (Kushner, 42–44). Evil does exist, but so does an all-powerful, benevolent God who is wisely working out his plan for the ages. Critizing God's motive or ability because we don't understand what he is doing is the height of arrogance.

𝐂 Distraction 2: Money (5:10–17)

SUPPORTING IDEA: *Christians who live in affluent societies must fight against the ways in which wealth can deaden the soul.*

5:10. This verse warns against the *love* of money, not money itself. In Scripture we find that having money is assumed to be a possibility among certain believers. In fact, the apostle Paul's teaching on this subject does not prescribe the giving away of all wealth. Rather, he exhorts us "not to be arrogant nor to put [our] hope in wealth . . . and to be generous and willing to share" (1 Tim. 6:17–18).

Some may wish to invoke the rich young ruler, who was unwilling to heed Jesus' words to sell everything he had (Luke 18:22). It seems that this was a *description* of one person's struggle. Jesus' words were not necessarily meant to be a *prescription* for all Christians. Earlier, in the same Gospel, Jesus called three different people to consider giving up three different things (comfort, money, and family) in order to follow him (Luke 9:57–62). One person's obstacle to following Jesus may not be another's.

5:11. One problem with having lots of money is the proper management of wealth. These could be either "creditors or hangers on." Either way, the bottom line is that there is not "the opportunity to really enjoy its [wealth's] fruit" (Longman, 165).

5:12. Great anxiety and restlessness may bother the person who has much wealth. The person of average means doesn't typically have the headaches that go along with great wealth—embezzlement, lawsuits, and questioning whether people like you or your money.

Many examples of the paranoia and fear that come from having great amounts of wealth could be given. Sir William Burwell was a wealthy Scottish ship owner who spent much of his life amassing an extraordinary collection of art. He gave his work to his native city of Glasgow but never lived to see it displayed publicly. He lived his last years as a recluse for fear that fire or theft would take away his precious art (Keddie, 67).

The important point to remember is not whether the rich experience sleepless nights because of "worry or indigestion" (Longman, 165; cf. Seow, 206, 220; Young, 113). The relevant point is that they do not experience joy and contentment.

5:13. Solomon observed that some people may be tempted to think that riches will bring life. Riches are deceptive, and they beckon us with their seductive allure. He wanted people to know that the outcome of such a belief is spiritual death. Finding life is a result of losing one's life (Matt. 16:25).

5:14. Riches can be lost. We see this all the time when we read that some multimillionaire is filing for bankruptcy. Why live for something that is uncertain and can't survive beyond the grave? Why not live for the true riches that remain even when a fortune is lost (Hab. 3:17–19)?

5:15. It is foolish to love money when such bad fruit comes from avarice and greed. Loving money also blinds us to the fact that we have brought nothing into the world and we will leave it just as we entered (Job 1:21; 1 Tim. 6:7).

Saint Anthony's words about earthly possessions are worth pondering:

> Some of those who stop in inns are given beds, while others having no beds stretch themselves on the floor and sleep soundly as

those in beds. In the morning, when night is over, all alike get up and leave the inn, carrying away with them only their belongings. It is the same with those who tread the path of this life: both those who have lived in modest circumstances, and those who had wealth and fame, leave this life like an inn, taking with them no worldly comforts or riches, but only what they have done in this life, whether it be good or bad (quoted in Willard, *The Spirit of the Disciplines*, 209).

5:16. None of us can control our birth or our death. Cryogenics will not save us any more than mummification saved the pharaohs of Egypt. There is no profit for the person who spends his entire life laboring for what is futile and perishable.

5:17. The person who is not empowered by God receives the bitter fruit of trying to find ultimate meaning in money. And as we have seen many times in the Book of Ecclesiastes, money does not give meaning to life. The phrase **frustration, affliction and anger** brings to mind many wealthy elderly people who have told me what a "pain" old age is—a theme that we will see graphically at the end of Ecclesiastes. Money, status, and power cannot hold back the certainty of death.

Ⅾ The Proper Perspective (5:18–20)

> **SUPPORTING IDEA:** *A person's relationship with God—not the circumstances of life—brings joy.*

5:18. The godly person lives with joy in the good provision of God. He is able to experience the joy of God, even in his work. This doesn't diminish the fact that we work "by the sweat of our brow," but it does mean that all areas of a believer's life are touched and transformed by the redeeming work of God (see comments on Eccl. 3:12–13). Realism mixed with hope is a common theme in Ecclesiastes. Great joy is our possession as believers, but Solomon doesn't shield us from the reality that our days on this earth are few (see Eccl. 9:9).

5:19. For those who have wealth, the only way to enjoy it is if God **enables** them. It is a gift from God to have such joy. Finding joy and fulfillment in possessions alone is not possible.

5:20. The righteous person is not preoccupied with his mortality. Rather, his relationship with God keeps him occupied, and this produces deep and abiding joy (cf. comments on Eccl. 2:24–26). The righteous person doesn't look back at his youth as the only good time of life. All of his life is empowered by God, so all seasons are marked by joy. This person experiences no "midlife crisis," nor does he become bitter with old age (cf. Eccl. 7:10).

In closing, note these two different perspectives on growing old:

> William Randolph Hearst, who amassed one of the great fortunes of
> our time, ended his days amidst all the opulence and splendor of the

castle which he built in southern California, sitting in a basement, playing over and over again the movies of his paramour from Hollywood, in a vain attempt to gain a degree of enjoyment from the past (Stedman, 68).

"Aging, accordingly, will become a process not of losing, but of gaining. As our physical body fades out, our glory body approaches and our spiritual substance grows richer and deeper. As we age we should become obviously more glorious" (Willard, *The Divine Conspiracy*, 396–97).

MAIN IDEA REVIEW: *Many things can distract us from worshiping God. Solomon speaks openly about a few of the major hindrances. Distractions such as the "love of money" keep us from the greatest treasure of all—an intimate relationship with the living God.*

III. CONCLUSION

Waiting on God

Athanasius mentions that the venerable Anthony, nearly 105 years old, gave some parting words for believers not to lose heart when they observed judges protecting the heretical Arian sect. Instead, he directed them to focus on "the holy faith in our Lord Jesus Christ, which you have learned from the Scripture" (Athanasius, 220).

We may be impatient like Ivan in *The Brothers Karamazov* who "must have justice, or I will destroy myself" (Dostoevsky, 126). But God may have us wait to see such vindication of his righteousness. In the meantime, we will grow to trust God if we grow in our ability to sit silently in his presence.

PRINCIPLES

- We need to hear from God much more than he needs to hear from us.
- The love of material wealth will keep us from the true treasure of knowing God.
- Those who know God experience joy during every circumstance of life.

APPLICATIONS

- Take a day alone with the Lord. Bring your Bible, notebook, or diary and your willingness to hear from God. Meditate over large sections of Scripture (e.g., Gospels, Psalms, and Isaiah) so you can be confident that you are hearing from God!

- Listen carefully to your own prayers. Do you find any problems with presumption or flippancy in addressing God?
- Since all Christians ought to be suspicious over how much they have bought into the "American dream," ask God to show you how much the "love of money" holds your attention.

IV. LIFE APPLICATION

A Verse for the Aging

I was living in Dallas and on my way to lunch at a friend's home. En route on one of the side streets, I happened upon a softball game. I slowed down and then stopped. Wistfully, I imagined being a seventy-five-year-old man sitting in the baseball stands, recalling my younger years when running fast and throwing hard were easy.

Although I was only twenty-five at the time (almost twenty years ago), I vividly recall how depressed I got thinking about this inevitable reality. My body at seventy-five (if I get that far) will not be able to cooperate with my desire to run like a young man.

It was shortly after this that I first memorized Ecclesiastes 5:20. This verse has come to mind on innumerable occasions since. Biblically, I have the freedom to be honest about my mortality, but I also can experience the profound joy of God in every season of life. Being seventy-five and watching baseball from the stands is no longer scary for me. In fact, I can say that I actually look forward to it . . . as long as my teeth can still sink into an apple!

The words of the pious Fr. Zossima in *The Brothers Karamazov* sum up what all Christians ought to say at the end of life: "My life is ending, I know that well, but every day that is left me I feel how my earthly life is in touch with a new infinite, unknown, but approaching life, the nearness of which sets my soul quivering with rapture, my mind glowing and my heart weeping with joy" (Dostoevsky, 152).

V. PRAYER

Father in heaven, keep me from being a mere babbler in your midst. May I grow to find increasing peace by being still in your presence. Amen.

VI. DEEPER DISCOVERIES

A. "Whoever Loves Money" (5:10)

Pastors find money a very awkward topic. This is unfortunate because the Bible has so much to say about money. As we see in this verse and its New

Testament companion (1 Tim. 6:10), it is the "love of money" that ultimately ruins us. We must remember that our hearts are only big enough for one all-consuming passion (Matt. 6:24). Like Paul we must learn contentment whether God has blessed us with little or with much (Phil. 4:12; cf. Prov. 30:7–9).

Money can be used for great good. In fact, Jesus was displeased when his followers did not seem to have the same amount of financial savvy that some non-Christians did (Matt. 16:1–13, esp. v. 8).

It is easy to deceive ourselves into believing that we don't "love money." It is imperative then that we experience true koinonia where the truths of God's Word are regularly shared (Eph. 4:11–16; Col. 3:12–17).

VII. TEACHING OUTLINE

A. INTRODUCTION

1. Lead Story: Quick to Hear and Slow to Speak
2. Context: Chapter 5 confronts us with the common error of speaking presumptuously in the presence of a holy God.
3. Transition: Godly prayer is characterized by a willingness to slow down and enter our Father's "unhurried world." To do so, we must value silence over productivity and worldly striving.

B. COMMENTARY

1. Improper Versus Proper Worship (5:1–7)
2. Distraction 1: Observing Injustice (5:8–9)
3. Distraction 2: Money (5:10–17)
4. The Proper Perspective (5:18–20)

C. CONCLUSION: WAITING ON GOD

VIII. ISSUES FOR DISCUSSION

1. Why do so many of us say the Lord's name over and over again in prayer, but rarely speak this way when conversing with one another?
2. According to the Bible, what are some of the characteristics of the person who "loves money"?
3. Considering God's first application in Micah 6:8 "to act justly," what should the church be doing to address various injustices around the world?

Ecclesiastes 6

The Futility of a Self-Made Paradise

Quote

"*We* may now have everything, but none of it means anything any more. The most we seem able to do is to take daily inventories of personal needs and then try to match up people, products, and opportunities with them. The irony is that this psychological hedonism, in which self is the arbiter of life, is self-destructive. Not only are we betrayed; we betray *ourselves.* Meanwhile, we also pay the price of destroying all interest in the Transcendent, the sole source of genuine meaning in life. God, the supernatural, moral absolutes—these have become strangers in our modern, secularized world. We are like Yeats's falcon, increasingly oblivious to the voice of the falconer. The center no longer holds. All is flung to the periphery, where its meaning is lost."

David F. Wells

IN A NUTSHELL

The descriptions of the people in this chapter and the one before it are in direct contrast to each other. If we just described the lifestyles of the people in the opening of this chapter and the last part of the preceding chapter, we would probably be inclined to think the person in this chapter is much happier. But lifestyle alone does not lead to happiness.

The Futility of a
Self-Made Paradise

I. INTRODUCTION

Rich and Clever People Still Die

*W*e tend to think that great wealth or ingenuity can bring fulfillment. The reason we think this is not totally unwarranted. Rich people do have advantages that others don't, and clever people can generally go further than those who aren't so gifted. But there are limitations to such advantages. Rich and clever people still die. They also don't have the ability to experience true joy and satisfaction unless God empowers them to do so.

II. COMMENTARY

The Futility of a Self-Made Paradise

> **MAIN IDEA:** *Solomon does not like religious platitudes. He deals too honestly with life's struggles to use catchy, religious phrases. But he does believe that "no God, no joy" properly depicts reality. He knows that meaning in life is not found in ease or the abundance of one's possessions.*

A Without God, Life Is a Waste (6:1–6)

> **SUPPORTING IDEA:** *Wonderful blessings such as long life and riches cannot be appreciated or enjoyed on their own. God is indispensable to a life characterized by joy.*

6:1. Solomon now makes another discovery. This particular observation is again made about "life under the sun." The evil that Solomon sees **weighs heavily on men**. The NASB construes this evil as being "prevalent among men." The most likely idea being conveyed here is one of frequency (Longman, 169).

6:2. This person has been blessed by God, but he doesn't know it! He undoubtedly thinks that "his hands have gotten him his wealth." In direct contrast to the righteous person of Ecclesiastes 5:18–20, this person is not empowered by God. Therefore, his enjoyment of life is confounded.

The statement that **a stranger enjoys them** has been understood in various ways. Maybe the wealthy person had his wealth stolen, or maybe he had no heir to whom his inheritance could be passed. Whatever the circumstance, the truth is clear: he is not empowered by God, so he cannot experience true or lasting joy. The life that has nothing but possessions is empty indeed (see Ps. 49:10–11).

6:3–5. In biblical times it was a sign of blessing to have many children (Ps. 127:3–5). Yet we hear Solomon's popular refrain: If a person has everything and not God, he really has nothing. To shock our sensibilities, Solomon says that it might have been better if this person had not been born. What does this sound like? None other than Jesus' words about Judas (Matt. 26:24; cf. Job 3:1–16).

6:6. Even long life, which is usually thought to be a blessing, is considered futile. No matter how long a person lives, it is impossible to avoid the inevitable—death. Observing the plight of those without God should give us great compassion for them. Those without God may be impressive and the envy of other human beings, but in reality they are bushes in the desert (Jer. 17:5–6)—unstable and lifeless.

B Without God, Cravings Can't Be Satisfied (6:7–9)

SUPPORTING IDEA: *Catering to the "true self" (a modern concept) does not fulfill us. Rather, it is in losing our lives that we find them (Matt. 16:25)—a proposition that flies in the face of our fleshly appetites.*

6:7. Workaholism apart from the redeeming work of God is useless. It provides no lasting satisfaction because the wrong goal is pursued. Robert Johnston comments:

> Man's efforts at self-justification are misplaced: the mystery of the world's order, the shared fate of its citizens, and the lack of discernible progress all militate for Qoheleth against an obsessive work-orientation. Instead Qoheleth calls his readers to approach life receptively, enjoying its gifts from God as they unfold (Johnston, 28).

6:8. In an ultimate sense, especially considering such inevitabilities as death (see v. 6), there are no advantages for the wise over the fool. There are only *relative* advantages for the wise person who does not know God (see comments on Eccl. 2:12–17).

The last part of the verse where the poor man knows how to walk before the living has resulted in various interpretations. The comments of Robert Davidson make good sense:

Suppose, he says, there is a poor man who knows how to cope with daily living—so what? There are obviously so many of the good things in life which a poor man, in Koheleth's eyes, can never have, just because he is poor. Deprivation is deprivation, whatever shape or form it takes. No romanticizing here about the value of the poor and simple life! It is as if Koheleth is casting his eye over all sorts and conditions of men—rich and poor, the wise and the fools—and saying to us that not one of them has found the key to unlock the innermost secrets of life (Davidson, 42).

6:9. There is much in Scripture that warns against using the senses to determine the "good life." All the way back to the garden of Eden where the tree of the knowledge of good and evil *appeared* delightful to Eve (Gen. 3:6), to David's lust toward Bathsheba, to John's teaching about the "lust of his eyes" (1 John 2:16), we find strong warnings.

Only God Can Explain the Riddle of Life (6:10–12)

SUPPORTING IDEA: *God is the ultimate reference point for all wisdom and knowledge. Our desire to understand more than we are able can fuel our frustration or drive us to a deeper trust in God.*

6:10. The attempts of man to understand the mysteries of life are futile because he is a contingent being. Someone much more powerful than man—God—has known man from the beginning and is the only source of true wisdom. One commentator put it this way:

To "give something a name" is to study or (as here) to appoint its character. Both the world (*what is*) and *man* have settled characters. *One who is stronger than he* is God. Thus the Preacher is underlining the impossibility of changing the basic character of life. Man cannot escape his limitations, nor can he completely unravel the world's anomalies (cf. 1:15). He may, like Job, wish to debate the matter with God, but God is altogether greater (Eaton, 107).

6:11. Instead of resting in the reality of being named by God and thereby recognizing one's great limitations to understand the world's mysteries, we typically get frustrated and "multiply words." But many words do not reflect a wise perspective. They are usually, *but not always* (Seow, 233), the sign of a fool (Eccl. 5:2–3; cf. Prov. 10:19).

6:12. Only God knows the future (cf. Eccl. 3:11), so it is senseless not to trust him (Brown, Fitzmyer, and Murphy, 538). Those who turn away from God end up destroying themselves (Rom. 1:18–32; cf. Deut. 6:24). Unfortunately, this is the option that most people choose (Eccl. 6:1–4; Matt. 7:13–14).

Shadows are spoken of elsewhere in the Bible where they "emphasize the frailty of human beings" (Longman, 178). Shadows have no real substance, they can easily switch directions, and they don't last. They can also startle us, emphasizing that man is weak and powerless.

Lack of hope is a clue that a person has exhausted every option for true happiness. The resulting disillusionment can be devastating. This striving to understand the riddle of life was articulated by David Levy, Dartmouth's top graduate in 1971. Listen to what he said in his valedictory address:

> Take pity on me, those of you who can justify the air you breathe . . . send me letters and tell me why life is worth living. Rich parents, write and tell me how money makes your life worthwhile. Dartmouth alumni, tell me how the Dartmouth experience has given value to your life. And if some one of you out there is also made like me, write me a letter and tell me how you came to appreciate the absurdity of your life (quoted in Richards, 24).

MAIN IDEA REVIEW: *Solomon does not like religious platitudes. He deals too honestly with life's struggles to use catchy, religious phrases. But he does believe that "no God, no joy" properly depicts reality. He knows that meaning in life is not found in ease or the abundance of one's possessions.*

III. CONCLUSION

The Only Source of Joy

Deep sadness and spiritual sobriety ought to grip us when we think of how easy it is to let idols capture the affections of the heart. Solomon has shown us that we must abandon the foolishness of believing that anything or anyone other than God is grand enough to bring deep and lasting joy. Only the majestic God revealed in the pages of Scripture can bring joy and satisfaction.

PRINCIPLES

- The circumstances of life don't determine a person's destiny; God's enablement does.
- Our insatiable appetite for meaning can't be met by the acquisition of more power or possessions.
- Only God has control of the future, so it is senseless not to trust him.

APPLICATIONS

- Pray about the opportunity to share the truths of this chapter with a non-Christian friend.
- Consider what idols impress you the most. Discuss this with a trusted Christian friend for prayer and accountability.
- Imagine yourself getting those things that you dream about having. What would it be like to have these apart from God?

IV. LIFE APPLICATION

"Stop Regarding Man"

It was my privilege to interview William F. Buckley at his home for a television special that aired nationally on PBS. You must know a little background to feel the full weight of what God taught me from this experience. Ever since I was a teenager, the question of what five people I would like to spend an hour with has always included Buckley. So you can imagine my excitement when I was given the opportunity not only to interview him but to spend time over several meals (at his initiative and expense).

As we got closer to the interview, God reminded me of a passage in Isaiah 2. This passage has ministered to me on a number of occasions when I'm tempted toward the idolatry of things or people. Verse 22 of Isaiah 2 really struck me the day before the interview: "Stop regarding man, whose breath of life is in his nostrils; for why should he be esteemed?" (NASB).

As a result, I was relaxed with Mr. Buckley and was able to treat him as a fellow human being. I am very thankful for the time spent with him. His interest in me and my work is a wonderful blessing, but I will always recall the important lesson God taught me about idolatry.

V. PRAYER

Father, help me to see that the idols of this world are a poor substitute for knowing you. As I repent daily of my idolatry, use me to "teach transgressors your ways" (Ps. 51:13). Amen.

VI. DEEPER DISCOVERIES

A. "God Does Not Enable Him to Enjoy Them" (6:2)

Attempts to downplay or diminish the sovereign prerogatives of God in this verse are ill advised. Typically, discussions about God's sovereign prerogatives, especially when it comes to salvation, cause many people to question the fairness of such a possibility. Many things need to be kept in mind when we consider this hotly debated topic.

First, there is an acute need to clarify what grace is all about. All of us are sinners (Rom. 3; 5); therefore, all of us deserve God's judgment. No one deserves heaven. If God wants to be gracious to some people, this does not make him unfair or unjust. All of us get what we deserve and some of us get far more than we deserve—a relationship with God!

Second, consider all of humanity on a level playing field. Either that playing field is marked by "equal freedom to choose or reject God" or it is marked by "all have sinned and run from God." I strongly lean toward the latter. Let me explain why.

If everyone has equal freedom to choose or reject God, why do some people choose to say yes to God while others don't? You may retort that some are more humble or see their sin more clearly. But this response doesn't answer the question *why?* Where do this humility and awareness of need for God come from? If they come from the "autonomous individual," then we must say that some people are less touched by sin than others—clearly a blasphemous idea. But if the playing field is marked by "all have sinned and run from God," then it must be God's initiative for salvation to occur. We simply respond in gratitude and faith for what God has set out to accomplish on our behalf.

Third, the sovereign prerogatives of God are not simply Paul's idea. Start at the beginning of the Bible with Genesis. See how God consistently chose the younger over the older, rightful heir (Isaac instead of Ishmael, Jacob over Esau, Joseph not Reuben, and Ephraim rather than Manasseh). Even Joseph, although he should have known better, was surprised to see his father Jacob bless his son Ephraim over the firstborn Manasseh (Gen. 48:14).

Fourth, we must maintain the tension points that Scripture gives us—a strong and clear description of God's sovereign prerogatives in salvation coupled with the desire of our heavenly Father to use us as the heralds of his truth (see discussion of Ezek. 37 in Eccl. 3:15).

Finally, we must be gracious with one another when discussing this issue. Christians have disagreed over this for many years. That acknowledgment however, is not meant to downplay the importance of this issue. It is extremely important and merits the honest, prayerful, and humble reflection of all Christians.

B. "His [Man's] Appetite Is Never Satisfied" (6:7)

We are shocked when we read stories in the Old Testament about the person who takes materials and makes an idol out of them (Isa. 44:12–15). What an idiot! How can someone be so lost? The excess materials not used on the idol help to keep him warm (Isa. 44:16). This only serves to heighten our amazement. How can anyone be so foolish that he would worship a man-made deity?

If we are honest, we will realize that we are tempted to do the same. We may not always use our hands to make an idol. Ambitious business people, just to list one example, are prone to create and then worship their corporate ventures. All of us make idols in our minds. Our minds are truly "perpetual forges of idols" (Calvin, 97). These "idol-factory" minds of ours delight in something or someone other than God.

Even more subtly, Christians might be tempted to question the wisdom of bowing to the God revealed in the pages of Scripture. The Lord says things about himself and acts in ways that offend our "sensibilities." So we begin to "tweak" and modify God. We create a God who is more palatable to the modern age—a God who doesn't judge anyone and is always quick "to believe the best."

So idolatry has many forms. Whatever its form, it always produces death, because the worshiper of idols becomes just like the false and dead images he adores (Pss. 115:8; 135:18).

VII. TEACHING OUTLINE

A. INTRODUCTION
1. Lead Story: Rich and Clever People Still Die
2. Context: We are introduced to a man who has "everything going for him." Sadly, he doesn't experience life the way it was designed to be lived, because he does not know the Designer.
3. Transition: This chapter jolts us into considering a different way of life than the one we have read about in the previous chapter.

B. COMMENTARY
1. Without God, Life Is a Waste (6:1–6)
2. Without God, Cravings Can't Be Satisfied (6:7–9)
3. Only God Can Explain the Riddle of Life (6:10–12)

C. CONCLUSION: THE ONLY SOURCE OF JOY

VIII. ISSUES FOR DISCUSSION
1. What light does Matthew 7:13–14 shed on Ecclesiastes 6:1?
2. If God must empower people to enjoy life, what role do we play in the lives of non-Christians?
3. What idols do you find the most attractive substitutes for God?

Ecclesiastes 7

Gaining Wisdom in Unlikely Places

"*T*hrough levity of heart, and small concern for our failings, we become insensible of the sorrows of our souls; but oftentimes we vainly laugh, when we justly ought to weep. There is no true liberty or right joy but in the fear of God accompanied with a good conscience."

Thomas à Kempis

Ecclesiastes 7

IN A NUTSHELL

*T*his chapter continues with some related themes that we find throughout the rest of Ecclesiastes. In the first half of the chapter, Solomon describes the wisdom of seeking God rather than worldly pleasures. In the second half, Solomon describes the temptation to sin rather than to trust God. Our desire to be independent of God makes it difficult for us to find wisdom.

Gaining Wisdom in Unlikely Places

I. INTRODUCTION

Sharing the Gospel

*I*t is not uncommon to find people who treat serious matters lightly while holding unimportant matters like sports to be the most significant issues of the day. Important matters such as the possibility of life after death are treated with scorn, humor, or worst of all, dismissed as not worthy of serious thought.

Years ago I was sharing the gospel with an undergraduate student at Stanford University. The conversation was quite civil until I got to the part about the consequences of not trusting Jesus. The idea of hell was laughable to this well-educated young man. In fact, he went on to articulate the popular notion that if hell existed it couldn't be so bad because all of his buddies would be there. It would be one big, happy party.

Solomon points to a better way in this chapter. He wants us to know there are matters which merit serious and sustained attention. Those who want to be wise are encouraged to go to the places where serious thought is encouraged.

II. COMMENTARY

Gaining Wisdom in Unlikely Places

> **MAIN IDEA:** *There are many paths to foolish living. The way of wisdom is narrow, but it brings great joy to those who continue on its course.*

◼ A A Sober Spirit Is Better Than Pleasure Seeking (7:1–10)

> **SUPPORTING IDEA:** *Certain places and people stimulate the pursuit of wisdom.*

7:1. There is something far greater than riches. Material prosperity can buy things like precious ointment, but they do not last. Ointment "smells good, gives a pleasant impression, but . . . it evaporates quickly" (Ellul, 78). A good name lasts. Perfume is concerned only with externals; a good name is something that comes from within (Keddie, 79). In our day and age we are mainly interested in externals. Fame and popularity have replaced genuine heroism. The former majors on image while the latter is based on character (Keyes).

The phrase **the day of death** [is] **better than the day of birth** has been understood in different ways. But the idea that a person's character and conduct are made clear at the end seems to fit Solomon's progression of thought (cf. Eccl. 8:10).

7:2–4. Much can usually be gained from thinking about the sobering realities of life such as death. But this is not always the case, since some people such as Freud can have a morbid fascination with death and dying (Becker, 102–3).

It is imperative that we internalize what Solomon is saying here. He says that it is **better** to go to a funeral than a wedding. This clearly does not mean that a funeral is more enjoyable! Funerals are a healthy wake-up call. They instill sobriety (Chrysostom, "Concerning the Statutes," 440; cf. Ambrose, "Letter LXIII," 472). All of us will die some day. "The shades of death" are a "fate no man can withstand" (Homer, *The Iliad,* 31). Ancient writers like Homer understood that "death is certain, and when a man's hour is come, not even the gods can save him, no matter how fond they are of him" (Homer, *The Odyssey,* 195). How different that perspective is from the view of Jesus in John 11:25–26!

Our mortality causes us to reflect on our lives and hopefully to make changes that will reduce the number of regrets we might have on the day of our death. Unfortunately, most of us don't ponder these realities. We tend "to live as though he [we] had unlimited time for doing the plan of God" (Wright, "The Interpretation of Ecclesiastes," 30).

It is not that Solomon believes *all* laughter to be wrong. Again, context determines meaning. Here he is speaking of a frivolous laughter that is not anchored to truth. Much better than such ungodly merriment is the sorrow that comes from honest reflection on the totality of life. Ironically, it is this person who is really the "winner" in life. Consider Peter Kreeft's observation: "Think of all the people you know. Is it not true that the ones who laugh the loudest and the most are usually the shallowest and the most foolish? And the wisest are usually the gravest? Perhaps the wise are grave because they remember the grave" (Kreeft, 39).

Externals, such as the boisterous laughter of an extrovert, are of little value. But the quiet, sorrowful musings of the reflective are highly prized. The wise thinks about what he learns from the **house of mourning,** while the fool is only concerned to remain where laughter resides.

We can learn much from Christians like Pascal and Jonathan Edwards who lived each day like it was their last. In the same way, William Law recommended that you

> represent to your imagination that your bed is your grave; that all things are ready for your interment; that you are to have no more to do with this world; and that it will be owing to God's great mercy if you ever see the light of the sun again or have another day to add to your works of piety. Then commit yourself to sleep as one that is to have no more opportunities of doing good, but is to awake among spirits that are separate from the body and waiting for the judgment of the last great day (Law, 151).

7:5–6. The rebuke of a wise man has characteristics similar to a funeral. It is hard to experience, but much good comes from it. A loving rebuke is better than the empty words of a fool. Fools are people-pleasers who love to flatter. The fool's input is a superficial song that only tells us what we want to hear (Prov. 27:5–6). Much to be preferred is the rebuke of a wise man because he thinks about the most important issues and gives counsel accordingly.

The comparison of a fool's laughter with **the crackling of thorns** may actually be a wordplay of sorts, similar to saying "nettles under the kettle" (Seow, 236–37, 247; Eaton, 110; Crenshaw, 133). This metaphor may depict loudness or possibly the fool's transitory influence. Thorns would be quickly consumed where coal would last much longer (Leupold, 152). Either way, the fool's counsel is of no value.

7:7–10. There are always areas to be warned about if a person wants to lead a moral and ethical life. The following four verses delineate several things which can prevent a person from living according to God's wise plan.

Injustice and the love of money have a disastrous effect on an otherwise noble life.

Injustice can confuse and anger us with questions such as, Where is God in the midst of this upheaval? (cf. Eccl. 3; 5). Money can lure us into the deception that the "good life" is attainable apart from God. Money's deceitful character can never be countered with too much vigilance.

Verse 8 warns us against the desire for immediate gratification. In a world where we have instant everything, we can't be warned enough. Waiting on God to bring true satisfaction is a major theme in the Scriptures, and it is certainly spoken of in Ecclesiastes. The next chapter will furnish another example.

A warning about anger reminds us that no one is exempt. Consider Moses. He was the most humble man of his time (Num. 12:3), but his anger kept him from entering the promised land (Num. 20:1–13). This shows how challenging it can be to lead others! Ungodly anger is a warning sign that shows we no longer believe God is sovereign or good. Those who trust in these two qualities of God can rest in him even when life is "unfair." Joseph is a great example in this regard. He was able to forgive his brothers because of his unswerving belief in God's sovereignty and goodness (Gen. 45; 50).

The last warning in this section is very common: the elderly person who derives little joy from the present and talks constantly about the "good old days." Sadly, this is heard quite frequently in places like retirement communities. Since we are to live in the present, it is safe to say that these people never truly live (see comments on Eccl. 3:19–22).

One commentator added the following hopeful note:

> The Bible does not commonly assess the present in terms of the past, but much more typically does so in terms of the future, with all its potential for change. Those who insist on harking back to the past often impose burdens on those who live in the present, from which they cannot escape. But to set the present in the context of the future is to set a path before someone else that allows the past to be left behind and a new way of being to be embraced (Provan, 145).

B The Wise Person Rests in God's Sovereignty (7:11–14)

> **SUPPORTING IDEA:** The wise person has a growing conviction that God's perspective of the "good life" is at odds with the world's perspective.

7:11. Wisdom is beneficial for all sorts of things, including the handling of money. Fools squander or worship wealth while the wise person is able to maintain a godly perspective on money.

7:12. Knowledge has been defined in various ways. We know that it is awareness of critical truth. Bringing in more of its moral dimension, it has been described as "the contemplative perception of the wise man" (Harris et al., 366). Wisdom is the character trait that actually carries out the *implications* of knowledge gained. Knowledge and wisdom are two sides of the same coin. In other words, knowledge is the discovering side of the coin and wisdom is the implementing side. Without knowledge, wisdom can devolve into zealotry. Without wisdom, knowledge is worthless theory and usually produces pride.

7:13. This verse has been interpreted in many ways. Some understand it as saying that God brings afflictions into our lives in order to test us (Kaiser, 84). Others see that the crooked is man's *perception* of what God is doing. God's plan looks wrong or crooked to us (Leupold, 160; cf. Eccl. 1:15). Whatever interpretation we accept, the sovereign purpose of God is clear. We cannot change what he has ordained.

7:14. Before we look at this verse, we must emphasize the biblical truth that God is never the *agent* of evil (Eccl. 7:29; cf. Gen. 6:12; Job 1:6–12;

Jas. 1:17). God has set aside a certain number of days that will be joyous. Others will be marked by sadness. We saw this truth earlier in chapter 3. Each day offers new opportunities, joys, struggles, and suffering. It is our responsibility to trust God through the good and bad times alike.

Furthermore, we must never lose sight of the redemptive work that comes from affliction. God allows affliction because he knows our tendency (like the people of Israel) to forget him during times of prosperity. As the psalmist said, "Before I was afflicted I went astray, but now I obey your [word.] . . . It was good for me to be afflicted so that I might learn your decrees" (Ps. 119:67,71; cf. Lam. 3:27).

God is our greatest good, yet we don't naturally pursue him. Affliction can be redemptive if it reminds us that we are dependent creatures who need to know the Father.

ⓒ All Have Sinned (7:15–22)

SUPPORTING IDEA: *A deep awareness of our sinfulness brings clarity and wisdom.*

7:15. These words remind us of Asaph's famous words in Psalm 73. Many times the righteous suffer while the unrighteous prosper. This kind of inequity can cause us to lose heart (see comments on Eccl. 5:8–9).

7:16. This is a very strange verse. It seems that Solomon's cynicism is getting the best of him. Actually, Solomon is describing the way things really are. Ray Stedman makes the point that this verb is reflexive, meaning a verb whose action is turned back or "reflected" on the subject of the verb. In other words, Solomon is warning us that we should be careful not to believe we are righteous apart from God (Stedman, 87; cf. Kaiser, 85–86; Keddie, 94–95).

Trying to curtail our "badness" through the energy of the flesh will produce self-righteousness (Augustine, "On the Gospel of John," 369). Trying to be good in our own strength is not only exhausting; it is impossible. Furthermore, righteousness, even the godly variety, ought always to be in tandem with mercy and kindness (Ambrose, "On Repentance," 329).

7:17. Just because the wicked may prosper (see v. 15) shouldn't lead us to conclude that their lifestyle is preferable. This is a false deduction, which Solomon seeks to address in the next verse.

7:18. There are a couple of truths to keep in mind. We are not to view ourselves as righteous apart from God. The other is not to cave in to worldliness simply because it looks like an easier life. But how do we hold on to these two truths in any consistent way? The fear of God is cited as the answer. Fearing God keeps us from pride in our own righteousness, and it motivates us to stay away from wickedness. We will see in the next chapter (esp. 8:11–12) how the person who fears God can persevere even while he observes the wicked who seem to get ahead in spite of their sin.

7:19–20. Wisdom continues to have much value (Ellul, 128–29), but we must never forget that we are sinners (Rom. 3:23). The fear of God gives us the ability to grow in wisdom without becoming arrogant and self-sufficient.

7:21–22. In case there is a person who believes he is righteous apart from God's gracious work, Solomon cuts through this unbiblical notion with these piercing words about the tongue. There is no one who is exempt from the vexing and destructive use of the tongue. All of us are prone to say things rashly (Prov. 12:18), to gossip (Prov. 18:8; 26:22), and to heap scorn on others by our words (Jas. 3:8–10).

We ought to be more humble (and therefore accurate) in our self-assessment. G. K. Chesterton was a good example of this. In answer to the question, "What's wrong with the world?" Chesterton said, "I am."

Ⓓ Wisdom Can Seem Elusive (7:23–29)

SUPPORTING IDEA: *A person can be turned away from the path of wisdom by many distractions.*

7:23–25. Solomon tells us that ultimate understanding about the world is elusive and mysterious. Even with all our discoveries about such things as DNA and quantum physics, we are reminded that there are many deep secrets that are inaccessible to the human mind.

7:26–28. Solomon knew firsthand the reality of verse 26 (cf. Prov. 5:1–4; 6:23–32). Women were a big part of his undoing. Solomon is simply reminding the reader that he never found a godly woman. Godly men were not particularly common, but evidently Solomon knew a few. Lest we think we are immune from sexual infidelity, we ought to recall that David, "a man after God's own heart," sinned in this way (Anonymous, 64). We should always be on guard.

7:29. Augustine made reference to this verse on a number of occasions. Among other things, he used it to show the error of the Pelagians (Augustine, *Sermons on New Testament Lessons*, 295).

This summary verse reminds us of the same reality as Romans 3:23. All of us have sinned. We alone are culpable for evil. The agency of sin always rests squarely on the shoulders of us humans (see comments on Eccl. 7:14). When God made us, he pronounced his work "very good" (Gen. 1:31). We are the ones who have made a mess of things, but we tend not to dwell on this truth.

MAIN IDEA REVIEW: *There are many paths to foolish living. The way of wisdom is narrow, but it brings great joy to those who continue on its course.*

III. CONCLUSION

Out for Revenge

Ted Kaczynski, the infamous "Unabomber," was a man on a mission. His passion to raise public awareness about the destructive effects of technology had a dark and twisted logic. In his April 6, 1971, journal entry, he stated, "My motive for doing what I am going to do is simply personal revenge."

Chilling words. But what about any sense of remorse or guilt? His September 15, 1980, entry includes the following: "Guilty feelings [after bombing the president of United Airlines]? Yes, a little. Occasionally I have bad dreams in which the police are after me. Or in which I am threatened with punishment from some super natural source. Such as the devil. But . . . I am definitely glad to have done what I have."

Amazingly, Ted Kaczynski believed that he had "much less tendency to self-deception than most people." He also believed that he "was a particularly important person and superior to most of the rest of the human race" (Van Boven and King, 38). Disregard for one's depravity coupled with an arrogant self-sufficiency is a lethal combination that produces fools.

PRINCIPLES

- Some of the most painful experiences in life can provide great opportunities for gaining wisdom.
- A deep sense of our sin is necessary if we are to have a life that honors God.
- The wise person is aware of the limits of human knowledge and understanding.

APPLICATIONS

- Be more attentive the next time you go to a funeral. Meditate on Psalm 90 before you go.
- Give thanks every day. Keep a journal of how God changes you through your expression of thanksgiving.
- Confess your "sins of omission" (what you left undone that you should have done) along with your "sins of commission." It will humble you and give a more accurate picture of your need for God's grace.

IV. LIFE APPLICATION

Sinners All

The brutality of the Unabomber may dull us into believing that we are "not that bad." Certainly, we sin, but our sins are inconsequential compared to the murder and mayhem wrought by Ted Kaczynski. Our sins may not have the same consequences as those of the person who commits murder, but the wise person embraces God's description of human beings apart from his grace. If you are looking for a good place to understand that description better, Romans 3:10–20 will be most instructive.

V. PRAYER

Teach me, Lord, to delight in the serious pursuit of a godliness without regrets. Amen.

VI. DEEPER DISCOVERIES

A. Maintaining a Godly Perspective in Suffering (7:14)

Not all suffering is for the purpose of teaching us "spiritual lessons." There are times when suffering is not tied to this purpose. Job and the man born blind (see John 9) are two such examples. But God does use all types of suffering for his glory and our good. We must be careful, though, lest we presume that we know all of what God is doing during times of intense suffering. Friends of sufferers should diligently seek to listen (Job 2:13), while the sufferers ought to ask God for wisdom in how to go through their trials (Jas. 1:2–5).

B. Taming the Tongue (7:21–22)

Control of the tongue is a true mark of godliness. The challenge to do this is an ongoing reminder of our fallen condition.

A commonly misunderstood verse is James 3:1. It tends to be interpreted that Bible teachers ought to know God's Word well and then teach it accurately. These are indispensable elements to teaching in a way that honors God, but James 3:1 is *ethical* in nature. The teacher of God's Word needs to have control over his tongue (see Jas. 3:2–12). In other words, he ought to be living what he is teaching (cf. Ezra 7:10). The warning about incurring "a stricter judgment" (NASB) is much more sobering than simply exegeting the text accurately!

C. "Not One Upright Woman Among Them All" (7:28)

A number of things ought to be kept in mind for a proper understanding of this verse. First, Solomon makes clear that all people, male and female, are sinners (Eccl. 7:20,29). No one is exempt.

Second, we must keep in mind that these words "are the findings of *one* man, as in the case of the psalmist who tells us in Psalm 37:25 that he has 'never seen the righteous forsaken or their children begging bread'" (Provan, 157, emphasis added). In other words, the genre of wisdom literature must be kept in mind. First Kings 11:3 says that Solomon "had seven hundred wives of royal birth and three hundred concubines, and his wives led him astray." The number *one thousand* in verse 28 does not need to be allegorized!

Third, wisdom in Proverbs is personified as a woman. Women are also described both positively (Prov. 31) and negatively (Prov. 2–7) in Proverbs. Even in the same chapter (Prov. 9), two women named "Wisdom and Folly" are contrasted (Seow, 272).

Fourth, the positive treatment of women in Ecclesiastes 9:9 (Murphy, 76) argues against reading this text in a manner that casts women in a poor light. The Bible clearly does not portray the character of women in any monolithic way. The mention of Jezebel with Ruth or Herodias with Mary reminds us of that reality.

VII. TEACHING OUTLINE

A. INTRODUCTION

1. Lead Story: Sharing the Gospel
2. Context: Where we go and who we know have an enormous impact for good or ill.
3. Transition: Solomon gives attention to various pitfalls that keep a person from living wisely.

B. COMMENTARY

1. A Sober Spirit Is Better Than Pleasure Seeking (7:1–10)
2. The Wise Person Rests in God's Sovereignty (7:11–14)
3. All Have Sinned (7:15–22)
4. Wisdom Can Seem Elusive (7:23–29)

C. CONCLUSION: OUT FOR REVENGE

VIII. ISSUES FOR DISCUSSION

1. Do you think it is a good idea to plan out the details of your memorial service? Why or why not?
2. How many of your friends are willing to confront you? If none come to mind, is it because you have surrounded yourself with people who say only what is agreeable?
3. How many serious-minded Christians do you know who model a winsome, joyful walk with God?

Ecclesiastes 8

Respect Your Authorities

I. **INTRODUCTION**
A Proper Attitude Toward Governing
Authorities

II. **COMMENTARY**
A verse-by-verse explanation of the chapter.

III. **CONCLUSION**
Imperfect Justice
An overview of the principles and applications from
the chapter.

IV. **LIFE APPLICATION**
The Limitations of Knowledge
Melding the chapter to life.

V. **PRAYER**
Tying the chapter to life with God.

VI. **DEEPER DISCOVERIES**
Historical, geographical, and grammatical enrichment of the commentary.

VII. **TEACHING OUTLINE**
Suggested step-by-step group study of the chapter.

VIII. **ISSUES FOR DISCUSSION**
Zeroing the chapter in on daily life.

"*What* I have done . . . [I] did according to my conscience, and to the best of my knowledge, filled with concern for my people, realizing the necessity of protecting its honor, in order to lead it again to a position of honor in this world. And should unnecessary sorrow or suffering ever come to my people because of my actions, then I beseech Almighty God to punish me."

Adolf Hitler

Ecclesiastes 8

IN A NUTSHELL

The popular slogan, "Question authority," is one that all of us can observe with little effort. The tendency to criticize, demean, and even antagonize authority figures is common in our culture. Generally speaking, there is wisdom in submitting to the reigning authorities. This chapter underscores that truth.

Respect Your Authorities

I. INTRODUCTION

A Proper Attitude Toward Governing Authorities

*O*nce again we see the practical ramifications of believing in the sovereignty of God. Here it applies to our relationship with the governing authorities. There are times where it is appropriate to disobey the governing authorities. The Hebrew midwives (Exod. 1); Shadrach, Meshach, and Abednego (Dan. 3); and the apostles (Acts 4) provide such examples. But note that in all of these examples the individuals did not take up arms against a corrupt government. They obeyed God and suffered the consequences of doing what was right.

The sovereignty of God should affect our perspective on *all* things. The apostle Paul, while a prisoner in Rome (or Caesarea), said that he was a prisoner of the Lord (Eph. 3:1; 4:1). Although Paul had a healthy respect for earthly rulers (see Rom. 13), he knew that God was ultimately sovereign in his life. God made Paul an "ambassador in chains" (Eph. 6:20). Earthly powers such as the Roman Empire can never thwart the advance of God's kingdom.

II. COMMENTARY

Respect Your Authorities

> **MAIN IDEA:** *Obedience to those in authority is a wise course of action.*

A Submit to the Governing Authorities (8:1–6)

> **SUPPORTING IDEA:** *Submission to the governing authorities is a wise—though not always easy—thing to do.*

8:1. This verse could easily serve as a wrap-up to chapter 7 or as an introduction to this chapter. In either case, it reminds us of the benefits that people derive from living wisely.

8:2–4. The phrase **obey the king's command** can be understood as "observe the king's face—that is, try to assess the king's mood from his expression" (cf. Prov. 16:15; Whybray, *Ecclesaistes*, 130). A person's obedience of the ruling authorities is linked with his fidelity to God. Furthermore, since it is wise "to heed the words of earthly rulers and be very reluctant to rebel against them, how much more should we honor and obey the word of

God?" (Moore, *Ecclesiastes,* 132). This certainly doesn't mean that we must obey the governing authorities at all times, but it does mean that we must submit to the role of the governing authorities in all matters that do not violate the will of God.

The desire to leave someone's presence can signify "disaffection and disloyalty" (cf. Hos. 11:2; Eaton, 118). It is wrong to cast off the governing authorities, because they are established by God (Rom. 13:1–2). It is also unwise because the king will continue to do whatever he wants to do anyway.

8:5–6. There are differing opinions over the interpretation of these verses. But the context and the overall argument of Ecclesiastes are well served with the following comments. It is wise to continue in one's loyalty to the governing authorities for the reasons described above. As a person does so, there may be times when he has room to suggest some positive change on certain issues.

Again, keep in mind that Ecclesiastes is wisdom literature. This genre describes the way things *usually* occur, but it does not cover every situation imaginable. Christians living in Cuba under a dictator like Fidel Castro may wonder how long it will be until they see true justice. On the positive side, political leaders, even cruel dictators, are often challenged and eventually conquered. Modern history has reminded us of this many times. Solomon also observed this reality (see comments on Eccl. 4:13–16).

Daniel is also a fitting example. He knew when to submit to the Babylonians (e.g., allowing his name to be changed), but he requested not to eat the king's choice food, since this would have been a violation of God's Word. Daniel's request was granted by the godless Babylonians and honored by God, and he grew more healthy than those who ate the king's choice food (Dan. 1:15).

B Fearing God in an Unjust World (8:7–17)

SUPPORTING IDEA: *Living our lives "before the face of God" will encourage faithfulness and steadfastness even when evil seems to be winning. There are many injustices in our world that can perplex, even cause doubt, for the thoughtful Christian. Solomon seeks to warn us about some of these.*

8:7–9. God has allotted a certain number of days for us to live (Gen. 27:2; Job 14:5; Ps. 139:16). We can't go beyond the boundary that he has set, no matter how much bran we eat. Eating right is a good and prudent thing to do. So are regular exercise and good sleep, because they affect the *quality* of a person's life. The *quantity,* however, is already determined by God.

There is a short period (relatively speaking) in which one person may oppress another. But in the end all of us die. If we don't believe that God will ultimately judge, we will look to sinful means for the arbitration of justice.

Wind (*rûah*) may be better rendered *spirit* in this context (Keddie, 107). The human spirit is ultimately beyond the control of any ruler.

8:10–13. Sometimes the pain caused by an unjust ruler is intensified by the fact that people remember him in a way that ignores his heinous actions.

> The wicked are praised in life and eulogized in death in the very cities where they practiced their injustices (8:10). It is one thing to observe the terms of the ancient maxim, *De mortuis nil nisi bonum* ("Say nothing but what is good of the dead"), but quite another to canonize an utter reprobate as if he were as pure as the driven snow! Injustice at this level also tests faith and tempts us to think that there may be no justice in the universe after all (Keddie, 109).

Because God's judgment is not meted out immediately, it causes ungodly people to sin even more. Even though the sinner may live a life free of pain (Ps. 73:4), it is still wise to fear God. It is better to fear God because there is not only peace of mind in this present world but also pardon at the final judgment. The judgment of God may be implied because the *immediate* benefits of fearing God do not seem apparent. In Ecclesiastes 12:13–14 it is explicitly stated.

8:14–17. God's will is not fully done on earth as it is in heaven. Inequities continue to abound. Righteous people suffer, and unrighteous people prosper. The unrighteous may also have little sense of right and wrong. What should a person do in a situation like this? Solomon reminds us to enjoy the "simple pleasures" of life such as eating and friendship. If a person is content with these things, there is still much joy that can be experienced even in a world of great injustice.

The closing two verses of this chapter continue with Solomon's graphic realism. Life is far too complex for any human to figure out how all its parts fit together. The most insightful people will continue to be mystified by much that life offers. The mystery of God's revelation reminds us of our rightful place in relation to it. "Yet if all were brought down to our poor level—if revelation contained no mysteries—if it were stripped of everything supernatural—surely its credentials, as professing to come from God, would be very doubtful" (Bridges, 207).

Although the believer in Jesus Christ is not exempt from questions over God's ways, he is at a distinct advantage. He knows that God will ultimately reward the righteous (Heb. 11:6) and "the earth will be filled with the knowledge of the glory of the LORD, as the waters cover the sea" (Hab. 2:14).

MAIN IDEA REVIEW: *Obedience to those in authority is a wise course of action.*

III. CONCLUSION

Imperfect Justice

Human standards of proper behavior are exposed for the mockery they make of true justice (Seow, 294). "Under the sun," there will never be true justice. Apart from the plumb line of God's righteousness, we humans are given to all kinds of bizarre notions about justice. Even Elena Ceausescu, the infamous wife of the former dictator of Romania, was remembered fondly by some of the people whom she oppressed (Drakulić, 122–25). We live in a twisted world where cowards and heroes are "held in equal honor, and death deals like measure to him who works and him who is idle" (Homer, *The Iliad*, 60).

PRINCIPLES

- As long as they don't ask you to disobey God or his truth, it is prudent to submit to the governing authorities.
- Fearing God is always the wisest option, even when it does not seem to yield any benefits.
- Even wicked people are often fondly remembered at their funerals.

APPLICATIONS

- Regularly pray 1 Timothy 2:1–5 for your local, state, and federal representatives.
- Read and meditate on Psalm 73.
- What are the practical implications of realizing that human beings can't fully understand life on earth?

IV. LIFE APPLICATION

The Limitations of Knowledge

Stuart Briscoe shares the following humorous exchange between a father and his son.

> Son: How far is it to the sun?
> Father: I don't know.
> Son: How far is it to Mars?
> Father: I don't know.
> Son: How far is it to the end of the Milky Way?
> Father: I don't know.

Son: Dad, you don't mind me asking you all these questions, do you?

Father: Not at all. How are you going to learn if you don't ask any questions?

There is nothing wrong with a godly curiosity that strives to understand God and his world. But we must always be aware of our limitations. Many truths belong to God alone (Deut. 29:29; cf. Isa. 55:8–9; 1 Cor. 13:12).

V. PRAYER

Thank you, God, for being my loving heavenly Father. Help me to have a healthy reverence and awe for who you are. Amen.

VI. DEEPER DISCOVERIES

A. "No Man Has Power over the Wind" (8:8)

The two options for interpretation of this phrase are summarized nicely by the following commentator:

> There is, however, an ambiguity here: *rûah* (*spirit*) can also mean "wind." Elsewhere Qoheleth uses it in both senses (e.g. wind, 1:6; 11:4; spirit or breath of life, 3:19,21; 11:5; 12:7). Here either meaning makes good sense: on the one hand, the theme of the wind as beyond man's control is echoed in 1:6, where the wind is taken as an example of the unalterable movements of the natural world; on the other, the thought that man is powerless to prevent the departure of the breath from the body (cf. 12:7) would neatly parallel the next clause, which states that he has no *authority over the day of death:* in other words, he can neither prolong his life nor determine when he will die (Whybray, *Ecclesiastes,* 133, emphasis added).

I lean toward translating *rûah* as *spirit* because it fits well with the following clause in verse 8: "So no one has power over the day of his death." *Rûah* translated as *wind,* especially with the uncertainty of the wind (see note on Eccl. 1:4–7), is also a good option that advances Solomon's argument in this chapter.

B. Shadow (8:13)

There is some debate among scholars over the meaning of *shadow.* This word can be a "figure of the insecurity of human life" (cf. Pss. 102:11; 109:23). It can also depict the idea that the "unrighteous will not flourish beyond the grave" (cf. Pss. 49; 73; Eccl. 3:16–21; 12:14; Eaton, 123). Whatever option a person chooses for this metaphor, it is clear that the person who does not fear God is living a precarious and transitory existence. God will not be mocked. There will be an ultimate "so what" to our decisions.

VII. TEACHING OUTLINE

A. INTRODUCTION

1. Lead Story: A Proper Attitude Toward Governing Authorities
2. Context: We should have a healthy fear for the various authority figures in our lives.
3. Transition: This chapter begins with the importance of submitting to earthly authorities. It moves to a discussion of our willingness to submit to almighty God.

B. COMMENTARY

1. Submit to the Governing Authorities (8:1–6)
2. Fearing God in an Unjust World (8:7–17)

C. CONCLUSION: IMPERFECT JUSTICE

VIII. ISSUES FOR DISCUSSION

1. What are we to make of those Christians like Dietrich Bonhoeffer, who plotted to kill Hitler?
2. Why are we so hesitant to speak "against the dead" even when they have done evil?
3. In what way is "the fear of the LORD" the *beginning* of knowledge or wisdom (Prov. 1:7; 9:10)?

Ecclesiastes 9

Remembering That We Are in the Hand of God

"*M*ay heaven grant you in all things your heart's desire—husband, house, and a happy, peaceful home; for there is nothing better in this world than that man and wife should be of one mind in a house. It discomfits their enemies, makes the hearts of their friends glad, and they themselves know more about it than any one."

Homer

Ecclesiastes 9

IN A NUTSHELL

*O*nce again Solomon reminds us of the uncertainty of our lives. We are not in charge—a point that Solomon has been making with ruthless clarity. God alone is sovereign. It is imperative that we remember these two basic truths, especially as we face this life with its many twists and turns.

Remembering That We Are in the Hand of God

I. INTRODUCTION

Finding Joy in the Midst of Suffering

*W*hatever one's political affiliation happened to be, deep sadness was the characteristic response upon hearing that President Ronald Reagan had Alzheimer's.

We are struck with sadness and insecurity as we contemplate the fact that the powerful do get sick and die. If one of the most powerful men in the world who also happened to be exceedingly fit gets a disease like Alzheimer's, what does that suggest for the rest of us? It's a question that levels pretensions of being in control that any of us might have. Our lives are marked by brevity, uncertainty, and an unnerving sense of vulnerability to all manner of evil.

For all its sadness, the drama of Reagan's Alzheimer's draws us in. Make what you will of Nancy Reagan's fascination with horoscopes or her penchant for meddling in the affairs of the presidency, you can't help but be impressed with her loyalty and devotion to Ronnie "until death do us part." The Reagans are part of a diminishing group of married couples who model much of what we see in this passage from Ecclesiastes.

II. COMMENTARY

Remembering That We Are in the Hand of God

> **MAIN IDEA:** *Life's uncertainties make trust in a sovereign and wise God the only reasonable option.*

Ⓐ The Predicament of Life Under the Sun (9:1–6)

> **SUPPORTING IDEA:** *Since everyone has a brief and transient existence, it is essential that we appreciate life while we still have it.*

9:1. This verse may go with the last part of chapter 8, and it certainly can be included here (see "Deeper Discoveries").

Our lives are marked by many uncertainties, but nothing surprises God. This counteracts a recent view of God called "Open Theism," in which God may voluntarily choose not to know what we will do in some situations. Man is clueless, but God is all-knowing. Therefore, the only proper response to God is fear and trust.

9:2–3. Everyone "under the sun" experiences the same fate—death. A noble life does not cancel out a person's mortality. It seems there should be a difference between the fates of the righteous and the unrighteous with respect to death and dying, but there isn't.

Apart from the grace of God, there is madness in our hearts. Keddie states the situation quite well:

> People dread mental illness with all its attendant problems. How much more should they flee from the madness of unbelief in God and unrepentance toward the Lord Jesus Christ! The worst madness in the world is the mind-set and heart commitment that runs from God to enlist with Satan's legion of spiritual terrorists. Sane sinners are in the grip of the most awesome insanity on earth (Keddie, 118).

9:4–6. Solomon continues his blunt commentary on life apart from God. All things being equal, it is better to be alive than dead. The living may discover a way to make some sense of this life and find some satisfaction in earthly existence. For the dead, those options don't exist. As Achilles said, "Say not a word in death's favor; I would rather be a paid servant in a poor man's house and be above ground than king of kings among the dead" (Homer, *The Odyssey,* 247).

A **live dog** may imply someone who is not very powerful from a worldly standpoint, and a **lion** may refer to someone who once was. In a relative sense, it is better to be alive and powerless than dead, even though once powerful. Since everyone eventually dies, it is foolish to chase after power and prestige.

The living have the distinct advantage of being able to reflect on their own mortality. By way of implication from the rest of Ecclesiastes, they also may make wise course corrections to reflect that undeniable reality. The dead simply do not have the option to make wise course corrections any longer. If people live their lives for earthly rewards or worldly accolades, they have not walked in the way of wisdom.

Passionate emotions such as love, hate, and envy that drove people to find the good life "under the sun" are now gone. The lesson is clear: powerful desires that are not anchored to the sovereign God will not preserve a person.

B God Makes Life Under the Sun Worthwhile (9:7–9)

SUPPORTING IDEA: *God offers joy in the midst of a world marked by pain and suffering.*

9:7. The connection of this section with the former section recalls the same sort of thing that we saw in 5:18 to 6:6 (see comments there). The reality of joy can occur only when God has invaded our lives. We have seen this reality in passages like Ecclesiastes 3:11 (receiving the gift of God) and Ecclesiastes 5:18–20 (being empowered by God). Only God makes mundane activities a joy (Eccl. 2:25).

9:8. Not surprisingly, these metaphors are descriptive of joy (Ps. 45:3; Isa. 62:3; Keddie, 124; Longman, 230). Joy, as we saw early on in Ecclesiastes, can occur only when a person is in right relationship with God. It may seem that some non-Christians are joyful, but once they focus on the important issues of life (see comments on Eccl. 2:1–11), they find there is no lasting meaning apart from God.

9:9. This verse is a wonderful response to those non-Christians who contend that Christianity does not address the harsh realities of life. Even a cursory reading of Scripture will demonstrate that God does not sugarcoat difficult issues.

In this verse we see the coupling of two important biblical themes. We see hope. Every single day with our spouse can be joyful. The idea that the first few years of married life are terrific and the rest tolerable finds no basis in the Bible. Unfortunately, this idea lives in the minds of many Christians (see "Deeper Discoveries" for Eccl. 3:8).

But all this talk about joy-filled married life doesn't negate the fact that this life is fleeting. The tension of enjoying our spouse every day yet remembering the brevity of life is the proper balance that must be maintained. If we forget about the great joy that is ours in marriage, we will tolerate a distant relationship with our spouse. If we forget how fleeting our lives are, we will not live prudently.

🄲 Working Harder Is Not the Way to Wisdom (9:10–12)

SUPPORTING IDEA: *An overemphasis on work is not the proper path to wisdom.*

9:10–12. The wise person gives his best effort with the available circumstances and opportunities. The temptation for all of us is to take this wise approach to life and push it to its unbiblical conclusion. For instance, it is irrational to be a workaholic because God ultimately gives us our work. Only he can bring any good out of it. We work, but he redeems. This truth need not promote passivity or sloppy work habits, but it does keep us from the folly of thinking that hard work alone will make for a rewarding life.

It is also irrational to be a workaholic because relationships will suffer. To have the kind of marriage depicted in verse 9 of this chapter takes a lot of unhurried time. This is an impossibility if we expend all our effort outside the home. The unchecked workaholism of so many people is also foolish because we do not know the day of our death. We ought to be wise in our use of time but watchful over a reckless attitude which thinks that more and faster is better.

D The "Peter Principle" Is Alive and Well (9:13–18)

SUPPORTING IDEA: *The world tends to elevate fools and marginalize the wise.*

9:13–15. The phrase **I also saw** is important. It is Solomon's "regular expression for actual incidents that stirred his reflections" (Eaton, 131). The world's value system is cruel, not the least of which is its forgetfulness. On earth a man does a noble and courageous deed, but it is forgotten. People have very short memories for such things.

My hometown is a little over an hour from San Antonio, home of the Alamo. We are told to "remember the Alamo" lest we forget what those brave people fought so valiantly to preserve. Many people can recall names like James Bowie, Davy Crockett, and Colonel Travis. There were others who were wise and brave, but they have been largely forgotten (see comments on Eccl. 1:11).

9:16. The idea of wisdom being better than strength is captured in the well-known belief that "the pen is mightier than the sword." The problem, as we have seen, is that wisdom from a person considered unimportant by society is either not heeded, or it is heeded and he or she is not given appropriate recognition. In God's economy, things are different. Not only does God use weak people (1 Cor. 1:18–31), but he enshrines their memory—as a quick read of the Gospels will show.

9:17–18. The quiet words of a wise person are superior to the boisterous shouts of politicians who want to call attention to themselves. Truth is conveyed through the mouth of a wise person, while the loud shouts of rulers are nothing but demagoguery. A country labeled a "superpower" but which is littered with foolish rulers is in trouble. Conversely, a country with wise rulers, though not stocked with weapons of war, is blessed. Indeed, "blessed is the nation whose God is the LORD" (Ps. 33:12).

MAIN IDEA REVIEW: *Life's uncertainties make trust in a sovereign and wise God the only reasonable option.*

III. CONCLUSION

Don't Give Allegiance to Fools

Solomon is always willing to poke holes in any delusional idea we may have about the possibility of experiencing lasting comfort "under the sun."

Here we get a pointed lesson on the world's tendency to give allegiance to fools.

PRINCIPLES

- Use your time wisely, since you don't know when it will run out.
- Special relationships like marriage can bring much joy, but they will never provide the lasting comfort that only God offers.
- It is foolish to live for the world's applause.

APPLICATIONS

- Take time to savor the "ordinary moments" that you spend with your spouse.
- Thank God for those people who are channels of his blessing to you.
- Thank one person whom the world does not honor but who has made an indelible impact on your life.

IV. LIFE APPLICATION

Joy and Sacrifice

The hope and realism of Scripture's view of marriage is described beautifully by Marvin Wilson. His comments are worth quoting at length.

> Like the cup of Jesus . . . the two cups of wine shared by Jewish marriage partners also dramatize the concept of common destiny. The first cup is called the "cup of joy." It reminds the couple that when joys in life are shared, they are doubled. The second cup is the "cup of sacrifice." In the midst of their celebration, the bride and groom are sobered by recognizing that burdens and problems will someday come into their marriage. But if these troubles are shared, they are halved.
>
> Contemporary Christian marriage can learn much from the symbolism of the Jewish marriage cup. In Christian marriage, a couple shares in the joys and challenges of a common destiny; each partner is bound to the other by love and mutual commitment. The cup of joy reminds the Christian of the need for celebration of life in a world daily marked by pain, tragedy, sickness, and death. Although marriage holds the potential of being one of the happiest experiences to be shared in life, it is also one of the most vulnerable; many enemies seek to destroy its unity and oneness. Thus, the cup of sacrifice sends a message to today's Church: hard times of testing

and discouragement may work at tearing a marriage apart. So, by God's grace, marriage partners must band together through personal sacrifice and mutual submission to sustain each other (cf. Eph. 5:21). Here is the support needed to insure the outcome of the relationship (Wilson, *Our Father Abraham*, 212).

V. PRAYER

Thank you, Father, for allowing me to face life with a hope that does not escape from the reality of suffering but always offers joy in the midst of life's storms. Amen.

VI. DEEPER DISCOVERIES

A. Determining the Flow of the Book's Outline (9:1)

This first verse of chapter 9 of Ecclesiastes has spawned considerable discussion. Is it better to place it with chapter 8 or chapter 9? Luther saw it as a commonly abused passage because some people would use it to instill "doubt and uncertainty about the grace and love of God toward us" (Luther, 3–4). Chapters 9 and 10 are also challenging because it is difficult to tell where the proper divisions ought to be placed (Longman, 224).

As others have said, the way we outline these chapters will not affect the overall argument of the book. In light of this, we will preserve the traditional divisions for chapters 9 and 10. Chapters 11 and 12, however, will be combined in the final section of this commentary.

B. "Time and Chance Happen to Them All" (9:11)

Chance is not the best word to use in this context, because it gives the impression that the world is a power untethered to the sovereign prerogatives of God. Iain Provan commented accordingly:

> The NIV's "chance" (*pega*ʿ) is an unhappy choice of translation, since this word connotes an impersonal and random force, whereas Qohelet is clear throughout the book that human fate lies ultimately in God's hands, no matter how random and impersonal what befalls us may appear. The verbal form *pg*ʿ means 'to meet, encounter.' A *pega*ʿ is simply something we encounter on the path of life—a circumstance or situation over which we have no control (Provan, 183).

VII. TEACHING OUTLINE

A. INTRODUCTION
1. Lead Story: Finding Joy in the Midst of Suffering
2. Context: Admiration for various types of fools will always take place "under the sun."
3. Transition: Solomon utilizes a "proverbial approach" to continue his observations of "life under the sun."

B. COMMENTARY
1. The Predicament of Life Under the Sun (9:1–6)
2. God Makes Life Under the Sun Worthwhile (9:7–9)
3. Working Harder Is Not the Way to Wisdom (9:10–12)
4. The "Peter Principle" Is Alive and Well (9:13–18)

C. CONCLUSION: DON'T GIVE ALLEGIANCE TO FOOLS

VIII. ISSUES FOR DISCUSSION

1. What are some of the worst results of denying one's mortality?
2. Do you think the growing revelations of the devastating consequences of unscrupulous business leaders will lead to greater promotion of those who are truly wise?
3. Why does the race not belong to the swift or the battle to the strong?

Ecclesiastes 10

Don't Despise Little Duties

Quote

"*F*lies are so mighty that they win battles, paralyse our minds, eat up our bodies."

Blaise Pascal

Ecclesiastes 10

 IN A NUTSHELL

*I*n this chapter Solomon gives us several examples of the "foolish life." Many of these matters seem insignificant, but grave consequences can come from such "small" things.

Don't Despise Little Duties

I. INTRODUCTION

Big Benefits from Doing Little Things

*M*any so-called "little things" can have a great impact for good or ill. For instance, we may label certain false statements "white lies," but they can exact a heavy toll. One of these "peccadilloes" is able to destroy trust and forever change the confidence we placed in another person.

On the other side of the coin are the amazing results that can accrue from consistently performing "small tasks." I think of my father in this regard. When he was in his late fifties, he asked me to help him set up a work-out routine. Although he was slim and had low cholesterol, he wanted to add some muscle. I will never forget watching my dad eke out a few push-ups on the living room floor. His trembling upper torso was a vivid testament to the difficulty of building dormant muscles. But my dad has kept at it. Now at seventy-seven, he does twenty-five push-ups every morning as well as other aerobic and anaerobic exercises.

Those of us who are impressed with the big and dramatic need to be reminded that it is the small and obscure activities that make or break people. The truly wise artist, doctor, or athlete knows how those hours of practice and preparation can lead to greatness.

II. COMMENTARY

Don't Despise Little Duties

> **MAIN IDEA:** *It is easy to downplay the significance of "little tasks," but they can determine the course of a person's life.*

"Little" Things Matter (10:1–4)

> **SUPPORTING IDEA:** *Indulging in a "little foolishness" may bring grave consequences.*

10:1. Flies possibly got into the ointment because someone failed to close the box that held the perfume (Bridges, 235). Many examples from all sectors of life can be given for this inviolate principle (Kreeft, 49–50; Ellul, 148). A little leaven certainly can affect the whole lump (1 Cor. 5:6).

The dynamic Christian life includes attending to the mundane affairs and routine activities done in obscurity. Faithfully applying all diligence to such matters results in a mature, stable, and joyous Christian life. Neglecting such matters will eventually break a person spiritually. This is one of the reasons so many gifted Christians compromise their testimonies. They place too much importance on public matters like speaking and writing and do not properly guard their own heart (Prov. 4:23; cf. 1 Tim. 4:16). Areas like private prayer, meditation on Scripture, and worship are neglected. This neglect eventually exacts a high toll.

Dallas Willard has talked about the need habitually to do the right things in order to be spiritually ready for whatever may come our way. I have heard Professor Willard use a baseball analogy to make the point. A good batter hits thousands of balls during practice in order to be ready for the real game. If the player has practiced adequately, he will be ready to respond automatically to the various pitches that come across the plate.

If we consistently avail ourselves of such things as private prayer, meditation on Scripture, and worship (individual and corporate), we will be better prepared for whatever challenges we might face. Not allowing "flies" to infest our spiritual life will preserve our sweet aroma before God.

10:2. It is the heart that directs a person. The heart is "not only the reason at work in arriving at a decision but also the will and direction one takes" (Murphy, 100). Whatever resides in the heart determines the direction a person will take (Eaton, 133).

10:3. Foolishness is a problem that does not stay in the deep recesses of the heart. What is imbedded in the heart must come out. The fool will demonstrate by his behavior that he does not value wisdom. This verse reminds us of a popular children's story, "The Emperor's New Clothes" (Bennett, 630–34). In the story a ruler roams around naked, believing that he has on beautiful clothes. Finally a small child exclaims, "The emperor has no clothes!"

What got the emperor into such a predicament? He believed the two strangers who came to town declaring that they could make clothes "that were made of the stuff which had the peculiar property of becoming invisible to every person who was unfit for the office he held or who was exceptionally stupid." Ironically, the emperor himself was "exceptionally stupid" because he trusted these shysters. The emperor was caught off guard because no one in his court was willing to tell him the truth (see Prov. 13:20).

10:4. Something as seemingly insignificant as not losing one's composure can have major ramifications (Prov. 15:1). It may even cause a great ruler to realize the error of his position. Hearkening back to Dallas Willard's illustration of the baseball player, we are reminded again of how important it is to do the right things consistently. A person never knows when those crucial situations will arise where he is called upon to exercise great restraint. If a person has not habitually lived according to wisdom, his foolishness will come out.

Foolishness Marks Life Under the Sun (10:5–7)

SUPPORTING IDEA: *Foolishness is on display at all levels of society.*

10:5–7. We need to be careful about the main point being presented in these verses. According to Solomon, some of the most qualified people are in lowly positions, while some of the most unqualified (**slaves on horseback**) are in positions of great influence. This point about slaves need not be taken to say that people from lowly backgrounds can never be wise rulers. Experience and common sense tell us otherwise. Solomon is saying that slaves generally would not have the ability or the training and background to be effective rulers.

Some interpreters take this passage as speaking about common people or slaves who take up arms against the reigning authorities. This interpretation seems improbable, given the context.

Work Smarter, Not Harder (10:8–11)

SUPPORTING IDEA: *Proper preparation is essential for any worthwhile task.*

10:8. Both of these situations depict the danger that may come from doing mundane activities. "There is always the possibility of an accident, even in the most pedestrian activity" (Murphy, 102; cf. Seow, 326).

10:9–10. Any activity can become dangerous if the proper precautions and preparations are not taken. The unwise continue to work even when the implements of labor are not properly prepared. Here a dull axe is still being wielded, even though its usefulness is limited. We need to take time for things like unhurried thinking and thoughtful reading of good books. Indeed, the wise person has God's view of time (Eccl. 3:1–11) for doing just that. We should not feel that it is a waste of time to pull back and sharpen our axes!

10:11. Another danger is a person who may have great skill yet fails to utilize his skill because he is lazy or allows himself to be distracted. Failing to use his skill exacts a heavy cost.

Vignettes on Foolish and Wise Living (10:12–20)

SUPPORTING IDEA: *Controlling the tongue is no small matter.*

10:12–13. Scripture has much to say about our speech. Words reveal the heart (Matt. 12:34–37). Our tongues can be a source of great healing or great hurt (Jas. 3:1–12). These two verses reveal that it is impossible to conceal what type of people we are. Our speech will give us away—whether we are wise or foolish.

10:14. A fool commits two errors. He tends to speak rashly (Prov. 12:18) and to say too much. Both can have disastrous consequences. It is better to hold one's tongue and wait for the best time to speak. A wise person knows when to be quiet (Eccl. 3:7; Jas. 1:19–20). It is interesting that Job's "counselors" were the wisest when they shut up (Job 2:13) and the most foolish when they began to speak. They spoke confidently about what was inaccessible to them and therefore not open to human understanding.

Another error that the fool makes is that he thinks he can figure out the future. Solomon taught us earlier that this is fruitless (Eccl. 3:11), yet the fool tends to believe he can be God! The fool from beginning to end is marked by folly, but that does not keep him from talking and speculating about the future. He is the classic example of a person who doesn't know what he doesn't know and who doesn't understand the proper boundaries or limitations of human knowledge.

10:15. The fool's laziness or neglect is so severe that he does not have the desire to do the needed preparations and planning for simple travel. What should be a simple task becomes impossible for the person who is not marked by wisdom. Furthermore, the fool is so clueless that he may have aspirations to do "great things," yet he is unable to do them because he can't accomplish the basic tasks of life.

10:16–20. Countries suffer greatly when they have people in power who are not qualified because of inexperience, immaturity, or lack of discipline. Rulers who are focused on ego gratification are a blight to any people (Luther, 166). Conversely, countries find great blessing with people who know how to restrain their carnal appetites.

Those who can control the so-called "private" areas of their lives cause much "public" good. If the eating patterns of our rulers are an important indicator about how they will lead, how much more so other areas! The modern notion that private morals don't affect public life finds no support in Scripture. A person who is faithful in a little will be faithful in much (Matt. 25:14–30).

Verse 18 reminds us of a recent tragedy in Turkey where homes were not properly built and could not withstand a severe earthquake. Lack of discipline has practical ramifications. "Little things" do matter.

Although verse 19 is somewhat enigmatic, it does seem to point to the fact that the fool believes that earthly things are the way to achieve the good life.

This chapter closes with additional teachings on the proper use of the tongue (cf. 10:12–14). The control of the tongue shows that a person is wise, but a fool's speech will come back to haunt him. God may withhold his judgment against us for using the tongue in a destructive manner (Eccl. 8:11–12). But we must realize that ultimately we will be held accountable for every careless word we speak (Matt. 12:36).

> **MAIN IDEA REVIEW:** *It is easy to downplay the significance of "little tasks," but they can determine the course of a person's life.*

III. CONCLUSION

Faithful to the Task

The history of Christian missions provides many stories about those who labored faithfully in obscurity and never got to see the fruit of their labors. Stephen, the first Christian martyr, never got to see how the Lord used his death to scatter the church and thus set in motion the furtherance of the gospel. We know that Stephen was a man who did not despise "menial" responsibilities. Doing the work of "waiting on tables" (Acts 6:1–5) was the mark of a great man.

PRINCIPLES

- Uneventful days of faithfulness are not to be despised.
- Place a premium on adequate preparation for any worthwhile endeavor.
- Guarding your heart will guard your tongue and save you from a world of hurt.

APPLICATIONS

- Make it a priority to eat healthy, get proper rest, and exercise on a regular basis. Find a friend who will "hold your feet to the fire" so these practices become a reality.
- Husbands, make a commitment to place a high priority on getting household chores done with excellence and enthusiasm.

IV. LIFE APPLICATION

Edifying Speech

Although the tongue is a "small part of the body," it can have a devastating and far-reaching impact (Jas. 3:5).

Since we have considered how "little flies" can exact a heavy toll, it is instructive to contemplate what Jonathan Edwards said in a discourse entitled "Christian Knowledge." Many things in this essay command our attention.

Edwards makes a strong case that all Christians ought to grow in their knowledge of God. Deep learning is not just for the clergy (Edwards, *The Works of Jonathan Edwards,* vol. 2, 157). Edwards would have agreed with the psalmist that a deep knowledge of God's Word is not a function of intellect or one's vocation. Rather, it demonstrates that a person loves God (see Pss. 1; 119).

One area that is especially relevant in light of the discussion about the tongue is Edwards's reminder that only those who grow in the knowledge of God's Word have the capacity to edify others with their speech (Edwards, 161–62). He observed that it was common for Christians to settle for superficial learning and unwholesome speech. May we be people who edify and encourage others with an expanding knowledge of our great and inexhaustible God!

V. PRAYER

Father in heaven, help me never to despise any of the responsibilities you entrust to me, no matter how "small and insignificant" they may seem. Amen.

VI. DEEPER DISCOVERIES

A. "If a Man Is Lazy, the Rafters Sag" (10:18)

This verse recalls the "seven deadly sins." They are called "deadly or capital because, as Thomas Aquinas explains, they are the head (caput), the principle cause or root of other graver sins, not because they are worse than other sins such as murder of the innocent and genocide for example" (Chan, 72).

The sin of laziness or neglect can be viewed as closely related to melancholy (Chan, 72). Others see it "as a boredom or apathy that leads to despair" (Allen, *Spiritual Theology,* 74). An important insight for us driven Americans is that the sin of laziness or neglect is not necessarily inconsistent with workaholism. This may sound contradictory, but it isn't. For example, a person may avoid certain responsibilities by giving too much attention to other matters. A neglectful husband may work eighty hours a week at a respectable job but fail to do the most basic of duties at home. If "the rafters sag," he is the classic hardworking but neglectful executive.

VII. TEACHING OUTLINE

A. INTRODUCTION
1. Lead Story: Big Benefits from Doing Little Things
2. Context: A foolish life comes incrementally. It does not happen overnight.

3. Transition: Wise and foolish ways to live continue to occupy Solomon's attention.

B. COMMENTARY
1. "Little" Things Matter (10:1–4)
2. Foolishness Marks Life Under the Sun (10:5–7)
3. Work Smarter, Not Harder (10:8–11)
4. Vignettes on Foolish and Wise Living (10:12–20)

C. CONCLUSION: FAITHFUL TO THE TASK

VIII. ISSUES FOR DISCUSSION

1. If "sharpening the saw" makes it easier for tasks to be accomplished with greater effectiveness, why do so many of us neglect adequate preparation?
2. Since it is possible to be a hardworking but neglectful person, how common is it for you to avoid addressing certain responsibilities at home by focusing on other matters?
3. Related to the previous question is the subject of hobbies. Although there is nothing wrong with hobbies, do you have one that consumes your time and causes you to neglect more important responsibilities such as those of a parent or spouse?

Ecclesiastes 11–12

Aging Gracefully

"*N*ow reckon yourself a young man in your best vigor—say, twenty years of age. Let there be another man, ninety years old. Both of you must die; both of you are in the cart being carried forward. His gallows and death stand within ten miles at the farthest, and yours within eighty. I don't see why you should think less of your death than he, even though your way is longer, since you are sure you will never cease riding till you come to it."

T h o m a s   M o r e

Ecclesiastes 11–12

I N   A   N U T S H E L L

*A*s the old saying goes, "Two things in life are certain: death and taxes." Solomon closes with poignant and practical counsel on living in light of aging and death.

Aging Gracefully

I. INTRODUCTION

A Venerable Old Uncle's Parting Counsel

*T*he final two chapters of Ecclesiastes have been combined because the traditional chapter breaks tend to interrupt the flow of Solomon's argument. The Book of Ecclesiastes addresses a wide array of issues. Some sections address matters that are especially pertinent during certain seasons of life. This final section clearly speaks to all of us, but it has a compelling message to young people. If young people would internalize the teachings of these final verses, they would save themselves from much trouble and live a life marked by wisdom.

I picture Solomon here as a venerable old uncle giving sage counsel to a young nephew or niece. How attentive will we be?

II. COMMENTARY

Aging Gracefully

> **MAIN IDEA:** *Realities like mortality and death may seem morbid to think about, but they actually produce wise living.*

A The Role of Diligence (11:1–6)

> **SUPPORTING IDEA:** *Work hard and be shrewd in conducting your business affairs because you never know what God may bless.*

11:1. Some commentators see this casting of bread more literally (Keddie, 143–44). Others see it as metaphorical. In either case, the bottom line is that taking calculated risks can be a valuable thing.

11:2. This verse may advocate philanthropy. Certainly the priority of generosity and benevolence is replete throughout Scripture. But it seems better to interpret this as instruction to have a varied portfolio (Garrett, 338). Putting all your assets into a single financial investment can be devastating. This verse and the previous verse provide a healthy balance. Calculated risks are good, but be wise by diversifying your investments.

11:3–6. Because of the uncertainty of life and because some people want to control their lives, it is tempting for them to do nothing until they have absolute certainty about a matter. This sort of passivity can be dangerous. As the old saying goes, "Doing nothing is not nothing; it is something." A person does not stay in a neutral zone. By doing nothing, you may miss a great opportunity. The phrase **whoever watches the wind** in verse 4 is taken by some as the human spirit, but the physical wind is surely in view (Moore, *Ecclesiastes*, 136).

Caution needs to be given with all advice. Obviously, there are many situations in which waiting for more information is wise. Many people get themselves into deep trouble by acting too impulsively. But this danger is not the one that Solomon now addresses.

Solomon highlights our ignorance with respect to what God is doing. Our emotional response may be to throw up our hands and quit. The biblical advice is to keep working because we never know when or how God may choose to bless our efforts. Not working due to discouragement is warned against (Eaton, 143–44).

The prescription in verse 6 to work hard must be held in check with what Solomon said earlier about work. It certainly does not advocate a reckless workaholism. Ecclesiastes 4:6 reminds us that "better one handful with tranquillity than two handfuls with toil and chasing after the wind."

Furthermore, the counsel to **sow your seed in the morning, and at evening let not your hands be idle** must be balanced with the teachings on God's sovereignty. It is God who ultimately brings about any good in work (Eccl. 3:11), and it is he who empowers people to enjoy the fruits of their labor (Eccl. 2:24–26; 3:13; 5:18–20; cf. 6:1–9).

B Instructions to the Young (11:7–12:1)

SUPPORTING IDEA: *Young people ought to enjoy the youthful season of life but never forget that everything they think and do will be judged by God.*

11:7–8. In the Bible the night is often depicted as a time of sorrow, fear, or uncertainty. The day, however, is shown to be a time of gladness. Here the idea of the "day" seems to be more than just the physical reality. It also seems to include the joy that comes from being young and not yet experiencing the sobering realities of old age.

Note the tension in verse 8. We have seen this sort of balanced teaching before, especially in Ecclesiastes 9:9. We are encouraged by the fact that every day can be joyful. But a person must never lose sight of the fact that he will die. Solomon has already given some important teaching on this subject in Ecclesiastes 7:1–6.

It is clear from this book that most young people as well as most old people do not live this way. Either people don't want to think about death, or they focus on it to the exclusion of experiencing any joy in the present. The wise person lives joyfully in the present (Eccl. 5:20; cf. 7:10) yet realizes the brevity and uncertainty of life.

11:9. Again, we find a good balance in the counsel that Solomon gives the young person. On one hand, the young are instructed to enjoy life and appreciate the freedoms that youth offers. But this advice is not advocating a bold jump into hedonism. Solomon wants this young man to keep in mind that God will judge him for everything he does, not to mention sins of omission. The young man's awareness of God's future judgment is of great importance to Solomon.

11:10. One of the sad things about youth is that so few really enjoy it the way God intended. The rise of suicide and depression among young people is alarming. Bitterness, grief, and anger ought not to be part of a young person's heart.

12:1. It is imperative that young people use these years to develop an intimate walk with God. Calling the young person to **remember your Creator** is not passive; it involves action (Kaiser, 118).

The intimacy with God and the convictions that can come during a person's younger years will serve him well when he becomes older. Getting on in years generally means more difficult circumstances on many fronts. The spiritual stability that comes from walking faithfully with God during the youthful years will help a person weather future challenges that will come with the passing of years. It's hard to imagine a more significant truth for Christian teenagers to grasp than this one!

Ⅽ The Brutal Reality of the Aging Process (12:2–8)

SUPPORTING IDEA: *A graphic description of the aging process should humble and sober us into loving life with far more of a "Godward focus."*

12:2. Commentators differ over what the following imagery means. I lean toward the idea that these images represent the changing physiology of the old person. The first part of this verse seems to refer to the loss of delight (cf. 12:1). Since light is deemed to be pleasant (11:7), the loss of it depicts the loss of pleasures. Solomon will come back to this idea in 12:5.

The phrase **the clouds return after the rain** has been understood in various ways. It could refer to fading memory or "gloom into which the elderly may fall" (Whybray, *Ecclesiastes*, 164). One commentator says this may be "the symptoms of glaucoma" (Crenshaw, 185).

12:3. Four common characteristics of aging are listed in this verse. First, **the keepers of the house tremble.** What typically guards a person's body are his hands, although some commentators are not so sure about this interpretation (Seow, 397). Instead of strength and stability, the hands tremble. What once gave a person comfort in being able to protect himself now shakes uncontrollably. This sparks fear because of the aged person's increased vulnerability.

Second, **the strong men stoop**. It is very rare to find elderly people with perfect posture. My father, who is in excellent shape, often jokes how he used to be six feet tall, but now is five feet ten inches.

Third, **the grinders cease because they are few** seems to refer to loss of teeth. Even some who are not ready to accept the "physiological interpretation" see merit to its possibility (Seow, 355).

Fourth, the problem of failing eyesight seems to be depicted.

12:4. The first part of this verse may refer to the fact that elderly people are shut off from business and daily commerce. It could also refer to the loss of teeth. Either way, old age limits a person's activities.

The second part of the verse also raises different possibilities. One possibility is that this depicts how elderly people are easily startled, even at the soft sound of a bird. Another interpretation moves more in the direction of saying that elderly people can't enjoy music or can't participate in singing any longer (see 2 Sam. 19:35). Either interpretation furthers the idea that Solomon is trying to get across about aging.

12:5. Fears over hurting one's body or being hurt by others becomes a growing concern with the passing of years. In ancient times it was not just bad hip joint, backs, and knees that caused discomfort for elderly people. Included were terrors on the road such as wild animals and bandits. Elderly people were especially vulnerable to such dangers.

When the almond tree blossoms is an interesting phrase, since almond trees blossoming in America forecast spring and have a pink petal. In the Middle East, almond trees blossom in midwinter and have a white petal toward the tip. Various commentators see this as the turning of the color of the hair that usually comes with old age.

The grasshopper drags himself along seems clear. The passing of years causes the elderly to develop a slower gait. **Desire no longer is stirred** (or "the caperberry is ineffective," NASB) is seen by many commentators as a description of loss of sexual desire, although "no evidence for the aphrodisiac qualities of the caper appears prior to the medieval Jewish commentaries" (Garrett, 342). Some extend it to refer to the loss of desire in general (Leupold, 282). This interpretation certainly has some merit because of what this passage may say about the loss of teeth and sight. Senses like taste and smell usually grow dull with age.

12:6. The phrase **the silver cord** may refer to the spinal cord. Taking it as household imagery, it could refer to an "oil lamp suspended on a cord" (Whybray, *Ecclesiastes,* 167). The **golden bowl** may be the head and the **pitcher** the heart. It may be that the imagery of the latter depicts the end of life "since mortals were viewed as earthen vessels made by the divine potter" (Seow,

366). The **wheel . . . at the well** is viewed by some as the organs of digestion, but this is not clear.

Again, we are told to **remember** the Lord (see 12:1). Otherwise a person may become bitter and angry over the challenges and limitations that come with the aging process. Just like Israel before going into the promised land, we need to remember God—but how easy it is to forget!

12:7–8. These verses move us toward the truth that there is indeed an afterlife.

It is easy to misunderstand verse 8 because of its close proximity to verse 7. Verse 7 is not saying that **the spirit returns to God** is a futile or empty hope. Rather, verse 8 seems to be a general reminder that the struggle of people to find meaning apart from God is vain. In particular, the aging process heightens this vanity. Since aging is inevitable and often brutal, it is ridiculous to live for this world.

🄳 The Conclusion (12:9–14)

> **SUPPORTING IDEA:** *A few basic truths will ensure that a person lives wisely.*

12:9–10. Solomon is the master teacher who takes ample time to discern the best way to communicate God's truth. Well-known Christian writers see the wisdom in following his lead (Kirkegaard, 13; Dillard, 24).

The job of communicating truth in a fresh way without diminishing its exacting nature is quite a challenge. On one hand we have some people who defer to creativity so much that the truth of God's Word takes a subordinate position. Instead of exposing and communicating what the text of God's Word says, it becomes an interpreter's clever opinions that take center stage. When biblical truth is eclipsed, it is impossible to see the full radiance and beauty of God's Word.

On the other side of things, there are those who—with an understandable desire to preserve the "holy, catholic and apostolic church"—fail to bridge the context of the ancient world with the modern world. As a result, people wonder how they can apply God's Word to the world in which they live. The Bible strikes them as antiquated and impractical.

Some pastors may also be reluctant to offer possible applications for fear that they are playing the role of the Holy Spirit. Their reasoning goes like this: since God is sovereign, his Spirit can tell people how they should apply the sermon. This sounds good, but it misses the point that God uses means to achieve his sovereign purposes. Even the Puritan pastors, for all their deep belief about the sovereignty of God, did not see that as a deterrent to giving specific applications (Packer, 116–17).

We also see that respect for language is a virtue. If Ernest Hemingway thought it appropriate to do one hundred rewrites of *Old Man and the Sea,* how much more should Bible teachers of God's Word look for the right choice of words that move people to follow Christ? Language that is persuasive, delightful, even timely (Seow, 385) should be used by ministers of the Scripture but always as a means to illuminate what the truth of God's Word reveals. We must take people back to the "ancient paths" (Jer. 6:16) but show how they relate to people's lives today.

12:11. Goads are sharp sticks used for prodding cattle, especially during plowing. Since the nails are the second tool of the shepherd, it makes sense that tent pegs may be in view.

So God's Word functions in these two ways. First, it spurs us on. Living according to what God's Word declares is the best thing for us. To fight against the law of God is painful and fruitless. God will achieve what he has purposed, regardless of our faithfulness. The apostle Paul learned firsthand how futile it is to "kick against the goads" (Acts 26:14).

Second, the Word of God produces stability (Jer. 10:4). The men or women who consistently yield to God's Word will not find themselves like those who are constantly "tossed back and forth by the waves, and blown here and there by every wind of teaching" (Eph. 4:14).

12:12. This verse does not warn against the reading of all books other than the Bible. It does warn against the danger of getting immobilized by the various views that are articulated by their respective advocates. This is clearly a situation where a person needs wisdom. John Wesley was a highly literate man, yet he described himself as "a man of one Book." Likewise, many Puritan pastors were steeped in the great works of Western culture, but they talked constantly about the importance of making the Bible primary.

12:13–14. Solomon finishes the Book of Ecclesiastes by giving three application points—fear God, obey him, and live in light of God's impending judgment.

Fearing God is a major theme in the Bible, yet it is rarely talked about any more. The common way of defining the fear of God as a "healthy respect" for God does not seem to do justice to *all* the teaching about this important topic. There are times when terror in the presence of God is appropriate. Even those who are in covenant relationship with God experience this at times (Isa. 6:1–7; Rev. 1:17–18).

Obedience to the Lord assumes acquaintance with the revealed will of God. It is impossible to obey God if we are unfamiliar with what the Scriptures say. Obedience to God is not done in the energy of the flesh. Rather, it is "faith working through love." Obedience to God's will is not burdensome (1 John 5:3; cf. Matt. 11:28–30). It is a joy. The words of Jim Elliot are instructive in this regard: "In my own experience I have found that the most extravagant dreams of boyhood have not surpassed the great experience of being in the Will of God, and I believe nothing could be better" (Elliot, 196).

Finally, the sobering reality of God's judgment is mentioned. It is interesting to note that the Masoretic Jews in putting together their translation of the Old Testament switched verses 13 and 14 because verse 14 was considered too "ominous" a note on which to end the book (Leupold, 301).

MAIN IDEA REVIEW: *Realities like mortality and death may seem morbid to think about, but they actually produce wise living.*

III. CONCLUSION

Admitting Our Age

A little while back I was perusing the Web site of AARP. Among other things, it is interesting that the American Association of Retired Persons seems no longer to want this label. It must make prospective members feel too old, which is a bit ironic considering that fifty years of age now makes you qualified to join this organization. This certainly raises the question of how many fifty-year-olds are able to retire!

In any case, the Web site made me reflect on how awkward and silly we can get in trying to deny our age. Solomon has shown a better way in these closing chapters of Ecclesiastes. We ought to enjoy the "younger years" because there are some great advantages to them, but we should continue to allow God to reveal his purposes for our latter years. Settling for anything less is foolishness.

PRINCIPLES

- Acting on your knowledge of God, especially as a young person, will yield good fruit later in life.
- Today's culture idolizes and idealizes youth. A biblical perspective leads us to enjoy that season of life but to maintain a sober attitude about human frailty.

APPLICATIONS

- Interview an elderly Christian. Ask that person to describe what things described in Ecclesiastes 12 have been most challenging for him or her.
- If you are young, begin to prepare yourself for the fact that one day, God willing, you too will be elderly.

IV. LIFE APPLICATION

Facing Our Mortality

The aging process can be met with foolishness by the young and old alike (Kierkegaard, 41; Houston, 205). Those who can honestly face their mortality find freedom and even humor, as former President George Bush so memorably conveys:

> As the summer finishes out and the seas get a little higher, the winds a little colder, I'll be making some notes—writing it down lest I forget—so I can add to this report on getting older. Who knows maybe they'll come out with a new drug that makes legs bend easier, joints hurt less, drives go farther [reference to golf], memory come roaring back, and all fears about falling off fishing rocks go away (Bush, 626).

The great artist Michelangelo modeled the proper attitude toward aging.

> When Michelangelo was eighty-eight, a medal was struck in his honor. On one side was his profile. On the other was a blind pilgrim with a staff, led by a dog, and an inscription from Psalm 51: "Then will I teach transgressors thy ways; and sinners shall be converted unto thee" (v. 13). The artist himself had chosen the psalm, wishing to picture himself as old and frail but submissive to the will of God (Guinness, 240).

V. PRAYER

Lord, give me the courage to face my mortality and in so doing live for the glories of your kingdom. Amen.

VI. DEEPER DISCOVERIES

A. Banish Anxiety (11:10)

One commentator defines *anxiety* (or "vexation" as the NASB puts it) as "whatever misleads, distracts or deceives us regarding the real meaning of life" (Moore, *Ecclesiastes*, 137). This does not fully describe the aspect of anger that is part of the word. A standard reference work reflects more fully the heart of the word by describing it as "to vex, agitate, stir up, or provoke the heart to a heated condition which leads to specific action" (Harris et al., 451). A popular commentator is correct when he sees this word as including "anger and resentment" (Swindoll, 339; cf. Eaton, 146).

B. "Of Making Many Books There Is No End" (12:12b)

This statement has spawned much discussion. One church father even mentioned this verse with the heretic Apollinarius to make the case that his false teaching was tied to his excessive writing (Basil the Great, 302). But several church fathers like Augustine also wrote voluminously.

Some interpreters believe the phrase refers to secular literature. For example, the Ryrie Study Bible has this brief comment on Ecclesiastes 12:12: "A warning against excessive devotion to secular literature" (Ryrie, 1000). That may be the correct interpretation, since obeying God is in view, and "secular" books can lead people astray. But this view does raise some important issues.

First, it is common to find stalwarts of the Christian faith like Augustine and Calvin who modeled the importance of knowing significant non-Christian works, not to mention the apostle Paul (Acts 17:22–28). Were they wrong to do so? It didn't seem to hurt their love for God, and it certainly seemed to enhance their ministries.

Second, just reading the Bible has gotten some people into trouble. Consider Victor Paul Wierwille, founder of the cult, The Way International. Getting impatient with Christians disagreeing about various doctrines, he deposited his three-thousand-volume library at the city dump. After that he asked God to teach him the truth unlike it had been known since the time of the apostles. The result was his repudiation of the cardinal doctrines of the Christian faith such as the deity of Christ.

Ryrie's comment about "excessive devotion" to non-Christian literature being the culprit certainly has merit, but the same warning ought to be issued about certain "Christian" books. At the very least, this would be a wise application of Ecclesiastes 12:12. Too much time with these books can hurt many people spiritually, not the least of which is that some have imbalanced or inaccurate teaching about God and the Christian life. In other words, some of the books Wierwille left at the dump found their appropriate home!

VII. TEACHING OUTLINE

A. INTRODUCTION

1. Lead Story: A Venerable Old Uncle's Parting Counsel

2. Context: Wise living results in proper preparation for eventual realities.

3. Transition: Solomon wraps up the Book of Ecclesiastes by reminding us of truths we tend to avoid.

B. COMMENTARY

1. The Role of Diligence (11:1–6)
2. Instructions to a Young Person (11:7–12:1)
3. The Brutal Reality of the Aging Process (12:2–8)
4. The Conclusion (12:9–14)

C. CONCLUSION: ADMITTING OUR AGE

VIII. ISSUES FOR DISCUSSION

1. Why is it rare to find young people who truly enjoy life especially when they are in a culture that caters so much to them?
2. Have you thought about how the aging process may show up in your body? Are such thoughts a waste of time?

Introduction to

Song of Songs

Although often called the Song of Solomon, the Hebrew title for the book is "Song of Songs." This is how the Hebrew language says "The Best Song." The book portrays the deep, genuine love between a man and a woman in marriage. The subject of the book is quite obviously sexual in nature. The intimacy and physical pleasure God intended for a man and a woman is tastefully and appealingly put on full display before us (cf. Gen. 2:15–25).

The book is a love song that clearly celebrates the joys of physical, intimate love within marriage. One of the book's distinctive messages is that sex is God's gift, his good gift, and that it should be enjoyed. The Song boldly proclaims the value and beauty of love and devotion between a man and a woman. The Song uses highly figurative and poetic language; it is easy to see its intent of exalting human love. The lovers' words portray a beautiful relationship expressed in the complete giving of themselves to each other in the marriage relationship.

Within the Song, the term *lover* refers to the man or groom and the term *darling* refers to the woman or bride. The desire of the darling for her lover is sung sweetly and beautifully. Likewise, the lover has strong feelings for his darling. This is no casual affair or brief infatuation. There is a genuine heartfelt love for each other. Separation is difficult to endure. The deepest expressions of pain and sorrow in the Song are evoked by separation. But here, separation does not end love. The message of the book is that sexual attraction is inseparably linked to the devotion of true love. The book is a scriptural song that exalts human love. Here, a sensual relationship between lifelong partners in marriage is depicted in a very positive manner. Moreover, this relationship is a marvelous and gracious gift from God.

The Song of Songs has a message that all married couples need to hear. It also has a helpful word for those anticipating marriage. The beauty of its language and thought elevate the sexual and physical relationship to a much higher level than the world does. Sexual feelings are accepted and affirmed. They are a part of God's plan for his people. In a very sensitive and winsome manner, the writer records for us several beautiful love poems that provide guidance for developing a marriage that is glorifying to God and satisfying for a man and a woman.

AUTHORSHIP

The title of the book reads "Solomon's Song of Songs" (literally, "The Song of Songs, which is to Solomon"). The meaning of this phrase can be a song *by* Solomon, a song *for* Solomon, or a song *about* Solomon. Traditionally, the Song was ascribed to Solomon, but the biblical text does not demand that conclusion. Solomon is referred to seven times in the book by name (1:1,5; 3:7,9,11; 8:11–12), and he is also spoken of as the king five times (1:4,12; 3:9,11; 7:5). There can be little doubt the song is about Solomon and his "darling." But this Song describes a quality of relationship with one woman that seems inconceivable for a man who had seven hundred wives and three hundred concubines (1 Kgs. 11:1–3), or in one who could not find one woman among a thousand (Eccl. 7:27). It may be that the book presents the one true love of Solomon's life, perhaps his first wife, or it may be an ideal presentation of love to which Solomon aspired.

If Solomon is the author of the book—and there is no compelling reason to reject the traditional view—he may have written it (1) early in life as a young man soon after he was married and before committing the sin of polygamy or (2) at the end of his life as he reflected on the ideal that God intended (and he missed). The language and style of the Song reflect the work of a single author. Indeed, the book reveals a marvelous unity and "a well-conceived layout designed both to achieve esthetic beauty and to reinforce some of the author's main themes" (Dorsey, 199).

DATE

Accepting Solomonic authorship, the book most likely would have been written sometime during his reign as king. This would be between 971 and 931 B.C. The mention of the ancient Canaanite city Tirzah along with Jerusalem in 6:4 would support dating the book in the tenth century. Tirzah served as the capital of the Northern Kingdom for approximately fifty years after the Southern and Northern Kingdoms split following Solomon's death. It was destroyed in the ninth century. Comparing Tirzah's beauty to that of Jerusalem fits well in the time of Solomon, but it does not seem appropriate after his death and the division and rivalry that followed (Carr, 146–47).

HISTORY OF INTERPRETATION

This book is certainly one of the more difficult books to interpret in all of the Bible. Judaism itself debated why the book should be included in the canon (cf. *Mishnah Yadaim* 3:5). The Jews allegorized the book as a picture of the love between the Lord and Israel. The church allegorized it as a story of the relationship between Christ and his church or Christ and the believer. Following this approach, Bernard of Clairvaux (1090–1153) delivered eighty-six sermons on the book and only reached the end of the second chapter before his death!

Some interpreters have seen in the Song the attempt by Solomon to seduce the young country girl away from her shepherd lover. Others have argued it is the marriage between Solomon and the daughter of Pharaoh. Delitzsch sees a relationship between Solomon and Shulammite in which she wins his heart away from polygamy to the highest level of conjugal love and from there to a picture of God's love for his people. Thus the book has been interpreted allegorically and typologically.

Song of Songs has been viewed as a collection of Syrian wedding songs, a collection of pagan fertility cult liturgies, an anthology of disconnected love songs, or even a drama. But it is best to interpret the book *literally* or *naturally*. There is no compelling reason not to do so, and such a reading grows naturally out of Genesis 1–2.

Further, the book involves two persons (Solomon and Shulammite), not three (Solomon, Shulammite, and the shepherd-lover). Solomon is the shepherd-lover, and Shulammite is his darling. The book narrates their courtship, wedding, and growth in marriage. The Song is a lyric poem, which demonstrates both unity and logical progression. It extols love, marriage, and physical pleasure within that covenant relationship.

The book emphasizes the supremacy of love in human relationships, especially that of husband-wife (analogous to that between God and believer). It draws attention to the beauty and purpose of physical/sexual enjoyment between a husband and wife in celebration of God-given oneness. This kind of love cannot be experienced apart from an equally passionate spiritual intimacy. The book is in the form of a dialogue, though monologue is prominent as well. This Song, indeed, is a literary masterpiece. It remains, "the Best of Songs."

THE SONG'S PLACE IN THE CANON

In the English Bible, the Song of Songs is located among the five books of Old Testament poetry: Job, Psalms, Proverbs, Ecclesiastes, and the Song of Songs. In Hebrew Bibles the Song of Songs was grouped in a different set of five made up of The Song, Ruth, Lamentations, Ecclesiastes, and Esther. The Jews refer to these five books as the five "Megilloth," the five small scrolls. Each was (and still is by practicing Jews) read at a different major festival celebrated in Judaism. The Song of Songs was read at Passover, Ruth at the Feast of Weeks, Lamentations at the ninth of Ab, Ecclesiastes at the Feast of Tabernacles, and Esther at Purim. As Barry Webb relates, "The adoption of the

Song of Songs as a lectionary reading for Passover has recently been described as a stroke of pastoral genius which saved redemption from ever being reduced to a mere dogma or ritual" (Webb, 28).

In other words, as the Jews conceived of the Song as a love story between the Lord and his people, reading the book at Passover each year reminded them that they were not redeemed from slavery in Egypt so that God could have slaves but "because the Lord loved you and kept the oath he swore" to Abraham, Isaac, and Jacob (Deut. 7:8). They were redeemed so they could love the Lord their God with all their hearts, souls, and abilities (Deut. 6:5). Year by year the Song reminded them of the love between God and his people.

Paul House makes some stimulating observations on the relationship between the Song and the rest of the Old Testament wisdom literature. Noting that throughout Proverbs the importance of seeking a virtuous wife is underscored, the theme then culminates in the famous section on an excellent wife (Prov. 31:10–31). He points out that the little Book of Ruth serves as a fitting illustration of the way a noble woman interacts with her husband, her family, and her community. House then concludes:

> If Proverbs 31 highlights sound advice on seeking a suitable mate and Ruth demonstrates the way that God brings the righteous together for marriage, the Song of Songs illustrates free and passionate love between a man and a woman. Ecclesiastes . . . states plainly that human love cannot take the place of one's respect and love for one's Creator. Thus Song of Songs is introduced and qualified within the canonical context (House, 464).

One final observation on the Song's place in the canon should be noted. Five times the Song addresses Solomon as king (1:4,12; 3:9,11; 7:5). In view of the whole Bible, the royal, messianic overtones conveyed by addressing the male in the Song as "king" should not go without comment. To summarize briefly the hope for the coming king found throughout the Bible, we note that Abraham was promised that kings would come from him (Gen. 17:16); Moses spoke of the day when the nation would have a king whom the Lord would choose (Deut. 17:15); Hannah sang of a king whom God would strengthen and exalt (1 Sam. 2:10); David was promised that one of his descendants would reign forever, that he would even be a son to the Lord (2 Sam. 7:12–14); the Psalms often sing of God's king (e.g., Pss. 2:6–12; 45; 110); the prophets proclaim the coming of the expected ruler (e.g., Mic. 5:2; Zech. 9:9); and when we reach the New Testament, Jesus is greeted with the words, "You are the Son of God; you are the King of Israel" (John 1:49).

While it is perhaps true that at times the allegorizing of the Song of Songs has gotten out of hand, it is no less true that marital relations are to be an earthly picture of the relationship between Christ and the church (Eph. 5:32). In the Song of Songs we are given an idealistic portrayal, replete with imagery fit for the garden of Eden (e.g., Song 4:12–5:1), of the relationship between the king and his bride. While maintaining that the Song is about human love, human love does not exhaust the greatest Song humanity has ever encountered. Indeed, the Bible sings the beauty of the love of God.

PURPOSES OF THE BOOK

First, the Song is a revelation of the nature of genuine human love between a man and a woman, love as God intended it to be. The book reveals that a crucial element of love is *mutual satisfaction*. As John Piper wrote, "The reason there is so much misery in marriage is not that husbands and wives seek their own pleasure, but that they do not seek it in the pleasure of their spouses. The biblical mandate to husbands and wives is to seek your own joy in the joy of your spouse" (Piper, 175).

We find rest in our spouse at all levels—emotional, physical, spiritual, and intellectual—as God satisfies our hearts in our mate. Mutual satisfaction is not only complementary; it is also *exclusive*. True satisfaction demands a commitment to exclusivity. "Forsake all others!" is fundamental (cf. Gen. 2:23–24). Further, love is seen as probably the strongest human emotion a person can experience in life. You cannot buy it (Song 8:7), nor can you demand it; indeed it is as strong as death (Song 8:6). The Song witnesses to the reality that love can be cultivated. We must nurture it over a lifetime.

Second, the Song shows us several fruits of true love. In true love there is *rest* in our mate (Song 3:1; 8:5). In true love there is *joy* with our mate (Song 1:4). In true love there is *courage* on behalf of our mate (Song 3:2; 8:6).

A POSSIBLE STORY BEHIND THE BOOK

King Solomon lived in the tenth century B.C. He was Israel's wisest and richest king. He owned vineyards all over the nation—one of them close to Baal Hamon in the northernmost part of Galilee, near the foothills of the Lebanon mountains. While visiting this vineyard, Solomon met a country girl called Shulammite. She captured his heart. They fell in love. For some time he pursued her and made periodic visits to see her.

Finally, he asked her to marry him. Shulammite gave serious consideration to whether she really loved him and could be happy in the palace of a king, and she finally accepted his proposal of marriage because she also loved him.

Solomon sent a wedding procession to escort his new bride-to-be to the palace in Jerusalem. There they married. The details of their first night together are intimately and beautifully described, and the first half of the book closes.

The second half of the book deals with the joys and problems of married life. She refused his sexual advances one night, and he left. She, realizing her foolishness, got up and tried to find him, eventually did, and they had a time of reconciliation and renewed intimacy.

While she lived at the palace, the new queen often longed for the mountains of Lebanon where she grew up. She finally asked Solomon to take her there on a vacation. He agreed, and the book closes with their return to her country home, their enjoyment of sexual intimacy, and their pledge of mutual and devoted love for each other.

THE SONG OF SONGS'S MESSAGE FOR TODAY

The Song of Songs is an important part of the Bible because it displays the beauty of human love in freedom and spontaneity. Its neglect has been the church's loss. At a time when marriages are struggling more than ever to survive, its recovery and study would be a significant move forward. The speakers in this beautiful Song are dramatic and captivating throughout. The highly figurative phrases of the work have caused much disagreement concerning interpretation, but it is best to understand the Song as the dialogue of two lovers with all their feelings and emotions for each other.

Because of the frequent comparison in Scripture between the marriage relationship and the spiritual relationship, many have taken the book a step further to view it as an illustration of that greater union of love in the mystery of redemption. Regardless of the implications of the book for the love story of redemption, it is refreshing to find such a book in the Bible that shows the sanctity of the marriage relationship in its beauty and exquisite pleasure. This book is a precious gift from our Creator and Redeemer, which we neglect at our expense.

Song of Songs 1:1–8

How to Begin a Love Story

"*T*he bride says to the groom, 'I am lucky to have you as my husband.' Or the husband says to his wife, 'I thank my lucky stars that I married you.' That's terrible theology! Our lives are not controlled by luck or lucky stars. God has ordained whom our mates will be. He brings us together."

Chuck Swindoll

Song of Songs
1:1–8

I N   A   N U T S H E L L

*G*od is something of a cosmic romantic. He ordains and enjoys a good love story. Song of Songs paints the portrait of such a love story and right from the beginning provides principles to get us off to a good start. How do you begin a love story between a man and a woman?

How to Begin a Love Story

I. INTRODUCTION

Love, Romance, and Marriage Through the Eyes of Children and Skeptical Adults

*W*hat do love, romance, and marriage look like through the eyes of a child? I came across some answers that kids gave which might interest you.

To the question, "How do you decide whom to marry?" Allen, age ten, said, "You've got to find someone who likes the same stuff. Like, if you like sports, she should like it, and she should keep the chips and dips coming." Kristin, age ten, replied, "No person really decides before they grow up who they're going to marry. God decides it all the way before, and you got to find out who you're stuck with."

When asked, "How can a stranger tell if two people are married?" Derek, age eight, said, "Married people usually look happy to talk to other people." A boy named Eddie responded, "You might have to guess based on whether they seem to be yelling at the same kids."

When asked, "Why do people go out on a date?" Lynette, age eight, was rather straightforward from the female perspective: "Dates are for having fun, and people should use them to get to know each other. Even boys have something to say if you listen long enough."

And responding to the question, "How do you make a marriage work?" a seven-year-old boy, wise beyond his years said, "Tell your wife that she looks pretty, even if she doesn't."

What do love, romance, and marriage look like through the eyes of a modern Washington writer and businessman? The opinion held by Philip Harvey is not nearly as hopeful or positive as that of the adolescent children surveyed above:

> A reasonable level of divorce may be a symptom of a healthy and mobile society, a society in which men and women are living unprecedentedly long lives, lives for which the companionship of but a single other person for 30 or 40 or 50 years may simply be inappropriate. . . . That most Americans categorically oppose divorce on principle is a function more of our aspiration to the ideal state than a realistic acceptance of how we humans actually behave . . .
>
> The freedom to have more than one mate over a 75 year lifespan may be a positive thing. Is it not possible that the ideal companion for our younger child-rearing years will not be the ideal companion for

our middle and later years? Is it not reasonable to suggest that the radical differences in the way we live in our fifties and sixties and beyond may be under many circumstances, most appropriately lived with a different person from the one with whom we reared children? . . . The interests of children must be given a very high priority. But allowing for that, it seems to me that a reasonable level of divorce is more likely to be a quality of a mobile and healthy modern society than a sign of moral decay (Harvey, "Divorce for the Best," *Washington Post*, 11 August 2000).

Harvey is not alone in his rather pessimistic prediction of one man with one woman for life. James Dobson in his January 2000 *Focus on the Family* newsletter shared these observations from an article he found in *The Washington Post*:

Sandy Burchsted, an unmarried "futurist" from Houston, estimates that one hundred years from now, the average American will marry at least four times and routinely engage in extramarital affairs with no fear of public humiliation. Miss Burchsted, who is writing a book on marriage in the year 2100, identified what she believed will be four different types of marriage at a World Future Society conference in July, 1999. The first union is called the *icebreaker marriage* (usually lasting about five years) in which couples will learn how to live together and gain sexual experience. Once disillusionment sets in, claims Burchsted, it will be perfectly acceptable for the couple to divorce. If one of the partners decides to marry again, he or she will enter a *parenting marriage,* which lasts between fifteen and twenty years. These couples will view raising children as their primary purpose, although child-rearing in the future will be in communal settings, not nuclear families.

After the second marriage is terminated, couples might enter a third union, which Burchsted calls the *self-marriage.* This relationship will be focused on self-discovery and personal awareness. "We see marriage as a conscious, evolutionary process," says Burchsted, "so this marriage will be about consciously evolving yourself." Finally, there is a fourth category of marriage, which will emerge as a result of the theory that people in the twenty-first century will be living until at least the age of 120. Burchsted calls this late-in-life marriage the *soul-mate connection,* characterized by "marital bliss, shared spirituality, physical monogamy and equal partnership." *The Washington Times* says that Burchsted's theories are based on "trends showing women becoming more financially independent, marriage and childbearing becoming more 'delinked,' 'serial monogamy' becoming more acceptable and extramarital sexual affairs occurring more frequently and with less public outcry" (Cheryl Wetzstein, "Researchers See Marriage as a Weakening Institution," *The Washington Times,* 28 October 1999).

II. COMMENTARY

How to Begin a Love Story

MAIN IDEA: *Solomon provides sound principles for getting started right in a relationship.*

A Anticipate the Rewards of Being with Your Mate (1:1–4)

SUPPORTING IDEA: *True love is accompanied by many blessings.*

1:1. This book is titled "Song of Songs" or "Solomon's Finest Song." First Kings 4:32 indicates that Solomon wrote 1,005 songs, but out of all of them this is his **Song of Songs**—this is his best. The second-century rabbi Akiba ben Joseph said of the Song of Songs, "In the entire world there is nothing to equal the day in which the Song of Songs was given to Israel. All the writings are holy, but the Song of Songs is the holy of holies" (*Mishnah, Yadaim* 3:5).

In other words, this was the number one song of the Jerusalem hit parade in 1000 B.C.! First Kings 4:29–31 also teaches that God blessed Solomon with wisdom that excelled all his contemporaries. Here Solomon looks at the issue of marriage and romance. Marriage is God's good gift. It should be a blessing. It should be rewarding. What kind of rewards does Solomon outline for us?

1. Desire the physical pleasures of marriage.

1:2. Marriage is the context in which physical passion and pleasure is set free. The kiss is a universal expression of desire and affection, and the woman (she is called Shulammite in 6:13) expresses her desire for her lover to kiss her and to kiss her deeply and repeatedly. The senses of touch and taste both came together, and the resulting passion was more than she could handle. She said, **Your love is more delightful than wine.** By describing his romantic, affectionate kisses in this way, she was saying, I find the touch of your lips and the embrace of your mouth sweet, powerful, intoxicating. It sweeps me off my feet. It sets my head spinning. The passionate kiss, we have discovered, is a sign of a healthy, romantic marriage, even more than sex. "The passionate kiss (average length one minute) reveals a lot about your relationship. Considered even more intimate than sex, passionate smooching is one of the first things to go when spouses aren't getting along" (*Marriage Partnership*, 10).

Several years ago I heard of a survey taken in Germany that revealed that if a man kissed his wife in the morning before leaving for work, he would: (1) live five years longer; (2) have fifty percent fewer illnesses; and (3) make twenty to thirty percent more money than the man who doesn't! Proverbs 5:18–19 says, "May you rejoice in the wife of your youth. A loving doe, a graceful deer—may her breasts satisfy you always, may you ever be captivated by her love."

2. Experience the personal pleasures of marriage.

1:3. The word *love* occurs repeatedly in verses 2–7. A careful examination reveals love's connection to the mind, will, and emotions. Not only does love connect our intellects and our desires; it keeps them in proper balance. Love is to be a delightful experience that expresses itself in many ways. Love has a physical dimension, but it is not just physical. The Song gives us four avenues whereby lovers should enjoy each other.

a. Delight in their fragrance.

The thought of the physical caresses of romance called to mind not only the intoxication of wine but also the swell smell of his cologne. He tasted good, and he smelled good. Without stretching the text, he brushed his teeth and used mouthwash. He took a bath, used soap, and then anointed himself with "good ointments." This is good counsel for every man at any time! Already we see the senses of taste, touch, and smell come together in the pursuit of romance and love. Here was a man sensitive to the things his woman found attractive. She was appreciative and responded in kind.

b. Delight in their fame.

His kisses were intoxicating. His smell was exhilarating. His reputation was unquestioned. **Your name** [meaning his reputation and character] **is like perfume poured out.** A person is more than his or her physical appearance. Who one really is goes beneath the skin. A wise person, when dating, will not only form an opinion of the person with whom he is involved; he will also listen and hear what others have to say. No matter how strong the physical attraction, he will also listen to public opinion. Is he honest? Trustworthy? Does she have a calm spirit? A level head? Is he known as a playboy? Does she have friends who believe in her? We should carefully consider what others say about the person we date and the person we would consider marrying. We all have blind spots. Love can indeed be blind. We must not let our emotions override good decision-making, even if it hurts.

Shulammite knew this man was respected. He was known as a person of character and integrity. She was not only physically attracted to him; she could respect him. She could admire him.

c. Delight in their friends.

1:4. Solomon was a much-desired man. He was indeed a catch! Verse 3 says, "No wonder the maidens love you!" In verse 4 these same women exclaim, concerning Shulammite's good fortune, **We rejoice and delight in you; we will praise your love more than wine.** The esteem of other women enhanced Shulammite's love and admiration for the man in her life. In essence they were saying, "If you don't get him and keep him, then we are going after him." Any woman would be fortunate to have such a man as her own.

d. Delight in their faithfulness.

While potential rivals were lurking about, this woman was so secure in her relationship with her man that she could rejoice in the praise and admiration showered on him by others. Love, to be sure, is jealous (cf. 8:6), yet it can also be generous when the bond is secure. She knew at the right time she could ask him to **take me away with you—let us hurry** (v. 4) and he would. He was her king, and she was his queen. Their love was majestic and royal. On one plane she could share him publicly and with others. On another level she possessed him as her own, and there were things that only the two of them shared, and that, in private. He brought her, and only her, into his chambers, his bedroom. Already she anticipated the love that would be consummated on their wedding night (4:1–5:1). Theirs was an exclusive love that dared not be shared with another.

In a survey, *Glamour* magazine asked men which marriage vow was the hardest to keep: Nineteen percent said it was to love "in sickness and in health;" nineteen percent said it was to love "for richer or for poorer." The toughest of all, said sixty percent of the men, was "to forsake all others" (*Entertainment Today*, 2 January 1997). A woman should be confident in her man's faithfulness. Shulammite had this from Solomon. Verse 4 concludes with his affirmation of the judgment of the maidens (or friends), **How right they are to adore you!** Ephesians 5:33 says it well: "Each one of you [husbands] love his wife as himself" (HCSB).

B Accept the Realities of Being with Your Mate (1:5–7)

SUPPORTING IDEA: *Marriage is the real deal. There are ups and downs. There will be good times and tough times.*

1:5–6. Marriage has its romance, its rewards. It also has its rough spots and realities. Men anticipating marriage may think, *Wow! We'll spend all of our time in bed.* Well, I've got news for you. Hopefully, you will enjoy some marvelous time in bed and in other places. You will, however, spend the majority of your time out of bed, and you will need to face head-on some of the realities that will confront you as you try to build your marriage. Note two realities a man must face when living with a woman. This list, by the way, is by no means exhaustive. It's just a place to start.

1. A woman can be ambivalent concerning her appearance.

Women change. It is their prerogative as females. It is built into their genes. They change, and they can change quickly and often. A man must be alert and sensitive. Like a weather radar, he must be able to see what is on the horizon.

How a woman thinks she looks is extremely important to her. It goes to the very foundation of her self-worth. In particular, she wants to know that she is attractive to the man in her life. But men, we must understand that what she thinks about how she looks matters more to her than what we think about how she looks.

a. She may be delighted with her appearance.

Shulammite knew she had a natural beauty. She believed that she was pretty and attractive, lovely and pleasing in appearance. She was sensitive to the fact that men are creatures of sight and that they are moved by what they see. She was confident he would like what he saw when he looked at her. Of herself she could say, "I am . . . **lovely.**"

b. She may be defensive about her appearance.

A tan was not grand in Solomon's day. Women prized fair skin and the "indoor look." This would signify the lofty social standing of the well-to-do city girl. In contrast, Shulammite was deeply sun-tanned and **dark.** She was a country girl who had been "looked upon" negatively by both the sun of nature and the sons of her mother who forced her to labor in the vineyards. "She had been doubly burned, **by the sun,** and by her brother's anger" (Gledhill, 104). The **tents of Kedar** speaks of "the Bedouin tribes whose tents, made from the hair of the black goats so common among them, are a frequent sight on the fringes of the deserts" (Carr, 78). The **curtains of Solomon** draw a different analogy. These curtains would be beautiful and valuable, of "exquisite craftsmanship . . . she is both hardened by the elements and yet beautiful" (Garrett, 387).

c. She may be disappointed with her appearance.

She worked hard to tend the vineyards in the field. As a result, her own vineyard, her body, had been neglected. The **vineyard** will be used several times in the Song as a metaphor of the woman's body. Unable to give the time, attention, and care she would have liked, her physical appearance, at least to her way of thinking, was less than the best. One easily senses her pain, her insecurity.

Tom Gledhill wrote:

> Her vineyard represents everything that conveys her essential femininity. Her looks, her complexion, her dress, her status, her sexuality—all those considerations which would make her attractive to a man. . . . In these verses we are brought face to face with the problems of our own self-image. How do we view ourselves? When we look at our own reflection in the mirror, do we like what we see? Can we accept ourselves as we really are, with all our quirks, idiosyncrasies and limitations? Do we like the way we look? Or are we always wishing we were like someone else? (Gledhill, 105).

A woman's appearance is an important element in her life. It requires great sensitivity and understanding on the part of a man. Men should make sure they praise their wives and build them up.

2. A woman can be anxious about a husband's absence.

Security is important to a marriage. A man feels it when his woman praises him. A woman feels it when her man is present. A marriage is destined to suffer, and suffer greatly, if there are extended periods of unhealthy separation.

a. A husband's absence can be a source of personal sorrow.

1:7. This verse tells us Solomon was gone. Why we are not told, though the imagery implies he was about the normal duties of life. Here the picture is that of a shepherd tending his sheep. She missed him. She longed for him. To speak so frankly exposed her heart, but it would also excite the heart of her lover. At noon the sheep would sleep. The other shepherds would be resting. There would be time just for them. No distractions. No interruptions. Furthermore, what a creative woman we see. Their meeting would be outside in the wide open spaces, perhaps under a shade tree? Perhaps in a temporary hut or shelter? Even as she sorrowed over his absence, she strategized about how to make their time together new, exciting, and memorable. But you can't love them if you're not with them.

b. A husband's absence can be a source of personal shame.

To wear a veil as she wandered among the flocks and shepherds would be embarrassing. It could, in that day, give the impression that she was a prostitute or possibly in mourning. (Later she would adorn herself with the veil in the privacy of her bedroom and for her husband on their wedding night [cp. 4:1].) A prostitute has many men, but she has no man she can call her own. There is no one at whom she can point and say, "That man is my man, and this woman is his woman." She did not want to have the slightest doubt that he was hers and she was his. For there even to be a question of their fidelity and commitment to each other would be shameful.

Shulammite knew there was a cost, a price to be paid, in committing herself for a lifetime to another person. She was aware of the fact that a marriage relationship can sometimes become high profile and take on a fishbowl type of scrutiny. Knowing the facts, she was willing to accept and live up to such a challenge.

Acknowledge the Risk of Being with Your Mate (1:8)

SUPPORTING IDEA: *We must grow to know our mate. Study him. Learn more about her.*

Romance is risky business. You take a chance. You roll the dice. But there are ways to improve the odds in your favor. Verse 8 is best understood as a mild, maybe even a playful, rebuke of Shulammite. She was looking to "hook-up" with her man. What did she need to do?

1. Know where you can find him.

1:8. Shulammite is called **most beautiful of women**, yet she is teased for not knowing where her man is. Perhaps she did not, as of yet, know him as well as she should. After all, marriage is a lifelong learning process. It is imperative that we grow in knowledge of our mate, of her needs, dispositions, gifts, weaknesses, and inclinations. To love him we must know him and know where and how to find him when we want him.

2. Go where you can find him.

Knowledge must be accompanied by action. How often is it true in a relationship that we know what the right thing to do is but we do not do the right thing? Shulammite is told to **follow** what, in essence, were familiar paths or **tracks** that Solomon was known to walk. If she followed the familiar paths she would find him.

MAIN IDEA REVIEW: *Solomon provides sound principles for getting started right in a relationship.*

III. CONCLUSION

Marriage Is Hard Work, but It Is Worth the Investment

Researchers Howard Markman and Scott Stanley of the University of Denver help us understand, in part, why good marriages work and bad marriages fail. It's not sex, money, or how many fights you have that make for a happy union. Marriage-wise couples aren't afraid to accept influence from each other. They connect on a daily basis in many small ways, think about their partner periodically when they're apart, take time-outs to soothe tempers, use humor as a coolant in arguments, and have softer start-ups when fighting. Even in conflict, their ratio of positive to negative actions—from a simple "mmmmh" or "yeah" to a pat on the arm—are 5 to 1 as opposed to 0.8 to 1 for unstable marriages (Shirley Barnes, "Keeping It Together," *Seattle Tribune,* 2 August 1998).

This is sound advice. We should be influenced by each other. The Lord should influence us. We should learn from each other. We should learn from God. We must grow in our knowledge of each other. Solomon and Shulammite have made a good start, a nice beginning. We can learn from both of them.

PRACTICAL PRINCIPLES AND APPLICATIONS

- Physical, sensual desire, and longing for intimate sexual consummation is a characteristic of romantic love, and it is a good thing within the bonds of marriage (intoxicating and sweet as wine).
- The character (as well as the physical appearance and fragrance) of a person is vitally important in the selection and enjoyment of one's spouse.
- Acknowledge your imperfections up front, but recognize the special value and potential they have for God to work in your life. (Imperfections are wonderful pricks to keep us humble, and who doesn't need to be humble in a marital relationship!)
- We must count the cost involved before committing ourselves for a lifetime to another person.
- A Christian's relationship to his or her spouse will often take on a fishbowl type of scrutiny! Accept it, and live up to the challenge.

IV. LIFE APPLICATION

Getting Started on Thinking About Marriage

If we would raise our marriages to the level God intends, we must guide them with principles that focus more on "we" than "me" and that esteem the other better than self. What we are after is having the mind of Christ (Phil. 2:3–5).

Here are seven areas that need our careful *thinking* and *commitment.*

Educationally

- Study marriage; become a real student of it.
- Study the opposite sex; at least try to become an expert on him or her (be ready for a lifetime adventure!).

- Study your spouse; really get to know her or him.

Sexually

- Be faithful to each other for life. Put boundaries in place now and commit never to compromise them.
- Know the difference between your needs and your wants.
- Exercise self-control (avoid and resist temptations).
- Never bargain with sex. Don't become a marital prostitute (to play you must pay!). This is a lose-lose proposition.
- Make sure there is mutual consent to all you and your spouse decide to do (1 Cor. 7:1–7). If a spouse cannot say no when circumstances warrant it, how can that spouse be sure that he or she is not a slave?
- Do not expect your spouse to have the same appetites and desires that you have. Strive for compatible appetites.

Individually

- Do not make unilateral decisions that affect your relationship.
- Do not depend primarily on your spouse for a sense of self-worth. Look to God.
- Own up to your mistakes. Be willing to say the seven magical words, "I am sorry, will you forgive me?" (Eph. 4:32).
- Deal with your own sins first before dealing with your mate's (Gal. 6:1).

Publicly

- Keep confidential matters confidential.
- Never criticize your spouse in public or in front of others.
- Guard the way you dress; check your motives and your judgment.

Rearing Children

- Set up disciplinary policies jointly and stick to them (Eph. 6:1–4).
- Do not argue about discipline in front of the children.
- Be loving, and always restore fellowship after discipline.
- Discipline in a manner that is appropriate to the child's action, age, and maturity.

Financially

- Set up financial priorities jointly and stick to them.
- Remember, no one is entitled to a "superior status" just because one earns the money to pay the rent, buy the groceries, etc. Keep-

ing the house clean and guiding the home front efficiently are just as important and just as worthy of appreciation and praise.

- All who share in the labor to maintain the family ought to share in everything the family earns or produces.

Relationally

- Take each other seriously (but not too seriously).
- Nurture each other (Eph. 5:29–30).
- Set up a problem-solving strategy.
- Be respectful and courteous at all times, treating your mate like a good friend, even a best friend.
- Spend time with your spouse and family (both quality and quantity time).
- Make room for intimacy and affection without pushing for sex (guys, are you listening?).
- Treat each other as equals because you are.
- Be honest with each other; always speak the truth in love (Eph. 4:15).
- Give your spouse practical and relational priority in all aspects of your life.
- Be slow to anger, slow to speak, and quick to listen (Jas. 1:19).
- Do not let the sun go down on your anger (Eph. 4:26).
- Never stop caring about pleasing your spouse (Phil. 2:3–4).
- Seek unity and do not feel threatened by disagreement (Phil. 2:2).
- Honor each other's rights and needs (1 Cor. 7:1–7).
- Do not impose your will on the other. Be peaceful and kind and use persuasion, not coercion.
- Seek to be best friends to each other.
- Try to deal with facts rather than feelings.
- Minister to rather than manipulate each other.
- Put your spouse before all others, including the children.
- Honor the Creator's structure for marriage (Eph. 5:21–33).
- Be approachable, teachable, and correctable (even by, and especially by, your spouse).
- Do not try to control everything.
- Confront each other with tenderness, compassion, and loving concern.
- Be willing to sacrifice for your loved ones.
- Do not neglect your responsibility to provide for your own.
- Be willing to communicate and to listen.
- Despise divorce and determine it will never be an option.
- Eat as many meals with each other as possible.

- Whenever possible, postpone doing things you want to do for yourself to the times when your spouse is busy with other things.
- Do not stop trying to make time for your spouse just because it seems so impossible to do so.

V. PRAYER

Heavenly Father, the most important decision I ever made was to repent of my sin and put my trust in your Son, the Lord Jesus, for my salvation. I believe the second greatest decision I will ever make is who I will spend my life with in marriage. Help me to recognize the gravity of this covenant. I ask you first of all to make me the right person for this relationship. I long for a love that will last. I desire a marriage that will glorify you. Take your Word and plant it deep in my heart that I may only be satisfied in what and who you have for me. I pray this in Jesus' name. Amen.

VI. DEEPER DISCOVERIES

A. Sex

Sex was God's idea. Yes, I know it is hard to believe, but God is the one who came up with this fantastic idea. He gave it to us as a wonderful gift for our *pleasure* and *procreation* (Gen. 1:26–31). God is pro-sex. He believes in it. He is for it. Our study of the Song of Songs (or Song of Solomon) makes this abundantly clear. This gift is intended for *partnership* and *protection*. When sex and marriage are experienced and enjoyed together as God intended, the joys and blessings that are ours are seldom, if ever, surpassed in this life (Gen. 2:18–25).

So what's the problem? Why is it that so many marriages end in divorce? Why is it that more and more persons are dissatisfied with their sex life both inside and outside of marriage? I believe the answer is really quite simple: we have forgotten or ignored what God has to say about sex, love, intimacy, and marriage. We have failed to read and heed the *Master's Manual for Marriage*, and the price many people have paid has been high indeed. However, it can be different if we will do things God's way.

God is so interested in and committed to the intimate, romantic and sexual aspects of marriage that he gave us an entire book of the Bible dedicated to the subject. It is called the Song of Songs.

This side of heaven, outside of having a personal relationship with Jesus Christ the Son of God, the best thing going is marriage and family. When we *do* marriage and family God's way, it is great. It is awesome. It is wonderful. The Song of Songs teaches us how to do marriage God's way, and it leaves nothing out. A beautiful love song, it portrays the deep, genuine love that a man and woman should enjoy in marriage. It teaches us that a successful marriage requires *commitment* and involves *work,* but that it is worth every investment we make. The book celebrates the joys of physical, intimate, sexual love. Sex is good; it is God's gift. It should be enjoyed and enjoyed often. This good gift of God will find its fullest expression when a man and a woman give themselves completely to each other in the marriage relationship (1 Cor. 7:1–7).

God knows nothing of "casual sex," because in reality there is no such thing. What is often called casual sex is always costly. Sexually transmitted diseases, unexpected pregnancy, and psychological and spiritual scars are some of the results, and the price paid, because we have approached God's good gift of sex in a casual manner. Sexual attraction is inevitable. It is what God intended. But unless we follow God's plan, we will miss out on his best and suffer the painful and tragic consequences in the process.

The Song of Songs explains the purpose and place of sex as God designed it. When we make love the way God planned, we enjoy the security of a committed relationship, experience the joy of unreserved passion, and discover the courage to give ourselves completely to another person in unhindered abandonment (Prov. 5:1–23).

B. Solomon

Solomon was the tenth son of David and the second son of Bathsheba. He became the third king of Israel and reigned forty years (971–931 B.C.). Born to David and Bathsheba after the death of their first son (2 Sam. 12:24), he was crowned king after his mother and Nathan the prophet intervened with David and secured David's decision to have Solomon succeed him (1 Kgs. 1–2). Solomon is remembered for his wisdom, his building programs, and his wealth generated through trade and administrative expertise.

Solomon is also remembered as having written 3,000 proverbs and 1,005 songs (1 Kgs. 4:32). His wisdom is seen in the Bible in the accounts of the two prostitutes who claimed the same surviving child (1 Kgs. 3:16–28) and by the visit of the queen of Sheba (1 Kgs. 10).

While Solomon's temple was the most famous of his building projects (1 Kgs. 5–8), it was by no means the only one. Solomon fortified a number of cities that helped provide protection to Jerusalem, built "store-cities" for stockpiling the materials required in his kingdom, and established military bases for companies of charioteers (1 Kgs. 9:15–19). The temple complex in Jerusalem was composed of several buildings, including Solomon's palace, the "house of the forest of Lebanon," the hall or "porch of pillars," the hall or "porch of the throne," and a palace for one of his wives, the daughter of the pharaoh of Egypt (1 Kgs. 7 KJV).

Solomon divided the country into administrative districts that did not correspond to the old tribal boundaries (1 Kgs. 4:7–19) and had the districts provide supplies for the central government. This system, combined with control of vital north-south trade routes between the Red Sea and what was later known as Asia Minor, made it possible for Solomon to accumulate tremendous wealth.

Solomon had great weaknesses as well as great strengths. The "seven hundred wives, princesses, and three hundred concubines" came from many of the kingdoms with which Solomon had treaties (1 Kgs. 11:1 KJV). He allowed his wives to worship their native gods and even had altars to these gods constructed in Jerusalem (1 Kgs. 11:7–8). This spiritual compromise indicates a weakness in Solomon not found in his father David.

Solomon was an ancestor of Jesus (Matt. 1:6–7) and is mentioned in Jesus' teaching on anxiety (Matt. 6:29; Luke 12:27). Jesus noted that the queen of Sheba came a long way to see Solomon and that something "greater than Solomon is here" (Matt. 12:42; Luke 11:31). Stephen noted that though David wanted to find a place for God, it was Solomon who "built the house for him" (Acts 7:47).

C. Geographical References

The Song of Songs mentions numerous locations from all over ancient Palestine. These include places both in northern Israel (Sharon, Lebanon, Hermon, and Carmel) and in the southern territory of Judah (Jerusalem and En Gedi). This geographic outlook reflects a time when all Israel was unified and even territories in the Transjordan were under Israelite dominion. These conditions did not prevail after the death of Solomon.

Kedar, mentioned in 1:5, was originally a personal name meaning "mighty" or "swarthy" or "black." It was the name given to the second son of Ishmael (Gen. 25:13; 1 Chr. 1:29). The name occurs later in the Bible as a reference to a tribe that probably took its name from Kedar. Little is known about this group. It appears that the descendants of Kedar occupied the area south of Palestine and east of Egypt (Gen. 25:18). They seem to have been nomadic, living in tents (Ps. 120:5; Song 1:5) and raising sheep and goats (Isa. 60:7; Jer. 49:28–29,32), as well as camels, which they sold as far away as Tyre (Ezek. 27:21). "Tents of Kedar" referred to the dark, beautiful black goat hair used to make the tents.

D. Cultural Insights

The imagery of the Song of Songs reflects an age of great prosperity. This supports the view that it was written in Solomon's day. During this time Jerusalem possessed the spices, perfumes, and luxuries mentioned in the book as well as great quantities of gold, marble, and precious jewels (Song 5:14–15; see 1 Kgs. 10:14–22).

E. Wine

This drink was made from fermented grapes, which grew throughout ancient Palestine. Even in areas with limited rainfall, enough dew fell at night to support thriving vineyards. Wine was made by pressing the juice from the grapes in large stone vats with a small drain at one end. The juice was collected in troughs, poured into large jars, and allowed to ferment while stored in cool, rock cisterns. Scripture condemns drunkenness and overindulgence but pictures wine as a part of the typical ancient meal. In the Song of Songs, wine is a symbol of intoxicating joy and sweetness.

VII. TEACHING OUTLINE

A. INTRODUCTION: LOVE, ROMANCE, AND MARRIAGE THROUGH THE EYES OF CHILDREN AND SKEPTICAL ADULTS

B. COMMENTARY

1. Anticipate the Rewards of Being with Your Mate (1:1–4)
   a. Desire the physical pleasures of marriage.
   b. Experience the personal pleasures of marriage.
2. Accept the Realities of Being with Your Mate (1:5–7)
   a. A woman can be ambivalent concerning her appearance.
   b. A woman can be anxious about a husband's absence.
3. Acknowledge the Risk of Being with Your Mate (1:8)
   a. Know where you can find him.
   b. Go where you can find him.

C. CONCLUSION: GETTING STARTED ON THINKING ABOUT MARRIAGE

VIII. ISSUES FOR DISCUSSION

1. Do you give attention to good hygiene before seeing your date or your mate? This issue is more important than most people realize!
2. Do you miss your partner when he or she is away? If so, is it healthy or unhealthy? Try to be honest.

3. What kind of reputation does your partner have? Can you truly hear what others say?

4. Being the right person is more important than finding the right person. Do you believe that?

5. How do you see yourself? Do you have a positive or negative sense of self-worth?

6. How does God see you right now? Is he pleased?

Song of Songs 1:9–14

The Power of Praising Our Partner

I. **INTRODUCTION**
The Gift of the Blessing

II. **COMMENTARY**
A verse-by-verse explanation of these verses.

III. **CONCLUSION**
Kindness and Respect Are Necessary for Healthy Romance
An overview of the principles and applications from these verses.

IV. **LIFE APPLICATION**
A Premarital Inventory
Melding these verses to life.

V. **PRAYER**
Tying these verses to life with God.

VI. **DEEPER DISCOVERIES**
Historical, geographical, and grammatical enrichment of the commentary.

VII. **TEACHING OUTLINE**
Suggested step-by-step group study of these verses.

VIII. **ISSUES FOR DISCUSSION**
Zeroing these verses in on daily life.

Quote

"*I* can live for two months on a good compliment."

Mark Twain

Song of Songs
1:9–14

IN A NUTSHELL

Words are powerful weapons. They can bless or curse, build up or tear down. Praising our partner with words of encouragement and respect will strengthen our love and nurture our relationship as we grow together in marriage.

The Power of Praising
Our Partner

I. INTRODUCTION

The Gift of the Blessing

In their outstanding book *The Gift of the Blessing*, Gary Smalley and John Trent give us some biblical and practical tips on how we can *bless* rather than *curse* those we love. When it comes to marriage and our mate, their counsel is crucial.

God has put us together in such a way that we have emotional and physical needs that can only be met by affirmation, acceptance as to intrinsic worth, encouragement, and unconditional love. We all have the desire and need to receive "the blessing" from others. Others include our heavenly Father but it should also include our spouse. Neither is to be excluded if we are to receive true holistic blessings. "The essential elements of the blessing include five things:

A meaningful touch. This includes handholding, hugging, kissing, and all types of bodily contact that have the purpose of communicating love and affection.

A spoken word. This element can demonstrate love and a sense of worth by the time involved, and the message(s) delivered. Its repetitive nature is crucial.

Expression of high value. This involves our passing along a message to others that affirms their intrinsic worth and value as a person. Praising them as valuable is the key idea.

Picturing a special future. This is the uniquely prophetic aspect of the blessing. What do our words tell others we believe the future holds for them? How do our present descriptions (nicknames) of others lay the foundation for future attitudes and actions on their part? How often it is that children, for example, fulfill the earlier expectations and predictions of a parent and friends, for good or bad. Positive words of encouragement as to future possibilities are those which will bless rather than curse.

An active commitment to see the blessing come to pass. This characteristic is both God-ward and man-ward. Godwardly, we are to commit others to his blessing and will. Manwardly, we are personally to make the commitment to spend whatever time, energy and resources necessary to bless others" (Smalley and Trent, 1993).

Blessing others involves both what we say and what we do. Words are important. Actions matter. Further, what we say and do cannot be occasional. It must be constant. It also must be specific, sacrificial, and even sensual. Song of Songs 1:9–14 tells us there is power in praising your partner. Here we see important and essential aspects of how to praise, how to bless our partner.

II. COMMENTARY

The Power of Praising Our Partner

> **MAIN IDEA:** *Praising our partner is essential to a satisfying and meaningful relationship.*

A Be Specific in Your Praise (1:9–10)

> **SUPPORTING IDEA:** *Be precise, not general, in your words of praise.*

1:9. Verse 9 shifts the scene from the simple world of the shepherd to the splendid world of the Egyptian Pharaoh. Solomon was aware of Shulammite's ambivalence and insecurity about her appearance and his absence (1:5–8). She needed him to bless her, to affirm her, to tell her she was the best. That is exactly what he did.

1. Tell her she is special.

Solomon began by calling her **my darling** (the NKJV has "my love"). This is the first—but not the last—time Solomon addressed her in this way (cf. 1:15; 2:2,10,13; 4:1,7; 5:2; 6:4). Repeatedly (nine times!), Solomon told her of his love. Unlike her brothers who hurt her in verse 6, Solomon will treat her with TLC. He will be her provider and protector, her lover and friend.

Solomon then did something that, if a man in America were to do this in our day, he would probably find himself in a hole from which he would never extricate himself. He compared his darling to a horse! Specifically, he said she was like **a mare** (or filly) **harnessed to one of the chariots of Pharaoh.** We are stunned by such a statement. But she would have been greatly honored. Pharaoh's chariots were pulled by stallions. A mare among them would have caused quite a commotion. She is likened to an only female in a world of males! What incredible value she possessed. She was, in his estimation, utterly priceless. She was desired not just by him but also by others. Yet he was the fortunate one who had captured her heart. She was unique; she was special.

2. Tell her she is beautiful.

1:10. Solomon now focused on one of the areas of her insecurity: her looks. Her **cheeks** were lovely, **beautiful**. They were enhanced with the dangling **earrings**, the ornaments and jewelry that graced them. Her **neck** was also beautiful **with strings of jewels**. She was regal and impressive. A stately dignity emanated from her person. The bridles of chariot horses were often decorated in beautiful and elaborate jewelry, and Solomon may have had the image of the lovely mare in mind. However, by now it was in the back of his mind as he gazed upon the beauty of his love. Her adornments did not detract from but enhanced her appearance. Solomon was not looking at some "overdressed glittering Christmas tree" (Gledhill, 113). There was nothing extravagant or excessive about her. A simple beauty is perhaps the best beauty. In Solomon's opinion, she had no equal, and he told her so.

Words are powerful weapons. "Sticks and stones may break my bones, but words can never hurt me" is not true. I have a scar over my eye where my cousin hit me in the eye with a baseball bat when I was a small boy. I have another scar on my right ear where my brother body slammed me on a marble coffee table one day when we were wrestling. Mom was gone somewhere, thank goodness. I have yet another scar right under my chin where a friend (I think!) rammed his football helmet while we played "bull-in-the-ring" before a big game one Friday night. Now let me tell you, all three of those events inflicted serious pain on me. They hurt! But none of the three wounded me as badly as have some words that have been fired at me at different times in my life.

Steve Stephens reminds us, "A healthy marriage is a safe haven from the tensions of everyday life. We need to hear positive things from our mate." He then lists thirty-seven things we should say to our spouse. Any spouse will be blessed by the following:

- "Good job!"
- "You are wonderful."
- "That was really great."
- "You look gorgeous today."
- "I don't feel complete without you."
- "I appreciate all the things you've done for me all these years."
- "You come first in my life, before kids, career, friends, anything."
- "I'm glad I married you."
- "You're the best friend I have."
- "If I had to do it over again, I'd still marry you."
- "I wanted you today."
- "I missed you today."
- "I couldn't get you out of my mind today."

- "It's nice to wake up next to you."
- "I will always love you."
- "I love to see your eyes sparkle when you smile."
- "As always, you look pretty today."
- "I trust you."
- "I can always count on you."
- "You make me feel good."
- "I'm so proud to be married to you."
- "I'm sorry."
- "I was wrong."
- "What would you like?"
- "What's on your mind?"
- "Let me just listen."
- "You are so special."
- "I can't imagine life without you."
- "I wish I were a better partner."
- "What can I do to help?"
- "Pray for me."
- "I'm praying for you today."
- "I prize every moment we spend together."
- "Thank you for loving me."
- "Thank you for accepting me."
- "Thank you for being my partner."
- "You make every day brighter."

(Steve Stephens, "37 Things to Say to Your Spouse," in *Stories for the Heart,* compiled by Alice Gray, Multnomah, 1996, 177–78).

Be particular in your praise. It will speak to your mate's heart and create an environment of romance. This is essential for building the intimate aspects of a relationship.

B Be Sacrificial in Your Praise (1:11)

SUPPORTING IDEA: *Actions sometimes speak louder than words.*

1:11. Solomon's praise of Shulammite inspired the praise of others. It seems the friends of verse 4, the daughters of Jerusalem (v. 5) joined Solomon in honoring his lady. Note the **we will make**. What we publicly say about our mate will often influence the opinion of others about him or her. Solomon had told her she was special and beautiful. She was the best. She deserved the best not just in words, but also in actions. When a man wants to be a blessing to his wife, here are two things he should always remember:

1. *Be specific.* **Earrings** (or ornaments) **of gold, studded with silver** were presented to Shulammite. Gledhill, in his free paraphrase, says, "We'll crown you with more royalty, O maiden queen, with costly gems, with rings of golden sheen and sparkling spikes of silver" (Gledhill, 66). Socrates said, "By all means marry. If you get a good wife, you'll become happy. If you get a bad one, you'll become a philosopher."

I am convinced that the issue is not so much a man "getting" a good wife as it is a man "gaining" a good wife by the way he loves her, by the way he cares for her. Women love specific and creative ideas. A man who invites his wife out on a date only to tell her it doesn't matter where they go or what they do doesn't know women. Love is specific. Praise is specific.

Judy Bodner in her book *When Love Dies: How to Save a Hopeless Marriage* drops a few hints in this context to help men out: (1) leave notes and love letters around; (2) plan detailed getaways; (3) set aside time alone just for the two of you; (4) share your feelings with each other; (5) make sexual intimacy attractive by creating a bedroom that is inviting and pleasant, a place of beauty. These are excellent suggestions that will be heeded by wise men.

2. *Be sincere.* The gifts of Solomon were genuine and from the heart. He was not trying to bribe her or buy her. His desire was to bless her, and to do so in a way that spoke to her heart. The gift of costly earrings of gold would accomplish this beautifully. Solomon had learned—or was at least in the process of learning—to speak her "love language." Gary Chapman in his wonderful book, *The Five Love Languages,* points out that every person speaks at least one of five love languages. Some people are even equipped to speak several, and with varying dialects. But it is rare that a husband and wife speak the same love language. After all, opposites do attract. Chapman identifies the five love languages as:

- *Words* of Affirmation
- Receiving *Gifts*
- *Acts* of Service
- Quality *Time*
- Physical *Touch*

In my marriage it is clear that my wife Charlotte and I have two love languages each. Not surprising, they are distinctively different. Hers are receiving gifts and quality time. Mine are words of affirmation and physical touch. I always strike a chord in Charlotte's heart if I bring her a gift. Cost is never a factor; it truly is the thought that counts. When I block off time for the two of us, she always responds in a positive and receptive manner. I've often wondered if her love languages are somehow related to her childhood and teenage years. You see, Charlotte's parents were alcoholics, and they divorced when she was a little girl. She has told me that she had some rather unspectacular birthdays and Christmases. At about the age of nine, she and her brother and sister were placed in a children's home where she spent the next ten years of her life. She really never saw either her mom or her dad during those years except for a couple of times early on. Time spent with family and the receiving of gifts from the same just wasn't there.

I'm certain these experiences have, at least in some measure, shaped her two love languages. Let me add before I move on that one wonderful thing did happen to Charlotte while she was in the children's home. She received Jesus Christ as her personal Lord and Savior, and God became her perfect Heavenly Father. Since then he has been molding and shaping her into the beautiful and godly woman, wife, and mother she is today.

My love languages are different from my wife's. I love it when she praises me, when she affirms me with her words. It means the world to me. I also love her touch and in lots of ways and places! One in particular is especially needful: my feet. I love to have my feet rubbed. When I get to heaven, I have already put in a request for two angels: one to rub and massage the left foot and one to rub and massage the right foot. I remember one evening Charlotte asked me to watch a movie with her (her love language of time) called *Sense and Sensibility*. It was immediately clear to me that this would be a chick flick, not an action-packed thriller. I quickly began to offer my best excuses on why I just couldn't "waste"—I mean "give up"—that much time.

To my amazement she didn't argue with me. As she said OK and walked away, she casually said, "I understand. I'm sorry you'll miss out on the two-hour foot massage that accompanies the popcorn and the movie."

I had only one response to that: "What time does the movie start?" A couple that grows in their knowledge of each other will learn to speak the love language of their mate. They will do it specifically, and they will do it sincerely.

Be Sensual in Your Praise (1:12–14)

SUPPORTING IDEA: *Love, loyalty, and longing are unique ways in which we praise our mate.*

1:12. Shulammite was moved to respond to the loving overtures of Solomon. Her insecurities had vanished. Her anxieties were put to rest by his words and actions of love. She now returned the favor. What we see is the two of them trying to outdo the other in the game of love. This will continue for several verses. What a wonderful contest for a couple to engage in! This woman had strong desires for her man. They were personal, physical, and sensual. They were particular and passionate. How do we, with intentionality, make our desires and our feelings known to our mate?

1. Desire is made known by love.

Again the man is addressed as a **king**, as royalty. Reclining "on his couch" or **at his table** indicates a time of rest and relaxation. Men have as a basic need "home support and serenity" (we will address this later). Shulammite knew what her man needed, and she provided it. Her **perfume**, nard, was expensive and "derived from a plant native to the Himalayan region of India. The scarcity, and hence the value, of this exotic **fragrance** made it much in demand as a 'love-potion'" (Carr, 84–85). Appealing to his self-worth and sense of smell, Shulammite, who was aroused herself, sought to elicit the same from her man. He was her king and worthy of a sensual and expensive display of affection.

2. Desire is made known by loyalty.

1:13. In genuinely erotic words, the woman said, **My lover is to me a sachet of myrrh resting between my breasts.** Carr says that myrrh

> is a resinous gum gathered from a species of a South Arabian tree. . . . In liquid form it would be carried in small bottles like nard, but it was also used in solid form. This way it could be carried in a small cloth pouch or sachet and worn next to the body. . . . The myrrh was mixed with fat . . . as the fat melted from the body heat, the aroma of the myrrh . . . would fill the room (Carr, 85).

Shulammite compared Solomon to this precious, sweet-smelling bundle that lay all night between her breasts, close to her heart. "Her thoughts of him are as fragrant and refreshing as the perfume that rises before her. . . . She carries those fragrant thoughts of him through the night in peaceful sleep" (Glickman, 37). Nestled between her breasts against her beating heart, there was an intimate bond of love, longing, and loyalty that could not be broken. There was a connection, a commitment that virtually transcended words.

In an article titled "The Danger of Divorce" Norman Bales says, "Perhaps the strongest deterrent to divorce is commitment. Every marriage will be tested at some point. What's the difference between those who survive the test and those who don't? Commitment tops the list" (Normal Bales, *All About Families Newsletter,* 26 July 2000). There was a commitment, a loyalty between Shulammite and Solomon. All night he lay as a precious perfume between her breasts, close to her heart.

3. Desire is made known by longing.

1:14. Again Shulammite referred to Solomon as **my lover.** Theirs was an exclusive love relationship. He was a one-woman kind of man, and she was a one-man kind of woman. But she said more. He was refreshing, like **a cluster of henna blossoms from the vineyards of En Gedi.** The henna bush can reach a height of ten feet. It has thick yellow and white flowers in clusters and smells like roses. A semitropical vegetation, it grows at the En Gedi Oasis on the western shore of the Dead Sea, south of Jerusalem. They are beautiful to see and sweet to smell and a very rare find in a dry desert climate.

The analogy is striking. Solomon was like an oasis with its surprising pleasures and provisions in a desert. He was a rare find and therefore of inestimable value. It is as if the woman was saying, "All I have seen is a desert of men until I met you. You are my oasis with your beauty and fragrance. No man refreshed me until I met you. I dream about you. I think about you. I dream about us. I think about us." Unbelievable, is it not, the passion that flows from a little praise? Passion in the bedroom is preceded by passion in all the other rooms. There truly is power in praising your partner.

> **MAIN IDEA REVIEW:** *Praising our partner is essential to a satisfying and meaningful relationship.*

III. CONCLUSION

Kindness and Respect Are Necessary for Healthy Romance

Tommy Nelson said, "Kindness is a mark of respect. Respect is necessary for romance" (Nelson, 26). We have seen a couple who deeply and genuinely respected each other. We have seen a couple sensitive to the needs of the other. We have seen a couple determined to bless the other. We have seen a couple learning to speak each other's love language. What we have seen is wonderful. What we have seen can be our experience as well when we do romance God's way.

For a marriage to be healthy and vibrant, five elements require consistent attention: (1) communication; (2) finances; (3) sex; (4) children; and (5) in-law relationships. If any of the latter four get into trouble, mark it down: communication broke down. To walk together for a lifetime requires that we talk—and on a regular basis. From serious conversations to general chit-chat, we must connect verbally if our marriage is to do well. Essential to "good connection" will be words of praise. A wise person said it well: "A courtship begins when a man whispers sweet nothings and ends when he says nothing sweet."

PRACTICAL PRINCIPLES AND APPLICATIONS

- Praising your mate as unique and special is a wonderful remedy for his or her feelings of inferiority and insecurity (1:9–11,14).
- Jewelry should enhance and not detract from a person's appearance (1:10–11).
- Little things can mean a lot in a relationship (1:10–11).

- Verbal praise of our mate will often influence the opinion of others with reference to our spouse (1:11).
- We should strive to make the very thought of our lover a source of mental and sensual pleasure (1:12–14).
- All the senses should participate in expressions of love toward our mate (1:9–14).

In Summary

- Love should be shown verbally (1:9).
- Love should be shown tangibly (1:10–11).
- Love should cherish, protect, and adore the mate whom God has given to us. Communicate that no one else compares to him or her in your life (1:9,12–14).

IV. LIFE APPLICATION

A Premarital Inventory

Basics to be answered together:

How long have you known each other? _____

How long have you been engaged? _____

Do you plan to ❑ Rent?   ❑ Buy?   ❑ Live with relatives?

Are you church members? _____

    If so, where? _____

    How often do you attend church? _____

    Do you go together? _____

    Do you plan to keep it the same? _____

Are you planning family devotions? _____

    If so, when? _____

Have you discussed together your ideals,
goals, and life work? _____

    Are you in agreement here? _____

Do you read the Bible?   ❑ Daily?   ❑ Together?

How do you plan to settle arguments and differences of opinion when they arise? _____

Groom:

What attracted you to your fiancée? _____

What are the three most important qualities you see in her?

    1. _____

    2. _____

    3. _____

What are the three most important qualities you'd like to find in your wife?

    1. _____

    2. _____

    3. _____

How much work should the husband be expected to do around the house to help the wife? _____

    What specifically do you plan to do? _____

In preparation for marriage, what has been the source of your knowledge of sexual relationship? ❑ Parents ❑ Books ❑ School ❑ Siblings ❑ Church (Pastor) ❑ Friends

What is your relationship to Jesus Christ? What does he mean to your life?

_____

_____

Do you have confidence that you will go to heaven when you die? _____

Why? _____

_____

Bride:

What attracted you to your fiancée? _____

What are the three most important qualities you see in him?

    1._____

    2._____

    3._____

What are the three most important qualities you'd like to find in your husband?

    1._____

    2._____

    3._____

Do you desire a career or to be a homemaker? _____

In preparation for marriage, what has been the source of your knowledge of sexual relationship? ❑ Parents ❑ Books ❑ School ❑ Siblings ❑ Church (Pastor) ❑ Friends

How many nights do you expect to go out on a date? _____

What type of entertainment do you think proper for a husband and wife to enjoy? _____

How many children do you think are the ideal number? ____ For you? ____

What is your relationship to Jesus Christ? What does he mean to your life?

_____

Do you have confidence that you will go to heaven when you die? _____

Why? _____

V. PRAYER

Dear Lord, words truly are powerful weapons. Sometimes I forget the impact they have, for good or bad. Your Word teaches me how hard it is to tame the tongue, but Jesus, I need it to be controlled, and controlled by you. Help me to remember that my tongue is wed to my heart. What is in my heart will eventually find its way to my mouth. Fill me with your Spirit, your love, your wisdom. Let me speak words that will bless, not curse; that will help, not hurt. As Lord of my life, be the Lord of my tongue as well. Amen.

VI. DEEPER DISCOVERIES

A. En Gedi

En Gedi literally means the "place of the young goat." It was a major oasis along the western side of the Dead Sea about thirty-five miles southeast of Jerusalem. The only natural waterfall in Israel is located at En Gedi. The springs of En Gedi are full, and the vegetation is semitropical. Both biblical and extrabiblical sources describe En Gedi as a source of fine dates, aromatic plants used in perfumes (1:14), and medicinal plants. It was a chief source of balsam, an important plant used for perfumes, and a major source of income for the area. En Gedi apparently lay on a caravan route that led from the eastern shore of the Dead Sea around to its south, then up the western side to En Gedi. From there the road went up to Tekoa and then to Jerusalem.

En Gedi, also called Hazazon Tamar (2 Chr. 20:2), was inhabited by Amorites in the time of Abraham and was subjugated by Chedorlaomer (Gen. 14:7). In the tribal allotments, it was given to Judah (Josh. 15:62). When David was fleeing from Saul, he hid in the area of En Gedi (1 Sam. 23:29). Saul was in a cave near En Gedi when David cut off a piece of his robe but spared his life (1 Sam. 24).

B. Myrrh

Myrrh was an aromatic resin with many uses in the Ancient Near East. It was traded along with spices (Gen. 37:25), used as an ingredient in anointing oil (Exod. 30:23), applied as perfume (Esth. 2:12; Song 1:13), placed in clothes to deodorize them (Ps. 45:8), given as a gift (Matt. 2:11), and used to embalm the body of Jesus (John 19:39).

In our text a small sachet held the sweet-smelling myrrh between the breasts of the woman. In the great heat of that land she would naturally perspire. This would melt the myrrh and produce an elegant fragrance. The myrrh resting between her breasts also speaks of the special place Solomon had in her heart.

C. Chariots

Chariots were two-wheeled vehicles, made of wood and strips of leather, and usually drawn by horses. They were used widely in Mesopotamia before 3000 B.C. and were introduced into Canaan and Egypt by the Hyksos about 1800–1600 B.C. Their primary function was as platforms in battle. They were also used for hunting, for transportation of dignitaries, and in state and religious ceremonies.

Egyptian chariots were the first to be mentioned in the Bible (Gen. 41:43; 46:29; 50:9). The iron chariots of the Philistines were fortified with plates of metal. This made them militarily stronger than those of the Israelites (Judg. 1:19; 4:3,13–17; 1 Sam. 13:5–7).

Chariots became an important part of Solomon's army and his commercial affairs (1 Kgs. 4:26; 9:15–19; 10:28–29). The military strength of Israel under Ahab was noteworthy because of the number of chariots available for use. According to Assyrian records, Ahab brought two thousand chariots into the Battle of Qarqar in 853 B.C.

VII. TEACHING OUTLINE

A. INTRODUCTION: THE GIFT OF THE BLESSING

B. COMMENTARY

1. Be Specific in Your Praise (1:9–10)
   a. Tell her she is special.
   b. Tell her she is beautiful.
2. Be Sacrificial in Your Praise (1:11)
   a. Be specific.
   b. Be sincere.
3. Be Sensual in Your Praise (1:12–14)
   a. Desire is made known by *love*.
   b. Desire is made known by *loyalty*.
   c. Desire is made known by *longing*.

C. CONCLUSION: KINDNESS AND RESPECT ARE NECESSARY FOR HEALTHY ROMANCE

VIII. ISSUES FOR DISCUSSION

Marital Intimacy Test

(Answer: 4—often, 3—often enough, 2—not enough, 1—rarely, or 0—never for each.)

How often do you show affection for each other?	_____
How often do you laugh at each other's jokes?	_____
How often do you say something nice to each other?	_____
How often do you compliment your partner in front of others?	_____
How often do you enjoy sexual intimacy?	_____
How often are you playful with each other?	_____
How often do you look each other in the eyes while talking?	_____
How often do you give each other a little surprise?	_____
How often do you say "please"?	_____
How often do you say "I'm sorry"?	_____

(Add up your points and divide by 10. You will get your score on a 4.0 scale, just like when you were in school!)

Song of Songs 1:15–2:7

Fanning the Flames of Love

I. **INTRODUCTION**
Marriage Is Out; Casual Sex and Low Commitment Are In

II. **COMMENTARY**
A verse-by-verse explanation of these verses.

III. **CONCLUSION**
True Intimacy Is a Wonderful Gift in Marriage
An overview of the principles and applications from these verses.

IV. **LIFE APPLICATION**
Thinking About Sex
Melding these verses to life.

V. **PRAYER**
Tying these verses to life with God.

VI. **DEEPER DISCOVERIES**
Historical, geographical, and grammatical enrichment of the commentary.

VII. **TEACHING OUTLINE**
Suggested step-by-step group study of these verses.

VIII. **ISSUES FOR DISCUSSION**
Zeroing these verses in on daily life.

"At the heart of mankind's existence is the desire to be intimate and to be loved by another."

Gary   Chapman

Song of Songs
1:15–2:7

 IN A NUTSHELL

Mutual admiration and desire for each other should be expressed clearly and repeatedly in fanning the flames of love.

Fanning the Flames of Love

I. INTRODUCTION

Marriage Is Out; Casual Sex and Low Commitment Are In

Reuters' News Service reported on June 6, 2000:

> Romance and marriage are out while casual sex and low-commitment relationships are in among young Americans, researchers said.
>
> A study by Rutgers University's National Marriage Project found that young men and women in their twenties, unlike generations before them, aren't interested in finding marriage partners when they date. Instead, they are more concerned with "Sex Without Strings, Relationships Without Rings."
>
> "Today's singles scene is not oriented toward marriage, nor is it dedicated to romantic love as it has been in the past," said David Popenoe, codirector of the National Marriage Project and a sociology professor at Rutgers in New Jersey.
>
> To be sure, young Americans today did not invent the concept of "free love," such as existed during the 1960s. The difference is that young people today are more concerned with economic and sexual self-gratification than past generations.
>
> Young people in America today are more concerned with having fun and making money and less focused on forming lasting relationships that lead to marriage and raising a family.
>
> The report said that young Americans (1) favor living together as a try-out for marriage or as an alternative to marriage; (2) believe sex is for fun and has no strings attached; (3) have a fear of divorce; and (4) see marriage (and divorce) as a potential economic liability.
>
> Oddly, however, most of the young men and women who participated in the study expected some day to meet and marry somebody who fulfilled their emotional and spiritual needs.
>
> The problem, researchers said, is that their current mercenary mating habits do not easily lead to the fulfillment of that goal. Barbara Dafoe Whitehead said the men and women in the study, because of the high incidence of divorce among their parents, did not count on having lasting relationships with each other. Instead, they focused more on themselves.

While the men and women in the study shared similar mating habits and goals in their early twenties, as the late twenties approached women much more than men wanted a committed relationship. But women also became more disenchanted with the pool of prospective partners and the likelihood of finding a mate.

Whitehead said, "We may be seeing a massive change that would mean that romantic love and courtship might be giving way to something altogether new. Or we may be in a period of cultural cluelessness."

What a tragic but realistic picture of the mating and marriage scene today. However, Iris Krasnow of the *Washington Post* (September 11, 2000) helps put all of this in perspective with her commentary on the HBO blockbuster "Sex and the City." In an article entitled "Being Single, Seeing Double" she writes:

I'm looking at the recent *Time* magazine cover that pictures the four buffed stars of HBO's "Sex and the City," women who talk dirtier and have more sex than anyone I have ever met. Front and center is Sarah Jessica Parker, with her tumbles of long locks, perfectly highlighted and curled, falling to breasts encased in a white strapless gown. Her lips are glossed into an iridescent purple pout; the look in her cat-green eyes says, "Take me now."

Decked for an evening of prowling, these women appear to be appropriate cover art for an article titled "How to Snag a Mate." Instead the "Sex and the City" sirens are a tease for a story on "Who Needs a Husband?" which points to a growing trend defined this way: "More women are saying no to marriage and embracing the single life. Are They Happy?"

Happy is not among the first words that come to mind. They are clearly stunning on the outside, but they do not exude real joy from within, and any single woman who has been dating too long and too much can tell you why: Sex in the city feels good for fleeting moments; it's no ticket to a satisfaction that endures. And there lies the ancient reason why most Americans still choose to get married. Being single is lonely. Humans need long-term companionship.

Most women don't want intimacy on the fly with a carousel of lovers. Most women want to find a partner who looks beyond the bottle-gold fibers of highlighted hair, and into the fiber of their being. Most women want to be able to skip shaving their legs once in a while and still feel beautiful in the eyes of their men.

Bottom line: men and women have not changed deep down inside where it really counts. All of us—no one is excluded—are looking for love, and a love that will last. However, once we do find it, how do we keep it and keep it for a lifetime? Solomon would say, "By fanning the flames."

God's Word is interested in a love that lasts, a love that daily needs the flames of its fire stoked to a passionate burning. How is such a love achieved? In Song of Songs 1:15–2:7 we discover three helpful suggestions: (1) praise your partner; (2) proclaim their provision; and (3) prepare for passion.

II. COMMENTARY

Fanning the Flames of Love

> **MAIN IDEA:** *Admiration of and desire for our mate must be expressed in clear and precise language that he or she will understand and appreciate.*

Praise Your Partner (1:15–2:2)

> **SUPPORTING IDEA:** *Affirm your mate's attractiveness, thoughtfulness, and uniqueness.*

Praising our partner is a constant theme in the Song of Songs because it is an essential ingredient for a healthy marriage. Again and again we see the man praising his woman and the woman praising her man. Communication that consists of gracious and kind words is the currency that buys and builds a lasting love relationship. Previously, the blessings were listed that flow when we say positive things to and about our mate. It might be uncomfortable, but it is probably helpful if we also examine some things we should not say.

Steve Stephens is a big help when he writes:

> There is nothing more painful than having unhealthy communication with the one you love. It is through communication that we connect and our spirits touch. If that connection becomes contaminated, it is only a matter of time before the whole relationship is poisoned. In the process of communication, wisdom is [sometimes] knowing what not to say rather than what to say.
>
> Therefore, I gathered together some close friends and asked them what *not* to say to your spouse. Here is their list:
>
> - "I told you so."
> - "You're just like your mother."
> - "You're always in a bad mood."
> - "You just don't think."
> - "It's your fault."
> - "What's wrong with you?"

- "All you ever do is complain."
- "I can't do anything to please you."
- "You get what you deserve."
- "Why don't you ever listen to me?"
- "Can't you be more responsible?"
- "What were you thinking?"
- "You're impossible!"
- "I don't know why I put up with you."
- "I can talk to you until I'm blue in the face, and it doesn't do any good."
- "I can do whatever I like."
- "If you don't like it, you can just leave."
- "Can't you do anything right?"
- "That was stupid."
- "All you ever do is think of yourself."
- "If you really loved me, you'd do this."
- "You're such a baby."
- "Turnabout's fair play."
- "You deserve a dose of your own medicine."
- "What's your problem?"
- "I can never understand you."
- "Do you always have to be right?"

("27 Things Not to Say to Your Spouse," in *Stories for the Heart*, 175–76).

Both Solomon and Shulammite knew the importance of words. Both were interested in fanning the flames of love. They continue their contest to see who can "outpraise" and "outcompliment" the other. What are the particulars of their praise which challenge us?

1. Admire his or her attractiveness.

1:15. Solomon said to his bride, **How beautiful you are, my darling!** "My darling" can also be translated "my love." This is not the first time Solomon has complimented her appearance. Perhaps once is not enough.

Solomon also said to Shulammite, **Your eyes are doves.** "Beautiful eyes were a hallmark of perfection in a woman (cf. Rachel and Leah, Gen. 29:17). Rabbinic tradition identifies beautiful eyes with a beautiful personality" (Carr, 86). Solomon, as he looked into her eyes, saw gentleness and tranquillity, purity and simplicity. Her eyes were an eloquent witness to the radiant woman on the inside. Our eyes are a very significant communication device. Outside of our words, they are our most important and effective means of communication.

When we lived in Dallas, Texas, there was a woman who attended our church who was one mean woman. I have often said, somewhat playfully, that on any night there was a full moon over Dallas you could see her circling the city on her broom! Well, one Sunday after church, we finished a conversation with this woman, speaking to her as nicely as we could. We then got into our van to go home. Charlotte and I are the parents of four sons, the oldest two being twins. One of the twins (they were probably eight or nine years old at the time) came up front as we were about to leave and said, "Daddy, you know that woman you and mama were talking to? She scares me." I started to say, "She scares me, too!" But I didn't. I did the proper daddy thing and said, "Oh? Why does she scare you?" His answer: "Well, she smiles with her face, but she has real mean eyes."

Eyes sometimes speak louder than our words. Shulammite smiled not just with her face. She also smiled with her eyes. Solomon admired and was captivated by her attractiveness, by her beauty on the outside as well as her beauty on the inside. Eyes are, after all, windows into the soul.

1:16. Shulammite now returned the favor of her man's compliment. It was given willingly and honestly. **How handsome you are, my lover! Oh, how charming!** The word *handsome* is the same Hebrew word translated as "beautiful" in verse 15, except it is in the masculine gender. "The word occurs fourteen times in the Song, but only this once in the masculine form" (Carr, 86).

There is an intensity in her words of praise. She continued by saying he was **charming** or "pleasant." He calmed her spirit. He put her at rest. He set her heart at peace. The kindness of his words in verse 15 was thoughtful. They met her at her point of need, and they spoke to her heart. The words are important. The man behind the words is essential. A woman is impressed by a man who understands and respects her personal and emotional needs. She loves a man who talks, who communicates. She is attracted to a man who, in strength and masculinity, says to her, "You have first place in my affections." She will respond with enthusiasm and energy to a man who treats her this way.

1:17. Shulammite continued her praise of Solomon by pointing out, "Our bed is verdant" (v. 16). **The beams of our house are cedars; our rafters are firs**. Three times the word *our* occurs. His thoughtfulness in preparing a home for them was a source of security. No wonder her eyes spoke tranquility and peace. John Snaith noted interestingly, *"Our couch* [bed] denotes in Amos 6:4 particularly stylish and magnificent couches used for feasting; so the couch here . . . is not . . . any old bed" (Snaith, 25).

Solomon's thoughtfulness has provided a strong, sturdy (even royal) home. Their home will be safe and secure, a responsibility God expects a man to bear. It will also be sexual and sensual. "Our bed is lush with foliage,"

(v. 16 HCSB) It is alive, fresh, fruitful. It will be a place of activity and growth, an environment conducive to the passionate lovemaking God says is a good thing in the marriage bed. Solomon was no insensitive male, and Shulammite appreciated and acknowledged his thoughtfulness.

2. Affirm his or her uniqueness.

2:1–2. Shulammite saw herself as the **rose of Sharon, a lily of the valleys.** Solomon then added, **Like a lily among thorns is my darling among the maidens.** This woman was utterly unique, rare, and special to Solomon. His words lifted her heart and self-worth to new heights. "Rose of Sharon" is more accurately "a wild autumn flower of the valley" (Patterson, 45). Sharon was a low coastal plain, which stretched from Mt. Carmel to the Egyptian border where wild flowers grew in great abundance. "Lily of the valleys" may refer to a lovely white blossom with six leaves and six petals. "This flower was especially associated with nuptial occasions" (Patterson, 45).

Shulammite, because of Solomon's praise, saw herself as a beautiful wild flower, free and untamed by any gardener. She was unique and uniquely Solomon's. She possessed a natural beauty and a natural desire for her man. No one had cultivated this unpicked flower. That was an assignment and privilege reserved for her husband, and him alone.

Solomon's statement that she was **like a lily among thorns** only reinforced the imagery of uniqueness. Shulammite was not just a flower among many flowers. She was a lily, a beautiful wild flower amidst thorns. She was a flower. All other women were thorns. By comparison, other women brought pain and were totally undesirable. She alone was his love. She was like an only flower in a world of thorny weeds. Such praise would not cause other women to applaud him. But it would cause his love to adore him. There was not another like her as far as he was concerned. This is how to fan the flames of love.

B Proclaim Their Provision (2:3)

SUPPORTING IDEA: *Let others know both the protection and the pleasure you get from your mate.*

2:3. Verse 3 is specific and sensual. The passion of love is running full throttle. Solomon has told Shulammite some of the real joys she brings to him and how she is the only woman in his life. The confidence she feels in their relationship frees her to give herself even more in unreserved abandonment. Solomon has created a romantic atmosphere. He has built his bride up by focusing on her positive features and gifts. Her response is nothing short of awesome.

1. Tell others how they protect you.

An apricot or apple tree in the woods would be rare and something you would not expect to find. It, of course, would be sweet to the taste, and would provide needed sustenance. Solomon said she was a flower woman among thorny women. Shulammite said that Solomon was a special tree among common woods. Finding him had brought her great delight, and she decided to sit down in his shade. She delighted in him. She was comforted by him. She was protected by him and only him, and as never before. "I never knew love before, then came you" could be the song of Shulammite's heart.

2. Tell others how they please you.

Apples were believed by some people in the ancient world to have sensual and erotic qualities. Shulammite was secure and safe in Solomon's shade, his watchful care. She now longed for physical intimacy, for lovemaking and sexual union. She simply said, **His fruit is sweet to my taste**. The language is chaste and appropriate. It is not lewd or out of bounds. It is also highly suggestive and erotic: "What I find in him I like. What I taste, smell, and feel is sweet and causes me to want more and more." Romance truly is an environment that prepares us for sexual union. As they anticipated their wedding night (4:1–5:1), the flames of passion were under control but burning.

Ⓒ Prepare for Passion (2:4–7)

SUPPORTING IDEA: *Do not rush love. Give it time.*

These verses continue the theme of romance. Interestingly, there is both encouragement and warning. Sex is a powerful gift. It is intoxicating. It has unbelievable potential for good or evil, to build up or tear down, to delight or destroy. Solomon gives us some additional instruction to ensure maximum sex, maximum safety, and maximum satisfaction. This is the great sex God has planned from the beginning.

1. Make love in the right place.

2:4. The man took his bride into **the banquet hall**, literally, "the house of wine." This scene anticipates the wedding night and the marriage bed. The open vineyard with all its beauty and encouragement to love may be in view. Regardless it will be a place reserved only and exclusively for them. The imagery of wine again speaks of the sweet and intoxicating love they will share.

2. Make love with the right commitment.

The phrase **his banner over me is love** speaks of the protective love of her lover, and the safe place to which he brought her. It also testifies that the love the king had for her was evident to everyone. He did not say one thing to her in private and contradict that in public. He was not warm and considerate when they were alone but cold and sarcastic when they were with others. He was not ashamed of his love for her. He was glad for all to see. No wonder she grew more and more secure in his love.

Carr notes that some translate the Hebrew text, which is admittedly difficult at this point, in a way that is even more strikingly sensual: "And his wish regarding me was love-making," or more simply, "His intentions were to make love" (Carr, 91). Solomon wanted her, and she wanted him. They were the right partners. They had the right passion. They had the right place. But all the essential ingredients were still not present.

3. Make love in the right way.

2:5. Shulammite said she was in the midst of a great feast, and she thought about their lovemaking. Her mind carried her away to the joys of marriage which were just around the corner. The Bible teaches that we should feast on our mate and that God smiles when we do. Shulammite was so overcome with the passion of the moment that she felt faint. "For I am lovesick" (NKJV) is translated in the NIV as **I am faint with love**. The "I" is emphatic. "I myself am swooning in the rapture of the moment." Did she wish to bail out and bring all of this to a sudden halt?

On the contrary, she asked for raisins and apricots to strengthen and restore her that she might enjoy more. **Strengthen** and **refresh** are imperatives. She demanded the necessary nourishment she needed to continue. Both **raisins** and **apples** were viewed as highly erotic and sensual. There is no question of the intent or intensity of her desire. One can hardly imagine the reciprocal response all of this would have brought about on the part of Solomon.

2:6. In the passion of their love, Shulammite had not lost sight or sense of the warmth, intimacy, and security of their relationship. With one hand he cradled her head. With the other he held and caressed her. It is interesting that the word *embrace* is used in the Old Testament "both of a friendly greeting (Gen. 48:10) and of sexual union (Prov. 5:20)" (Carr, 93). He was her friend and her lover. Both were important to her. Both are important to all women. No man should forget this.

4. Make love at the right time.

2:7. Sexual relationships should take place at the right place with the right person in the right way at the right time. Not any time is a good time. There is indeed a proper time—a God time. Verse 7 is a recurring theme in the Song (cf. 3:5; 8:4), and its repetition underlines its importance. So crucial is it that it takes the form of an oath. The word **charge** means "to adjure or urge." Shulammite was directing her words to the sorority of females (**Daughters of Jerusalem**) as she warned them to pursue passion at the proper pace.

The **gazelles** and **does of the field** were both beautiful female animals, vigorous and sexually active in season. She understood that though men are usually viewed as the more sexually active and interested, God created women as sexual beings with sexual desires.

All of us are susceptible to our passions getting out of control, overriding both our reason and will, and causing massive hurt and damage. We must understand and understand well: God gave us sex as a wonderful gift to be enjoyed between a man and a woman within the bonds of marriage. This plan of his will never change. He gave us such a plan not to "rain on our parade" or "steal our fun." He gave us this plan because it brings him glory and it is for our good.

Therefore, Shulammite warns us, **Do not arouse or awaken love until it so desires**—until the time is right. Passion is great when the place for its expression is the marriage bed. Duane Garrett says it well: "Girls should not allow themselves to be aroused sexually until the proper time and person arrives. The natural joy of sexual awakening is ruined by premature experimentation" (Garrett, 392–93).

MAIN IDEA REVIEW: *Admiration of and desire for our mate must be expressed in clear and precise language that he or she will understand and appreciate.*

III. CONCLUSION

True Intimacy Is a Wonderful Gift in Marriage

Maximum sex is marriage sex. Great sex is marriage sex. The best sex is believers' sex. Why? Because through a relationship with Jesus Christ you see sex as one of the most beautiful aspects of life. You come to understand that it is more enjoyable to give than to receive, that bodily pleasure can also be spiritual, that men and women have equal rights to sexual pleasure, and that the quality of a sexual relationship is more than just physical pleasure, but it is not less than physical pleasure. God has given us a great gift. Let us enjoy it as he designed it. You will find the delights to be greater than you ever imagined. But before moving on, let's put a realistic face on this important subject.

Romance for men is a three-letter word: SEX. For women, romance can mean lots of things. It is very difficult for men to understand, but for women, romance may or may not include sex. Indeed, women find some of the most interesting things romantic. For example, if a man will pray with her, help her wash the dishes, clean out the garage, or run a warm bubble bath and light a candle, his wife will often find these romantic. All of these things are strange to the ears of a male, but they speak deeply to the heart of a woman.

The simple fact is men and women are wired differently when it comes to the area of romance.

For men, romance is highly visual; it is what they see. For women, romance is extremely relational and personal; it is what they feel. Men indeed are creatures of sight; they are moved more by what they see. Women on the other hand are creatures of the ear and of the heart; they are moved more by what they hear and by what they feel. This point is so crucial it might be worth our digressing for just a moment. What do men say is romantic to them? The following list of fifteen suggestions from Gary Chapman's wonderful book, *Toward a Growing Marriage,* is not exhaustive, but it is helpful as a woman tries to understand where a man is coming from in this area of romance.

1. Be attractive at bedtime—nothing in the hair or strange on the face. Wear something besides granny gowns and pajamas.
2. Do not be ashamed to show you enjoy being with me.
3. Dress more appealingly when I am at home (no housecoats, slippers, etc.).
4. Do things to catch my attention: remember that a man is easily excited by sight.
5. Communicate more openly about sex.
6. Do not make me feel guilty at night for my inconsistencies during the day (not being affectionate enough, etc.).
7. Be more aware of my needs and desires as a man.
8. Show more desire and understand that caressing and foreplay are as important to me as they are to you.
9. Do not allow yourself to remain upset over everyday events that go wrong.
10. Do not try to fake enjoyment. Be authentic in your response to me.
11. Do not try to punish me by denying me sex or by giving it grudgingly.
12. Treat me like your lover.
13. Listen to my suggestions on what you can do to improve our sexual relationship.
14. Forgive me when I fall short of what I should be.
15. Tell me what I can do to be the sexual partner you desire.

On the other hand, what suggestions have wives made to their husbands about how they can make romance and sexual relations more meaningful? Again, Gray Chapman gives us a list to help us get the idea.

1. Show more affection; give attention throughout the day; come in after work and kiss me on my neck and ask me about my day (and stay around and listen!).
2. Be more sympathetic when I am really sick.

3. Accept me as I am; accept me even when you see the worst side of me.

4. Tell me that you love me at times other than when we are in bed; phone sometimes just to say, "I love you!" Do not be ashamed to tell me, "I love you" in front of others.

5. While I am bathing or showering, find soft music on the radio or dim the lights and light a candle.

6. Honor Christ as the head of our home.

7. Talk to me after our lovemaking; make caresses after our lovemaking and hold me.

8. Be sweet and loving (at least one hour) before initiating sex.

9. Show an interest in what I have to say in the morning.

10. Help me wash dinner dishes and clean the kitchen.

11. Pay romantic attention to me (hold hands, kiss) even during relatively unromantic activities (television watching, car riding, walking in the mall, etc.).

12. Help me feel that I am sexually and romantically attractive by complimenting me more often.

13. Pray with me about the problems and victories you are having; let me express my own needs to you.

14. Do not approach lovemaking as a ritualistic activity; make each time a new experience.

15. Think of something nice to say about me and do it in front of others often.

Here is wise counsel for men and women alike, as we work together to fan the flames of love.

IV. LIFE APPLICATION

Thinking About Sex

If only because one is a man and the other a woman, married couples usually have quite different appetites, attitudes, and approaches to sex. Furthermore, many people may come to marriage with varying beliefs and expectations. The following attitude assessment tool is designed to open up discussion about these differences. Take it with your partner and see what you can learn about each other.

Attitude Assessment Tool*

	Agree	Disagree	Uncertain
Sex is one of the most beautiful aspects of life.			
It is more enjoyable to give than to receive.			
Bodily pleasure is fleshly and not spiritual.			
Sexual intercourse is primarily for physical release.			
Our religious beliefs have the greatest influence on our attitudes toward sexual behavior.			
Men and women have equal rights to sexual pleasure.			
There are sexual activities that I would consider wrong for a married couple to practice. If you agree, list these: 1._____ 2._____ 3._____ 4._____			
To be truly satisfying, intercourse must lead to simultaneous orgasm.			
Sexual fantasies are normal.			
The male always should be the aggressor in sexual activity.			
In general, women don't enjoy sex as much as men.			
Men should be allowed more freedom in sexual behavior than women.			
The quality of a sexual relationship is more than just physical pleasure.			

*Adapted from *Sexual Fulfillment in Marriage: A Multimedia Learning Kit* by Clifford and Joyce Penner, Family Concern, Inc., 1977. Available through the Penners at 2 N. Lake Avenue, Suite 610, Pasadena, CA 91101.

V. PRAYER

Father, patience on my part and trust in you are essential when it comes to marriage, both before and after the wedding. Increase my faith and inspire my obedience so I will approach marital intimacy in the right way and with the right commitment, waiting for the right time. Help me to remember my body belongs to you (1 Cor. 6:19–20). You bought me with a price, the precious blood of Jesus! Let me honor you with my body now and forever. Amen.

VI. DEEPER DISCOVERIES

Biblical Principles Governing Sex

- Sexual relations within marriage are holy and good. God encourages intimate relations and warns against their cessation (1 Cor. 7:5).

- Pleasure in sexual relations is both healthy and expected (the bodies of both parties belong to each other; Prov. 5:15–19; 1 Cor. 7:4).

- Sexual pleasure is to be guided by the principle that one's sexuality is to be other oriented ("rights" over one's body are given in marriage to the other party; Phil. 2:3–4).

- Sexual relations are to be regular and normal. No exact number of times per week is right or correct, but the biblical principle is that both parties are to provide adequate sexual satisfaction so that both "burning" (sexual desire) and temptation to find satisfaction elsewhere are avoided (1 Cor. 7:9).

- The principle of satisfaction means that each party is to provide sexual enjoyment (which is "due" him or her in marriage) as frequently as the other party requires. Other biblical principles (moderation, seeking to please another rather than oneself, etc.) also come into play. Consideration of one's mate is to guide one's requests for sexual relations.

- In accordance with the principle of "rights," there is to be no sexual bargaining between married persons (I'll not have relations unless you . . ."). Neither party has the right to make such bargains. This is a form of "prostitution" and must be avoided.

- Sexual relations are equal and reciprocal. The Bible does not give the man superior rights over the woman or the woman superior rights over the man. Mutual stimulation and mutual initiation of relations are legitimate (a constant theme in the Song of Songs).

- Whatever is safe, pleasing, enjoyable, and satisfying to both is acceptable. The body of each belongs to the other (1 Cor. 7:4). Neither should demand from the other what is painful, harmful, or distasteful to him or her.

VII. TEACHING OUTLINE

A. INTRODUCTION: MARRIAGE IS OUT: CASUAL SEX AND LOW COMMITMENT RELATIONSHIPS ARE IN

B. COMMENTARY

1. Praise Your Partner (1:15–2:2)

   a. Admire his or her attractiveness.

   b. Affirm his or her uniqueness.

2. Proclaim Their Provision (2:3)

   a. Tell others how they protect you.

   b. Tell others how they please you.

3. Prepare for Passion (2:4–7)

   a. Make love in the right place.

   b. Make love with the right commitment.

   c. Make love in the right way.

   d. Make love at the right time.

C. CONCLUSION: THINKING ABOUT SEX

VIII. ISSUES FOR DISCUSSION

1. How can you put *thought* and *effort* into creating a romantic "atmosphere" for your spouse?

2. Think of some positive ways you can build up your spouse by concentrating on his or her positive features and gifts.

3. Explore the joys and opportunities for love. Three biblical principles to guide you: (1) unselfish love, (2) mutual agreement, and (3) Christlike submission and humility.

4. Is communication really vital for intimacy? Why or why not? How would you rate your communication skills?

5. Are the right mate and the right moment worth waiting for? Why?

6. What does 1 Corinthians 13 have to say about how to fan the flames of love? How can verses 4–8 be applied specifically to marriage?

Song of Songs 2:8–17

Spring Fever

I. INTRODUCTION
Men Are Dogs, and Women Are Cats!

II. COMMENTARY
A verse-by-verse explanation of these verses.

III. CONCLUSION
The Eight-Cow Wife

An overview of the principles and applications from these verses.

IV. LIFE APPLICATION
Premarital Discussion Questions

Melding these verses to life.

V. PRAYER
Tying these verses to life with God.

VI. DEEPER DISCOVERIES
Historical, geographical, and grammatical enrichment of the commentary.

VII. TEACHING OUTLINE
Suggested step-by-step group study of these verses.

VIII. ISSUES FOR DISCUSSION
Zeroing these verses in on daily life.

Quote

"*We* have to work hard at marriage.

It's the most fun work in the world, but it's still work."

A n n e   O r t l u n d

Song of Songs
2:8–17

I N   A   N U T S H E L L

As we prepare for marriage, in the joy of that "spring fever" feeling, we need to look at things honestly and ask some hard questions. Remember, relationships are uniquely sensitive things, especially married relationships.

Spring Fever

I. INTRODUCTION

Men Are Dogs, and Women Are Cats!

I have often said men are like dogs and women are like cats, and with good reason. Think about it. A man is very much like a dog. If you will feed him, praise him, and play with him on a regular basis, you will have a happy man. On the other hand, a woman is far more complex and mysterious, very much like a cat. A cat can walk into a room, and you look at it, and it looks at you. It walks over to you and begins to purr and rub up against your leg in a sweet and gentle fashion. The cat then quickly turns around and walks out of the room, and you say, "That was a really sweet cat."

However, a few minutes later that same cat walks into the room, you look at it and it looks at you. Suddenly without provocation or warning the cat leaps for your face, attempting to claw your eyeballs out! This was the same cat that came in so sweet and gentle a few moments ago. Something happened while that cat was out of the room. You have no idea what it was, but it certainly changed the disposition of that cat in a matter of seconds.

I do see some significant similarities between a cat and a woman! A friend of mine heard me draw this analogy some years ago, and he sent me something that reinforced and added additional supporting evidence to my thesis that men are dogs and women are cats. Let me share the insights of some very smart person somewhere.

Is it a cat? Is it a woman? Maybe it's both! Why?

1. They do what they want.
2. They rarely listen to you.
3. They're totally unpredictable.
4. They whine when they are not happy.
5. When you want to play, they want to be alone.
6. When you want to be alone, they want to play.
7. They expect you to cater to their every whim.
8. They're moody.
9. They can drive you nuts and cost you an arm and a leg.
10. They leave their hair everywhere.

Conclusion: Cats are tiny little women in fur coats.

Is it a dog? Is it a man? Maybe it's both! Why?

1. They lie around all day, sprawled out on the most comfortable piece of furniture in the house.
2. They can hear a package of food opening half a block away, but they can't hear you even when you're in the same room with them.
3. They leave their toys everywhere.
4. They growl when they are not happy.
5. When you want to play, they want to play.
6. When you want to be left alone, they still want to play.
7. They are great at begging.
8. They will love you forever if you feed them and praise them.
9. They do disgusting things with their mouths and then try to give you a kiss.
10. They can look dumb and lovable, all at the same time.

Conclusion: Dogs are tiny little men in fur coats.

Yes, men and women really are different, and they are different in some very significant ways. In marriage we do "sweat the small stuff," and it is "the little foxes" (v. 15) that can be our undoing if we are not on the lookout for these marital pests.

As we look forward to spending our life with someone who causes our palms to sweat, our pulse to race, and butterflies to fly wildly in our stomach, we need to take a hard look at the realities of marriage. We also need to ask some tough questions.

II. COMMENTARY

Spring Fever

> **MAIN IDEA:** *Good, hard questions need to be asked as we think about marriage. Marriage is one of God's greatest gifts to us, but it requires hard work before and after the wedding if we are to "go the distance" together.*

A Question 1: Is He Transparent in His Actions? (2:8–9)

> **SUPPORTING IDEA:** *Study and watch your (prospective) mate carefully. Is he or she transparent and clear in his or her intentions?*

2:8–9. The scene has shifted from the city and the palace back to the country and Shulammite's home. The wedding day of the couple in love is just a few days away. Still, every word and every action should be carefully weighed right up until the time of the ceremony. One cannot have too much information when it comes to this momentous decision.

The most important decision a person will ever make is whether he or she will trust Jesus Christ as Lord and Savior. The second most important decision is who he or she will marry. It is possible to have too little information before marriage, and the results are often tragic. Shulammite was a wise woman. She was a student of Solomon. She watched every move he made. Was he the real deal? Was he authentic? Were his true intentions apparent? What clues did she gather?

1. Watch his or her actions.

It is a truism: "actions speak louder than words." When Solomon acted, Shulammite watched, and she liked what she saw. Five times in verses 8–17 she calls Solomon **my lover**. Both words are important. He is *my* lover. He is my *lover*. A tender love affair had been growing for some time. Everything seemed to be falling into place. The hearts of two lovers were being knit together. Did Shulammite find Solomon's actions to be in concert with what her heart was telling her?

Indeed she did. She heard his voice calling out to her as he came for her. She complimented his agility (**leaping** and **bounding**) and his attractiveness (**like a gazelle or a young stag**, honored for their strength, form, and beauty). His advance was a clear indication of his desire for her and only her. He was enthusiastic. He was above board and open about his love. He was not ashamed to be public about his affection. He made this clear as he came up to the wall of the home. No one doubted his feelings for this woman.

2. Watch his or her eyes.

"Eyes are windows into the soul." Solomon looked and gazed through the **windows** and **lattice** of the house. His eyes spoke, and they spoke loudly. They also made clear his desire for Shulammite. He wanted her, but he approached her with honor and respect. He came close with loving, penetrating glances, but he would maintain a certain distance until they united their lives in marriage. She was more than a sex toy he longed to play with. She was a wonderful woman deserving of his best behavior, both now and later. His present actions were an indication of his future behavior as well.

Several years ago I was scheduled to do a family life conference in another state. A week or so before I was to go, I received an anonymous card in the mail from a woman with a broken heart. Here is what she wrote:

> Dear Dr. Akin,
> I hope you receive my card before the marriage conference. . . . I recently married a member of [our] church (he will be attending your seminar). This past Valentine's Day he did not acknowledge the

romantic holiday, and I was very hurt. I watched as my coworkers received flowers. To make things worse, he joked about it in front of one of my friends. My mom told me I should have known what to expect since he never gave me flowers while we were dating. This may sound selfish and petty on my part. I am just so discouraged!

After I come home from my job, I do all the housework and cooking and shopping. I wouldn't mind so much if he would just occasionally show his appreciation. The only time he has ever given me a gift is on my birthday and at Christmas. It would mean so much to me if just once he would give me something just because he loves me. I exercise and try to look nice. I iron all his clothes and cook his favorite meals. He has thousands of dollars to invest in the stock market, but he has never spent one dollar on a romantic gift for me. I know flowers will eventually wilt, but they are so beautiful. I'm afraid my love will eventually wilt. Will you pray for me?

What an out-of-touch husband! This man probably loves his wife, but he has no clue how to show it. In fact, it appears he never has. He was insensitive before they married, and he is insensitive after they married. But this woman should have seen it coming. We can't criticize the man for not being transparent. What she saw is what she got. Transparency, you see, is a two-way street. What is he or she showing? What are you seeing? We must work at full disclosure on one end and honest evaluation on the other.

B Question 2: Is He Tender with His Words? (2:10–14)

SUPPORTING IDEA: *Words are powerful weapons. They are also powerful messengers. Listen carefully.*

USA Today reported on a study that found how we talk—even more than what we say—can predict whether a marriage will succeed or fail.

How newlyweds talk to each other, more than what they actually say, can predict which couples will divorce with 87 percent accuracy, a new government-sponsored research says. The results of the ten-year study from the University of Washington, Seattle, add to the growing body of research sponsored by the National Institute of Mental Health that seeks to identify what saves marriages.

Interviewed within six months of marriage, couples who will endure already see each other "through rose-colored glasses," study co-author Sybil Carrere says. "Their behavior toward each other is positive." Those who will divorce already see each other "through fogged lenses," seeming cynical and unable to say good things about each other (Karen S. Peterson, "Sweet Nothings Help Marriages Stick," *USA Today,* 30 March 2000).

How we say things can be as important as what we say. A kind attitude and a tender tone will foster receptive ears on the other end. For the third time Shulammite referred to Solomon as her "beloved," her "lover." With gentleness and tenderness in his voice, he spoke and she listened. What kind of things should we listen for in a potential mate, a lifelong spouse?

1. Listen for praise.

2:10,13. In verses 10 and 13, Solomon invites Shulammite to **arise** and **come** away with him. He was again completely transparent in his intentions. He was also precious with his words. He called her his **darling** (NKJV "love") and his **beautiful one**. She was a joy to his heart and eyes. He loved her, and he found her irresistibly beautiful. He did not keep his thoughts to himself. He did not assume she knew how he felt; he told her how he felt. He praised her publicly and precisely.

2. Listen for particulars.

2:11–13. Solomon was an atypical man when it comes to romance. He understood that the way to a woman's heart is often in the details, the little things. In verses 11–13 Solomon invites Shulammite not to have sex but to take a walk in the countryside. She would have found this romantic. Furthermore, the details with which he described the passing of **winter** and the coming of spring are startling, especially for a man. His attention to detail is a model for all men everywhere. It is quite likely that Solomon's elaborate description has a double focus. Springtime is universally a time for love. Falling in love is like experiencing springtime all over again. Everything is fresh, new, and alive. Things simply look different when you are in love. You see things and notice things that you previously missed or overlooked.

For this young couple in love, winter and the rainy days were gone. Flowers were blooming, birds were singing, spring was in the air. You could see it and smell it. Love could be found everywhere you looked.

3. Listen for passion.

2:14. When two people are in love, they want to spend time alone, just the two of them. Solomon extended his invitation again, calling Shulammite his **dove** (cf. 1:15). Doves are gentle and beautiful. They often nestle in the clefts of the rock out of sight and safely hidden. Solomon compared Shulammite to such a dove and urged her to come out to him. She had kept herself safe and secure until God brought the right man into her life. She had saved herself for marriage. Now the right man had arrived, and he asked her to come to him.

One senses the passion of his request when he said he desired to see her lovely face and to hear her sweet voice. Keel's comments strike home the thrust of Solomon's words: "The voice is just as infatuating (or 'sweet'; cf. Prov. 20:17) as the face is ravishing. . . . The usual translations ('pleasant,' 'lovely,' etc.) are too pallid, failing to do justice to the intensity that enlivens this little song" (Keel, 107).

Craig Glickman wrote:

> One good indication of real love is the desire to communicate, a wish to discover all about this person whom you love so much. No detail seems too trivial to be related. No mood or feeling of one is unimportant to the other. And you care about the details and the feelings because you care so much about the person. That which would be insignificant or boring to even a good friend is eagerly received with genuine interest by the one who loves you. . . . The mere voice of the one loved is enchantingly special just in itself. One could read from the telephone book and the other would raptly listen simply for the sound of the voice (Glickman, 47–48).

[C] Question 3: Is He Tenacious in His Commitment? (2:15)

SUPPORTING IDEA: *Little things can become big things in a marriage.*

2:15. "Foxes were notorious in the ancient world for damaging vineyards. . . . Some ancient sources also suggest that foxes were particularly fond of grapes" (Snaith, 41). Here the **little foxes** represent those dangers and problems that can sneak into a relationship and do untold damage almost without notice, until it is too late. Even in the very best relationships a couple is vulnerable to potentially destructive problems. Here the proverb is certainly true: "An ounce of prevention is worth a pound of cure." A couple must be determined and tenacious in their commitment to **catch** the little foxes. The word *catch* is an imperative, a word of command from the Lord. We should take to heart at least two important truths in this regard.

1. Trouble is usually in the small things.

Foxes are little animals. You hardly notice them, and they are good at hiding. Only when the damage is done do you realize they were there. Issues like role responsibilities, conflict resolution, goals, expectations, finances, sex, spiritual compatibility, interpersonal compatibility, and social compatibility do not just naturally work in a relationship. They must be addressed and worked through continually if a marriage is to grow and develop.

2. Remember, relationships are uniquely sensitive things.

Solomon said, **our vineyards . . . are in bloom**. They were vulnerable to attack, and so is our marriage. We must provide necessary and essential protection. In our words, actions, and attitude, we must resolve to nurture and tend our relationship with great care. Any wise couple will consider a number of questions as they contemplate the prospects of marriage. It will help us in catching those foxes. They address several small things that could become big things if not faced head-on.

1. Have you discussed and come to agreement on what the Bible means when it says that the husband is to be a loving leader and the wife is to be a submissive helper (Eph. 5:21–33)?
2. Have you agreed always to tell your partner the truth (Eph. 4:15)?
3. Have you committed never to criticize your partner in public?
4. Are you in agreement on how decisions will be made when disagreement occurs?
5. Are you both committed to intimacy in your communication as a couple and to the effort this will require?
6. Do you both want to be used of God to help each other come to full maturity as a Christian?
7. Do you like the outlook on life and the values of your partner?
8. Are you personally committed to making your marriage a success whatever the cost or sacrifice?
9. Have you determined premarital sexual standards by open discussion so that each feels the decision reached honors the Lord (1 Cor. 6:18–20)?
10. Does the wife-to-be realize that men move from the visual to the physical and therefore need a healthy sexual relationship with their spouse to deter temptation?
11. Does the husband-to-be realize that women move from the emotional to the sexual and therefore need love demonstrated in verbal and practical ways?
12. Do you have complete confidence that your partner will be faithful to you (that is, could you trust him or her with a member of the opposite sex)?
13. Can you identify a day or time period when you placed your faith in Jesus Christ for salvation (John 1:12; Rom. 10:9–10,13)?
14. Do you have the certainty that your partner has come to faith in Jesus Christ?
15. Has your partner demonstrated a lifestyle of similar spiritual commitment as you have?

16. Have you decided where you will attend church and to what degree you will become involved?
17. Are you comfortable sharing feelings, desires, and goals with your partner?
18. Do you experience a sense of emotional pain when you are separated from your partner?
19. Have you demonstrated a willingness to be flexible in your relationship?
20. Have you been able to forgive your partner for an offense, then to reconcile and forget the matter (Eph. 4:32)?
21. Are both sets of parents in agreement with your intentions?
22. Have you looked objectively at your partner's family to see the major influences in shaping his or her life?
23. Do you respect your partner, and are you proud to have people for whom you have high regard meet him or her?
24. Do you find generally that you like the same people?
25. Have you observed differences in your social backgrounds that might cause conflicts?

Dealing with these types of questions will provide a helpful and healthy protection that will make it extremely difficult for those little foxes to do their damage.

𝔻 Question 4: Is He Trustworthy for Life? (2:16–17)

SUPPORTING IDEA: *Trust is an essential foundation for building a meaningful, happy, and lasting marriage.*

Solomon and Shulammite were realistic about their romance. They loved each other, but they also knew problems were inevitable. They had an initial strategy for facing difficulties when they arose (v. 15). Still, did they have what it takes to go the distance? Were they serious about the words "till death do us part"? I believe they were, and so must we be as well. "How will I know if he (she) really loves me," and will he (she) love me for life?

1. You must know you belong to each other.

2:16. There is a confidence and commitment in a healthy relationship. Each will know of the love and devotion of the other. Shulammite could say with bold assurance, **My lover is mine and I am his**. They enjoyed an intimate and exclusive love. Like ninety percent of Americans, they believed extramarital affairs are wrong. However, unlike the thirty-five percent of women and forty-five percent of men who allegedly cheat on their spouses (*Psychology Today*, July/August 2000, p. 10), they were determined to be true to each other. The phrase **he browses among the lilies** indicates he enjoyed the love and pleasures she had to offer. Again, because she was confident of their relationship, she freely gave herself to him. Security is essential to maximum sexual and marital enjoyment.

2. You must know you want each other.

2:17. The couple longed for marital union and sexual consummation. Because they belonged to each other, they wanted each other with no barriers standing in the way. Thinking ahead to what they would enjoy, Shulammite invited Solomon to come to her with the agility, strength, and beauty of a **gazelle** or **young stag** (cf. v. 9). The **rugged hills** (NKJV "mountains of Bether") is literally "hills or mountains of separation." This would seem to be a not-so-subtle reference to the woman's breasts (cf. 4:6). With all her desire and passion she welcomed him. **Until the day breaks** (literally, "breathes") **and the shadows flee** away (in other words "all night"), be my lover and enjoy the fruits of our love.

Shulammite has come a long way in her own personal self-evaluation. The unreserved love of this man who had entered her life had brought about a great change. She was now the woman God created her to be. Together the two of them were far better and more beautiful than they could have ever been alone. Love will do that when we pursue it God's way and with all our heart.

> **MAIN IDEA REVIEW:** *Good, hard questions need to be asked as we think about marriage. Marriage is one of God's greatest gifts to us, but it requires hard work before and after the wedding if we are to "go the distance" together.*

III. CONCLUSION

The Eight-Cow Wife

Norman Wright tells the story of "The Eight-Cow Wife." Before you wonder if he has lost it, read on and see if God doesn't teach us something very valuable through this story.

> When I married my wife, we both were insecure and she did everything she could to try to please me. I didn't realize how dominating and uncaring I was toward her. My actions in our early marriage caused her to withdraw even more. I wanted her to be self-assured, to hold her head high, and her shoulders back. I wanted her to be feminine and sensual.
>
> The more I wanted her to change, the more withdrawn and insecure she felt. I was causing her to be the opposite of what I wanted

her to be. I began to realize the demands I was putting on her, not so much by words but by body language.

By God's grace I learned that I must love the woman I married, not the woman of my fantasies. I made a commitment to love Susan for who she was—who God created her to be.

The change came about in a very interesting way. During a trip to Atlanta I read an article in *Reader's Digest*. I made a copy of it and have kept it in my heart and mind ever since. It was the story of Johnny Lingo, a man who lived in the South Pacific. The islanders all spoke highly of this man, but when it came time for him to find a wife the people shook their heads in disbelief. In order to obtain a wife you paid for her by giving her father cows. Four to six cows was considered a high price. But the woman Johnny Lingo chose was plain, skinny, and walked with her shoulders hunched and her head down. She was very hesitant and shy. What surprised everyone was Johnny's offer—he gave eight cows for her! Everyone chuckled about it, since they believed his father-in-law put one over on him.

Several months after the wedding, a visitor from the United States came to the islands to trade, and he heard the story about Johnny Lingo and his eight-cow wife. Upon meeting Johnny and his wife, the visitor was totally taken back, since this wasn't a shy, plain, and hesitant woman but one who was beautiful, poised, and confident. The visitor asked about the transformation, and Johnny Lingo's response was very simple. "I wanted an eight-cow woman, and when I paid that for her and treated her in that fashion, she began to believe that she was an eight-cow woman. She discovered she was worth more than any other woman in the islands. And what matters most is what a woman thinks about herself" (H. Norman Wright, "The Eight-Cow Wife," *Marriage Magazine,* May/June 2000).

PRACTICAL PRINCIPLES AND APPLICATIONS

- It's the small stuff that ruins a marriage. Always be on the lookout for the little foxes that can slip in unawares and damage your relationship.
- Grow in your knowledge of each other. Ask your mate some tough, probing qustions. Ask yourself some tough, probing questions.
- Identify and resolve potential problems such as communication; background; aspirations and goals; children (number? discipline?); expectations; in-law relations; finances and debts; attitudes toward sex; attitudes about alcohol, drugs, sexually explicit materials, etc.

IV. LIFE APPLICATION

Premarital Discussion Questions

In preparing for marriage, we can never have too much information. Really knowing the person you plan to marry is essential if the marriage is to start well, continue well, and end well. Following are some important questions prospective couples should discuss together before the "I do's."

1. What does love mean to you? What does it look like?
2. Do you believe the one you love is a mature person?
3. How do you try to please the person you love?
4. Who comes first usually—you or the person you love?
5. How often and in what way do you express feelings of warmth, tenderness, and appreciation to the person you love?
6. What activities will you desire to continue to do separately once married?
7. How long do you want or expect your marriage to last? Why?
8. What are your strengths and weaknesses as you see yourself?
9. What do you see as your responsibilities (role) in marriage?
10. What was the degree of happiness or unhappiness of your parents?
11. What feelings do you have toward each of your parents? Your brothers and sisters?
12. Did you come from a home where there were quarrels and fights? How were differences and problems solved by your parents?
13. Did you favor either parent? Were you the favorite child of either parent?
14. How did you cope with your parents when they argued?
15. How do you anticipate dealing with your parents once married? How do you anticipate dealing with your in-laws?
16. How much time do you feel you want to spend with your parents or in-laws in the first year of your marriage? After that?
17. How near do you plan to live to your parents or in-laws?
18. If a problem should come up with your parents or in-laws, whom do you think should handle it?
19. Is your marriage going to be like the marriage of your parents, your in-laws, or neither? Why?
20. Is the person you love too close with either parent?
21. What form of entertainment do you like? Does the person you love enjoy the same kinds of entertainment?
22. Do you like the friends of the person you love?
23. Do you have many friends, and how close are you to them?

24. After you marry, how will you choose friends? Spend time with friends?
25. Do your feelings about God or spiritual matters play a part in your relationship with the person you love?
26. Do you attend church regularly? Does the person you love do so? Will you attend regularly and together once married?
27. Do you have a personal relationship with Jesus Christ? If not, would you like to?
28. Will any future children you may have be brought up in church and taught to love God?
29. What are your goals in life?
30. Do you like sympathy and attention when you are ill?
31. As a general rule, do you enjoy the companionship of the opposite sex as much as that of your own sex? How, if any, will that change after marriage?
32. How much praise do you feel you need?
33. Do you think it will be a good idea to allow your future spouse an appropriate amount of the family income to spend as he or she so chooses, without giving an account to you?
34. Do you like to tease the person you love in front of others? Why?
35. Who is more intelligent, and how do you feel about this?
36. Do you ever feel depressed? Is this ever noticeable in the person you love?
37. Do you perceive yourself as a "talker" or a "listener"?
38. What interests, sports, or hobbies do you two share?
39. Do you like children? How many children do you want? How many does he or she want?
40. Would you express your feelings on family planning and discipline?
41. How will finances be handled in your marriage? What are your thoughts about debt?
42. Do you plan to use a budget? Have you ever tried to draw up a projected budget?
43. What sexual experience have you had? Is this known to the person you love?
44. Could you express your ideas on the need for affection and sex in your forthcoming marriage?
45. Do you think your sexual needs are more or less than those of the person you love? Have you discussed this much? At all?
46. Do you think your sexual and affectional needs are more or less than those of the person you love?
47. Who informed or instructed you on the so-called facts of life? Are you sufficiently knowledgeable in this area?

48. Do you usually remember birthdays and special occasions? How do you recognize them?
49. How would you feel about getting professional help from a marriage counselor should you not be able to work out a problem in your marriage?
50. Do you know many happily married couples?

V. PRAYER

Heavenly Father, marriage is a very serious issue. I really need to know who I am getting and what I am getting into. Give me wisdom and courage to ask good, hard questions of my prospective mate. Help me to realize I cannot know too much before saying "I do," but I could know too little. Spring fever feels good, but winter will come sooner or later. Guide me to make wise preparation for marriage. After all, this decision involves the person with whom I will spend the rest of my life. In Jesus' name. Amen.

VI. DEEPER DISCOVERIES

Foxes

Foxes were notorious pests in the ancient world. Poets wrote about them (Theocritus of Comatas, c. 275 B.C.), and they have been described as "guileful, riddling creatures in fables and proverb; and thus comparable to the cunning serpent" (Landy, 240). Given this historical and literary insight, what might we say are some of the more prominent activities of the foxes of our day that slip in and attempt to destroy our marriages? Let me highlight seven.

Warning 1 (the fox of role reversal). A marriage will get into trouble when God's role for the husband and the wife is reversed or abused.

Warning 2 (the fox of intimacy stagnation). A marriage will get into trouble when initial, sensual love fails to develop into true intimacy.

Warning 3 (the fox of silence or stonewalling). A marriage will get into trouble when it is not being nourished by regular and genuine communication.

Warning 4 (the fox of time ill spent). A marriage will get into trouble when forces or persons outside the marriage encroach on the time the two of you need alone to build and maintain a healthy relationship.

Warning 5 (the fox of outside interference). A marriage will get into trouble when real and personal needs are being met more and more outside the marriage.

Warning 6 (the fox of fatigue). A marriage will get into trouble if the wedding vows are considered conditional, marriage is no longer considered a sacred covenant before God, and divorce begins to be considered as a possible solution to an unhappy situation.

Warning 7 (the fox of misunderstanding). A marriage will get into trouble if the man and woman fail to understand and appreciate and enjoy just how different they really are from each other.

VII. TEACHING OUTLINE

A. INTRODUCTION: MEN ARE DOGS, AND WOMEN ARE CATS!

B. COMMENTARY

1. Question 1: Is He Transparent in His Actions? (2:8–9)
   a. Watch his or her actions.
   b. Watch his or her eyes.
2. Question 2: Is He Tender with His Words? (2:10–14)
   a. Listen for praise.
   b. Listen for particulars.
   c. Listen for passion.
3. Question 3: Is He Tenacious in His Commitment? (2:15)
   a. Trouble is usually in the small things
   b. Relationships are uniquely sensitive things
4. Question 4: Is He Trustworthy for Life? (2:16–17)
   a. You must know you belong to each other.
   b. You must know you want each other.

C. CONCLUSION: THE EIGHT-COW WIFE

VIII. ISSUES FOR DISCUSSION

If we are to beat the little foxes, we must recognize that this is a battle that will take place on a day-by-day basis. The victories of yesterday will not be sufficient for the battles of tomorrow. Indeed it is absolutely essential that we grow a little bit every day in our relationship with each other. Several years ago, Harry Chapin wrote a song titled "We Grew Up a Little Bit." Harry Chapin was a ballad singer. He did not have many answers, but he sure knew how to raise the right questions. Listen to the words of this song, and see if they will not challenge your heart and your commitment to each other, to at least grow a little bit every day in this wonderful relationship we call marriage.

We got married early and just a little bit late.
Baby came too early, but some things just can't wait.
We were just beginning but it was very clear
We grew up a little bit that year.
I caught on as a meter man. You were caught at home.
When I started night school you ended up alone.
But you had another baby while I had my career.
And we grew up a little bit. We grew up a little bit.
We grew up a little bit that year.
They put me in an office job, the young man on the move.
We bought a house in Shaker Heights. You supervised the move.
We were cashing checks. You were changing children while
I played engineer.
And we were growing ever faster every year.
But I got bored of kilowatts and you were tired of kids.
I started staying out at night, and soon that's what you did.
At parties we'd go separately. You'd wiggle and I'd leer.
And we were growing faster. We were growing ever faster.
We were growing ever faster every year.
Well you learned to live in silence. I learned to live in lies.
And we both ignored the empty spaces growing in our eyes.
Your breath became a gin and tonic while mine became a beer.
And we grew up a little more last year.
Today at work they passed me by and promoted John instead.
I came home to find you'd wrecked the car. I guess I lost my head.
Well, I can't believe I hit you, but the rage came on so strong.
Ah, where did we go wrong?
As you sit there crying I wonder who you are?
The partner-stranger-friend and foe who's come with me this far.
We stand here in the ashes, and I guess it is quite clear.
We did not really grow too much each year.
So you say we're going nowhere. Well, I know that's where we've
been.
But I still can't help wondering can we begin again?
I feel so full of questions, curiosity, and fear.
But could we grow a little bit? Could we grow a little bit?
Can we grow a little bit this year?

Harry Chapin, "We Grew Up a Little Bit," *Dance Band on the Titanic*, Electra/Asylum Records, 1977. Used by permission.

Song of Songs 3:1–5

A Lover's Nightmare

I. INTRODUCTION
God Knows Best About Sex, Marriage, and Children

II. COMMENTARY
A verse-by-verse explanation of these verses.

III. CONCLUSION
Berry Mauve or Muted Wine?
An overview of the principles and applications from these verses.

IV. LIFE APPLICATION
Ways in Which Men and Women Are Different
Melding these verses to life.

V. PRAYER
Tying these verses to life with God.

VI. DEEPER DISCOVERIES
Historical, geographical, and grammatical enrichment of the commentary.

VII. TEACHING OUTLINE
Suggested step-by-step group study of these verses.

VIII. ISSUES FOR DISCUSSION
Zeroing these verses in on daily life.

Quote

"*A* successful marriage is always a triangle:

a man, a woman, and God."

C e c i l   M y e r s

Song of Songs
3:1–5

 I N   A   N U T S H E L L

*A*s the author of marriage and family, God knew what he was doing when he designed them as he did. God truly "knows best" when it comes to issues like marriage, sex, family, and children.

A Lover's Nightmare

I. INTRODUCTION

God Knows Best About Sex, Marriage, and Children

*M*arriage is one of the greatest things going. In a book titled *The Case for Marriage,* Linda Waite and Maggie Gallagher argue convincingly, and against conventional wisdom, that married people are "happier, healthier, and better off financially." Amazing, isn't it? We are now discovering in popular culture what many of us already know: God knows best! Yes, even scientific research is now vindicating the Creator's idea of marriage and the family. For example, when we examine evidence on *sex,* we discover God knows best.

God knows best about sex.

1. In 1993 it was reported that 68,000,000 Americans had a sexually transmitted disease (Patricia Donovan, "A Prescription of Sexually Transmitted Diseases," *Issues in Science and Technology,* 1993, vol. 9, no. 4, p. 40). Approximately 15.3 million Americans contract a sexually transmitted disease (STD) annually. One in four of the victims is under age twenty. Five of the eleven most common reportable infectious diseases in this country in 1998 were sexually transmitted. And that doesn't include the most common—herpes and human papillomavirus (HPV); the Centers for Disease Control and Prevention (CDC) don't collect data on these. HPV causes over 90 percent of cancer and precancer of the cervix, which, in turn, is causing the deaths of approximately five thousand American women yearly.

The number of sex partners is highly correlated with the likelihood of contracting an STD. Studies from the CDC clearly show that, on average, the younger a person is when he or she starts to have sex, the more partners he or she is likely to have. Hence, delay sexual activity until marriage and avoid STDs. Furthermore, the likelihood of contracting a STD during marriage is negligible. Thus, more marriage means fewer STDs (Joe S. McIlhaney, "Improve Nation: Boost Marriage," *Knight Ridder/Tribune News Service,* 29 September 2000).

And keep this in mind: many STDs are incurable; others can render you sterile; and some are potentially fatal. It is an amazing reality to think if we would simply do sex God's way—one man with one woman within the covenant of marriage for life—every single STD would disappear in one generation.

2. We now know sex is more satisfying for those who wait until marriage. A survey of sexuality, which was called the "most authoritative ever" by

U. S. News & World Report, conducted jointly by researchers at State University of New York at Stony Brook and the University of Chicago, found that of all sexually active people, the people who reported being the most physically pleased and emotionally satisfied were married couples (Robert T. Michael, John H. Gagnon, and Edward O. Lauman, *Sex in America: A Definitive Survey,* Boston: Little, Brown & Co., 1994, 124).

One writer put it rather straightforwardly:

> "Promoting marriage in America will make for a lot more happy men and women." *Sex in America* reported that married sex beats all else. For example: "Married women had much higher rates of usually or always having orgasms, 75 percent, as compared to women who were never married and not cohabiting, 62 percent." And, the researchers wrote, "Those having the most sex and enjoying it the most are the married people" (Joe S. McIlhaney, "Improve Nation: Boost Marriage").

3. Not only is sex better in marriage; it is best if you have had only one sexual partner in a lifetime. We now know "physical and emotional satisfaction start to decline when people have had more than one sexual partner" (Michael *et al,* 125). Great sex is godly sex. God knows best about sex.

God also knows best about marriage.

1. We have discovered that married people have healthier unions than couples who live together. Research from Washington State University revealed, "Cohabiting couples compared to married couples have less healthy relationships" (Jan E. Stets, "The Link Between Past and Present Intimate Relationship," *Journal of Family Issues,* 1993, vol. 114, p. 251).

2. Married people are generally better off in *all* measures of well-being. Researchers at UCLA explained that "cohabiters experienced significantly more difficulty in [subsequent] marriages with [issues of] adultery, alcohol, drugs and independence than couples who had not cohabited" (Michael D. Newcomb and P. M. Bentler, "Assessment of Personality and Demographic Aspects of Cohabitation and Marital Success," *Journal of Personality Assessment,* 1980, vol. 44, p. 21). In fact, marriages preceded by cohabitation are 50 to 100 percent *more* likely to break up than those marriages not preceded by cohabitation (William Axinn and Arland Thorton, "The Relationship Between Cohabitation and Divorce: Selectivity or Casual Influence?" *Demography,* 1992, vol. 29, p. 358).

3. "Wife beating" should more properly be called "girlfriend beating." According to the *Journal of Marriage and the Family,* "Aggression is at least twice as common among cohabiters as it is among married partners" (Jan E. Stets, "Cohabiting and Marital Aggression: The Role of Isolation," *Journal of Marriage and the Family,* 1993, vol. 53, pp. 669–70).

4. Married people enjoy better physical and mental health. Dr. Robert Coombs, a biobehavioral scientist at UCLA, conducted a review of more than 130 studies on the relationship between well-being and marital status, concluding that "there is an intimate link between the two." Married people have significantly lower rates of alcoholism, suicide, psychiatric care, and higher rates of self-reported happiness (Robert Coombs, "Marital Status and Personal Well-Being: A Literature Review," *Family Relations,* 1991, vol. 40, pp. 97–102).

5. Those in married relationships experienced a lower rate of severe depression than people in any other category (Lee Robins and Darrel Regier, *Psychiatric Disorders in America: The Epidemiologic Catchment Area Study,* New York: Free Press, 1991, p. 72). The annual rate of major depression per 100 is as follows:

Married (never divorced)	1.5
Never married	2.4
Divorced once	4.1
Cohabiting	5.1
Divorced twice	5.8

A recent study of the mental health of the married and unmarried looked at a nationwide sample of nearly thirteen thousand people. Married women were about 33 percent more likely than unmarried women to rate their emotional health as "excellent." Unmarried women were more than twice as likely as married women to rate their emotional health as "poor."

6. Researchers at the University of Massachusetts say married people experience less disease, morbidity, and disability than do those who are divorced or separated. Their explanation: "One of the most consistent observations in health research is that the married enjoy better health than those of other [relational] statuses" (Catherine K. Relssman and Naomi Gerstel, "Marital Dissolution and Health: Do Males or Females Have Greater Risk?" *Social Science and Medicine,* 1985, vol. 20, p. 627). One study concerning men in particular revealed that nine out of ten men married at forty-eight will still be alive at sixty-five, while only six out of ten single men will be.

7. Men and women are at much greater risk of being assaulted if they are not married, reported the U.S. Department of Justice in 1994 (U.S. Department of Justice, Office of Justice Programs, Bureau of Justice Statistics. "Criminal Victimization in the United States, 1992," NCJ-145125, March 1994, 31). The rates per 1,000 for general aggravated assaults against:

Males

Married	5.5
Divorced or separated	13.6
Never married	23.4

Females

Married	3.1
Divorced or separated	9.1
Never married	11.9

God knows best about marriage.

God also knows best about children.

1. The best place to raise children is in a home with a father and a mother who are married to each other. On average, children do better in all areas when raised by two married parents who live together. The most authoritative work done in this area is by Dr. Sara McLanahan of Princeton University. In *Growing Up with a Single Parent,* she explains, "Children who grow up in a household with only one biological parent are worse off, on average, than children who grow up . . . with both of their biological parents, regardless of the parents' race or educational background" (Sara McLanahan and Gary Sandefur, *Growing Up with a Single Parent,* Cambridge: Harvard University Press, 1994, p. 1).

2. Adolescents who have lived apart from one of their parents during some period of childhood are:

- twice as likely to drop out of high school;
- twice as likely to have a child before age 20;
- one-and-one-half times as likely to be idle—out of school and out of work—in their late twenties (McLanahan and Sandefur, 1).

A study conducted at the University of Utah said that parental divorce hurts young children because it often leaves them in the care of highly stressed and irritable mothers (*Family in America,* February 2000 p. 2).

3. Children without fathers more often have lowered academic performance, more cognitive and intellectual deficits, increased adjustment problems, and higher risks for psychosexual development problems (George Rekers, "Research on the Essential Characteristics of the Father's Role for Family Well-Being." Testimony before the Select Committee on Children, Youth and Families, U.S. House of Representatives, 99th Congress, 2nd session, February 25, 1986, 59–60). Violent children are eleven times more likely not to live with their fathers and six times more likely to have parents who are not married. Children not living with both biological parents are four times as likely to be suspended or expelled from school (*Business Daily,* November 12, 1997).

The *Heritage Foundation* noted in June 2000: "A million children a year see their parents divorce. Only 42 percent of teens aged 14–18 live in a 'first family,' an intact, two-parent married family." Children of divorce experience "anger, fear, sadness, worry, rejection, conflicting loyalties, lowered self-confidence, heightened anxiety, loneliness, more depressed moods, more suicidal thoughts," says the Heritage report, "The Effects of Divorce on America" by Dr. Patrick Fagan and Robert Rector.

Compared to kids in intact homes, children of divorce face startling risks. They are: twelve times more likely to be incarcerated as juveniles; fourteen times more prone to be physically abused by a single mother, and thirty-three times more at risk if she cohabits; three times more apt to get pregnant, and males commit suicide at sixfold higher rates.

The report also notes that "many children of divorce become dysfunctional adults: Even thirty years after the divorce, negative long-term effects were clearly present in the income, health, and behavior of many of the grown offspring." They have more failed romantic relationships, a greater number of sexual partners, are two to three times as apt to cohabit, are less trusting of fiancées, less giving to them and are twice as likely to divorce. When both are from divorced homes, their risk of divorce is as much as 620 percent higher in the early years of marriage. Thus the "marital instability of one generation is passed on to the next" (Mike McManus, "Heritage Foundation Calls for Political Leadership on Marriage," *Ethics & Religion,* 22 June 2000, Column #982).

Dr. David Popenoe, a noted family scholar from Rutgers University, explains that there can be no serious debate over this issue:

> I know of few other bodies of data in which the weight of evidence is so decisively on one side of the issue. On the whole, for children, two-parent families are preferable. . . . If our prevailing views on family structure hinged solely on scholarly evidence, the current debate never would have arisen in the first place" (David Popenoe, "The Controversial Truth," *New York Times,* 26 December 1992, A-21).

Further, a sociologist at the University of Pennsylvania said: "Most studies show that children in stepfamilies do not do better than children in single-parent families; indeed, many indicate that, on average, children in remarriages do worse" (Frank F. Furstenberg Jr., "History and Current Status of Divorce in the United States," *The Future of Children,* 4, no. 1, Center for the Future of Children, Spring 1994, p. 37). It is disturbing to note that stepfamilies are the second-fastest growing family structure in America. The fastest is created by out-of-wedlock births (David Blankenhorn, *Fatherless America: Confronting Our Most Urgent Social Problem,* New York: Basic Books, 1995, p. 307).

4. Even the death of a parent is not as devastating to a child as losing one by divorce or desertion. Why? Single-parent families created by the death of a spouse have a natural protective mechanism distinguishing them from other single-parent families. Dr. James Egan, a child psychiatrist at Children's Hospital in Washington, D.C., provocatively asserts, "A dead father is a more

effective father than a missing father" (James Egan, M.D., "When Fathers Are Absent." Address given at the National Summit on Fatherhood, sponsored by the National Fatherhood Initiative: Dallas, 27 October 1994).

When a father (or mother) dies, he still maintains a place of authority, influence, and moral leadership in the home. Parents who have departed due to death usually leave positive reputations. Their pictures remain on the wall, they are talked about positively, and negative behavior on the part of a child can be corrected with a simple reminder: "Would your dad (or mom) approve of that kind of behavior?" If the father has abandoned the child or was never identified, the answer to that question is either "Who cares?" or, even worse, "Who?"

In an article titled "How Kids Mourn," *Newsweek* reported: "'The death of a parent can have devastating psychological consequences, including anxiety, depression, sleep disturbances, underachievement and aggression. But so can a lot of other things, and losing a parent [by death] is actually less devastating than divorce. We know that children tend to do better after a parental death than a divorce,' says sociologist Andrew Cherlin of Johns Hopkins, 'and that's a stunning statistic, because you'd think death would be harder'" ("How Kids Mourn," *Newsweek,* 22 September 1997, p. 58).

Actually there is nothing stunning about this at all. When a child, big or small, loses a parent by death, his or her mind reasons something like this: "If my daddy *could* be here, he would be here. But he's dead and so he can't." On the other hand, if a child loses a parent by desertion or divorce, his or her mind reasons differently: "If my daddy *wanted* to be here, he would be here. I guess he *doesn't want* to be here, and . . . it must be my fault." This is the devastating fallout on children wounded by a divorce, a wound we now know often follows them into adulthood (see the major work on this by Judith Wallerstein, *The Unexpected Legacy of Divorce*).

And now as a new millennium begins, additional new research has come forth that makes the argument for marriage with even greater force. As noted earlier, in their blockbuster, *The Case for Marriage: Why Married People Are Happier, Healthier and Better Off Financially,* authors Linda Waite, a professor of sociology at the University of Chicago, and Maggie Gallagher, director of the Marriage Project at the Institute for American Values in New York, reveal married women living with their husbands are much less likely to be victims of domestic violence and even violence from strangers than are their single, separated, divorced, or cohabiting sisters. For most women, marriage is a safe place to be. Marriage changes the relationship of the marriage partners for the good, giving them a stake in the well-being of each other and the family in a way other forms of "partnership" cannot.

The public promise of marriage "changes the way you think about yourself and your beloved; it changes the way you act and think about the future; and it changes how other people and other institutions treat you as well." An extensive survey of the data on marriage shows that married people, in general, are significantly healthier, both physically and mentally, than their non-married peers: They are far more affluent, even when living on only one income; women are safer, and men, even from backgrounds at high risk for violence, are far less likely to commit crime; they report more satisfying sex lives than their single peers, even those who are cohabiting; and overall they are significantly happier than folks in any other kind of relationship "arrangement" (Betsy Hart, "Both Sexes Thrive in Marriage," *Scripps Howard News Service,* 6 October 2000).

God knows best. The evidence is overwhelming and indisputable. He knows best about sex, marriage, and children. And yet we can still have doubts, worries, anxieties, and questions as we approach this divinely ordained institution. Fear can almost paralyze us. How can I know? How can I be sure this is the right person? Has the "case for marriage" received a positive verdict in my own heart? Let me encourage you to keep in mind four things given to us by Solomon as you attempt to settle this issue.

II. COMMENTARY

A Lover's Nightmare

MAIN IDEA: *God designed marriage in exactly the right way.*

🅰 Marriage Is the Right Place to Enjoy Sexual Passion (3:1–2)

SUPPORTING IDEA: *Sex in marriage maximizes protection and pleasure.*

3:1–2. Many scholars believe this portion of the Song of Songs is a dream Shulammite had one night shortly before her marriage to Solomon. It was not a pleasant dream at first. In fact, it was more like a nightmare. Still, in the midst of it we learn something of the passionate love she had for Solomon. We also receive counsel about passion and its relationship to marriage.

1. Satisfy yourself this is the right mate.

Her desire and passion for Solomon was an all-night affair, and it was intense. She was completely consumed with him in her thoughts. In her bed where he would soon join her, she longed to have him now and she longed for him **all night**. It is interesting to note the themes of "seeking" and "finding" occur four times in these verses. The word translated **looked** or "sought" (NKJV) can also mean "to desire, yearn, or long for." There is a feverishness in the word. There is passion. She was certain in her heart (**I looked for the one my heart loves**). He was the right man for her.

2. *Save yourself for the right moment.*

She looked for or sought Solomon, but she did not find him. She arose and, at night, went into and about the city—something dangerous and inappropriate for a young woman in the Middle East. This supports the idea that she was having a dream. So great was her desire for Solomon that she abandoned proper decorum and went in search **for the one my heart loves**. Still, she did not find him. Why? The answer is simple: he was not there—yet! She had saved herself for her wedding night. In so doing, she had honored both God and her husband.

Sex, as we have noted, is God's good gift and one to be enjoyed, but only in marriage. Hebrews 13:4 teaches us the marriage bed is undefiled. It is a place where God says to enjoy the pleasures of sexual passion and do so fully.

Solomon was not at the present time in her bed at her side, or even in the city, but he would be soon. She had saved herself for the right moment. She wanted that moment to be *now,* and she missed him not being with her. This is the passion God wants us to have for each other in marriage. It will be an indication you have found the right person. Marriage is the right place to enjoy sexual passion. Marriage is the right place to find great sex.

B Marriage Is the Right Place to Examine Potential Problems (3:3)

SUPPORTING IDEA: *We should carefully consider obstacles to a healthy relationship.*

3:3. In her dream Shulammite met **the watchmen** of the city as she searched for Solomon. The significance of the watchmen in her dream is not clear. They could represent nothing important at all. On the other hand, they could represent persons of authority and importance, persons of wisdom and counsel who could lend valuable assistance. These were men who "go about the city" (NKJV). They were wise in the ways of the street. They had observed the habits of humanity. They had seen things. "They know. . . ." Interestingly, they found her, and she questioned them, **Have you seen the one my heart loves?** Two lessons can be learned from this simple encounter.

1. *Pursue your spouse with healthy abandonment.*

She again called Solomon **the one my heart loves**. She was not ashamed for anyone, even strangers, to know how she felt. She loved him and was looking for him. She missed him and needed him. Her anxiety at his absence was normal and to be expected. As time goes on after they are married, it will be a healthy sign in their relationship that they miss each other when they are apart but that a security has developed in the relationship that puts fears and anxieties to rest. That there would ever be a day they would enjoy being apart would be a telltale sign that their marriage was in serious trouble.

2. Pursue your spouse with helpful advice.

Shulammite's asking for help in finding Solomon again reminds us that asking questions—lots of questions—before marriage is a wise and good thing. We should ask questions of others and of each other. It is impossible to know too much. It is impossible to have too much information before making this awesome decision about who you will spend the rest of your life with.

C Marriage Is the Right Place to Experience Natural Protection (3:4)

SUPPORTING IDEA: *We should find and experience a sense of security in our spouse.*

3:4. Shulammite's persistence paid off as is often the case when it comes to romance. The watchmen left, and suddenly there was Solomon—the one she loved. Notice two things she did that would let him know of her love and that we would do well to emulate.

1. Hold on to him.

She **held him and would not let him go**. Shulammite was no passive wallflower or hesitant lover. She was appropriately and passionately aggressive at this moment. She had found her man, and she was not about to lose him again. She grabbed hold of him and would not let him go. She needed him. She wanted him. She felt protected and secure when he was with her, and I suspect he felt the same.

2. Honor him.

She took Solomon back to her maternal home, a place that would also feel safe and secure. She was certain he was the man with whom she wished to spend the rest of her life. There is no indication of resistance on Solomon's part. He loved her and desired her as much as she did him. He was honored by her attention and her intentions. This was indeed the woman for him as well. In sickness and in health, for better or for worse, until death do them part, they would be there for each other.

Ⓓ Marriage Is the Right Place to Exercise Spiritual Patience (3:5)

SUPPORTING IDEA: *There is a right person, place, and time for making love.*

3:5. Marriage is as much about being the right person as finding the right person. When you are the right person, you can wait on God and trust both his plan and his timing. When you are the right person, you are ready for God to bring the other right person into your life. For the second time in the Song (cf. 2:7), we hear the refrain calling us to patience, to wait. The refrain is in the form of an oath, a vow. Although the vow is made by **the gazelles** or **the does**, I believe ultimately it is to the Creator of these beautiful and active animals that Shulammite looked. What was her counsel? In a sense we come full circle back to verse 1.

1. Make a commitment to God to wait for the right person.

We have received good counsel in how we can identify the right person. Be patient. Wait on the Lord. God always gives his best to those who leave the choices with him.

2. Make a commitment to God to wait for the right time.

God's time is always the right time. When we wait and do marriage, sex, and romance on his schedule, we discover what we should have known all along: God, indeed, knows best!

MAIN IDEA REVIEW: *God designed marriage in exactly the right way.*

III. CONCLUSION

Berry Mauve or Muted Wine?

I came across a story by T. Suzanne Eller titled "Berry Mauve or Muted Wine?" that provides a beautiful witness as we make the case for marriage. See if you don't agree.

> He found me weeping bitterly in the hospital room. "What's wrong?" Richard asked, knowing that we both had reason to cry. In the past forty-eight hours, I learned that I had a cancerous lump in my breast that had spread to my lymph nodes, and there was a possible spot on my brain. We were both thirty-two with three young children.
>
> Richard pulled me tight and tried to comfort me. Our friends and family had been amazed at the peace that had overwhelmed us. Jesus

was our Savior and comfort before I found out I had cancer, and he remained the same after my diagnosis. But it seemed to Richard that the terrifying reality of my situation had finally crashed in on me in the few moments he was out of the room.

As he held me tight, Richard tried to comfort me. "It's all been too much, hasn't it Suz?" he said.

"That's not it," I cried and held up the hand mirror I had just found in the drawer. Richard looked puzzled.

"I didn't know it would be like this," I cried, as I stared in shock at my reflection in the mirror. I didn't recognize myself. I was horribly swollen. After the surgery, I had groaned as I lay asleep and well-meaning friends had freely pushed the self-dispensing medication to ease what they thought was pain. Unfortunately I was allergic to morphine and had swelled like a sausage. Betadine from the surgery stained my neck, shoulder and chest and it was too soon for a bath. A tube hung out of my side draining the fluid from the surgical site. My left shoulder and chest were wrapped tightly in gauze where I had lost a portion of my breast. My long, curly hair was matted into one big wad. More than one hundred people had come to see me over the past forty-eight hours, and they had all seen this brown-and-white, swollen, makeup-less, matted-haired, gray-gowned woman who used to be me. Where had I gone?

Richard laid me back on the pillow and left the room. Within moments he came back, his arms laden with small bottles of shampoo and conditioner that he confiscated from the cart in the hall. He pulled pillows out of the closet and dragged a chair over to the sink. Unraveling my IV, he tucked the long tube from my side in his shirt pocket. Then he reached down, picked me up and carried me—IV stand and all—over to the chair. He sat me down gently on his lap, cradled my head in his arms over the sink and began to run warm water through my hair. He poured the bottles over my hair, washing and conditioning my long curls. He wrapped my hair in a towel and carried me, the tube, and the IV stand back over to the bed. He did this so gently that not one stitch was disturbed.

My husband, who had never blow-dried his hair in his life, took out a blow-dryer and dried my hair, the whole while entertaining me as he pretended to give beauty tips. He then proceeded, based on the experience of watching me for the past twelve years, to fix my hair. I laughed as he bit his lip, more serious than any beauty-school student. He bathed my shoulder and neck with a warm washcloth, careful to not disturb the area around the surgery, and rubbed lotion into my skin. Then he opened my makeup bag and began to apply makeup. I will never forget our laughter as he tried to apply my mascara and blush. I opened my eyes wide and held my breath as he brushed the mascara on my lashes with shaking hands. He rubbed my cheeks with tissue to blend in the blush. With the last touch, he held up two lipsticks. "Which one? Berry mauve or muted wine?" he asked. He applied the lipstick like an artist painting on a canvas and then held the little mirror in front of me.

I was human again. A little swollen, but I smelled clean, my hair hung softly over my shoulders and I recognized myself.

"What do you think?" he asked. I began to cry again, this time because I was grateful. "No, baby. You'll mess up my makeup job," he said and I burst into laughter.

During that difficult time in our lifes, I was given only a 40-percent chance of survival over five years. That was seven years ago. I made it through those years with laughter, God's comfort and the help of my wonderful husband. We will celebrate our nineteenth anniversary this year, and our children are now in their teens. Richard understood what must have seemed like vanity and silliness in the midst of tragedy. Everything I had ever taken for granted had been shaken in those hours—the fact that I would watch my children grow, my health, my future. With one small act of kindness, Richard gave me normalcy. I will always see that moment as one of the most loving gestures of our marriage.

(From *Chicken Soup for the Couple's Soul*, edited by Jack Canfield, Mark Victor Hansen, Mark and Chrissy Donnelly, and Barbara De Angelis [Deerfield Beach, FL: Health Communications, Inc., 1999]. © 1998 by T. Suzanne Eller.)

PRACTICAL PRINCIPLES AND APPLICATIONS

What are some basic, everyday gifts you can give your spouse?

- Affection
- Affirmation
- Companionship
- Compliments
- Emotional support
- Encouragement
- Excitement
- Faithfulness
- Friendship
- Handyman skills
- Hard work

- Help
- Housekeeping skills
- Insights
- Listening skills
- Loyalty
- Material support
- Openness to change
- Organization
- Physical love
- Responsibility
- Roots
- Steadiness
- Support
- Time
- Understanding
- Unselfishness
- Willingness to spend time
- Others:
- _____
- _____
- _____

IV. LIFE APPLICATION

Ways in Which Men and Women Are Different

1. Men and Women Communicate Differently
   - Listening is hard work for men; it brings happiness to women.
   - Talking can intimidate men; it nurtures intimacy for women.
   - Men tend to report facts; women want to share feelings.
   - Men feel compelled to offer solutions; women want affirmation and assurance.
   - Men tend to compartmentalize; women think more integratively.
   - Men don't respond to hints; women are subtle and coded in their conversation.
2. Men and Women View Romance Differently
   - Romance for men means sex; for women it can mean lots of things.
   - Romance for men is highly visual; for women it is extremely relational and personal.
   - Romance for men is what they see; for women it is what they feel.
3. Men and Women Have Needs Differently
   - Women need to feel valued; men need to feel successful.

- Women need to be heard; men need to be praised.
- Women want to be interdependent; men want to be self-sufficient.

4. Men and Women See Self-Worth Differently
   - Women value relational moments; men value occupational achievements.
   - Women fear neglect; men fear failure.

5. Men and Women Think About Time Differently
   - Men do not think about time; women value quantity and quality time.
   - Men go with the flow; women appreciate specific and creative ideas.

6. Men and Women Parent Differently
   - Mothers nurture; dads provide strength and a child's sense of self-worth.
   - Mothers provide the emotional support for children; dads provide a sense of security.

V. PRAYER

Father, it is normal to approach marriage with fear and apprehension. After all, this is a big decision that should last for life. I need your help, your wisdom, your guidance. I need for your will to be done in my life more than ever. I know your ways are the best in every area of life. I want only what you want for me when it comes to my marriage. I want a marriage that will be to your glory and for my good. Help me to wait on you and trust your timing. In Jesus' name I pray. Amen.

VI. DEEPER DISCOVERIES

A. Watchmen

These men were city guards stationed on the city walls (cf. 5:7, 2 Sam. 13:34; 18:24–27; 2 Kgs. 9:17–20; Ps. 127:1; Isa. 52:8; 62:6) and the city gates (cf. Neh. 3:29; 11:19; 13:22). Apparently they also patrolled the city, especially at night, to provide order and safety. For Shulammite to venture out at night and alone would be extremely unusual and dangerous, especially since she was a woman. This adds support for the idea that she was having a dream. It also highlights her desire and love for Solomon. She longed for his presence to such an extent that she would put her own life in danger to find him.

B. Mother's House

This phrase has two possible understandings. First, it refers to the actual home, and probably the bedroom, of her mother. In the Song this is a place of security and intimacy. It is potentially an invitation to making love in the safety and privacy of this location. Second, it, along with the idea of "conceiving," could refer to the womb or the sexual parts of a woman. If this interpretation is correct, the invitation to making love is even more pronounced and direct. Given the fluidity of Ancient Near Eastern poetry, such an understanding is entirely possible.

VII. TEACHING OUTLINE

A. INTRODUCTION: GOD KNOWS BEST ABOUT SEX, MARRIAGE, AND CHILDREN

B. COMMENTARY

1. Marriage Is the Right Place to Enjoy Sexual Passion (3:1–2)
   a. Satisfy yourself this is the right mate.
   b. Save yourself for the right moment.
2. Marriage Is the Right Place to Examine Potential Problems (3:3)
   a. Pursue your spouse with healthy abandonment.
   b. Pursue your spouse with helpful advice.
3. Marriage Is the Right Place to Experience Natural Protection (3:4)
   a. Hold on to him.
   b. Honor him.
4. Marriage Is the Right Place to Exercise Spiritual Patience (3:5)
   a. Make a commitment to God to wait for the right person.
   b. Make a commitment to God to wait for the right time.

C. CONCLUSION: BERRY MAUVE OR MUTED WINE?

VIII. ISSUES FOR DISCUSSION

Consider the following "Thirty Questions Most Frequently Asked by Young Couples Looking Forward to Marriage"

1. Where should a couple stop in petting before marriage?
2. Is jealousy part of love for your mate?
3. Who should control the purse strings?
4. When both are working, is the wife's money hers or theirs? If both work, who should support the family while (if) the husband continues his schooling?
5. Is there any reason why the wife should not support the family while the husband continues his schooling?

6. Should the husband help with housework?

7. Should couples have a will drawn up soon after marriage?

8. Should a young couple carry insurance?

9. What are the effects of frequent business travel or unusual working hours on marital happiness?

10. To what extent should we discuss our pasts?

11. Is it true that people are not really "in love" until after they have been married for some years?

12. When we differ, how can we work out a happy adjustment?

13. Is it true that quarrels are never necessary?

14. If we come from divided families, can we profit by our parent's mistakes?

15. When we belong to two quite different churches, how do we work out our differences and what about children?

16. How can a couple keep in-laws in their place but still make them feel loved and necessary?

17. What if he feels she does not give enough and she feels he does not give enough? If they talk about it and still feel this way, what is suggested?

18. How soon after marriage should a couple plan to have children?

19. When considering having children, should the decision be primarily economic?

20. Are contraceptives safe to use? Do they lead to cancer or sterility?

21. What part does each partner have in the love play preceding and during intercourse?

22. Is every couple able to have satisfactory intercourse?

23. Is it harmful or wrong to have intercourse during menstruation?

24. Is there danger of constantly arousing sexual desires and not fulfilling this desire, in both male and female?

25. How does a woman know when she reaches a climax?

26. Do women undergo emotional changes during pregnancy and menstrual periods?

27. How important is it for couples to know their RH factor?

28. Are regular times for prayer important?

29. Are there occasions in marriage when divorce seems a reasonable and even proper solution?

30. If we find difficulties arising in our marriage, what immediate steps should we take?

Song of Songs 3:6–11

The Wedding Day

"*M*arriage involves a covenantal agreement to meet all of your spouse's needs for companionship (on every level: sexual, social, spiritual, etc.) for the rest of your life. It is, therefore, a final act."

J a y   A d a m s

Song of Songs
3:6–11

 I N   A   N U T S H E L L

*C*hristian marriage is a divine covenant between God, a man, and a woman. It is a time of celebration and commitment. The covenant is a binding commitment for life testified to by a public ceremony (3:6–11) and a private consummation (4:1–5:1).

The Wedding Day

I. INTRODUCTION

Marriage Versus Cohabitation

*W*eddings and marriage for life are out! Cohabitation, trial runs, and prenups are in. At least this is the picture you get if you listen to the prophets of popular culture.

Monica Schmidt: "It's just a piece of paper to me. I consider myself married without that . . . There's more freedom; I'm allowed to do whatever I like."

John Nielsen: "It's outmoded. I'm just as committed to the relationship as I would be if I were married." Claiming to be emotionally abused from his parents, divorced, and now in therapy, John adds, "Anything that comes before my recovery has to go. If I'm not putting myself first, the children are not going to see someone who is looking after themselves."

Robin Hill, in a cohabiting arrangement: "I've got a life too. If I thought 'Oh, this isn't doing anything for me,' I'd move on." When asked about a wedding and marriage, she joked, "I thought 'well, we do need a new toaster!' but I can't see the need to be married" (Bettina Arndt, "Cohabitors: The New Breed, *The Age,* Australia, 7 December 1999).

Aline Fesquet and Frank Embert, who entered into a "civil solidarity pact" in France: "For us, it is a step forward in our relationship, but without the family and all the baggage" (Suzanne Daley, "French Couples Take Plunge That Falls Short of Marriage," *New York Times,* 18 April 2000, 1A).

The numbers would certainly indicate that cohabiting is the rage of the day. The number of cohabiting couples has risen from 439,000 in 1960 to 4.2 million in 1998 (Debra Gaskill, "Shacking Up Strikes Out," *Kettering–Oakwood Times,* Dayton, Ohio, 2 May 2000). With so many couples adopting this new lifestyle, it must be producing some really good results, right? Wrong. Consider the following data:

1. Only about one-sixth of live-ins last at least three years, and only one-tenth endure five years or more (Karen S. Peterson, "Wedded to Relationship but Not to Marriage," *USA Today,* 18 April 2000).

2. Living together before marriage increases the risk of divorce. One study found an increased risk of 46 percent. Living together outside marriage increases the risk of domestic violence for women and the risk of physical and sexual abuse for children. One study found that the risk of domestic violence for women in cohabiting relationships was double that in married relationships; the risk is even greater for child abuse. Unmarried couples have

lower levels of happiness and well-being than married couples (David Pope-noe, "Cohabitation: The Marriage Enemy," *USA Today*, 28 July 2000).

3. Couples who live together first are more likely to have an affair during marriage than those who don't (Brian Holman, "Co-habiting First May Not Improve Marriage," *Scripps Howard Foundation Wire*, 5 August 2000).

4. Cohabiting couples are three times more likely to say "hitting, shoving, and throwing things" occurred between them and their partner the previous year (CMFCE@smarriages.com). Pamela Smock summarized the situation well:

> While common sense suggests that premarital cohabitation should offer couples an opportunity to learn about each other, increasing their chances for a successful marriage, the evidence suggests just the opposite. Premarital cohabitation tends to be associated with lower marital quality and increased risk of divorce ("Living Together: Facts, Myths, About 'Living in Sin,'" Ann Arbor, 4 February 2000).

So what is the problem? Rita DeMaria hit the nail on the head when she said, "Being single is a choice that most people do not choose. People want to be married." However, "some people have never seen a good marriage" (Murray Dubin, "A Mission to Remedy Marriage," *Philadelphia Inquirer*, 6 August 2000).

For far too many people, their perspective on marriage can be summed up 1, 2, 3. First comes the *engagement* ring, then comes the *wedding* ring, and then comes the *suffering*. Perhaps the "case against marriage" is really not too hard to understand, given what some people have seen and experienced. This radical skepticism toward God's divine plan was pointedly addressed by Larissa Phillips in an article titled "The Case Against Matrimony: If Marriage Is Risky, Doomed and Expensive, Why Bother?" It is lengthy, but the message is worth hearing. She wrote:

> The National Marriage Project at Rutgers University recently announced the findings of a new study: the marriage rate has dropped 43 percent since 1960, and increasing numbers of young people are choosing to stay unmarried. The U.S. Census Bureau came out with related big news last week: The number of babies born to unwed parents has increased fivefold since the 1930s, owing, for the most part, to more and more couples rejecting marriage, even after the birth of a child. Suddenly everyone is scrambling to understand. Well, I get it, and I didn't have to scramble to understand.
>
> In fact, what interests me is not why the members of my generation (X, if you will) are getting married less, but why anyone is surprised. What did everyone—i.e., the baby boomers—expect? As the unmarried mother of a new baby, I am the object of much indignant

scrutiny among the older generations, who seem to have conveniently forgotten the past 30 years, in which almost everyone I know has been emotionally pummeled in some way by divorce. As my boyfriend asked at a recent family gathering, while playing a board game in which you have to prompt the other players to supply a particular word: "What must you do before you get married?" The answer, of course: get divorced. My father and his wife thought this was hilarious. And yet aging boomers seem shocked and befuddled that someone would choose to avoid the whole swampy mess of broken vows and failed traditions that they've left in their wake.

People over 40 flinched with disdain when I first announced my pregnancy. "Oh," they would exclaim, barely masking their disapproval. "And . . . what do your parents think?" They struggled to understand my lack of panic. "Are you going to keep it?" they asked, wide-eyed. As if the '60s, '70s and '80s never happened. As if at least one-third of marriages don't fail. As if everyone in my family and my boyfriend's family, grandparents included, hadn't broken their marriage vows. At least once. "What's with all these people in our family having babies without getting married?" my middle-aged uncle (who is divorced and recently broke up with his live-in girlfriend) asked my 40-ish aunt (who recently divorced her husband because he'd taken up with a married woman, who is now his third wife; my aunt is now living with her boyfriend). The worst is from my parents. "Marriage is very important," my mother said. "It establishes a bond that you just can't get otherwise."

I wanted to argue with her, but she was getting ready to leave the country with her new husband. They spend their summers at their cottage up in Nova Scotia, a good 20-hour trip away from the rest of us. "Studies show that married couples are better off financially than single people," my father's youngish second wife insisted. It's probably true that she is better off financially since marrying my father, but I wasn't sure how that applied to me. When my boyfriend and I looked into getting married, we found out that we would pay an extra $2,000 each year in taxes. If marriage is risky, doomed and expensive, well, why bother?

"You just should," my father offered in that magnanimous, ain't-life-grand manner he developed shortly after re-entering the singles scene when I was a teenager. My father is big on the "shoulds" of life, with some reason. He has always done everything he was supposed to, even as a divorced father; he never even bad-mouthed my mom (nor did she ever trash him, for that matter). But the fact that my parents divorced well—and they really did—doesn't grant them immunity from their actions. The fact that my uncles and aunts and grandparents and family friends felt they had absolutely no choice other than to divorce doesn't change the outcome. They still got divorced, all of them. They still showed my generation, by example and by forcing us to go along with their example, that marriage was something easily and amicably exited from.

Marriage, they said, was not that big of a deal. Premarital sex is fine. (Or at least that's what they implied when they presented their boyfriends and girlfriends at the breakfast table—before we were even out of high school.) Families, they said, do not need to stay together if things become too boring. I would have more sympathy for divorced people if their lives had improved by getting out of terrible marriages that (apparently) couldn't be survived for another moment. But the ones I'm familiar with continue to associate with flawed human beings. These second and third marriages still seem to require work, and still have shortcomings.

My mother and father, for example, still struggle with the same issues that plagued their marriage to each other. The only difference is, older and wiser, they both seem more willing to compromise, to sacrifice and to accept. I am not whining about or regretting the events of the last three decades. When my parents divorced in the late '70s, we children went along with it like troopers. When they started bringing home boyfriends and girlfriends in the '80s, we ultimately accepted these new people into our family. Sometimes, the new people went away. And we dealt with the divorces and separations all over again. And accepted the new people all over again.

Fine. Exhausting, but fine. It's a wonder we 18- to 35-year-olds even have the energy to date. (And maybe some of us don't.) But for myself, the scattered, patchwork concept of family I grew up with has only increased my quest for commitment. I've seen firsthand the pain and futility of divorce culture and I don't intend to relive it, or to drag my children through the nightmare of watching their parents flirt with strangers.

My decision not to marry does not indicate a desire for a life of debauchery and half-formed commitments. Quite the opposite . . . but we have no fantasies about coasting through the next 50 years on the coattails of a weakened and disparaged contract that, thanks to boomer innovation, now includes options like pre-nup clauses. Considering everything we've seen, bearing the weight of our relationship on our own backs seems a lot wiser than leaning on the white-laced and satin-cummerbunded follies of our parents. Thanks, but we're looking for more than just a party, a round of toasts and a validity stamp from Uncle Sam to get us to that golden anniversary.

Our parents, on the other hand, seem to believe in marriage more than they do in monogamy. Like I said, that's fine. Every generation has its torch to carry. But when this particular generation, which grooved to its own beat and stomped on every tradition that seemed too square, too inhibiting or just plain boring, turns around with nostalgia in its eyes and questions my choices, I have to protest. My generation would just as soon steer clear of the fatuous, feel-good mess of getting divorced and remarried. The tradition that was passed down to us—in which divorce is a logical and expected conclusion to a marriage—is one we would just as soon pass by. . . . Of course marriage is on the decline. But don't blame us. The boomers started it (Larissa Phillips, "The Case Against Matrimony," *Salon*.com, 18 November 1999).

We could easily get depressed from all of this until we realize that there is a common thread that runs through all the stories we have heard. It could be put in the form of a simple question: Where is God in all of this? He doesn't even get "honorable mention." Marriage, after all, was his idea. He has a pattern. He has a plan. Marriage can be different when we invite the holy Trinity to honor the wedding and direct the marriage. Our expectations, hopes, and dreams can and will be radically altered and transformed, and all for the better.

In this study the focus is on what begins a marriage: the wedding. This is what is described in Song of Songs 3:6–11. It is a beautiful scene. There are some distinctive characteristics and elements of the wedding God has planned for each of us. God's Word addresses four things in this text.

 ## II. COMMENTARY

The Wedding Day

> **MAIN IDEA:** *A Christian wedding should involve celebration and commitment.*

🄰 A Great Wedding Will Be a Public Celebration (3:6)

> **SUPPORTING IDEA:** *A wedding is to be a time of joy and happiness.*

A wedding should be one of the most exciting and important days in any person's life. It should not be entered into lightly or without careful consideration. God's plan is that you experience it only once unless death parts you and your spouse. It legitimately should be a time of joy and laughter, happiness and hope. Solomon notes two facets of a public celebration.

1. A wedding is a time that should be special.

3:6. Marriages in the Ancient Near East were civil rather than religious affairs. Most often they took place in a home. A central aspect of the wedding ceremony was a procession to the bride's home led by the groom. He would go and gather her to himself, then escort her back to their new home where the actual wedding ceremony would take place. The wedding feast sometimes would last up to a week. The marriage, however, would be consummated on the first night. The marriage was a special ritual in which the man publicly pledged himself to his bride and she to him.

Solomon and his entourage went to Shulammite's home to get her. The pageantry and procession would honor Shulammite and appropriately sanctify the day in all of its significance. The wedding day is not just another day. It is a once-in-a-lifetime event. It is indeed special.

2. A wedding is a time to make a statement.

Solomon wanted the world to know how much he loved this woman. As Shulammite came out of the wilderness and into the city, columns **of smoke** appeared to accompany her. We learn, however, that it was actually **myrrh and incense** mingled with **the spices of the merchant**. The burning of these spices would appeal to the senses of sight and smell. These spices also would have been costly. This day would be the beginning of their new life together. Their commitment to each other was strong and secure. The celebration—and even the extravagance—of the procession was appropriate for such an important occasion. They intended to make a statement.

Without being opulent and ostentatious, a wedding should be a celebration. It should be festive but also spiritual. It should be a public testimony of the value we place on our mate and the worth of his or her companionship. It is not God's plan that it take place quietly behind closed doors. It is a public affair!

B A Great Wedding Contains a Promise of Protection (3:7–8)

SUPPORTING IDEA: *A wedding involves a promise of one life to another.*

When Solomon came for Shulammite, he did not come alone. He brought his companions. He brought his best. An escort of striking presence accompanied him. They enabled Solomon to make two statements about the marriage he and his bride would enjoy.

1. Marriage provides safety.

3:7. The **sixty warriors, the noblest of Israel** were friends of the groom. They were Solomon's closest and most trusted confidants. Most likely they were his royal bodyguard, whose duty it was to protect the king and his family. By their presence they served as a pledge of safety from Solomon to Shulammite. They were warriors of the nation Israel. They surrounded Solomon's "royal litter" or **carriage**. She was safe under his protective care and concern. He would spare nothing to assure her heart and mind that she would be well taken care of.

2. Marriage provides security.

3:8. The sixty warriors were **experienced** and skilled. Shulammite could put to rest any fears that might trouble her heart. They had their weapons and were experienced in the affairs of battle. Even at night when evil and wicked persons were especially active to do their shameful deeds, she could be at peace that all was safe and secure. Her man would see to it. He would be her champion and defender.

This marriage was no shaky situation with nagging doubts and unanswered questions. Shulammite was not marrying some cad who would abuse her. She was marrying a man who would love and protect her.

Tommy Nelson provided a helpful word at this point in the context of the wedding ceremony:

> Part of the safety and security of the wedding ceremony will be evident in the people who serve as your best man, maid or matron of honor, groomsmen, and bridesmaids. Choose godly people who will support you fully in the vows you make. As a whole, those who witness your marriage should be like a holy hedge of protection around you, keeping you focused toward each other inside the circle of matrimony, and keeping out anybody who might try to destroy your marriage.
>
> Don't ask someone to stand up for you who isn't completely committed to you, to your marriage, and in general, to the sanctity and value of marriage. Such a person will not encourage you to work through problems in your marriage. Such a person will not do the utmost to help you and your spouse when you need help. And they may embarrass you at rehearsal dinner! (Nelson, 76).

C A Great Wedding Includes a Pledge of Commitment (3:9–10)

SUPPORTING IDEA: Commitment *is the key word missing in too many marriages today.*

The missing word in cohabiting relationships is the *c* word: *commitment*. When a man and woman come together to say the "I do's," commitment envelopes each and every vow. There is a pledge of physical, spiritual, emotional, and personal commitment. In particular, two things are said in this text.

1. All that I have belongs to you.

3:9–10a. The **carriage** in which Solomon brought Shulammite to their wedding was fine. It was made of the very best materials money could buy. The **wood** was **from Lebanon**. The timbers from those forests were in great demand throughout the Ancient Near East (Carr, 111). It was from this wood that Solomon had carved his "sedan chair" or carriage. Added to this were **posts . . . of silver**; a **base of gold**, and a **seat . . . with purple**. All of this was exquisitely beautiful and expensive. It was Solomon's way of saying, "I will keep nothing back from you. All I have now belongs to you. You will always get my best."

Today, sometimes even in marriage, all that we have is not shared with our mate. In 1999, I was sad to learn that the best-selling book in Amazon.com's marriage category was *How to Write Your Own Premarital Agreement*. It is a book on prenuptial contracts. A publicist at Source books, where they hang a congratulatory plaque, said, "Kind of funny, isn't it? We put out all these books on love and marriage, and this is the bestseller" (Kathy Kristof, "Love and Marriage and Money," *L.A. Times,* 14 September 2000).

A wedding that honors God and our mate does not come with strings attached or things held back. If you are not confident that your potential mate is worthy of all that belongs to you, perhaps you should reconsider your potential mate and why you are even thinking about marrying this person in the first place.

2. All of my love belongs to you.

3:10b. The interior of Solomon's carriage was unusual. It was "paved with love by the daughters of Jerusalem" (NKJV). No more precious materials could have been used. Some students of the Bible believe mosaics depicting love adorned the interior of the carriage. Duane Garrett suggested that "inlaid with love" alludes to an association between "sedan chair" and "bed" and is a subtle hint at their approaching wedding night (Garrett, 402). Whatever is true of the particular details, the main point is clear: they loved each other, and they pledged that love to each other at their wedding.

D A Great Wedding Has the Approval of Others (3:11)

SUPPORTING IDEA: *Make sure those who know you and love you are supportive of your marriage.*

Sociologist Barbara Dafoe Whitehead has said, "Courtship is dying, lasting marriage is in crisis . . . kiss marriage goodbye. . . . Today it's hookup, breakup and get even. Is everybody happy?" (*Manhattan Institutes City Journal,* Summer 1999). Newspaper columnist Suzanne Fields says in today's world women are not winning but losing, and losing big time. She directs our attention to the self-help section of our bookstores for a quick perusal of titles: *The Heartbreak Handbook; Getting Over Him; How to Heal the Hurt by Hating; Dumped: A Survival Guide for the Woman Who's Been Left by the Man;* and my personal favorite: The *Woman's Book of Revenge: Getting Even When "Mr. Right" Turns Out to Be All Wrong.*

You know, sometimes Mr. Right turns out to be Mr. Wrong. Cinderella turns out to be a Wicked Witch. Is there one last word of counsel that Solomon might give us to guide us away from such a disaster? Yes, and it is simply this: Make sure you have the approval and blessing of others. There is wisdom in the counsel of many.

1. Our friends will approve.

3:11. Notice that the **daughters** (or young women) **of Zion** came out to join in the celebration of the wedding. This is probably the same group identified as the daughters of Jerusalem elsewhere (cf. 1:5; 5:16). They approved. They were excited. In their mind this was a good and wonderful thing that was about to happen. They liked Solomon when he was with Shulammite. She brought out the best in him, not the worst, when they were together. The same was true for Shulammite. She was a better and more beautiful woman when she was with Solomon. That is a good sign for which we should be on the lookout. My mate makes me better, and others notice.

2. Our families will approve.

Solomon's **mother** approved of Shulammite. The potential for in-law problems did not loom over the wedding, as is too often the case. She had prepared for him a **crown** similar to an Olympian laurel wreath, which symbolized the gladness and joy of his wedding day. According to rabbinic tradition, crowns were worn by the bridegroom and the bride until the destruction of Jerusalem in A.D. 70 (Snaith, 57). This was a day of happiness not only for the king and his queen but for all who shared in this wonderful event. Those who loved Solomon and Shulammite most were confident this marriage was meant to be and meant to last. Their approval was no guarantee, but it was an indication of the confidence both family and friends had in the rightness of this union. This is something every wise couple will consider carefully as they work to have a great wedding and a great marriage.

MAIN IDEA REVIEW: *A Christian wedding should involve celebration and commitment.*

III. CONCLUSION

An Unusual Worship Service at a Baptist Seminary

On April 13, 2000, a very unusual thing occurred on the campus of a Baptist seminary in Wake Forest, North Carolina. Approximately 550 couples, hand in hand and heart to heart, reaffirmed their marriage vows in a worship service and signed a covenant pledging to "exalt the sacred nature and permanence of the marriage covenant." The vows, penned by Dr. Paige Patterson and his wife Dorothy, beautifully mirror the language of Ephesians 5:21–33 and are a wonderful expression of the covenantal commitment a husband and wife should pledge to each other on the day of their wedding. They also express the devotion and commitment that should characterize a marriage until death separates.

Husbands

My precious and honored wife, this day I renew before God my covenant with you. I covenant today, sacrificially to love you as Jesus loves his church. I covenant to bestow always upon you abundant honor. I will seek to know your needs and to provide for them materially, physically, mentally, and emotionally. I will seek your well-being, happiness and success above my own. Above all, I covenant to be the spiritual leader of our union, to provide a spiritual example through my walk with Christ, to teach the Bible, and to pray for my family, to lead family worship. I will be faithful to you physically, mentally, and emotionally and to avoid all that is pornographic, impure, or unholy. I will not be angry or bitter against you or allow the sun to go down on my wrath. I will not keep books on evil. I will cultivate tender affection for you both in private and in public. I will compassionately give to you my body and spirit in the union which we alone enjoy together. I covenant this day to accept the role of servant leader. And to be to my children and grandchildren, should God grant, a compassionate, encouraging, and guiding father. This day I seal this covenant for as long as we both shall live.

Wives

My precious and honored husband, this day I renew before God my covenant with you. I covenant this day to love and respect you with all the fervency of my being. I covenant to make our home a place of repose and comfort. I will honor you as the spiritual leader of our home. I will devote myself to you and the offspring God may give above all others. I will graciously submit to your servant leadership, never allowing the sun to go down on my wrath. I will not keep books on evil. I will regard my responsibilities as wife and mother as priority above all else except God. I will seek your well-being, happiness, and success rather than my own. I will compassionately give to you my body and spirit in the union that we alone enjoy together. This day I seal this covenant for as long as we both shall live (Melissa King, "Marriage Vows Renewed by the Pattersons and 1,100 Others at Southeastern Seminary, *Baptist Press,* 20 April 2000).

PRACTICAL PRINCIPLES AND APPLICATIONS

- A wedding is the public attestation of two becoming one.
- A wedding should be a time set apart—an event.
- A wedding should be a celebration and not an ordeal.
- A wedding involves personal commitment to a binding covenant on the part of the man and the woman.

IV. LIFE APPLICATION

Ten Practical Secrets for Staying Happily Married

1. *Dream a dream.* Develop a vision of everything you believe your marriage can be. Begin dreaming before the wedding.
2. *Be steadfast.* A happy marriage requires thoroughly committed partners.
3. *Build the trust factor.* Spouses in a solid relationship have complete faith and confidence in each other.
4. *Stay healthy.* A good marriage is encouraged by two emotionally, physically, and spiritually healthy people.
5. *Work on chemistry.* Maximize passion, romance, and affection. Be sensitive to each other's needs.
6. *Learn to talk.* Become good communicators.
7. *Never say die.* Conflict is inevitable, so learn to handle it productively, not fatally!
8. *Seek a mutually satisfying sexual relationship.* A great sex life results from and also builds intimacy in marriage.
9. *Get connected.* Recognize the important role of children and friends in making your marriage successful.
10. *Pursue spirituality.* Partners in great marriages find significance in their spiritual lives. Seek to grow in your walk with Jesus.

V. PRAYER

Dear Father, I want my wedding to honor and please you. Let my mate and me show others what a truly Christian wedding looks like. Help us to demonstrate our commitment to Jesus as Lord of our marriage. Help us to show our commitment to each other. Our marriage is for life. Divorce will not be an option. By your grace, may our marriage go the distance. In Jesus' name and for his glory I pray. Amen.

VI. DEEPER DISCOVERIES

Marriage Poems

There is only one other marriage poem in Scripture. It is Psalm 45. It is a seventeen-verse song of praise written also for the king on his wedding day. Most likely it was sung on more than one occasion, as would be the case with our text here in the Song of Songs. It would not have been unlikely or inappropriate for common people to have these texts sung or read at their weddings.

Like Song of Songs 3:6–11, Psalm 45 has messianic overtones (Ps. 45:6–7 is quoted in Heb. 1:8–9). It is not difficult to see similarities in both texts to the classic New Testament text on marriage found in Ephesians 5:21–33. Further, it is readily evident why God uses marriage as an analogy for the salvific relationship of Christ and the church. Jesus Christ, the Son of God, is not only the bride's groom; he is also her king. The parallels are too striking to be coincidental.

VII. TEACHING OUTLINE

A. INTRODUCTION: MARRIAGE VERSUS COHABITATION

B. COMMENTARY

1. A Great Wedding Will Be a Public Celebration (3:6)
   a. A wedding is a time that should be special.
   b. A wedding is a time to make a statement.
2. A Great Wedding Contains a Promise of Protection (3:7–8)
   a. Marriage provides safety.
   b. Marriage provides security.
3. A Great Wedding Includes a Pledge of Commitment (3:9–10)
   a. All that I have belongs to you.

    b.   All of my love belongs to you.

  4. A Great Wedding Has the Approval of Others (3:11)

    a.   Our friends will approve.

    b.   Our family will approve.

C. CONCLUSION:AN UNUSUAL WORSHIP SERVICE AT A BAPTIST SEMINARY

VIII. ISSUES FOR DISCUSSION

Love or Lust: What's the Difference?

LOVE

1. *Focuses on the other.* "Let each of you look out not only for his own interests, but also for the interests of others" (Phil. 2:4 NKJV).

2. *Leads to fulfillment.* "To know the love of Christ which passes knowledge; that you may be filled with all the fullness of God . . . who is able to do exceedingly abundantly above all that we ask or think, according to the power that works in us" (Eph. 3:19–20 NKJV).

3. *Brings satisfaction.* "No discipline seems pleasant . . . but . . . later . . . it produces a harvest of righteousness and peace for those who have been trained by it" (Heb. 12:11).

4. *Encourages self-control.* "I discipline my body and bring it into subjection" (1 Cor. 9:27 NKJV).

5. *Desires to live by the Spirit.* "Live by the Spirit, and you will not gratify the desires of the sinful nature" (Gal. 5:16).

6. *Includes Christ.* "Clothe yourselves with the Lord Jesus Christ, and do not think about how to gratify the desires of the sinful nature" (Rom. 13:14).

7. *Seeks God to gain its desires.* "Delight yourself in the LORD and he will give you the desires of your heart" (Ps. 37:4).

8. *Prevents sin.* "'Love your neighbor as yourself.' But if you bite and devour one another, beware lest you be consumed by one another" (Gal. 5:14–15 NKJV).

9. *Nourishes the soul.* "May God himself, the God of peace, sanctify you through and through. May your whole spirit, soul and body be kept blameless" (1 Thess. 5:23).

10. *Commits to each other* (free love is a contradiction in terms). "You . . . have been called to liberty; only do not use liberty as an opportunity for the flesh, but through love serve one another" (Gal. 5:13 NKJV).

LUST

1. *Focuses on self.* "You . . . have been called to liberty; only do not use liberty as an opportunity for the flesh" (Gal. 5:13 NKJV).

2. *Leads to frustration.* "You want something, but don't get it. You kill and covet, but you cannot have what you want" (Jas. 4:2).

3. *Continually wants more.* "They are . . . separated from the life of God . . . [and] have given themselves over to sensuality so as to indulge in every kind of impurity, with a continual lust for more" (Eph. 4:18–19).

4. *Enslaves self.* "To whom you present yourselves slaves to obey, you are that one's slaves. . . . You have presented your members as slaves of uncleanness, and of lawlessness" (Rom. 6:16,19 NKJV).

5. *Desires to gratify the sinful nature with things contrary to the Spirit.* "The sinful nature desires what is contrary to the Spirit. . . . The acts of the sinful nature are obvious: sexual immorality, impurity and debauchery; idolatry and witchcraft; hatred, discord, jealousy, fits of rage, selfish ambition, dissensions, factions and envy; drunkenness, orgies, and the like" (Gal. 5:17,19–21).

6. *Excludes Christ.* "Since they did not think it worthwhile to retain the knowledge of God, he gave them over to a depraved mind. . . . They have become filled with every kind of wickedness, evil, greed and depravity" (Rom. 1:28–29).

7. *Sins to gratify its desires.* "All of us also lived among them at one time, gratifying the cravings of our sinful nature and following its desires and thoughts" (Eph. 2:3).

8. *Entices with evil desires.* "But each one is tempted when, by his own evil desire, he is dragged away and enticed" (Jas. 1:14).

9. *Wars against the soul.* "I urge you, as aliens and strangers in the world, to abstain from sinful desires, which war against your soul" (1 Pet. 2:11).

10. *Avoids commitment and leads to tragedy.* "Don't lust for their beauty. Don't let their coyness seduce you. For a prostitute will bring a man to poverty, and an adulteress may cost him his very life" (Prov. 6:25–26 TLB).

(Dennis Rigstad, "Is It Love or Lust?" *Psychology for Living,* February 1988)

Song of Songs 4:1–5:1

The Wedding Night

I. **INTRODUCTION**
What the Bible Really Says About Sex

II. **COMMENTARY**
A verse-by-verse explanation of these verses.

III. **CONCLUSION**
The Lover's Quotient Test

An overview of the principles and applications from these verses.

IV. **LIFE APPLICATION**
A Sex Education Questionnaire

Melding these verses to life.

V. **PRAYER**
Tying these verses to life with God.

VI. **DEEPER DISCOVERIES**
Historical, geographical, and grammatical enrichment of the commentary.

VII. **TEACHING OUTLINE**
Suggested step-by-step group study of these verses.

VIII. **ISSUES FOR DISCUSSION**
Zeroing these verses in on daily life.

Quote

"*The* spiritual beauty of sexuality is seen in service,

lovingly meeting the physical desires and needs of our mate.

The spiritual meaning of a Christian's sexuality

is found in giving."

Gary Thomas

Song of Songs
4:1–5:1

IN A NUTSHELL

There is both beauty and blessing planned by God for the
Christian bedroom.

The Wedding Night

I. INTRODUCTION

What the Bible Really Says About Sex

*I*n an article titled "What They Didn't Teach You About Sex in Sunday School," Peggy Fletcher Stack wrote, "Many people assume the Bible has just one message about sex: Don't do it" (Religious News Service, 13 October 2000). Anyone who says this obviously has not read the Bible. God, in his Word, has a lot to say about sex—and much of it is good.

Sex as God designed it is good, exciting, intoxicating, powerful, and unifying. Although the Bible is not a book on sex, it does contain a complete theology of sexuality: the purposes for sex, warnings against its misuse, and a beautiful picture of ideal physical intimacy as set forth in the Song of Songs. The "one-flesh" relationship (cf. Gen. 2:24) is the most intense physical intimacy and the deepest spiritual unity possible between a husband and wife. God always approves of this relationship in which husband and wife meet each other's physical needs in sexual intercourse (cf. Prov. 5:15–21).

Paul indicates that sexual adjustment in marriage can affect the Christian life, especially prayer (cf. 1 Cor. 7:5; see also 1 Pet. 3:7). Both husband and wife have definite and equal sexual needs which are to be met in marriage (1 Cor. 7:3), and each is to meet the needs of the other and not his own (Phil. 2:3–5).

God gave us the good gift of sex for several important reasons. These purposes include: knowledge (cf. Gen. 4:1), intimate oneness (Gen. 2:24), comfort (Gen. 24:67), the creation of life (Gen. 1:28), play and pleasure (Song 2:8–17; 4:1–16), and avoiding temptation (1 Cor. 7:2–5).

A husband is commanded to find satisfaction (Prov. 5:19) and joy (Eccl. 9:9) in his wife and to concern himself with meeting her unique needs (Deut. 24:5; 1 Pet. 3:7). A wife also has responsibilities. These include availability (1 Cor. 7:3–5), preparation and planning (Song 4:9–16), interest (Song 4:16; 5:2), and sensitivity to unique masculine needs (Gen. 24:67). The feeling of oneness experienced by husband and wife in the physical, sexual union should remind both partners of the even more remarkable oneness which the spirit of a man and a woman experiences with God in spiritual new birth by faith in Jesus Christ (John 3).

There is beauty and blessing in the Christian bedroom. Here God says eat and drink deeply (Song 5:1). We have come to the wedding night. The bride and groom are alone with only God as the unseen but welcomed guest. Here before us the couple consummates their marriage in intimate sexual union.

Our passage, in exquisite poetry, provides for us a portrait of what a Christian bedroom can and should be.

II. COMMENTARY

The Wedding Night

> **MAIN IDEA:** *Sex is God's good gift to be enthusiastically enjoyed within the context of marriage.*

A Let It Be a Place of Satisfying Attractiveness (4:1–7)

> **SUPPORTING IDEA:** *Men and women should strive to meet each other's most basic and intimate needs in marriage.*

4:1–7. These verses are a song of admiration from the groom to his bride. The time for the sexual consummation of their marriage has arrived, and yet it will not be until verse 16 that this will happen. True romance is "an environment of affection" in which sexual union will occur more often and with greater satisfaction. In other words, there are some essential preliminaries before it is time for the main event.

Unfortunately, this is not always clear to a male. Having been aroused sexually, he is now on the prowl as a predator, and his bride can certainly feel the part of prey. Solomon was sensitive to this, and so he began with the most important sex organ we have: *the mind!* Thinking about how his new wife might feel, he chose first to cultivate an atmosphere of acceptance through carefully chosen words.

1. Men, meet your wife's need for verbal support.

4:1,7. Three times, both at the beginning and at the end of this song, Solomon told Shulammite she was **beautiful**. Twice he called her his **darling**. In verse 7 he says there is **no flaw in you**. In his eyes she was the perfect woman for him.

Women are verbal creatures. They are moved by what they hear and by what they feel. "To a great extent, she thinks and feels [about herself] the way a man leads her to think and feel" (Nelson, 89). A man must learn to touch her heart (her mind) through her ear. This helps her feel good about herself, and it relaxes, prepares, and motivates her to give herself in passionate lovemaking to her husband. A wise man will understand the value of words, the right words, in preparation for sexual intimacy.

A study in *Psychology Today* noted that women are more likely to be disappointed with marriage than men, especially in the context of romance. Why?

One explanation is that as compared with men, they have higher expectations for intimacy, and thus they react more negatively to conjugal reality. In a major national survey conducted in 1976 by the Institute for Social Research at the University of Michigan, more wives than husbands said they wished their spouse talked more about thoughts and feelings, and more wives felt resentment and irritation with husbands than vice versa.

The researchers conclude: "In marriage . . . women talk and want verbal responsiveness of the kind they have had with other women, but their men are often silent partners, unable to respond in kind" (Carlin Rubenstein, "The Modern Art of Courtly Love," *Psychology Today,* July 1983, p. 49). The way to a woman's heart is often through the ear. Solomon was sensitive to this, as every husband should be.

2. Women, meet your husband's need for visual stimulation.

4:1–6. If a woman is a creature of the ear, a man is a creature of the eye. He is moved by what he sees. Verses 1–6 are a continuation of Solomon's song of admiration as he praised eight different parts of his wife's body. This would continue to meet her need for verbal support, especially as we unlock the doors to the Ancient Near Eastern images we encounter. At the same time these verses also teach us something about the male and how visual he is when it comes to sex. A brief survey of these verses makes clear that Shulammite was not clothed in sweats, flannel, or burlap! Apparently, only a veil covered her eyes. The rest of her body was in full view, and Solomon liked—he loved—what he saw. Still, his patience and understanding were singularly remarkable. What an incredible example he sets for men everywhere.

4:1. Women in the Ancient Near East would wear a veil on the day of their wedding. Solomon said, **your eyes behind your veil are doves**. The veil both hid and enhanced her beauty. His likening of her eyes to doves conveys ideas of peace and purity, tranquility and tenderness, gentleness and innocence (cf. 1:15; 2:14; 5:2). Her eyes spoke; they communicated to her husband that she had been calmed and set at rest by his kind and affirming words.

The phrase **your hair is like a flock of goats descending from Mount Gilead** would probably not get a man very far in our day, but it would have been lovely music to the ears of Shulammite. Viewed from afar, a herd of black goats streaming or skipping down a mountainside as the sun glistened on their black hair was a beautiful sight. As Shulammite prepared to give herself to her husband, she let her hair down. Cascading down her neck and across her shoulders, her beautiful wavy locks enticed the sexual desires of Solomon. Mount Gilead was a mountain range east of the Jordan River and northeast of the Dead Sea. It was known for its fertile pastures. Shulammite was herself vigorous and fertile on this, their wedding night. Letting her hair down signaled to Solomon her readiness for him.

4:2–3. These verses focus on the beauty of her mouth. Her **teeth** were clean, bright, and white; none were missing. Her **lips** were **like a scarlet ribbon** (literally, "thread"). Indeed, her **mouth** was beautiful. It was beautifully shaped and enticing to her man. There is some question, because of the unusual Hebrew word used here for "mouth," whether Solomon had in view physical or verbal pleasures that came from her mouth. An either/or decision is unnecessary. "Her mouth is . . . a fertile oasis with lovely words flowing out of it—not to mention possible heavy wet kissing" (Snaith, 61). Both her lips and her words were prizes of pleasure.

Her brow or **temples** behind the veil are compared to **the halves of a pomegranate**. They blushed red with desire, and the sweetness of their fruit invited Solomon to kiss them. Pomegranates were considered an aphrodisiac in the ancient world. Attractive to the eye and sweet to the taste, the image appealed to the senses of sight and taste.

4:4. Her **neck** was like **the tower of David** constructed in layers with the shields and weapons of Solomon's warriors, his mighty men (cf. 3:7–8). She stood tall and graceful. She was neither cowed nor timid. Why should she be in the presence of a man who loved and admired her with such passion? The image "conveys a sense of unassailable strength. No man could conquer her, and her suitor is awed by the dignity she carries. Her love is a gift; it could never become plunder" (Garrett 1993, 405).

4:5–6. Verses 5 and 6 draw attention to Shulammite's **breasts**. First, they are compared to **twin fawns of a gazelle that browse among the lilies**. They were soft and attractive, tender and delicate, making her husband want to touch and caress them gently. Second, he describes them as two mountains: one a **mountain of myrrh** and the other a **hill of incense** (or frankincense). Both spices were expensive and used as perfume for the body and the marriage bed (Proverbs 7:17 informs us that the harlot perfumes her bed with myrrh, aloes, and cinnamon). Now the senses of sight and smell were aroused. So enraptured was Solomon that he desired to make love to his wife all night long: **until the day breaks and the shadows flee**.

Time and tenderness are essential twins for a sexually and romantically attractive bedroom. Here we see that slow, romantic foreplay is underway. Solomon visually and literally, I believe, undressed his bride. He praised her specifically and in detail for everything he saw. He gave before receiving. He was as much concerned, if not more so, for her pleasure and satisfaction as he was for his own. He was loving her as Christ has loved us (Eph. 5:25–33).

4:7. It is interesting to note that we do not know what Shulammite looked like. What we do know is what she looked like to Solomon. In his eyes she was **beautiful**, gorgeous; no one compared to her. This bedroom was a place of satisfying attractiveness to both Solomon and Shulammite.

Ⓑ Let It Be a Place of Sensual Anticipation (4:8–11)

SUPPORTING IDEA: *It is proper and honoring to God and our mate to anticipate sexual satisfaction from our mate.*

A recent survey states that humans are apparently the only creatures on the planet who see sex as fun, with the possible exception of dolphins and pygmy chimps (*U.S. News and World Report*, 4 August 1997, p. 62). I am not sure what to make of that, if anything. I do know we humans think about and anticipate the sexual experience, almost without exception. We give this area of life a lot of time and attention. People attend seminars like "Getting the Love You Want," "Resexing Marriage," "Resurrecting Sex: The Passionate Marriage Approach," "Marital Sex as It Ought to Be," and "Hot Monogamy."

Yes, we think and talk a great deal about sex, but far too often we do not understand it, at least not as God intended. The results of going our own way have not been pretty. Perhaps God has had it right all along. When it comes to sensual anticipation, what counsel do we receive from him?

1. Invite your mate to come to you.

4:8. Solomon's complete attention has been on his wife. There is only one first-person reference in the first seven verses (v. 6). Biblical sex will always be focused on one's mate before it looks to one's self. Then, and only then, is it the right time to take lovemaking to the next level. Solomon has called Shulammite his darling. Now he called her his **bride**. He called her to leave where she was and **come** to him. Lebanon was near her home. The other mountain ranges mentioned are in the general area as well.

The **lions' dens and the mountain . . . of the leopards** perhaps represent fears Shulammite may have had. Solomon did not charge her; he called to her. He did not demand; he invited. He invited her to leave her home and her fears behind. He would care for her. He would love her. She was his love, his darling. She was his bride, his wife. Five times in verses 8–12 Solomon referred to her as his bride. Sensual anticipation must be clothed with words of safety and security if it expects a warm reception. Solomon's invitation was beautifully delivered.

2. Indicate how your mate captivates you.

4:9. It would seem that Shulammite responded in a positive manner to Solomon's invitation. Solomon's words in verses 9–11 would seem to affirm this. He began by saying Shulammite had **stolen** or "ravished" his heart. Her love was so overpowering that he could not resist her. Her love had captured his heart, and he could not escape. Just a **glance** of her eye or seeing one link in her necklace sent him swooning out of control. She was enchanting, and he was powerless to resist her spell.

Solomon then said something that is very strange to our ears. He again called Shulammite his **bride**, but he also referred to her as his **sister**, something he would do no less than five times (cf. 4:9–10,12; 5:1–2). Again we must understand the use of the word in its historical context. In the Ancient Near East, *sister* was a term of affection and friendship. In addition to its literal meaning, it could indicate a close and intimate relationship that a husband and wife enjoyed. True lovers will also be true friends, even best friends. This is something Solomon understood quite well.

4:10. Repetition is often a wonderful teacher. In verse 10 Solomon again called Shulammite his **sister**, his **bride**. He told her that her love was **delightful** and that it was **more pleasing . . . than wine**. Wine is intoxicating and sweet, but it could not compare to this. He was drunk with love for her. Charles Spurgeon, the great British preacher of the nineteenth century, said her love was better than wine because it could be enjoyed without question, would never turn sour, would never produce ill effects, and produced a sacred exhilaration (cited in Patterson, 73).

Her smell also got Solomon's attention. The **fragrance** or scent of this woman was superior to "all spices" (v. 10 NKJV). For a man, sight is closely followed by smell in the sensual realm. Shulammite knew this, so she prepared herself in a way that would draw her man to her.

4:11. Verse 11 moves us into even greater sensual and romantic territory. Her **lips**, Solomon said, **drop sweetness as the honeycomb**, and **milk and honey are under your tongue**. The idea that a particular kind of kissing began in France is put to rest by this verse! Deep, wet, sweet, and passionate kissing is at least as old as this Song. Canaan was a land of milk and honey (cf. Exod. 3:8). It was a land of joy, blessing, and satisfaction that God graciously provided for the nation of Israel. It was a land of sweetness to a people who had been enslaved for over four hundred years. Solomon found immeasurable joy in the deep, long, and intimate kisses of his bride.

Besides smelling good herself, she also applied attractive fragrances to her clothes. Lebanon flourished with cedar trees (cf. 1 Kgs. 5:6; Pss. 29:5; 92:12; 104:16; Isa. 2:13; 14:8; Hos. 14:5–6). The fresh aroma of those mountain cedars filled the nostrils of Solomon as he undressed his bride and made preparation for lovemaking. Virtually all the senses—taste, touch, smell, sight, and sound—have played a role in this sensual symphony in this bedroom. The lovemaking that we enjoy will only be enhanced as we follow this example.

◖ Let It Be a Place of Specific Availability (4:12–15)

SUPPORTING IDEA: *Our virginity is one of the greatest gifts we can give to our mate.*

One of the greatest gifts a person can give his or her mate in marriage is exclusive and exciting sex. To enter marriage as a virgin is a precious treasure to bestow on our spouse. Unfortunately, it is also a far too rare treasure. The Bible is clear on the issue: any sex outside of marriage is sin in the eyes of God. This includes premarital sex, extramarital sex, or unnatural sex (homosexuality, bestiality, etc.). "Flee sexual immorality" (1 Cor. 6:18 NKJV) is God's command. Shulammite had listened to the voice of her God about her sexuality. Note the beautiful imagery Solomon used to describe his bride on their wedding night.

1. God is pleased when we keep ourselves pure.

4:12. Shulammite is described as **a garden locked up** and **a sealed fountain**. Each pictures her purity and virginity. She had sealed up herself for her husband. She had saved a precious treasure that belonged only to him. I have never known a woman, or a man for that matter, who regretted saving herself sexually for marriage. I have, however, known many who regretted not doing so. In particular, I think of a letter written to Josh McDowell years ago that probably expresses the regrets of many people who have been scarred by the sexual revolution.

> Dear Mr. McDowell,
>
> Having premarital sex was the most horrifying experience of my life. It wasn't at all the emotionally satisfying experience the world deceived me into believing. I felt as if my insides were being exposed and my heart left unattended. I know God has forgiven me of this haunting sin, but I also know I can never have my virginity back. I dread the day that I have to tell the man I truly love and wish to marry that he is not the only one—though I wish he were. I have stained my life—a stain that will never come out.

God is pleased, we are protected, and a mate is honored when we keep ourselves pure.

2. God is pleased when we give each other pleasure.

4:13–14. Solomon extended the imagery of the garden in verses 13–14, describing his bride as an exotic array of fruits, flowers, plants, trees, and spices. She was unique and valuable, rare and desirable. She was a fantasy garden, a lover's dream. To find **pomegranates, choice fruits, henna and nard, saffron, calamus, cinnamon, incense, myrrh, aloes,** and all the **finest spices** in one garden was unimaginable, and yet in his bride, he found them all. She would satisfy his senses of taste, sight, and smell. He could never be bored. He would enjoy the multiple pleasures discovered in this garden. Each time would be an exciting time, a new and different adventure.

4:15. Solomon now thinks of "his wife" as **a garden fountain, a well of flowing water streaming down from Lebanon**. To other men she was locked up, enclosed, and sealed. For her husband she was wide open, accessible, and available. Indeed, her love was overflowing and streaming for him. What she once held back from others she now gave to her husband with unreserved passion and abandonment. And why? Because she had saved herself for this day and this man. She was no casualty of sexual promiscuity. She did not have the wounds of a young twenty-one-year-old who said with pain and sadness in her voice, "I have had seventeen partners—too many, I think" (Patricia Dalton, "Daughters of the Revolution," *Washington Post*, 21 May 2000). Purity and pleasure go hand in hand when it comes to sex. Be specific in your availability. It is worth the wait.

D Let It Be a Place of Sexual Affection (4:16–5:1a)

SUPPORTING IDEA: *Richard Baxter, the great Puritan, was right when he said to a husband and wife, "Keep up your conjugal love in a constant heat and vigor."*

What do happy couples say about sex? *Reader's Digest* published an article that answers that question with the caption, "With a dash of surprise, a pinch of romance and a word or two at the right moment, love can be kept simmering even in the longest marriage." Adapting their list slightly and adding a couple of other suggestions, I think at least twelve things can be said.

1. They make sex a priority; it is important to them.
2. They make time for sex.
3. They stay emotionally intimate.
4. They know how to touch and what works.
5. They keep romance alive by meeting each other's needs.
6. They keep their sexual anticipation alive.
7. They know how to play and foreplay (both in and out of bed).
8. They know how to talk to each other.
9. They remain lovers and friends.
10. They maintain a sense of humor and know how to laugh.
11. They want to please each other.
12. They cherish each other as a sacred and precious gift of God.
    ("What Happy Couples Say About Sex," *Reader's Digest*, February 1989, pp. 13–16)

Shulammite and Solomon certainly intended to fall into the "happy couple" category when it came to their sex lives. For the first time in our passage, Shulammite speaks, and her words would have gotten her husband's attention immediately.

1. Encourage your mate to make love with you.

4:16. In beautiful and enticing poetry, Shulammite invited Solomon to make love to her. She who had been told twice not to awaken love until the right time (cf. 2:7; 3:5) now said, "The time is right. I am yours. Come and take me." North winds are strong and south winds more gentle. In lovemaking Shulammite wanted and needed both. She had been listening to every word spoken by her husband because she picked up on the imagery of the garden. She was that garden and her lover was welcome to come in and enjoy. She invited him, she guided him, she told him what she was feeling and what she wanted.

Great sex is the result of good communication. All the physiological parts fit when a man and woman come together, but sex is no mere mechanical union. It is a personal and spiritual union nurtured by careful communication. We cannot be certain of all that is meant by the imagery of coming to the garden and tasting the choice fruits. It is not difficult to imagine that many good things are intended.

2. Encourage your mate after love with you.

5:1a. The marriage has been consummated. The couple has made love. They were not disappointed. They had planned for it, saved themselves for it, studied up on it, and talked about it. All of their time and effort had been rewarded.

It is beautiful to note Shulammite invited Solomon to come to "his garden" in 4:16. Now in 5:1a he called her **my garden**. In fact, nine times in this one verse he uses the word *my*. Don't miss that it is used in this manner after, not before, their lovemaking. In tender words he called Shulammite his garden, his sister, and his bride. Coming in to her was indeed a garden delight. She smelled good, tasted good, and felt good; and he told her so. Their lovemaking had been good. It had been wonderful. She invited him to come to her, and he did. He no doubt hoped for many more times together just like this, and so he romantically and tenderly expressed the pleasure she had given him.

In a study by Susan Sprecher, a professor of sociology at Illinois State University, sexual satisfaction was greater in relationships in which partners initiated equally or in which women sometimes initiated sex. Why then do so many couples fall into the pattern of the man being the only one to suggest having sex? Sprecher and other sex researchers speculate that society's norms suggest that men should pursue and women should be pursued. The result may be that women tend to be less comfortable initiating sex. Or it may be that women tend to use subtle, indirect cues—which may not be consciously noticed—to initiate sexual activity, while men use more direct verbal requests and other measures. Women who initiate sex frequently are often very sexually satisfied to begin with, Sprecher believes, and this enables them to be more at ease about expressing their sexual desires.

A woman who initiates sex also often stimulates her partner's sex drive and his desire for her, which helps drive this entire pattern. Several studies have found that many men like it when their female partner initiates sex. Matt Sess, of New York City, says that he has always been the primary initiator in his relationship with Laura, his wife of eight years. "But when she initiates sex, it's definitely a turn-on," he says. "It doesn't happen a lot, but when it does, it's a pleasant surprise" (Julie Walsh, "Who's Lighting the Fire?" *WebMD Medical News,* 16 March 2000).

No doubt Solomon found Shulammite to be something of a "turn-on," and he let her know it—a wise man, indeed.

E Let It Be a Place of Spiritual Approval (5:1b)

SUPPORTING IDEA: *God's gift of sex is an expression of his goodness and his grace. He delights in the activity of the believer's bedroom.*

5:1b. The last part of verse 1 has created quite a bit of interpretive discussion. Exactly who encouraged this man and woman in their lovemaking? Some believe it was the friends of the couple. However, the intimate knowledge of this speaker of all that had transpired in their bedroom would rule this out. Others believe it to be the voice of the wind again, personified from 4:16. Clearly it cannot be either Solomon or Shulammite since they are the ones being addressed.

Though his name never appears directly in the entire Song of Songs (but see 8:6), I believe the one who speaks here is God. He was the unseen but present guest in their bedroom. He had observed all that had happened this night, and he told us what he thought about it all.

1. Sex in marriage enjoys divine approval.

Eat, O friends, and drink; drink your fill (or "deeply"), **O lovers**. The love shared by Solomon and Shulammite, together with the gift of sex, was given to them by God. As Glickman observed:

> He lifts His voice and gives hearty approval to the entire night. He vigorously endorses and affirms the love of this couple. He takes pleasure in what has taken place. He is glad they have drunk deeply of the fountain of love. Two of His own have experienced love in all the beauty and fervor and purity that He intended for them. In fact, He urges them on to more. . . . That is His attitude toward the giving of

their love to each other. And by the way, that's also His attitude toward couples today (Glickman, 25).

Yes, God was there, and he was pleased with what he saw. "He sees the passion. He hears the sighs of delight. He watches the lovers as they caress one another in the most intimate places. He is witness to the fleshly, earthly sights, sounds, and smells. . . . God desires for us to rejoice in our sensuousness, to give in to it" (Dillow and Pintus, 17).

2. Spouses in marriage enjoy divine affection.

A term of tender affection flowed from the mouth of God as he looked upon the couple enjoying his good gift of sex. He called them **lovers** or **friends**. God loved them, and he loved what he saw. How foreign this is to the thinking of so many persons when they try to imagine what the Creator thinks about sex. He loves us, and he likes it when we are engaged in the passion of lovemaking within the covenant of marriage. It can truly be revolutionary and transforming when we accurately and correctly get the Creator's perspective.

We can become like a woman named Beth who said:

> Loving my husband can become an act of worship to God. As my husband and I lie together, satiated in the afterglow of sexual ecstasy, the most natural thing in the world is for me to offer thanksgiving to my God for the beauty, the glory of our sexual joy. I don't even think about what I am doing; my heart just turns to the Lord and offers praise. Truly his gift of sex is a wondrous thing (Dillow and Pintus, 19).

MAIN IDEA REVIEW: *Sex is God's good gift to be enthusiastically enjoyed within the context of marriage.*

III. CONCLUSION

The Lover's Quotient Test

Some men need a little assistance in preparing for romance, and so I have included an adaptation of Jody Dillow's "Lover's Quotient Test" for husbands and wives to take together. As you will see, I will advise you not to take the results too seriously but to take them seriously enough. The scale runs from 0 to 360. I confess that the first time I took it I made a 90. (You can look up the results yourself!) Since then, I have progressed to a 170 and recently a 220. Believe me, progress has been made in more than one area.

I was motivated to get to work after giving this silly test one time at a marriage conference in Lawton, Oklahoma. You see, the next night a beautiful and elegant woman in her late 40s or early 50s came up to me to tell me the score her husband had achieved on the test. Her pastor later told me this was perhaps the finest and godliest woman he had ever known. Well, her husband scored a 270! To this date (over ten years and two hundred fifty conferences later), that is still the highest first-time score I've seen recorded. As you might suspect by now, I am a rather playful person, and so I said, "Well, I have only one thing more to ask. Is he really that good?" I will never forget her response. She said, "Yes, he is. I am quite certain that I am married to the most wonderful man in all the world." And with those words she kindly and graciously walked away.

God spoke to my heart that night through that precious woman. I began to think: *Wouldn't it be wonderful, if someone were to ask my wife Charlotte, "Is Danny that good?" and with honesty and integrity she could say, "Yes, he is. I'm quite certain I am married to the most wonderful man in all the world." * Few things could be said about a man, a husband, that would be a greater honor than that. So guys, don't take the test too seriously, but do take it seriously enough. If you will, you will find that the beauty and the blessings of the Christian bedroom will be so much more than you would have ever imagined.

Lover's Quotient Test

We need to find out just how creative you are as a husband! Let's take the following Lover's Quotient Test. Give yourself ten points for each item on the following list if you have done it once in the past six months. If you have done any item on the list two or more times, you get twenty points. Don't take the results too seriously—but do take them seriously enough!

- Have you phoned her during the week and asked her out for one evening that weekend without telling her where you are taking her? A mystery date is what we have in mind!
- Have you given her an evening completely off? You clean up the kitchen; you take care of the kids; you get things settled for the night.
- Have you gone parking with her at some safe and secluded spot and kissed and talked for an evening?
- Have you drawn a bath for her after dinner? Put a scented candle in the bathroom, added bath oil to the bath, sent her there right after dinner, and then you cleaned up and put the kids to bed while she relaxed. (In order to get any points for this, you must also clean up the tub!)
- Have you phoned her from work to tell her you were thinking nice thoughts about her? (You get no points for this one if you asked her what was in the mail or what is for dinner!)
- Have you written her a love letter and sent it special delivery? (First-class mail will do.)
- Have you made a tape recording of all the reasons you have for loving her? Given it to her wrapped in a sheer negligee?

- Have you given her a day off? Send her out to do what she wants. You clean the house, fix the meals, and take care of the kids. (My wife says you ought to get thirty points for this one!)
- Have you put a special-effects recording of ocean waves on tape and played it while you had a luau on the living room floor? Other creative evening adventures may be substituted!
- Have you spent a whole evening (more than two hours) sharing mutual goals and planning family objectives with her and the children?
- Have you ever planned a surprise weekend? You make the reservations and arrange for someone to keep the children for two days. Tell her to pack her suitcase, but don't tell her where you are going (just be sure it's not the Super Bowl or the Final Four!). Make it someplace romantic.
- Have you picked up your clothes just one time in the past six months and put them on hangers?
- Have you given her an all-over body massage with scented lotion? (If not, why not?)
- Have you spent a session of making love to her that included at least two hours of romantic conversation, shared dreams, and much variety of approach and caresses?
- Have you repaired something around the house which she has not requested?
- Have you kissed her passionately for at least thirty seconds one morning just before you left for work or one evening when you walked in the door?
- Have you brought her an unexpected little gift like perfume, a ring, or an item of clothing?
- Have you replaced her old negligee?

This ridiculous test has been given to men all over the country. Let's see how your scores compare with theirs:

200–360: Lover. Awesome! You are the man! You undoubtedly have one of the most satisfied wives in the country. You are in the top 1 percent!

150–200: Good. Way to go! Very few make this category. You are a top-ten candidate! Your wife probably smiles a lot!

100–150: Average. This husband is the norm and usually not very exciting as a lover. You are steady, but there are not many fireworks in the area of romance from your wife's perspective.

50–100: Klutz. Boring! You can do better than this! Too many men score in this category. I hope you will begin to work to move up soon.

0–50: Typical Husband. Ouch! Sad! There is a huge difference between a "typical husband" and a "lover." The only reason your wife is still married to you is that she's a Christian. She has unusual capacity for unconditional acceptance (of you!), and there are some verses in the Bible that sustain her (adapted from Jody Dillow's "Lover's Quotient Test").

IV. LIFE APPLICATION

A Sex Education Questionnaire

There's a widespread misconception that in the wake of the sexual revolution, everyone knows the basics of human sexuality. A Christian wife wrote to a family magazine: "We were both virgins when we married, and I don't regret that for a minute. However, I thought my husband would know a lot more about sex than he does. How is it possible that he can be so clueless at times about what brings me pleasure?" (*The Healthy Marriage Handbook,* p. 85).

Answer the following questions to see how much you know about human sexuality (some questions can be answered with a simple "yes" or "no").

1. Can you properly and accurately describe the main sex organ of the male and female bodies? ❏ Yes ❏ No

2. Are you able to explain what orgasm is for both the man and woman and how it is achieved? ❏ Yes ❏ No

3. Do you sometimes become embarrassed when sex is being discussed, even in a wholesome manner? ❏ Yes ❏ No

4. Would you agree that a minister is usually the best qualified to teach sex education? ❏ Yes ❏ No   If not, then who? _____

5. When a father is asked a question about sex by his daughter, do you think he should answer it? ❏ Yes ❏ No

6. Are you ever ashamed of your interest in sexual matters?
❏ Yes ❏ No   Should you be? ❏ Yes ❏ No

7. In teaching or discussing sex education, do you give ample time to discussing the many wholesome ways of showing affection other than by kissing and petting? ❏ Yes ❏ No

8. Do you think sex education should continue after marriage?
❏ Yes ❏ No   Why? _____

9. Can people tell by your actions and your talk that you have a wholesome, reverent regard for marriage? ❏ Yes ❏ No

10. Could you turn to Scripture passages that discuss aspects of sex education? ❏ Yes ❏ No

11. As a parent, when do you instruct your children in sex education?

_____

12. How much should you tell a five-year-old when he asks where babies come from? _____

13. How can you guide your children toward wise, sexual standards?
_____

14. Why might a teenager dwell excessively on sex matters?
_____

15. What would you say is the main characteristic of true love?
_____

V. PRAYER

Dear Father, thank you for your gracious and good gift of sex. Thank you for designing it for maximum protection, pleasure, and partnership. Help me and my mate to honor your gift and to enjoy your gift! Each time we make love, help us to remember we do so with your approval and pleasure. In Jesus' name. Amen.

VI. DEEPER DISCOVERIES

Lebanon

Lebanon was famous for its great cedar trees. Today only patches of the once formidable forests remain. At one time Palestine contained vast forests, but never did it have anything like that of Phoenicia. Solomon contracted with Hiram, king of Tyre, to provide beams and paneling for building the temple in Jerusalem. The most noticeable aspect of cedar is its aroma. The odor is not offensive to humans, but insects resist it. Solomon found the smell of the cedars of Lebanon on the clothes of Shulammite pleasing and delightful (4:11).

Some of these cedar trees grow to heights of 120 feet, but most are 60 to 80 feet in height. The girth of some trees is 30 to 40 feet. Like the ancient olive trees in the garden of Gethsemane, some cedars of Lebanon are thought to be about 2,000 years old.

The cedars of Lebanon not only furnished timbers and paneling for building purposes; they also were a symbol of strength, splendor, longevity, and glory. Ezekiel compared the king of Assyria to a great cedar of Lebanon (Ezek. 31); David indicated the cedars of Lebanon to be an example that caused the powerful voice of God to break (Ps. 29); the cedars of Lebanon are listed among other items like the oaks of Bashan that are lofty and lifted up (Isa. 2:13); in a lamentation, Ezekiel included the cedars as a point of boastfulness which would cause the downfall of Tyre (Ezek. 27:32); other references appear in Psalm 80:10; Song 1:17; Isaiah 33; Jeremiah 22:15; and Zechariah 11:1.

The Lebanese today think much of their cedars. They have made them their national symbol. They are the monarchs of the evergreens.

VII. TEACHING OUTLINE

A. INTRODUCTION: WHAT THE BIBLE REALLY SAYS ABOUT SEX

B. COMMENTARY

1. Let It Be a Place of Satisfying Attractiveness (4:1–7)
    a. Men, meet your wife's need for verbal support.
    b. Women, meet your husband's need for visual stimulation.
2. Let It Be a Place of Sensual Anticipation (4:8–11)
    a. Invite your mate to come to you.
    b. Indicate how your mate captivates you.
3. Let It Be a Place of Specific Availability (4:12–15)
    a. God is pleased when we keep ourselves pure.
    b. God is pleased when we give each other pleasure.
4. Let It Be a Place of Sexual Affection (4:16–5:1a)
    a. Encourage your mate to make love with you.
    b. Encourage your mate after love with you.
5. Let It Be a Place of Spiritual Approval (5:1b)
    a. Sex in marriage enjoys divine approval.
    b. Spouses in marriage enjoy divine affection.

C. CONCLUSION: THE LOVER'S QUOTIENT TEST

VIII. ISSUES FOR DISCUSSION

Seven Questions About Marriage

1. Have you faced the myths of marriage with honesty? Myths can include that both partners expect the same thing out of marriage—"everything bad in my life will disappear"—or, "my spouse will make me whole."
2. Can you identify your love style? The word *love* can mean different things to people, often translated into an emphasis on passion, intimacy, commitment, words, or service.
3. Have you developed the habit of happiness? Happy couples are that way because both partners *decide*—they make a decision—to be happy, regardless of their circumstances. They trust God in good times and bad times.

4. Can you say what you mean and understand what you hear? Good communication, not just talking, can make the difference in whether a marriage thrives, just survives, or dies.
5. Have you bridged the gender gap? Men are from Mars; women are from Venus. Actually, men are from earth and women are from Earth. Understanding differences is the key.
6. Do you know how to fight a good fight? Conflict is inevitable, but knowing how to "fight fair" is critical.
7. Are you and your partner soul mates? Marriage thrives when the spiritual dimensions of both participants are nourished (adapted from "Saving Your Marriage Before It Starts" by Les and Leslie Parrott).

Song of Songs 5:2–8

A Bad Night in the Bedroom

Quote

"*L*ove is a heart that moves . . . away

from the self and toward the other."

Dan Allender and

Tremper Longman III

Song of Songs
5:2–8

I N   A   N U T S H E L L

A bad night in the bedroom may be unavoidable, but it need not be fatal. Sensitivity to the needs of the other (Phil. 2:3–5) is the key to navigating this marital minefield successfully.

A Bad Night in
the Bedroom

I. INTRODUCTION

The Best Sex Is Married Sex

"*L*awyers can't cope as divorce epidemic sweeps the United Kingdom," reported the *London Observer* (9 January 2000). An outbreak of "matrimonial millennial madness" led one of Britain's leading divorce law firms, Lloyd Platts & Co., to refuse to take on any new clients. Said Vanessa Lloyd Platts, "If couples continue to separate at the current rate, there won't be anybody left to divorce in 10 years." Feminist writer Natasha Walter argued, "This means people don't want to put up with second best anymore! Marriage isn't keeping up with the way we conduct our relationships and what I see much more of is that a lot of men and women are looking for love but not necessarily within the framework of one partner for life."

Julia Cole, a spokesperson for *Relate,* said the beginning of a new century had prompted a new scrutiny of relationships. Sexual problems, always uppermost in people's minds . . . seem especially widespread. "There is an expectation that along with the perfect lunch, the perfect presents, the perfect New Year's Eve, there will be lovely, perfect sex. The contrast between expectations and reality is often enormous" (*London Observer,* 9 January 2000).

Obviously, far too many people are experiencing significant disappointment with their marriage, and problems often find their way into the bedroom. However, most problems in a marriage do not *begin* in the bedroom, but many problems in a marriage do *end up* in the bedroom. No marriage will be all that God intended if the intimate life is not meaningful, satisfying, and enjoyable.

Proverbs 5:18 says, "Let your fountain be blessed, and rejoice with the wife of your youth" (NKJV). Notice it did not say "only in your youth"! In February 1999, the *National Health and Social Life Survey* completed what was identified as the most comprehensive study of American sex lives ever. The results were published in the *Journal of the American Medical Association* with some interesting findings (*World Magazine,* 27 February 1999).

1. Sexually active singles have the most sexual problems and get the least pleasure out of sex.
2. Men with the most "liberal attitudes about sex" are 75 percent more likely to fail to satisfy their partners.

3. Married couples by far reported the happiest satisfaction with their sex lives.
4. The most sexually satisfied demographic group of them all: married couples between fifty and fifty-nine!

Oh, but the news gets even better. A November 29, 1999, news release noted that when University of Chicago researchers set out to discover which religious denominations have the best sex they learned that the faithful don't do all their shouting in church. Conservative Protestant women, their 1994 survey found, report by far the most orgasms: 32 percent say they achieve orgasm every time they make love. Mainline Protestants and Catholics lagged five points behind. Those with no religious affiliation were at 22 percent.

So, *Newsweek* may run a story that asks: "Was it virtually good for you? Sex: the best lovemaking of your life is now just a few nanobots and a body suit away," touting the virtues of techno, virtual-reality sex (*Newsweek,* 1 January 2000)! And *Cosmopolitan* may challenge us with "Cosmo's 20 Favorite Sex Tips Ever" (*Cosmopolitan,* January 2000). But if you really are interested in the best sex possible, based on the data, find yourself a born-again mate and keep him or her around into his or her fifties and beyond because the best is yet to come!

Still, it is often the case that too many couples are suffering the hurt and disappointment of too many bad nights in the bedroom. When those bad nights come, what do we do? How should we respond? Might I offer a suggestion: let's *follow the Bible, God's Word.* Let's allow God to provide guidance on how we can avoid bad nights in the bedroom.

II. COMMENTARY

A Bad Night in the Bedroom

> **MAIN IDEA:** *Understand what causes bad nights in the bedroom and find ways to avoid repeat performances.*

A Understand the Desire for Love May Fail Because of Bad Timing (5:2)

> **SUPPORTING IDEA:** *A man must understand a woman's need for time and affection.*

5:2. Shulammite, Solomon's wife, was in bed. Perhaps she was dreaming or half awake, tossing and turning out of anxiety and disappointment. Many view this as possibly another dream. The issue is quite simple: he was late again. The flow of the text hints that she may have been hoping for, or expecting, a night of romantic intimacy with her love, her husband. However, he was out again and he was late in returning home. Why, we are not told. Her desires had been dashed. Why did this happen?

1. Work may cause the problem.

The Bible says his head was **drenched with dew**, and his hair **with the dampness of the night**. This is an example of Hebrew parallelism. The point is clear. It was late, near or after midnight. Perhaps he had to work late. This is not unlikely. After all, Solomon was the king of Israel. Struggling to make things come together in the tough, cruel world of a king required long, hard days. Sometimes those days turned into nights. Time is, and has always been, our most precious commodity. You can only spend it *one time* and at *one place*. On this particular evening, *work* won out over the *wife*, and the stage was set for a confrontation, a showdown in the bedroom.

2. Words may not cure the problem.

In the Ancient Near East, it was often the custom for a husband and wife to occupy separate bedrooms. Solomon had come home and was tired, but he was not too tired. He was, after all, a man. The fact is he was probably in need of both emotional and physical support and intimacy with his wife after a long, hard day. This is how God has wired a man.

A study notes that for men the secret of a happy marriage is emotional support and an active sex life. Women, though, would just like their husbands to take more interest in them. Women said they just wanted their husbands to take a greater interest in their opinions and a more active role in their social lives. Marriage counselor Sheron Li Yuet-Yi said, "Sex plays an essential role in building up a successful marriage. We have seen newlyweds who do not have any idea how to do it and we have seen some middle-aged couples who are either too lazy or too tired" (*South China Post*, 16 November 1999). Sometimes things just don't come together in the bedroom as we had hoped.

Solomon's approach with his wife was gentle and sensitive. Perhaps he sensed some tension. A locked door to the bedroom might tip a guy off! Note his four names of affection and the four uses of the possessive pronoun "my":

- **My sister** (cf. 4:9) emphasized their friendship and the permanency of their relationship.
- **My darling** (cf. 1:9; used nine times and always by Solomon) spoke of the one in whom he delighted and took pleasure. It is often used in the context of acknowledging her beauty.
- **My dove** (cf. 2:14) was perhaps a pet name. It described her gentleness.
- **My flawless one** means my "perfect" or "blameless" one—the one whom I know is wholly mine and no other's.

Solomon was *sincere* in his compliments and words of praise. Of course, this is not always the case with husbands, and our wives can become experts in deciphering some of our "code" phrases. A radio station in Louisville had some fun at male expense when they talked about "what men really mean when they say . . ."

- "It's a guy thing" really means: "There is no rational thought pattern connected with it, and you have no chance at all of making it logical."
- "Can I help with dinner?" really means: "Why isn't it already on the table?"
- "Uh-huh," "Sure, honey," or "Yes, dear" really means absolutely nothing; it's a conditioned male response.
- "It would take too long to explain" really means: "I have no idea how it works."
- "We're going to be late" really means: "Now I have a legitimate excuse to drive like a maniac."
- "Take a break, honey, you're working too hard" really means: "I can't hear the game over the vacuum cleaner."
- "That's interesting, dear" really means: "Are you still talking?"
- "That's women's work" really means: "It's difficult, dirty, and thankless."
- "We share the housework" really means: "I make the messes; she cleans them up."
- "You know how bad my memory is" really means: "I remember the theme song to *F Troop,* the address of the first girl I ever kissed, and the vehicle identification number of every car I've ever owned, but I forgot your birthday."
- "Oh, don't fuss. I just cut myself. It's no big deal" really means: "I have severed a limb but will bleed to death before I admit I am hurt."
- "Hey, I've got my reasons for what I'm doing" really means: "And I sure hope I think of some pretty soon."
- "I can't find it" really means: "When I look in the refrigerator, I can't move the milk jug because if the ketchup is not behind it, then the milk jug won!"
- "What did I do this time?" really means: "What did you catch me doing?"
- "I heard you" really means: "I haven't the foggiest clue what you just said, and I am desperately hoping that I can fake it well enough so you don't spend the next three days yelling at me."

Sometimes words—even our best ones—cannot overcome *bad timing* and prevent a bad night in the bedroom.

Ⓑ Understand the Details for Love May Feel Like Too Much Trouble (5:3)

SUPPORTING IDEA: *A woman must understand a man's need for sexual intimacy and pleasure.*

5:3. Shulammite was perhaps angry. She was certainly hurt. The most basic needs of her heart had not been met by her husband. Bob Turnbull in "What Your Wife Really Needs" reminds men that wives will dry up and wither on the inside without four things:

1. *Time.* The currency of a relationship; clearing space in your calendar for her says you are valuable to me.
2. *Talk.* This is how she connects with you. It is also one way in which she handles stress (men, on the other hand, walk or take flight).
3. *Tenderness.* It feeds her soul when she is nourished and knows she is cherished.
4. *Touch.* Nonsexual, affectionate touch is crucial to a wife, and if she only receives it as the pregame to sex, she will begin to feel used, like a marital prostitute (*Marriage Relationship,* Fall 1999).

Whether he meant to or not—and he probably didn't—Solomon failed this *4-T* test, at least in the eyes of his wife. This, however, did not justify how Shulammite responded, and her response was selfish and especially insensitive to the fragility of the male ego. An evening that once held promise for both the husband and the wife was about to go down the drain. What can we do to avoid this?

1. Guard against silly priorities.

Shulammite's response in twenty-first-century America would translate, "Not tonight; I have a headache" or "Not tonight; I'm too tired." Several Bible teachers note **I have taken off my robe** suggests she now lay naked, unclothed beneath the sheets. Is there perhaps a little dig hinting at "what you will miss because you stayed out too late"? In essence, Shulammite said, "My comfort is more important than your needs or desires. I waited; it's late. So sad. Too bad. If you can't get home at a decent hour, don't expect any special attention from me."

2. Guard against being a selfish person.

Washing the feet was an oriental custom before eating a meal or retiring for bed. Shulammite was washed up and ready for bed. It is implied that she had tired of waiting up for Solomon to come home. To have to get up, put on her clothes, and get her feet dirty was too much trouble. Self-centeredness is a deadly sin. It can and will destroy anything that gets in its path. It is also foolish because it never has an accurate picture of reality.

In this context let me address one new and specific danger to our marriages that has recently come on the scene. Computers are one of the marvelous inventions of the twentieth century. They have produced much good in many areas of life. Marriages, however, have suffered far too much from pornography, cybersex, and illusionary and unreal on-line romancing. In "Letters of the Century: America 1900–1999," 412 letters were compiled to show us something about our personal perspectives during the twentieth century. The very last letter selected came from the Shirley Glass AOL Electra Column. It was picked because it captured best the last decade and illustrated how the complexities of the computer age have changed us. It reads as follows.

> Dear Dr. Glass,
> I met a very interesting man on-line a couple of weeks ago, and have talked to him on the phone several times as well. He is enchanting, charming, and everything I could possibly want. The trouble is that I'm already married and all the way across the country from Mr. Wonderful. I really think I love this man, but what can I do?
> Sincerely,
> Confused and Charmed

Listen to Shirley's wise and direct counsel.

> Dear Confused and Charmed,
> Your "Mr. Wonderful" may be somebody else's philandering husband. Internet relationships create a romantic mystique because you can create exciting fantasies about the other person. Add a little dose of secrecy, emotional intimacy, and sexual innuendoes, and you've got a full-blown emotional affair. It is easy to be charming when you are not dealing with the everyday irritations of leaking roofs and noisy kids. The love that you feel for this man is based on romantic idealization, whereas your marriage is based on reality. Furthermore, stable long-term relationships are seldom as exciting as stage 1 (the honeymoon) relationships. What does your on-line search for companionship and romance indicate about your marriage? Talk to your husband about your wants and needs and try to put some energy back into your marriage.

Selfishness and self-centeredness are death to a relationship. They will never build up but only tear down. They are unrealistic. They are harmful. They are sin. Further, they result in regret. They are certain to produce a bad night in the bedroom and possibly many lonely nights as well.

◎ Understand the Denial of Love May Flower Only Temporarily (5:4–7)

SUPPORTING IDEA: *Sorrow and disappointment are certain to follow selfish and self-centered decisions in marriage.*

5:4–5. Six times in verses 2–8 Shulammite called Solomon her **lover** or "beloved" (NKJV). She had been angry with him, but she did love him. His tender words have worked their way into her heart. Now Solomon, being the typical male, followed up with one last advance. He gently placed his hand on the latch (the opening of the door). Because of the poetic, symbolic, and erotic nature of this book, numerous scholars have noted the male hand is sometimes used euphemistically for the sexual parts of a man (cf. Isa. 57:8,10; Jer. 5:31; 50:15). If this is so, the latch or opening corresponds most certainly to the female counterpart. What is the response to this kind, sensitive, and sensual overture?

1. You may reconsider saying no.

Her "feelings were stirred" for her husband. She was touched by his kindness. With the words, **I arose**, she moved into action. The "I" is emphatic. She now wanted to make things right. The **myrrh** was left by Solomon as a sign of his love and regret that things had gone sour, or on the hand of Shulammite who quickly prepared herself for the now-desired sexual rendezvous. She now felt a desire for marital intimacy with her husband.

It is tragic that in many marriages the bedroom becomes a war zone and a battlefield because wives are convinced their husbands always want sex, and husbands are convinced their wives like to say no as often as possible. A friend of mine who does marriage counseling told me about a woman who came to him who was having marriage problems. The issue was sex. It seemed to her that sex was all her husband was interested in, and he was constantly putting pressure on her for activity in that department. She was just about at the end of her rope, so she came looking for help.

My friend is an insightful and wise person, and he gave the woman an interesting assignment. He asked her to go back home and for the next week to become a "huntress" in her relationship with her husband. He told her to track him down again and again, several times a day if she could, and engage in sexual relations. He asked her to call him at the end of the week and tell him about the results of this plan. Well, my friend did not get a call at the end of the week. He received a phone call just two days later. The woman said, "I think your plan worked. My husband is lying over in the corner of our bedroom waving a white handkerchief! In fact, this whole day, when I come into a room where he is, he tries to get out as fast as he can!"

She went on to tell him that they both felt very foolish. They had, after fifteen-plus years of marriage, come to realize that their sexual appetites, though not identical, were quite similar and definitely compatible. He was always pressuring her because he thought she always wanted to say no. If he didn't turn up the heat, they would never have sex, he thought. She, on the other hand, was in the "resistance mode" because she thought having sex was all he ever wanted to do, and if she didn't say no at least some of the time, they would be having sex all the time. Better communication could have saved this couple many years of stress and hurt. Better communication can save us from these things as well.

2. You may reap from saying no.

5:6. Studies now offer preliminary evidence that actual physical changes occur during marital conflict. For example, marital conflict affects the heart rate. These studies also show that marital fights can weaken the immune system (especially in women), raise blood pressure, and speed up the heart rate. For women, simply discussing angry feelings can lead to these stressed-out body reactions. For men, the stress seems to be accompanied by the act of talking louder and faster or walking away in retreat. The greatest benefits regarding health and long life come to those who are happily married. Those who are happily married seem healthier overall than any other group.

Marital conflict indeed has the potential for suffering and sorrow in many areas. Our text addresses two.

He may walk. It has been well said, "More belongs to marriage than four bare legs in a bed." Though men like that idea, their needs run so much deeper. Yvonne Turnbull, in "What Your Husband Really Wants," notes four things a husband longs to receive from his wife:

1. *Being his cheerleader.* A man thrives on his wife's approval and praise.
2. *Being his champion.* A wife's respect and encouragement lift a man's spirit and his sense of self-worth.
3. *Being his companion.* A man wants his wife to be his best friend.
4. *Being his complement.* A woman is necessary to complete a man (*Marriage Partnership,* Fall 1999).

A single friend of mine says, "Being single makes for lonely nights but peaceful days." A married man longs for both *peaceful days* and *intimate nights.* If he does not receive them, he may walk away (withdraw) or even out of the relationship. Such was Solomon's response on this occasion. Shulammite sadly said, **I opened for my lover, but my lover had left; he was gone.**

He may not talk. Wounded males almost always go into a shell. Most husbands will not fight their wives physically or verbally. They walk and they won't talk. Marriage counselor Howard Markman said, "Men don't want to spend their lives fighting, so they start withdrawing; that's a typical pattern of development of marital distress." Shulammite's heart sank. She looked for Solomon but he was gone. She called but he did not answer. Men have not changed much in three thousand years.

3. You may regret saying no.

5:7. This verse is best taken symbolically of Shulammite's own disappointment in herself. It is hard to imagine the **watchmen** literally beating the queen. It is the pain she felt not from her mate but from *herself* and, I believe, from *God's Spirit*. If our spouse hurts us or wrongs us, we should give God some time to work in his or her heart. Shulammite responded not from a tongue-lashing by Solomon but from within her own heart. She felt beaten and **bruised** over what had happened.

You may be alone. John Gottman, a nationally respected marriage counselor and professor of psychology at the University of Washington, says men and women kill their love with criticism, contempt, defensiveness, stonewalling, and the failure to repair the hurt caused by these harsh styles. When these unhelpful strategies for dealing with disappointment are not corrected, people commonly end up alone and heartbroken. This is clearly what Shulammite felt and experienced.

You may be ashamed. Her **cloak** (or veil) was taken away. She felt as if everything valuable and important to her was gone. Why? Because God had worked in her heart. Distance had made the heart grow fonder. Without the interference of a griping, whining, and nagging mate, the Lord had done what only he can do. She was genuinely repentant and sorry for her actions. The stage was now set for reconciliation and reunion.

🅓 Understand the Drive of Love May Flame with Testimony (5:8)

> **SUPPORTING IDEA:** *The right words at the right time given in the right way can often move us toward reconciliation.*

5:8. The **daughters of Jerusalem** are the chorus group that appears throughout the book at strategic times. They are called by Shulammite and charged as solemn witnesses to what she is about to say. These will be important words—words from the heart and words she hopes will be trumpeted throughout the land.

1. Tell others of your love.

Here are the right *words* from the right *heart* at the right *time* and, yes, to the right *persons*. She was his *cheerleader* and he was her *champion,* and she said this to others. This spoke loudly to his male ego, to who and what he was as a man on the inside. Herbert Stein raised the issue, "why a man needs a woman" and wrote: (1) she is a warm body in bed to cuddle and comfort; (2) she provides intimate conversation (interest, understanding, and trust); (3) she serves his need to be needed. "To this woman you are irreplaceable at any price" (*Reader's Digest,* December 1999). Shulammite told the world of her love for Solomon. This would speak deeply to his heart.

In the context of sex, Douglas Wilson said:

> There is a sexual relationship at the center of the home which should be obvious to all who live there—hugs, kisses, and romantic attention. . . . There is nothing wrong with children knowing that their father is male and their mother is female and that they have a sexual relationship. There is something wrong with them not knowing (Wilson, *Reforming Marriage,* 109–10).

Shulammite had no fear of others knowing of her sexual desire for her husband.

2. *Tell your mate of your love.*

Someone said that "the tragedy of love is indifference." Alphonse Kerr said, "Love is the most terrible, and also the most generous, of the passions; it is the only one which includes in its dreams the happiness of someone else." Shulammite was saying in verse 8: "I can't last another day without you. Am I too weak or disinterested to make love to him? Don't be foolish. How could I not want more? I have lovesickness. The only remedy is my husband." We will discover Solomon's response to this in 6:4 and following.

MAIN IDEA REVIEW: *Understand what causes bad nights in the bedroom and find ways to avoid repeat performances.*

III. CONCLUSION

LOVE May Be Best Spelled T-I-M-E

Love is a beautiful four-letter word. Sometimes in both marriage and family, it is best spelled T-I-M-E. Men do not think much about time. Women, however, value both quantity and quality of time. Solomon certainly discovered this the hard way. Baby boomers have subjected themselves willingly to a great lie. We have told ourselves that though we did not give our spouses or children quantity time because of the busyness of our schedules, we more than made up for it with quality time.

But we now know that for a child, and for that matter, a spouse, quality time is quantity time. Both spouse and children want you when they want you, and if you're not there, they don't get you. Men in this context tend to go with the flow. We have to be honest; most of us are not very creative. This is a tragedy. Women are thrilled beyond words when their men show their appreciation for them with specific and creative ideas.

How many times has a man blown it on a date night with his wife? He realizes that it has been some time since he took his wife out for a date, so he approaches her and says, "Honey, how about a date this Friday night?" She of course passes out, and he is forced to call 911 to have emergency service to revive her! But once she has regained consciousness, she quickly responds with an enthusiastic "yes!" She then asks the question that has been building within her soul since she heard her husband's offer: "What are we going to do?"

Then tragically and shamefully there comes out of the mouth of a male perhaps some of the dumbest words that have ever been uttered by human lips, "Oh, it doesn't matter to me." When a man utters those words, he basically crushes the heart of his wife, and he destroys any possibility for good that could have come out of a romantic evening. A wise man will not only invite his wife out for a date; he will also be creative and specific in planning out the entire event (including taking care of the baby-sitter!). The bottom line is this: Tell me where you spend your time, and I will tell you what you love.

Reba McIntyre, a country singer, recorded a song several years ago that could tragically be the theme of many boys or girls as they reflect on this issue of time as it relates to their father. Do not neglect what these words may also say about your marriage.

The Greatest Man

The greatest man I never knew lived just down the hall
And every day we said, "Hello," though we never touched at all.
He was in his paper, and I was in my room.
How was I to know he thought I hung the moon?
The greatest man I never knew, I guess I'll never know.
He worked late almost every night;
He never had too much to say; too much was on his mind.
Now it seems so sad that everything he gave us took all he had.
Days faded to years and the memories to black and white.
He grew cold like an old winter wind that blew across my life.
The greatest words I never heard, I guess I'll never hear.
The man I thought would never die has been dead almost a year.
He was good at business, but there was business left to do.
He never said he loved me; I guess he thought I knew.

(Written by Layng Martine and Richard Leigh. ©Layng Martine Songs. Used by permission.

PRACTICAL PRINCIPLES AND APPLICATIONS

- When problems arise, look for the positive in your spouse, not the negative.
- Listing those characteristics you appreciate in your mate will help rekindle former feelings of love.
- Forgiveness and acceptance of forgiveness are essential for relational restoration.
- Life partnership precedes sexual partnership.
- New and fresh evidence of your love creates conditions for a long and happy marriage.
- Seek to move from ingratitude to appreciation toward your mate.
- Seek to move from pride to humility in relation to your mate.

IV. LIFE APPLICATION

A Marital Intimacy Checkup

Checkups are a vital part of life. In all dimensions of our lives, we look at what's happening in light of a standard. We have physical checkups, performance evaluations at work, and we listen to the Word of God to test our hearts and actions against it. In a relationship as vital and intimate as marriage, periodic checkups are needed so corrective action can be taken.

As you view your present relationship from your perspective, how would you evaluate your degree of satisfaction or dissatisfaction with the following as it relates to you and your spouse? Circle the number that best describes your feeling about each item.

1 = Very Dissatisfied
2 = Somewhat Dissatisfied
3 = Neutral
4 = Somewhat Satisfied
5 = Very Satisfied

1. Spiritual Intimacy (oneness before God and devotion to Jesus Christ)   1 2 3 4 5
2. Work Intimacy (sharing common tasks)   1 2 3 4 5
3. Intellectual Intimacy (closeness in ideas and viewpoint)   1 2 3 4 5
4. Recreational Intimacy (relating in fun and play and other activities)   1 2 3 4 5
5. Emotional Intimacy (being on the same wavelength or feeling level)   1 2 3 4 5
6. Crisis Intimacy (closeness in problems and pain)   1 2 3 4 5

7. Conflict Intimacy (understanding and resolution in facing and struggling with differences)   1 2 3 4 5
8. Creative Intimacy (sharing in acts of creating together)   1 2 3 4 5
9. Commitment Intimacy (mutual fulfillment from shared efforts)   1 2 3 4 5
10. Aesthetic Intimacy (sharing experiences of beauty)   1 2 3 4 5
11. Sexual Intimacy (growing in knowledge and joy of sexual union)   1 2 3 4 5
12. Communication Intimacy (feeling of availability and openness in every area)   1 2 3 4 5

What corrective actions do you and your spouse need to take in order to raise the level of intimacy in your marriage?

V. PRAYER

Dear Lord, selfishness is a terrible sin, and it can be deadly to my marriage and family. No one ever gave to others like Jesus. Please help me day by day to be like him, especially where it really matters: in my marriage and in my family. In Jesus' name I pray. Amen.

VI. DEEPER DISCOVERIES

Flowers, Plants, and Spices in Song of Songs

1. *Aloes* (4:14). From a large, aromatic tree that produces resin and oil for making perfume. Used to perfume nuptial robes (Ps. 45:8).
2. *Apple tree* (2:3,5; 7:8). Symbol of strength, sweetness, and fragrance. May be a reference to the apricot.
3. *Calamus* (4:14). Tawny-colored, reedlike stem grown in wet places in India. Use obscure, but from context apparently the stem had a flower with a sweet, aromatic smell.
4. *Cedar* (1:17; 5:15). Coniferous tree esteemed for its durability and aroma. Some grow to over 120 feet with 40-foot girth. Used in constructing Solomon's palace and sedan carriage.
5. *Cinnamon* (4:14). Similar to the modern spice. Also used with other spices for producing a sweet smell.
6. *Fig tree* (2:13). Refers to figs that ripen at various times from August onward, some remaining until the following spring.
7. *Fir* (1:17). Evergreen tree used for ships, buildings, and musical instruments.
8. *Flowers* (2:12). Reference to wildflowers, which appear after the rains of March and April.

9. *Frankincense, incense* (3:6; 4:6,14). A tree that grows in southern Arabia that exudes clear resin from incisions in the bark, hardening into small yellow beads with a strong odor.

10. *Henna, henna blossoms* (1:14; 4:13). A shrub with fragrant white blossoms, growing to a height of twelve feet. Leaves were made into a paste and used to color hair and nails.

11. *Lily of the valley* (2:1–2; 4:5; 5:13; 6:2–3). Probably a lotus or anemone. Described as "glowing red," the common "madonna lily" was plentiful in Palestine.

12. *Mandrakes* (7:13). Dark green, low-growing plant, like lettuce, with purple flower and forked root. Bright red fruit ripens in May and is the size of a small apple.

13. *Myrrh* (1:13; 3:6; 4:6,14; 5:1,13). A short, stubby balsam tree that dripped gum from its bark. It was highly prized for its aromatic qualities. It was used for anointing oil, female purification, cosmetics, and in burial shrouds.

14. *Palm tree* (7:8). Stately trees found in oases along with graceful cypress and tall cedar, often used as sensual, poetic images.

15. *Pomegranate* (4:3,13; 6:7,11; 7:12; 8:2). An apple-shaped fruit with thin, hard skin, containing pulp of rosy color. Often viewed as an aphrodisiac.

16. *Rose of Sharon* (2:1). A meadow flower resembling a tulip with a sweet fragrance. Found in abundance on the plain of Sharon.

17. *Saffron* (4:14). A plant of the crocus family, producing aroma and orange dye. Used in foods as well as therapeutically. Its flowers were white or purple.

18. *Spikenard, nard* (4:13–14). Plant with scented roots from which a fragrant oil was extracted.

19. *Vineyards* (2:13,15). Grove of grapes with fragrant blossoms.

20. *Wheat* (7:2). Pale, newly threshed, and winnowed wheat, often used to describe ideal skin color. Here used to denote the satisfying sustenance of the wife's love.

21. *Wood of Lebanon* (3:9). Probably refers to the cedar in this passage. It symbolized value, strength, and stability.

VII. TEACHING OUTLINE

A. INTRODUCTION: THE BEST SEX IS MARRIED SEX

B. COMMENTARY

1. Understand the Desire for Love May Fail Because of Bad Timing (5:2)
   a. Work may cause the problem.
   b. Words may not cure the problem.
2. Understand the Details for Love May Feel like Too Much Trouble (5:3)
   a. Guard against having silly priorities.
   b. Guard against being a selfish person.
3. Understand the Denial of Love May Flower Only Temporarily (5:4–7)
   a. You may reconsider saying no.
   b. You may reap from saying no.
   c. You may regret saying no
4. Understand the Drive of Love May Flame with Testimony (5:8)
   a. Tell others of your love.
   b. Tell your mate of your love.

C. CONCLUSION: LOVE MAY BE BEST SPELLED T-I-M-E

VIII. ISSUES FOR DISCUSSION

Here are some sound principles on how to have a "good fight." Talk through the ten ideas and evaluate how well you and your mate "fight fair."

1. Confront problems as soon as possible after they arise. Don't allow them to fester and cause bitterness.
2. Master the art of listening. If we fail to show others respect by listening to them, we shouldn't be surprised if they show us the same discourtesy. Ask for clarification if you don't understand.
3. Limit the discussion of the conflict to the here-and-now issue. Don't drag out yesterday's (or last year's) dirty laundry.
4. Use "I" messages in making your point and expressing your emotions. This not only allows you to take responsibility for your feelings, but it also allows the other person to hear about your feelings without feeling defensive. "You" messages tend to be perceived as attacks and criticism.
5. Avoid exaggerations such as "always," "never," etc. Such statements are seldom true simply because as inconsistent human beings we seldom "always" or "never" do anything.
6. Avoid character assassination (name-calling and put-downs). Pointing out character flaws or demeaning another person will do nothing but stir up greater disharmony.

7. Use appropriate words and actions for the matter at hand. Not all arguments are worth fighting at peak volume.

8. Don't be concerned about winning or losing the argument. It's better if both parties can be more concerned about resolving the conflict rather than who "wins" or "loses."

9. Determine limits. Comments that are hurtful or damaging must be avoided.

10. Choose to forgive. All people fail. If we don't give others a chance to start over after failure, our relationships will suffer. Complete forgiveness may take time, depending on the degree of hurt caused by the other person. It's important to have an attitude of forgiveness and keep asking God to help you get to the point where you can truly forgive.

Song of Songs 5:9—6:13

Keys to Harmony and Reconciliation

I. INTRODUCTION
Marriage Is Scary Business

II. COMMENTARY
A verse-by-verse explanation of these verses.

III. CONCLUSION
Why So Many Songs About Love?

An overview of the principles and applications from these verses.

IV. LIFE APPLICATION
Basic Needs of Men and Women

Melding these verses to life.

V. PRAYER
Tying these verses to life with God.

VI. DEEPER DISCOVERIES
Historical, geographical, and grammatical enrichment of the commentary.

VII. TEACHING OUTLINE
Suggested step-by-step group study of these verses.

VIII. ISSUES FOR DISCUSSION
Zeroing these verses in on daily life.

Quote

"*A* marriage will flourish when it is composed of two persons who will nurse each other; it may even survive when one is a nurse and the other is an invalid; but it is sure to collapse when it consists of two invalids, each needing a nurse."

S y d n e y   J .   H a r r i s

Song of Songs
5:9—6:13

I N   A   N U T S H E L L

*M*eeting each other's basic needs is crucial to marital harmony and reconciliation.

Keys to Harmony and Reconciliation

I. INTRODUCTION

Marriage Is Scary Business

*M*arriage is scary business to many people today. With so many unhappy couples sharing horror story after horror story, some persons will do almost anything to increase their odds for success. In New York some women are enrolling in a class called "Marriage Works," a 6-month, 276-hour course to help them land the right mate. The cost is a cool $9,600 (Abby Ellin, "A Class Feminists Might Abhor," *New York Times*, 5 March 2000).

To this class you can add the Divorce Busting Center's "Keeping Love Alive" workshop; the "Hot Monogamy" workshop (4 days, $1,800 per couple or $1,000 per person); Twogether, Inc.'s "Pairs Passage to Intimacy" (2 days, $499 per couple or $250 per person); "Getting the Love You Want: Workshop for Couples," (2 days, $575 per couple); Pairs for Love's "Language of Love" (1 day, $25), "If You Really Loved Me" (1 day, $225 per couple or $125 per person), "Passage to Intimacy Weekend" (2 days, $450 per couple or $250 per person), and the list goes on. I guess desperate times call for desperate measures.

God did not intend for marriage to end quickly. He did not intend for it to be painfully endured. He intended it to be wonderfully enjoyed. It was not his plan that it would be a burden. He wants it to be a blessing. In order for us to experience maximum marriage satisfaction, it is essential that we *grow to know* each other. A woman must come to understand the unique needs her husband has as a man. A man must discover the unique needs his wife has as a woman. All of this is hard work, lifelong work, but work that pays unbelievably rich dividends.

John Gray became a household name and an overnight millionaire with his best-selling book *Men Are from Mars, Women Are from Venus*. In his book he struck a cord that resonates in each of us. Men and women really are different. We *think* differently; we *see* things differently; we *feel* things differently. We are different and different by *design*: it is the way God made us and the way God intended. He did make us male and female and declared it a good thing (Gen. 1:27).

But John Gray in making his argument did make a small error. Men are not from Mars, and women are not from Venus. Men are from Earth and women are from Earth, and we have got to deal with it if we are to make marriage, sex, and romance work. Most marriages that get in trouble do so not over the big things but the little things. These little things are often grounded in male-female differences. We *do sweat the small stuff.*

Dorthy Rosby, in an article titled "It's Living Together That Makes Marriage Difficult," tells the story of the woman who shot her husband because he ate her chocolate. She wrote, "I probably read about that incident with a Hershey bar in my hand. At the time, I may have even thought he had it coming. But now that I think about it, even I, a confirmed chocoholic, think shooting was extreme."

She then adds:

> It truly is the little things that destroy relationships. Margarine, chocolate, nylons on the towel rack, hair in the sink. I once heard about a couple who fought for more than four hours—over a rubber band. He had it, and she wanted it. . . . It's the little things that happen when you're living together. Part of the problem is that God made opposites attract: savers marry spenders; neatniks pair up with slobs; and early birds team up with night owls. Opposing idiosyncrasies come together like weather fronts when couples live together (Dorthy Rosby, *First for Women*, 23 February 1998, 114).

In marriage a wife needs to put her husband where her heart is. A man, on the other hand, needs to love his wife. We do this by learning to meet some basic needs that are at the essence of who our mate is. For a man there are at least five. For a woman there are at least seven. A superb book that looks at the needs of men and women in a similar fashion is Willard F. Harley Jr.'s *His Needs Her Needs* (Grand Rapids: Revell, 1986). This book has greatly impacted my own thinking, and much of its contents are reflected in this chapter.

II. COMMENTARY

Keys to Harmony and Reconciliation

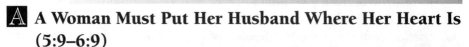

MAIN IDEA: *Meeting each other's basic needs allows a marriage to grow and mature into what God designed marriage to be.*

A A Woman Must Put Her Husband Where Her Heart Is (5:9–6:9)

SUPPORTING IDEA: *A man has basic needs that can be met only by his wife.*

Shulammite was growing in her knowledge of Solomon. Their relationship was maturing. They hit a bump in the road in 5:2–8, but they refused to let that sidetrack them. Out of that conflict they discovered a better understanding of each other and a greater commitment to move ahead. What did Shulammite discover about Solomon's basic needs?

1. He needs admiration and respect.

God has wired a man in such a way that he longs for and needs his wife's admiration and respect (cf. Eph. 5:33b). She understands and appreciates both his value and achievements more than anyone else. She reminds him of his gifts and abilities and helps him in the area of self-confidence. She is his biggest fan, and he is her hero. She is proud of her husband, not out of duty, but as an expression of genuine and sincere admiration for the man she loves and with whom she has chosen to share her life. She sees her husband as a gift from God.

In his February 1995 *Focus on the Family* newsletter, James Dobson provided some insightful marital counsel. In the process of challenging both husbands and wives, he "nailed" this issue concerning a man's need for admiration and respect.

> It is never too late to put a little excitement in your relationship. Romantic love is the fuel that powers the female engine. Unfortunately, most of us get so busy earning a living that we often drift away from the things that drew us together in the first place. . . . [Therefore] a gentle reminder to men: marriages must be nurtured or they wither like a plant without water. There is more than one perspective on every substantive issue, however, and we need to look at the other side of this one. The task of maintaining a marriage is not exclusively a masculine responsibility. Men and women should share it equally. Wives must understand and meet the needs of their husbands, too. That is an idea you may not have heard in a while.
>
> Let me be more specific. It is my conviction that Christian writers, myself included, have tended to overstate the masculine responsibilities in marriage and to understate the feminine. Men have been criticized for their failures at home, and yes, many of us deserve those criticisms. But women are imperfect people too and their shortcomings must also be addressed. One of them is the failure of some wives to show respect and admiration for their husbands. George Gilder, author of *Men and Marriage,* believes women are actually more important to the stability and productivity of men than men are to the well being of women. I am inclined to agree.
>
> When a wife believes in her husband and deeply respects him, he gains the confidence necessary to compete successfully and live responsibly. She gives him a reason to harness his masculine energy— to build a home, obtain and keep a job, remain sober, live within the law, spend money wisely, etc. Without positive feminine influence, he

may redirect the power of testosterone in a way that is destructive to himself and to society at large. . . . What should a woman do for a man that will relate directly to his masculine nature? In a word, she can build his confidence.

A wife's approval means the world to a man. Knowing that she is in his corner, that she loves and admires him, serves both to motivate and inspire him (see also Steven Nock, "Does It Pay for Men in America to Marry and Raise Children?" *Insight,* 29 May 2000, pp. 40–43).

5:9–15. Shulammite met Solomon's need for admiration and respect with a catalogue of praise in 5:10–15. Here she lauded both his appearance and character. She said, "My love is fit and strong, which may mean dazzlingly ruddy" (Glickman, 66). **His hair is wavy and black as a raven.** He was good-looking to her—tall, dark, and handsome. **His head is purest gold** is a statement of its great wealth and value. This is what he was to her.

Her description of **his eyes (like doves)** reflects peace and gentleness, calmness and tranquillity, brightness and alertness. They too were attractive, **washed in milk, mounted like jewels. His cheeks** were sweet scented, possessing a pleasant and desirable smell from his cologne. **His lips** had sweet, wet kisses that she longed to embrace. They were **lilies dripping with myrrh.** Her husband aroused her senses of smell and taste, and she told him so.

Physically he had prepared himself for her. **His arms** were strong and valuable like **rods of gold set with chrysolite. His body** was handsome, carved and cut like **polished ivory decorated with sapphires.** His attractiveness and worth were much to be admired, she said. **His legs** were strong and sturdy like **pillars of marble set on bases of pure gold. His appearance** was breathtaking and unimaginable compared to the beauty and grandeur of the tall and imposing cedar trees of **Lebanon.**

His was a rugged attractiveness, a masculine attractiveness. Shulammite told him he was handsome and valuable inwardly and outwardly, in appearance and character. He was the man with whom she had chosen to share and spend her life, and there were no regrets.

A woman is crucial to the success and well-being of a man. It is indeed the case that a great woman can take a mediocre man and raise him to the level of good. But a not-so-great woman can take a great man and pull him down to the level of mediocrity. A woman's admiration and respect for her man often provide the key and make the difference. Sandra Aldrich said women who want to be treated like queens need to treat their husbands like kings (Sandra Aldrich, "Husbands Don't Have Scriptwriters," *Today's Christian Woman,* March/April 1998, pp. 36–39).

2. He needs sexual fulfillment.

It is no surprise to discover in survey after survey that men say sexual fulfillment is their number one need. Now to be sure, it is high on the list of a male, but I am convinced it is not number one but number two. I am also convinced that a man's need for admiration and respect, and his need for sexual fulfillment, are intimately connected. If a woman fails to meet her husband's need for sexual fulfillment, she will also fail to meet his need for admiration and respect. Why? Because a man finds it impossible to believe that his wife admires and respects him if she does not desire him sexually. In other words, his ability to attract her and satisfy her sexually is essential to his sense of self-worth and his need for admiration and respect.

Shulammite knew this, and so she worked at becoming an expert sexual partner for Solomon. She studied her own desires and responses to recognize what brought out the best in her. She also *talked* and *communicated* this information to her husband to ensure that their sex life would be satisfying and enjoyable. In an article titled "Communicating About Sex Keeps Couples Loving," Dr. Maj-Britt Rosenbaum of Long Island Jewish Medical Center points out that opposite sexes sometimes have opposite views about sex. This can spell trouble for a relationship if it is not worked out.

Experts agree it is common for people to have different sexual styles. But couples who communicate about their differences can often resolve them, while those who view opposing styles as rejection or as a lack of love are on a collision course with disaster. There is no substitute for talking things out so the other person understands your feelings.

The article goes on to address areas of potential conflict such as Mr. "All the Time" versus Mrs. "Occasionally," "Planned Patti" versus "Spontaneous Sam," "Daytime David" versus "Nighttime Natalie," "Hurry Up Harry" versus "Slow Down Denise," "I Like the Darkness Diane" versus "I Love the Light Larry," and "One Track Mind Michael" versus "Instant Distraction Donna" (Gwen Yount Carden, *Dallas Times Herald,* 11 February 1989, 1E).

5:16–6:3. Shulammite speaks of the beauty of **his mouth** and the fact that he was altogether attractive. His mouth was **sweetness itself**. She desired him. She wanted him, and she told him so. In her mind, who would not want such a man? In 6:2–3 she says he **has gone down to his garden** for a time of enjoyment. This is a reference to Shulammite herself (cf. 4:16), and in particular to her giving herself in lovemaking. She provided for him **beds of spices**, a place of pleasure. There he fed and gathered what satisfied and pleased him. She was available to him. She was there for his enjoyment. The bedroom of this couple would never become a place of boredom!

It is important at this point to be honest and note that men and women do not approach sex in the same way and with the same perspective. It has been said that when it comes to sex men are like *microwave ovens* and women are like *Crock Pots* (not crackpots!). What does this mean? Simply put, men are creatures of sight and are moved by what they see. If a man sees what he likes, he can heat up in a hurry—like a microwave oven. On the other hand, a woman is more like a Crock Pot. She must simmer a while before she is ready!

Willard Harley has said that in marriage we must create an atmosphere of affection in which sex will be enjoyed more often and with greater pleasure. Phil McGraw, author of *Relationship Rescue: A Seven Step Strategy for Reconnecting with Your Partner,* says, "If you have a good sexual relationship, it's about 10% of the value of the relationship overall. If you don't have a good sexual relationship, it's about 90%" (Cecelia Goodnow, "Phil McGraw Draws Raves for 'No Bull' Approach to Rescuing Relationships," *Seattle-Post,* 4 March 2000).

"For many people, sex has become a labor rather than an adventure" (Peter Marin, "A Revolution's Broken Promises," *Psychology Today,* July 1983, p. 55). But no marriage will be everything God wants it to be without the beautiful gift of sex being active and satisfying for both partners. It requires communication and understanding. But if we will make it a priority and give it the attention it requires, we can find the full joy and satisfaction that the Song of Songs promises.

3. He needs home support.

6:3. Shulammite expressed great confidence in the relationship she enjoyed with Solomon. She said, **I am my lover's and my lover is mine**. She also noted that he was comfortable in her presence and in their home. **He browses among the lilies**. Not only did he find her *physically* satisfying; he also found her and their home *emotionally* satisfying. She had created a home that offered him an atmosphere of peace and quiet and refuge. She managed the home, and it was a place of rest and rejuvenation. Shulammite understood what all women need to understand: that the wife and mother is the emotional hub of the family.

There is a colloquial saying that is well-known by almost all married persons. It goes something like this: "In the home, if Mama ain't happy, then nobody is gonna be happy!" This may not be fair, but it is true. It is the way things are. I am fond of saying that a woman is the thermostat of the home. If her thermostat goes up to 90 or 95 degrees, it is not just hot for her; it is hot for everybody. On the other hand, if her thermostat goes down to 70 or 65 degrees, it is not just cool for her; it is cool for everyone.

A man will not hang around a woman who is continually badgering him and beating him up verbally. He will take one of two actions. Either he will fight or take flight. Most men will not fight their wives. They will not fight them physically because it is wrong, it strips away their masculinity, and they will also go to jail (and rightly so). Most men will not fight their wives verbally either. There is a simple reason for this. They almost always lose verbal battles. Women are indeed verbal creatures. It is said that the average male speaks somewhere between ten thousand and twelve thousand words per day. On the other hand, the average female speaks somewhere between twenty thousand and twenty-five thousand words per day with gusts of up to fifty thousand words! (I'm joking about the gusts!)

In other words women are well equipped for verbal battles and men are not. As a result, most men will not fight their wives physically or verbally; they choose instead to take flight. They become known as workaholics or persons engaged in multiple extracurricular activities. The reason for all of this is quite simple: it is quieter alone at the office or out in left field on a softball field. A woman must understand how crucial she is to providing a home that is a place of support for her husband. Michele Weiner-Davis, author of *Divorce Busting* and *Getting Through to the Man You Love*, said, "The key to dealing with men is to stop talking and start acting. . . . Women need to learn male friendly methods of persuasion and stop doing what doesn't work." Her suggestions include:

- Stop pressing your point when it's obvious he's heard you, even if he doesn't acknowledge it.
- Make your goals clear and action oriented.
- Pay attention to how your conflict ends.
- Ignore [some] undesirable behavior.
- Take a time-out.
- Emphasize the positive.

"It's far more efficient to praise than scold, to reward than punish" (Stephanie Dunnewind, "It's Time for a New Strategy When Nagging Doesn't Work," *Seattle Times*, 6 April 2000).

Interestingly, it is also in a woman's best interest to work toward home support. According to research done at Ohio State University College of Medicine, marital quarrels are harder on women than on men. Blood samples taken from ninety newlywed couples after they had a fight showed that women had higher levels of stress hormones. Researchers noted that men tend to withdraw from conflict or "tune out." Women, on the other hand, are more likely to be critical or demanding (*Today's Christian Woman*, March/April 1997, p. 19).

Professor Bob Montgomery at Bond University in Australia says the formula for a happy, nurturing relationship is simple: Five good times for every bad one.

If everything is basically good most of the time, a marriage can absorb the shocks and problems that are part of everyone's life—especially if both [partners] are able to put out the soothing response of humor when these crises emerge (Julie Macken, "The Mystery of Why Women Marry," *Financial Review*, 28 August 1999).

A man needs to believe and experience a home that is his castle. He has the need for home support, and the wife is essential to his receiving this.

4. He needs an attractive wife.

6:4–9. Shulammite had praised Solomon, and now he returned the compliment. Yet as he returned the compliment, we learn something more about a basic need that a man has: the need for his wife to be attractive. Solomon began by telling his love, his darling, that she was like two of the most beautiful and lovely cities in Palestine: **Tirzah** and **Jerusalem**. It is interesting to note that in Lamentations 2:15, Jerusalem is called the "the perfection of beauty." So unbelievable was her beauty that he said it was as if he were facing an awesome army with its **banners** in full display. Her beauty threw him off balance. So great was her loveliness that he was almost overwhelmed: **Turn your eyes from me; they overwhelm me**.

Going back to earlier descriptions, he again described the beauty of her **hair**, the brightness of her **teeth**, and the loveliness of her **temples**. His love for her had not diminished, and her beauty was as radiant as ever. Yet he did not stop there. He added to his previous praise. He told her she had a uniqueness that transcended all others. In verses 8–9, he said there might be **sixty queens** and **eighty concubines** and **virgins beyond number**, but none of them compared to her. Again he referred to her as his **dove**, and then he added that she was his "virtuous one" and utterly **unique**. This favorable opinion, he noted, was also shared by her mother, as well as other women. They, too, **called her blessed** and they also **praised her**.

A man longs for a woman who is possessed of an inner and outer beauty. A woman who is beautiful to her husband will cultivate a godly and Christlike spirit in her inner self (cf. 1 Pet. 3:1–5). She understands that being beautiful on the inside will make her more attractive on the outside.

She is also a woman who keeps herself physically fit with diet and exercise, and she wears her hair, makeup, and clothes in a way that her husband finds attractive and tasteful. Her husband is pleased and proud of her in public but also in private. Shulammite understood well the need for Solomon to have a wife whom he could be proud of physically and spiritually, publicly and privately.

5. He needs a best friend.

5:16. In the latter part of 5:16, Shulammite said of Solomon, **This is my lover, this my friend, O daughters of Jerusalem**. Shulammite was well aware of the fact that though a man may not always act like it, he needs his wife to be his best friend. How does a wife go about doing this? She develops mutual interests with her husband. She discovers activities her husband enjoys and seeks to become proficient in them as well. If she learns to enjoy them, then she joins him in them. If she does not enjoy them, she encourages him to consider other things that they can enjoy doing together. She works at becoming her husband's best friend so that he repeatedly associates her with those activities he enjoys the most.

I recognize that men are good at putting on acts and pretenses. However, I have become more and more convinced with each passing year of my own marriage that a man really does need to have a woman, his wife, who is his best friend.

I also believe a word of warning is essential at this point. I believe it is wise for a man to have an inner circle of three or four men who are his confidants and with whom he has great trust. I am also unalterably convinced that no woman should be a part of that circle. It is an unwise and dangerous course of action. But in addition to that, in his innermost circle, there must be only one person, and that one person should be his wife. She should be his closest confidant. She should be his closest companion. She indeed should be his best friend. Experts tell us that many long marriages wither from neglect rather than blow up.

So many times when couples get involved in careers and parenting their children, they lose that emotional connectedness with each other. "It slips away and they don't realize it," says Claudia Arp. "She's into her thing, he's into his thing, then when the kids leave—that reason for staying in the relationship goes, too." "In the past, marriages stayed together because society expected you to stay together," says David Arp. "Now if a marriage stays together, it's because the couple wants to stay together" (Kristen Kauffman, "Divorced After Decades," *The Dallas Morning News,* 15 September 2000).

A husband and a wife should be lovers. The Song of Songs has made this clear. But a husband and a wife should also be each other's *very* best friend. Our Song has also made this clear, and it is not surprising that there is usually an intimate link between being great lovers and being best friends.

B A Man Must Love His Wife (5:9,10b,16; 6:4,8–13)

> **SUPPORTING IDEA:** *A woman has basic needs that can only be met by her husband.*

Men and women are different in many ways. One area in particular is in the realm of needs. They are quite different, and therefore it is not surprising to see that women have needs that are significantly different from those of men. How has God put a woman together? What does she need from a man?

1. She needs a spiritual leader.

5:10b. Shulammite said that Solomon was **outstanding among ten thousand**. *Outstanding* means "chief" or "distinguished." It is clear that her primary focus was on his physical appearance, and yet I am convinced she made this statement as well because of the godly character that radiated from within. It would be difficult to imagine the Bible commending anyone simply on physical appearance alone. Even here in the Song of Songs, the spiritual character of a man is at least implicitly present.

The fact is, a woman's primary need is that her husband be a spiritual leader. She longs to follow a man of courage, conviction, commitment, compassion, and character. A woman needs a man who can be both steel and velvet. He can be a man's man, and at the same time he can be gentle, tender, and approachable. I have often said that a good woman is worth her weight in gold. However, a good man is worth twice his weight in gold because there are so few of them.

Time magazine (14 February 1994) published on its cover the body of a man with the head of a pig. The lead article was titled, "Are Men Really That Bad?" The fact is men have been beaten up quite severely over the past several decades, and many men deserve those whippings. But I sense that there is a new generation on the scene that is committed to being the kind of man that honors God and blesses a wife. Such a man will be a spiritual leader in the home. He will take the initiative in cultivating a spiritual environment for the family. He will be a capable and competent student of the Word of God, and he will live out before all people a life founded on the Word of God. He will encourage and enable his wife to become a woman of God, to become more like Jesus, and he will take the lead in training their children in the things of the Lord (cf. Eph. 5:25–6:4).

2. She needs personal affirmation and appreciation.

6:4. Solomon referred to Shulammite as his love, his **darling**. He told her how lovely, beautiful, and awesome she was. In verses 5–9 he detailed those qualities and attributes that he found so irresistible. There is no question that this would have met her need for affirmation and appreciation. A man who loves a woman will praise her for personal attributes and qualities. He will extol her virtues as a wife, mother, and homemaker. He will also commend her in the presence of others as a marvelous mate, friend, lover, and companion. She will feel that to him no one is more important in this world.

I remember telling men in a marriage conference that one of the ways they show their wife appreciation is by picking up the phone and calling her during the day to see how she is doing. He is not to call to ask what came in the mail or what's for supper! The following night a sweet young woman came up to me to tell me that her husband had obviously listened to what I had said the night before. She informed me that they had been married for a number of years and that her husband had never called her during the workday until today. On this day he called her five times!

At first I was quite proud of the impression I had made on the man, but then a frightening thought entered my mind. I asked her, "Well, what did he say in each of those conversations?" She informed me that he hadn't said much and that each conversation lasted no more than a minute. I began to apologize to her for the fact that things had not worked out so well. She quickly interrupted me, "Oh no, it was wonderful. Just the fact that he thought to call means everything. We can work on the words later! However, if he doesn't call, we have nothing to work on."

Charlotte and I had some dear friends in Dallas who would come over to our home for pizza on a regular basis. I remember on one occasion my wife was standing in the kitchen getting some food ready. Just sort of spontaneously and without really thinking about it, I said to her, "Charlotte, girl, I do believe you are the most beautiful thing I have ever seen." She smiled at me and I smiled back. Then one of my friends, whose name was Cathy, said to me, "Danny, I love it when you say nice things about Charlotte in front of other people, and you do it a lot."

I had not really thought about it that much before, and so I turned to Cathy and said, "You mean when John (her husband) says nice things about you in front of other people, it means a lot?" She responded with a twinkle in her eyes, "Hardly anything he does makes me feel more special."

Men, we need to be reminded that words of appreciation and affirmation, in front of other people, speak to one of the deepest needs in the life of our wives.

3. She needs personal affection and romance.

6:8–9,11–13. Romance for a man means sex. He cannot imagine romance without having sex. On the other hand, romance for a woman can mean lots of things, and sex may or may not be a part of it. Solomon recognized the need to cultivate an environment of romance, so he told Shulammite in 6:8–9 that no one compared to her when it came to other women. She was his **unique** one (v. 9). All those who saw her declared her fortunate and they sang her praises.

In verses 11–13, we find her response to the praise that had been showered on her by Solomon. She moved to the garden to see the beauty of it and the fresh evidences of their love. This is depicted by her desire to see whether the **vines had budded or the pomegranates were in bloom**. She went on to say that even before she was aware of it, her soul had been enraptured and she was set **among the royal chariots of my people**.

Verse 13 pictures her being swept away while those who looked on her beauty and perfection (at the encouragement of her husband, it should be noted) pleaded with her to return and not to go away. A woman who responds in this way has had her deepest need for affection and romance met by her husband.

It is crucial that a man learn how to speak to the needs of his wife's heart in the area of romance. He must demonstrate to her both in word and deed that he understands her unique needs and appetites in this area. The fact is that most men do not understand romance from the female perspective. Most of us of the male species would not recognize romance as women understand it if it were to slap us in the face or bite us on the nose. I became acutely aware of this when I came home one day when we were living in Dallas and I asked my wife Charlotte, "Honey, do you think I'm romantic?"

She yanked her head around so quickly, it is amazing to me that she did not permanently damage her neck. There was a look in her eyes that I had never seen before, but I was quite certain that I was not going to like what she would say. Well, being the loving wife that she is, she began by saying, "Let me start by saying that I do love you, and I cannot imagine being married to anybody else but you. You are a good husband and a wonderful father. However, I must tell you that the answer to your question is *no*. You are not romantic. I doubt that you would recognize it if it slapped you in the face or bit you on the nose."

Well, as you can imagine, my feelings were hurt, and so I responded in typical male fashion, "Well, I've been reading a lot about this stuff lately, and all these books that I have been reading say you need it." She responded by telling me that she did, and so I told her that I might try to begin to give it to her in the near future. I must add at this point, I had no idea exactly how that was going to happen, but I was pleased when she said, "Well the fact that you're even going to try, I find romantic."

Now I want all of you to know that what I am about to tell you is absolutely the truth with no embellishment. It was a Friday night when we were living in Dallas, Texas. I walked up behind Charlotte feeling that it was time to be romantic (you guys know what that means!). I began to rub her back and neck. After just a couple of moments, she turned around and looked at me and said, "Why don't you go on, leave me alone, and quit bothering me." I responded by telling her that I thought that was romantic. She informed me that it was not romantic now, nor would it be romantic later. I clearly understood what that meant, so I went off to bed early that night by myself. There was no need in waiting up.

The next morning my wife took a shower. Now when Charlotte takes a shower, she always loves to put on her body an Avon product called Skin-So-Soft. Those of you who are familiar with it know that it does three things:

(1) it smells really good, (2) it will slime your dry skin if it needs it, and (3) it also happens to be a wonderful insect repellent. Well, Charlotte will put this on her body and then wipe it off with a towel. Her towel was lying on the bed after she had gotten out of the shower. I walked over and did an unusual thing. I picked up her towel and I smelled it. I turned to Charlotte, and I said very innocently, "Honey, this towel smells like you." She responded by saying, "Now that's romantic."

I looked at her, stunned at her statement, and I said, "You don't have to make fun of me. I am really trying at this romance thing." She responded by telling me that she really did find my statement romantic and she walked out of the bedroom. At that point I looked up into heaven and told God there was no hope in this area as far as I could see. I would never be able to understand romance from the female perspective. God was gracious to me, and he gave me insight into how this romance thing works from the female perspective.

Romance is basically a game. It is a very specific game. It is the game of hide-and-seek. She hides it, and you seek it. Now if you find it, it is good. On the other hand, if you don't find it, you have one of two options. First, you can get nasty, mean, and bent out of shape and just be a miserable old grouch for the rest of your life. I have met a number of men just like that. Second, you can remind yourself: it's a game. Sometimes I win, and sometimes I lose. But that's the fun of playing the game. So it is the game of hide-and-seek.

There's a second part to this game, and this is not fair. But some things are not fair; it is just the way they are. Guys, you must understand. What is romantic to your wife, say, on Monday, may not necessarily be romantic on Tuesday. Indeed, women are adept at moving the romance on a regular basis, sometimes even hiding it in places where they cannot even find it. However, when you go searching for romance in the place where it used to be, but now you discover that it is no longer there, do not be surprised if looking over your shoulder is the woman that God gave you, and with her eyes she says something like this, "Yes, my darling. I moved the romance. It's somewhere else now. And I'm going to wait to see if you love me enough to look for it all over again."

Now again guys, you can get angry, mean, and bent out of shape, or you can remember that it's a game. And games can be fun. Sometimes you win, and sometimes you lose. But it's all a great game. Men, if you will approach romance in this way, not only will you find it fun but you will also get better at it along the way. Carlin Rubenstein reminds us, "The level of romance in a relationship is a kind of barometer of love: When romance is low, couples have sex less often, are less happy about love, and are more likely to consider divorce" (Carlin Rubenstein, "The Modern Art of Courtly Love," *Psychology Today,* July 1983, p. 46).

4. She needs intimate conversation.

5:16. Shulammite states that Solomon's **mouth is sweetness itself** and that **he is altogether lovely.** When one compares this verse with verse 13, it is clear that she had in mind, at least in part, his kisses and physical expressions of his love. Yet as we have seen in this book, statements are often capable of more than one meaning. At this point she was also complimenting him with respect to the words that proceeded from his mouth, and that they were sweet. A woman has a need for intimate conversation. She needs a husband who will talk with her at the feeling level (heart to heart). She needs a man who will listen to her thoughts about the events of her day with sensitivity, interest, and concern. Daily conversation with her conveys her husband's desire to understand her.

Wise men learn soon after marriage that women are masters of code language. They say what they mean and expect you to know what they mean, and the particular words may not be the key. Unfortunately, some men are simply ill prepared and a little dense at this point, and it often gets them into serious trouble. How often it is that a man will come into the house in the evening, walk into the kitchen, give his wife a kiss on the cheek, and ask her, "Honey, how was your day?" He will receive the response, "Fine." Now if he is listening to the tone in which the word *fine* is delivered, he will pick up that *fine* does not mean *fine*; *fine* means "bad." Unfortunately, he isn't listening. He retires to their family room and grabs that male therapy device, the remote control, unaware of what has just transpired.

However, about three hours later it hits him. *She didn't fix me any supper.* Men become amazingly sensitive when they're hungry. And so this starving warrior makes his way to the bedroom where he finds his wife, and he asks a simple question, "Honey, is anything bothering you?" She simply and curtly responds, "No." Now of course, this *no* means "yes." It also means this: "You weren't interested in finding out three hours ago, and I'm not about to tell you now. Indeed, this world will come to an end before you know what's bothering me."

Now a man could try to blame this whole episode on his wife, but the fact is that the blame lies at his feet. When he came in the kitchen and kissed her on the cheek and asked about her day, she screamed loud and clear, "I've had a horrible day. Nothing's gone right. I need you to stay here for a few moments and let me just vent and get some things out of my system." Ten minutes of undivided attention can revolutionize the way the rest of the evening will go. A man must learn to meet his wife's need for intimate conversation.

5. She needs honesty and openness.

6:10,13. Solomon was utterly transparent and open in his affection and love for Shulammite. In verse 10 he said that to him she shone **like the dawn,** was as beautiful **as the moon,** as **bright as the sun,** as **majestic as the stars in procession.** Nothing was hidden; everything was out in the open when it came to his love and affection for her. A woman needs her husband to be honest and open with her. She needs a man who will look into her eyes and, in love, tell her what he is really thinking (Eph. 4:15). He will explain his plans and actions clearly and completely to her because he regards himself as responsible for her. He wants her to trust him and feel secure. He wants her to know how precious she is to him. Growing openness and honesty will always mark a marriage when a man loves a woman.

6. She needs stability and security.

5:9. The young women of Jerusalem responded to the loving words of Shulammite in 5:8. They acknowledged that in her view, Solomon was better than any other. In 6:1, the young women of Jerusalem again requested of Shulammite the location of her love. It was clear in their mind that she knew where he was and that she was secure and certain in that knowledge. Even when he had "turned aside," she was aware of where he was located. In 6:13 where her friends called for her to return, it is clearly implied that she was in his presence and that he was carrying her away to be with him. He had placed her in his chariot, and they were together. She was secure in the love of her husband.

A man who loves a woman will firmly shoulder the responsibilities to house, feed, and clothe her and the family. He will provide, and he will protect. He will never forget that he is the security hub of the family for both his wife and his children. She will be aware of his dependability, and as our text indicates, so will others. There will be no doubt where his devotion and commitments lie. They are with his wife and his children.

7. She needs family commitment.

6:9. The family is not directly mentioned in the Song of Songs, and children are notably absent. Yet in 6:9 Solomon makes reference to the fact that she was **the only daughter of her mother,** perfect to the one who gave her birth. Solomon knew that drawing upon this family imagery would speak to her heart, and it would also impress upon her his interest in the family and the importance he placed on it. A woman longs to know that her man puts the family first. Such a man will commit his time and energy to the spiritual, moral, and intellectual development of the entire family, especially the children.

For example, he will play with them, he will read the Bible to them, he will engage in sports with them, he will go to their games, and he will take them on other exciting and fun-filled outings. Such a man will not play the fool's game of working long hours, trying to get ahead, while his spouse and children languish in neglect. A woman needs a man who is committed to the family. She needs a man who puts his wife and children right behind his commitment to the Lord Jesus Christ.

When fifteen hundred mall shoppers were asked what they wished for most when they blew out their birthday candles, men and women gave vastly different answers. The number one wish of women was "more time with spouse." Among men that wish came in at twenty-seventh on the list. (What did the guys wish for most often? A lower golf score.) (*New Man*, September 1997, p. 20). What a pitiful and pathetic answer by men.

Bill McCartney, former football coach at the University of Colorado and head of Promise Keepers, said, "When you look into the face of a man's wife, you will see just what he is as a man. Whatever he has invested or withheld from her, is reflected in her countenance" (*Men in Action*, April 1995).

MAIN IDEA REVIEW: *Meeting each other's basic needs allows a marriage to grow and mature into what God designed marriage to be.*

III. CONCLUSION

Why So Many Songs About Love?

"An anthropologist once asked a Hopi Indian why so many of his people's songs were about rain. The Hopi replied that it was because water is so scarce and then asked, 'Is that why so many of your songs are about love?'" (Gregory McNamee, quoted in *Reader's Digest*, May 2000, p. 87).

When a woman puts her husband where her heart is, she makes it her ambition to meet five basic needs in his life. When a man loves a woman, he makes it a life goal to meet seven basic needs of his wife. When a husband is committed in this way, and when a wife has the same commitment, it is not surprising that both husband and wife have a smile on their face and joy in their heart. This is the way God intended it from the very beginning. As those who are committed to God's plan for marriage, we should settle for and expect nothing less.

God made men to be men, husbands, and fathers. A man should never apologize for being a man, for being a masculine human being. God made women to be women, wives, and mothers. No woman should ever apologize for being a feminine person. You see, no one is as good at being a man as a man, and no one is as good at being a woman as a woman.

PRACTICAL PRINCIPLES AND APPLICATIONS

How to Be Attentive to the Needs of Your Mate

1. Keep in mind your dating schedule. If a couple of weeks (months!) have gone by and you and your spouse haven't done anything together, it's time to get out of the house, even if it's just for pie and coffee (or a Diet Coke!).

2. Make a point of talking every day, even if it's just for ten minutes. If your children are still small, you will find it difficult to "find" the time—you'll have to carve it out.

3. Take up activities or hobbies you can do together. Bicycling, tennis, golf, and the movies are just a few activities that couples can do together. Or you can develop common interests in collecting, cooking, volunteering, or working in the yard together.

4. Relearn walking. In addition to being good for you physically, short or long walks together are good for you emotionally. Time alone is provided just to commune and share your thoughts and heart with each other.

5. Share your daily schedules for the coming week. Not only will you each feel more involved, but you can schedule some time for each other. It allows you to feel a part of each other's lives.

6. Serve together in your church. This is a way to double your investment by serving your Savior and spending time with your spouse.

7. If you can tell something is bothering your spouse, ask him or her about it. Slowly draw out your spouse. Ask gently but directly, "Is anything bothering you, Honey? I'd really like to hear about it."

8. Remember the four Cs: *compassion, communication, compromise*, and *consideration*. Compromise is a key building block of marriage, but it works best when both sides have aired what's bothering them. In order for give-and-take to work, offer to hear what your spouse has to say first. Finally, heed this advice a father gave one of his adult sons: "Treat your wife with as much courtesy as you would a friend, even a stranger. If you can treat her like a best friend, you'll be fine."

IV. LIFE APPLICATION

Basic Needs of Men and Women

A wife makes herself irresistible to her husband by learning to meet his five basic needs:

1. *His need for admiration and respect.* She understands and appreciates his value and achievements more than anyone else. She reminds him of his capabilities and helps him maintain his walk with God and also his self-confidence. She is proud of her husband, not out of duty, but as an expression of sincere admiration for the man she loves and with whom she has chosen to share her life (Eph. 5:22–23,33).

2. *His need for sexual fulfillment.* She becomes an excellent sexual partner to him. She studies her own response to recognize and understand what brings out the best in her; then she communicates this information to her husband, and together they learn to have a sexual relationship that both find repeatedly satisfying and enjoyable (Prov. 5:15–19; Song 4:9–5:1; 1 Cor. 7:1–5; Heb. 13:4).

3. *His need for home support.* She creates a home that offers him an atmosphere of peace and quiet and refuge. She manages the home and care of the children. The home is a place of rest and rejuvenation. Remember, the wife and mother is the emotional hub of the family (Prov. 9:13; 19:13; 21:9,19; 25:24).

4. *His need for her to be attractive.* She is possessed of inner and outer beauty. She cultivates a Christlike spirit in her inner self. She keeps herself physically fit with diet and exercise, and she wears her hair, makeup, and clothes in a way that her husband finds attractive and tasteful. Her husband is pleased and proud of her in public but also in private (Song 1:8–10; 2:2; 6:13–7:9; 1 Pet. 3:1–5)!

5. *His need for a life companion.* She develops mutual interests with her husband. She discovers those activities her husband enjoys the most and seeks to become proficient in them. If she learns to enjoy them, she joins him in them. If she does not enjoy them, she encourages him to consider others that they can enjoy together. She becomes her husband's best friend so that he repeatedly associates her with the activities he enjoys most (Song 8:1–2,6).

A husband can make himself irresistible to his wife by learning to meet her seven basic marital needs:

1. *Her need for a spiritual leader.* He is a man of courage, conviction, commitment, compassion, and character. He takes the initiative in cultivating a spiritual environment for the family. He becomes a capable and competent student of God's Word and lives out before everyone a life founded on the Word of God. He leads his wife in becoming a woman of God, and he takes the lead in training the children in the things of the Lord (Ps. 1; Eph. 5:23–27).

2. *Her need for personal affirmation and appreciation.* He praises her for personal attributes and qualities. He extols her virtues as a wife,

mother, and homemaker. He openly commends her, in the presence of others, as a marvelous mate, friend, lover, and companion. She feels that to him, no one is more important in this world (Prov. 31:28–29; Song 4:1–7; 6:4–9; 7:1–9).

3. *Her need for personal affection (romance).* He showers her with timely and generous displays of affection. He also tells her how much he cares for her with a steady flow of words, cards, flowers, gifts, and common courtesies. Remember, affection is the environment in which sexual union is enjoyed and a wonderful marriage is developed (Song 6:10,13; Eph. 5:28–29,33).

4. *Her need for intimate conversation.* He talks with her at the feeling level (heart to heart). He listens to her thoughts (her heart) about the events of her day with sensitivity, interest, and concern. Conversations with her convey a desire to understand her, not to change her (Song 2:8–14; 8:13–14; 1 Pet. 3:7).

5. *Her need for honesty and openness.* He looks into her eyes and, in love, tells her what he really thinks (Eph. 4:15). He explains his plans and actions clearly and completely because he regards himself as responsible for her. He wants her to trust him and feel secure (Prov. 15:22–23).

6. *Her need for home support and stability.* He firmly shoulders the responsibility to house, feed, and clothe the family. He provides and protects, and he does not feel sorry for himself when things get tough. Instead he looks for concrete ways to improve home life. He desires to raise their marriage and family to a safer and more fulfilling level. Remember, the husband and father is the security hub of the family (1 Tim. 5:8).

7. *Her need for family commitment.* He puts his family first. He commits his time and energy to spiritual, moral, and intellectual development of the children. For example, he prays with them (especially at night by the bedside), reads to them, engages in sports with them, goes to their games, and takes them on other outings. He does not play the fool's game of working long hours, trying to get ahead, while his children and spouse languish in neglect (Eph. 6:4; Col. 3:19–20).

V. PRAYER

Father, you are a marvelous and wonderful Creator. We see evidence of it everywhere, including the way you made men and women. I am so grateful that we are equal in your eyes but different by design. I confess, however, that I never knew just how different I am from my mate until I got married. Wow! What an education. Lord, I am still learning about my mate. I suspect I will keep on learning until I meet you in rapture or death. Help me to work at this and to give my "marriage education" my very best. You deserve this, and my mate needs it. Thank you for putting a man and woman together in this fantastic partnership called marriage. In Jesus' name I pray. Amen.

VI. DEEPER DISCOVERIES

A. The Daughters of Jerusalem

This phrase as used in the Song of Songs has been variously interpreted to identify friends of the bride, women of the royal court of Israel, or merely a personification of the audience for Shulammite and Solomon (that is, a literary device rather than a group of real people). The epithets used by Shulammite (Song 3:5,11) are apparently parallel phrases used to address Hebrew women loyal to their king. The women mentioned in the Song were characterized by a willing spirit as they worked to make Solomon's carriage (a portable canopy chair or bed; 3:6–10) very beautiful.

B. Animals Mentioned in the Song of Songs

In the Ancient Near East, animals were vital and important for a number of reasons. The Song of Songs uses them in poetic imagery to highlight characteristics of each lover.

Dove. This bird personified innocence and purity, peace, and tranquillity and serves as a term of endearment (1:15) or pet name. Shulammite imagined the king urging her to come and alluded to the shy nature of doves as they rested high in the clefts of large rocks (2:14).

Fawns, gazelles, stags. These designations of deer were common in the poetry of this period. Gazelles were graceful and thus a symbol of feminine beauty. Each lover used this analogy for the other. She saw him as a young stag (2:9,17). Her breasts evoked thoughts of young fawns feeding (4:5; 7:3).

Filly (mare). The comparison of Shulammite with a mare of Pharaoh's chariots was intended as a high compliment, since stallions normally pulled his chariots. Also according to 1 Kings 10:28, Solomon introduced to the kingdom the finest thoroughbred Egyptian horses (Song 1:9).

Flock. This term is used repeatedly as the nation's economy was agricultural, involving flocks and herds. Shepherding patterns undergird the expressions of love (1:7–8).

Foxes. These little animals were crafty and swift, sly, and cunning. They are used to denote dangers that could harm the couple's marriage (2:15).

Goats. Probably the Nubian ibex, with glossy, beautiful, black hair, still found in this area (1:8; 4:1).

Lion, leopard. Symbolically, the lion is seen as a threat, stalking its prey; the leopard (panther) is highly intelligent and treacherous. Both lived in mountainous areas (4:8).

Raven. The shiny feathers of this sleek, black bird are used to describe the attractive hair of Solomon (5:11).

Sheep. The whiteness of newly washed wool serves as a description of her clean, bright teeth (4:2; 6:6), perfectly matching ("twins") and evenly set.

Turtledove. This bird (doves, NIV) is the wild pigeon that passes through Palestine at the beginning of springtime (2:12).

VII. TEACHING OUTLINE

A. INTRODUCTION: MARRIAGE IS SCARY BUSINESS

B. COMMENTARY

1. A Woman Must Put Her Husband Where Her Heart Is (5:9–6:9)
   a. He needs admiration and respect.
   b. He needs sexual fulfillment.
   c. He needs home support.
   d. He needs an attractive wife.
   e. He needs a best friend.
2. A Man Must Love His Wife (5:9,10b,16; 6:1,4,8–13)
   a. She needs a spiritual leader.
   b. She needs personal affirmation and appreciation.
   c. She needs personal affection and romance.
   d. She needs intimate conversation.
   e. She needs honesty and openness.
   f. She needs stability and security.
   g. She needs family commitment.

C. CONCLUSION: WHY SO MANY SONGS ABOUT LOVE?

VIII. ISSUES FOR DISCUSSION

Ann Douglas (*Chicago Tribune*, 2 January 2002) warns us of "Ten Traps" that can sabotage a marriage. Talk through these carefully and honestly with your mate. The checkup can do you good.

1. *Taking your partner for granted.* Let your partner know you appreciate him or her.

2. *Forgetting that a good marriage takes work.* Too many people think that having a happy marriage is magical. We must accept the idea that romantic love takes a great deal of work.

3. *Not talking through conflict.* Don't rely on heavy sighs, slammed doors, and other nonverbal communication when something is bothering you. Otherwise, problems will fester.

4. *Failing to romance your partner.* Everyone wants to feel special. Find your mate's "love language" and speak it often.

5. *Fighting dirty.* Resist the temptation to figure out what will hurt your partner most and then use that against him or her.

6. *Fighting over money.* Forty-three percent of married couples argue about money. Come up with a financial game plan that both of you can live with.

7. *Letting the passion fizzle.* "Have sex often—anytime either of you is in the mood," Kate Wachs says. "If you wait until both partners are in the mood, you won't end up having much sex at all and, over time, you'll end up drifting apart."

8. *Shutting down sexually when you're angry rather than dealing with issues.* Withholding affection can seriously damage a relationship. Never play "marital prostitution."

9. *Failing to understand that marriages have ups and downs.* Expect great times in your marriage; just don't expect them to happen every day. Marriage is the real world.

10. *Throwing in the towel too easily.* Don't view your partner as disposable. Vow to rekindle the flames rather than looking for a way out.

Song of Songs 6:13–7:10

A Lover's Praise

"*W*hen a man whose marriage was in trouble sought his advice, the Master said, 'You must listen to your wife.' The man took this advice to heart and returned after a month to say that he had learned to listen to every word his wife was saying. Said the Master with a smile, 'Now go home and listen to every word she isn't saying.'"

Anthony de Mello

Song of Songs
6:13–7:10

 IN A NUTSHELL

*G*od creates a man and redeems a man through Jesus Christ to behave beautifully in relation to his wife. Praise, pursuit, and passion are the three Ps for discovering the pleasures a marriage can provide.

A Lover's Praise

I. INTRODUCTION

Some Thoughts About Men

*M*en can be rather peculiar creatures. In the minds of women, they are often downright strange. A good friend of mine, Charles Lowery, is a marriage and family conference speaker who lives in Albuquerque, New Mexico. Several years ago he tried to help us get a handle on the mind of the male in a column he wrote. I think you'll find this both entertaining and right on target.

> A few years ago the Forester Sisters sang a song about men. It went something like this: "They buy you dinner, open your door, other than that what are they good for?" Men . . . Men do have problems, especially with relationships. We grow up playing baseball, football, king of the hill, and capture the flag. We grew up competing with each other— doing things and fixing things. We don't talk much, especially about our feelings. You might say that deep down, men are real shallow.

> A man thinks *talk* is a four-letter word. He thinks the relationship is going great if he doesn't have to talk. Putting him in a situation where he has to talk makes him very uncomfortable. That's why men go to the bathroom alone, the way God intended it.

> A man just has difficulty expressing himself. My daughter will call and I will say only three things: "How's the weather?" "Need any money?" "Here's your mother." A woman can talk on the phone for thirty minutes and you say, "Who was that?" She says, "I don't know, it was the wrong number."

> Things are simple with a man. Women are complex. They may even be smarter. Think about it. A woman's best friend is diamonds, and man's best friend is a dog. Yes, women are more complex. When a woman is going out, she has to decide if she is going to wear her hair up or down, flats or high heels, slacks or dress, casual or dressy dress, stockings, knee highs or socks, jewelry or no jewelry, lots of makeup or little makeup. A man picks up some clothes, smells them, and if there is no visible dirt he has himself an outfit! A man makes a fashion statement by turning the brim of his baseball cap backwards. Women dress to express themselves, and men dress so they won't be naked.

> Of course the bottom line is look at what women carry—a purse. It contains everything she might need. Men carry a wallet. It conveniently contains nothing but money, which means you can

buy whatever you need. Simple! But these differences affect many aspects of a relationship.

Let me tell you "simple" doesn't work when dealing with your wife, especially in the area of gifts. If your last gifts have been things like salad shooters, dust-busters, weed whackers, deluxe irons, and drywall compound, you are in serious trouble. They work, but they don't work with your wife.

Yes, men and women are different. That was God's plan. The difference is the dynamic. Together we can be more than we could ever have been apart. That's why God said it was not good for man to be alone. Then he made man a helper to complete him.

It is clear men and women think and act differently. Unfortunately, far too many men both think and act badly. In the fall of 1996, *NBC* introduced a sad, sick comedy called *Men Behaving Badly*. It depicted men as crude, rude lowlifes who are basically worthless. But the Song of Songs has a different take on men. It shows us men who behave beautifully, men behaving as God intended when he *created* them in his *image* and *saved* them through his Son Jesus Christ. What does this man, this husband, look like? Solomon highlights three truths.

II. COMMENTARY

A Lover's Praise

MAIN IDEA: *A man who behaves beautifully in marriage will praise, pursue, and be passionate about his wife.*

A He Advances in the Praise of His Mate (6:13–7:6)

SUPPORTING IDEA: *Praise your mate in every way you can imagine.*

We have already seen Solomon praise his wife twice for her physical beauty and priceless character (4:1–7; 6:4–9). In each description there is growth in appreciation for her. Each is more personal, intimate, and sensual. Repetition is a great teacher. God obviously thinks (and probably our spouses too) that we cannot say kind and uplifting things too often to our mates. In the Song, the repetition we discover is seldom, if ever, identical. There is growth and progress in the love, knowledge, and joy this husband and wife share. Solomon is advancing; he is growing up in the school of praise of his mate. What are some of the particulars we discover?

1. Praise her publicly.

6:13. Solomon swept his wife off her feet and placed her in his "royal chariots" (6:12). He publicly honored her. This display of affection drew the praise of her friends, who pleaded with her to return that they **may gaze on her**. Four times the imperative **come back** was voiced. But she was gone. She had left all for a man who was so public, in this instance even without words, in his love for his wife. The word **Shulammite** is used only here in the Song. It is actually the feminine form of "Solomon," literally "Solomoness." It means "perfect one" (Garrett, 419).

Shulammite was taken aback by the praise she received, and she responded with a question: **Why would you gaze on the Shulammite, as on the dance of Mahanaim?** (or "two camps"). This latter phrase is unclear. Mahanaim was a town east of the Jordan River where David fled and hid from his son Absalom (2 Sam. 17:24). The precise meaning intended by Solomon is unknown to us, but Shulammite's question and actions are not. They had praised her beauty, and she was appreciative. But there was another whose praise meant even more. That person was her husband.

His praise had freed her to express herself with unhindered, sensual abandonment. She would now dance, and dance nakedly and seductively. However, this dance was not for many but only for one. It would be a private performance reserved only for her husband. There was power in public praise.

2. Praise her physically.

7:1–5. This is the third—and most sensual—detailed, physical description by Solomon of his wife. Starting from her dancing feet to a woman's glory (her hair, see 1 Cor. 11:15), Solomon described physical features of his wife which drew attention to her beauty as a woman. One thing was obvious—she had removed her outer garments and danced in the light clothing of a shepherdess—or, more likely, she danced fully naked, appealing seductively to the male's heightened sense of sight (Carr, 156).

But we should keep this in perspective. What constitutes a sensuous and attractive woman is probably a badly misunderstood idea by most. A *USA Today* survey asked men what they first noticed about a woman. Interestingly, the number one answer was the eyes (39 percent). Second was the smile (25 percent). Only 14 percent said the first thing they noticed was the body ("Snapshots," *USA Today*, 9 June 1998, p. D1).

Different men find different kinds of women attractive. I think Linda Dillow and Lorraine Pintus said it best when they wrote, "Nothing is as 'sexy' as a woman who gives in to her sensuousness, a woman who enjoys sex and lets her husband know she loves to give and receive pleasure." Going on to quote Lisa Douglass, they added, "Nothing transcends the traditional definitions of beauty like the face and the body of a passionately aroused woman" (Dillow and Pintus, 60; see Lisa Douglass, "Orgasms: The Science," *New Woman*, June 1998, p. 126).

3. Praise her particularly.

Solomon focused on ten aspects of his wife's beauty. Although attention was on the physical, certain features also highlighted the attractiveness of her personality and character as well.

7:1. She danced before him, and so he mentioned first her **sandaled feet**. Her sandals would have left the top of her feet nearly bare. This would have been alluring and particularly attractive (Snaith, 100). His reference to her as a **prince's daughter** was a symbolic way of praising her noble character, and it testified to how her husband viewed and treated her. He honored her as God commanded (1 Pet. 3:7). There were no demeaning glances, no rude snapping of the fingers, no harsh words of contempt or criticism. She was a princess, a queenly maiden.

Her **legs** were shapely and priceless, the work of a skilled craftsman. The word refers to the upper part of the thigh where the legs begin to come together (Carr, 156). Like priceless **jewels**, they were attractive to see and precious to hold.

7:2. Verse 2 is badly translated in my judgment in virtually every English version. The problem is with the word **navel**. It simply does not fit the upward progression or description. The word almost certainly is a reference to the innermost sexual part of a woman, her vagina (vulva) (Carr, 157; Snaith, 101). Solomon's description makes no sense of a navel, but it beautifully expressed the sexual pleasures he continually received from his wife. Like **a rounded goblet** or bowl, it never lacked **blended wine**; she never ran dry. She was a constant source of intoxicating pleasure and sweetness.

The idea of blended or mixed wine could refer to the mingling of male and female fluids in the appropriate place of a woman's body as a result of sexual climax (Snaith, 103). Shulammite was an exotic garden (4:12,16) and an intoxicating drink (7:2) in her lovemaking. Seldom, if ever, was her husband disappointed.

He compared her **waist** to **a mound of wheat encircled by lilies**. This could refer to her gently curved figure and also to the fact that she was like food to him. She was wheat and wine, food and drink. She nourished and satisfied him in every way.

7:3–4. He again described her **breasts** as **two fawns** (cf. 4:5). They were soft and attractive, enticing him to pet them. Her **neck** was an **ivory tower** (cf. 4:4). She was majestic, stately, a confident and dignified woman. Her **eyes** were beautiful, pure, and refreshing (cf. 1:15, 4:1), like the Moabite city of Heshbon (cf. Num. 21:25), a city known for its reservoirs. The location of Bath Rabbim is unknown, though it is possibly the gate in Heshbon that led to the pools. Her **nose** was **like the tower of Lebanon looking toward Dam-**

ascus. She was strong in character, and there was a genuine sense in which he drew strength and security from her. He may also have been saying, "Her nose complements and sets off her facial beauty" (Garrett, 422).

7:5. Shulammite's **head** crowned her **like Mount Carmel**, Solomon said. The Carmel mountain range was considered one of the most beautiful in all of Palestine. She was beautiful and unique, majestic and awesome (cf. Isa. 35:2; Jer. 46:18). Her **hair** was **like royal tapestry**, purple (or deep red), and her husband was **held captive** by its beauty. He had been ensnared by her.

4. Praise her personally.

7:6. Solomon summarized his praise of his wife by telling her she was **beautiful** and **pleasing**, a love with **delights**. He was specific and personal. Physically she was stunning, and personally she was pleasant. She was his love and lover, and he associated nothing but delight with her. What man would not allow himself to be captivated by such a woman?

Ⓑ He Is Aggressive in the Pursuit of His Mate (7:7–9a)

SUPPORTING IDEA: *A man should zealously and creatively pursue the love of his mate.*

Solomon was creative and imaginative as he expressed his desire for Shulammite. He was not boring, nor did he display a one-track mind. He was always looking for new and fresh ways to communicate his love and affection.

1. Express a desire for her love.

7:7. Solomon compared his wife to a stately, swaying palm tree and her breasts to its clusters. Her breasts were a sweet and tasty fruit that he found irresistible. He moved quickly to express his intentions: "I will climb the palm tree; I will take hold of its fruit" (v. 8). Solomon had watched his wife dance before him as long as he could. His passion was at a fever pitch. He left nothing to chance. He did not assume his wife understood what he was feeling. He told her, and he told her plainly.

A man should not make assumptions when dealing with a woman, especially his wife. It can get him into serious trouble. In our first year of marriage, I made such an assumption. I assumed a particular object lesson would make the appropriate impression on my wife Charlotte.

We sat down one Saturday evening to eat a sandwich for dinner. As she placed a wonderful sandwich on the table, Charlotte also put beside it a Tupperware product that had inside of it—if you used your imagination and a magnifying glass—something that remotely resembled potato chips. Once these crumbs were placed in your mouth, you could easily have assumed it was a new variety of chewing gum. They were awful. I turned to Charlotte and said, "Honey, I don't like these. They're too small and stale. I want some big, fresh, crispy potato chips."

She responded, "Sweetheart, when all of these are gone, we can get some more."

That was not the answer I was looking for, so I said, "But Darling, I saw in the pantry on the way in here a brand new bag of fresh, crispy potato chips that has never been opened. I want those!"

Quick as a flash she shot back, "Well, Sugar Dumpling, when this container is empty, we can get those."

I then did something that a man would only do in his first year of marriage. I stood up, took her Tupperware, and dumped the chips in the floor! I then said, "This one is empty now. You can go and get the others." It probably will not surprise anyone that (1) she did not go get the other chips, (2) it was rather chilly at our house for several days, and (3) I learned the danger of assuming my wife would appreciate my creative object lesson.

2. Express delight from her love.

7:8–9a. Solomon told Shulammite that he wanted her and that he sensed that she wanted him. Her breasts, her breath, and her mouth were sources of sensual desire and delight. Her **breasts** were attractive and sweet. Her **breath** was fragrant, like apricots or **apples** (Carr points out that "breath" could be a reference, in the Hebrew text, to the nipples of her breasts; 162–63). The deep, sensual kisses of her **mouth** were intoxicating **like the best wine**. Shulammite had earlier described her husband's mouth in this way (1:2). He now returned the compliment. The stage had been set for a time of romantic lovemaking.

John Gries was on target when he wrote, "Jesus intended marriage to be happy for you. God expects regular sex in marriage, and sex is a learning process." In his book *Sex 101: Over 350 Creative Ways to Combine Sex, Romance, and Affection,* Gries points out seven essentials for satisfying sex. They include communication, time, patience, experimentation, understanding, being teachable, and humor. He notes that "every ingredient is very important" (*Baptist Press,* 1 November 2000).

Religious News Service reported that

> family, money, and religion are even more important to Americans than sex, according to a new survey on attitudes toward sexual health. But that does not mean Americans devalue sex. Of those surveyed, 82 percent said sexual satisfaction was important or very important. Loving family relationships received the most votes, with 99 percent considering it important or very important. Financial security was a close second, receiving 98 percent. Ranked third, religion and spiritual life was considered important or very important by 86 percent. . . . This survey is a "snapshot" in time that looks at how

American adults view issues related to sexuality and sexual problems as a whole, said Dr. Marianne J. Legato of Columbia University. Researchers also found that age did not affect the importance people placed on sex. The vast majority of respondents—94 percent, split almost equally between men and women—agreed that "enjoyable sexual relations add to a person's quality of life, even when they grow older."

Yes, we should expect delight from the love of our mate. And the good news is that it can get better with each passing year.

Ⓒ He Accepts the Passion of His Mate (7:9b–10)

SUPPORTING IDEA: *In a healthy marriage, there is giving and receiving with mutual satisfaction as the goal.*

It has been some time since Shulammite has spoken (6:13). She has been listening carefully and taking in all that her husband has said. He has gotten the attention of her heart, and again it was through her ear, through what she heard. Now it is her time to act, and act she does. What do we discover about the pleasures of passion in a good marriage?

1. Let there be mutual giving.

7:9b. Picking up on the imagery of wine, Shulammite expressed her desire to satisfy and bring pleasure to her husband. **May the wine go straight to my lover, flowing gently over lips and teeth.** They were making love to each other, and it was delightful—like fine, intoxicating wine. They exchanged kisses and intimate expressions of love that each found satisfying. His goal was to satisfy and please her. Her goal was to satisfy and please him. When there is mutual giving with the goal of pleasing your mate, the marvelous result will be that both spouses will experience the joy and pleasure God intended for us (cf. 1 Cor. 7:3–4; Phil. 2:3–5).

2. Let there be mutual gratification.

7:10. There had already been refrains or statements of mutual possession (2:16; 6:3). But this time the statement was different. Rather than read, "I am my lover's and my lover is mine" (6:3), we read, **I belong to my lover, and his desire is for me.** This was a strong affirmation of possession and gratification. She delighted in the fact that her husband's desire was only for her. What security! What satisfaction! What safety! She was so taken back by his love for her that she did not need to mention her possession of him. The word **desire** occurs only here and in Genesis 3:16 and 4:7. It speaks of a strong yearning. Solomon, as is true of all men, had an earnest desire for "the loving approval of his wife" (Patterson, 110). She was grateful for his desire for her, and he was grateful for her admiration and respect.

Passion is not an easy thing to keep aflame over a lifetime, but it is an essential thing.

MAIN IDEA REVIEW: *A man who behaves beautifully in marriage will praise, pursue, and be passionate about his wife.*

III. CONCLUSION

The Husband of Noble Character

Most of us are familiar with the "virtuous woman" of Proverbs 31. She is certainly a worthy model for all women to emulate. Several years ago Michael Jones, a fine student at Southern Seminary in Louisville, Kentucky, wrote something of a modern-day proverb that beautifully expresses what it means for a man to "flesh out" the biblical command to love his wife just like Jesus Christ loved the church and gave himself (in sacrificial death) for her (Eph. 5:25).

The Husband of Noble Character

A husband of noble character, who can find? He is worth more than winning the Publisher's Clearinghouse Sweepstakes. His wife has full confidence in him. He brings her good, not harm, all the days of her life.

He works hard to provide for his family. Getting up early, he helps get the kids ready for school, then dashes off to work. With his shoulder to the grindstone, he works with energy and vigor, as one who is working for the Lord. And while busy, he always finds time to call his wife during the day just to say, "I love you."

He promptly comes home from work and immediately pitches in with the chores, helping the children with their homework, or with making dinner. While hot dogs and baked beans are his specialty, he doesn't fear heating up a TV dinner or even making a meat loaf. He does this with such ease that all are amazed and in awe.

When his wife prepares a meal, he always eats with gusto and, when finished, never forgets to smile and tell her how great it was. Of course, he is always the first to volunteer to do the dishes, or at least to volunteer the children to complete the task! All in all, he is a joy to have in the kitchen.

As a father, there is no equal on the face of the earth. No matter how exhausted from work or other responsibilities, he always takes time for his children. Whether it's making funny faces at the baby, tickling the small child, wrestling or playing with an older child, or making pained and disbelieving expressions at his teenager, he is always there for them. He is a whiz at math, science, spelling, geography, Spanish, and any other subject his children are studying at school. And if he should be totally ignorant of the subject at hand, he skillfully hides his ignorance by sending the child to his mother. He can fix any problem—from a scraped knee to loose bicycle chains, from interpreting rules for a kickball game to refereeing sparring matches between his kids.

More importantly, he is also the spiritual leader in the family. He always takes the family to church. He shows his children, by life and example, what it means to love the Lord Jesus and to be a Christian. He teaches his children how to pray and the importance of knowing and loving God. He often rises early to pray for his wife and children, and he reads from his Bible at night before falling off to sleep. He disciplines his children with loving firmness, never yelling or with humiliating words. He is always more interested in teaching a lesson and building character than in simply punishing. During the day he meditates on God's Word and on how to live it. He shows Christ in all his dealings with others and is considered a valuable employee by his bosses. His coworkers respect his hard work, integrity, and kindness.

He always shows his wife the utmost respect, even opening the door for her. He is always quick with a word of encouragement and is constantly telling her how beautiful she is, even when she isn't wearing any makeup. A day seldom passes that he doesn't tell her of his love for her. Praise for her is always on his lips. Anniversaries and birthdays are never forgotten, and gifts and flowers are often given "just because." And he even makes superhuman efforts to be nice when her family is visiting.

He is full of compassion for the pain of others and willingly helps those in need. Whether it's changing a stranger's flat tire, helping with a friend's home improvement project, or feeding the poor at the local soup kitchen, he is the first to volunteer. He is not afraid to shed a tear with a friend in pain or to be rowdy in laughter at another's good joke. He loves life and lives it with passion.

His children, while not always calling him "blessed," have no doubts about his great love for them. His wife also calls him many things, among them "the best," and she thanks God for him. Many men do many great things, but he surpasses them all. Flattery is deceptive, and good looks, like hair, are fleeting; but a man who fears the Lord is to be praised. Give him the reward he has earned, and let his deeds bring him praise.

PRACTICAL PRINCIPLES AND APPLICATIONS

- Be personal and specific when you praise your wife.
- Praise your wife often.
- Avoid careless words.
- Giving and receiving are essential to a healthy marriage.

IV. LIFE APPLICATION

Extramarital Affairs

According to a *National Opinion Research Center* survey in 1994 (cited in *Newsweek*, 30 September 1996), 21 percent of men and 11 percent of women will have an extramarital affair in their lifetime. Tragically, the church is not immune to this widespread evil. Prevention is always the best cure. The first positive preventive step is developing an intimate, fulfilling relationship with your spouse.

V. PRAYER

Heavenly Father, too many men have behaved badly for too long. I do not want to be such a man. Help me to cultivate the character of Christ and to love and care for my wife like you love and care for me. Help me to grow in my praise of her. Help me to pursue her in a way that speaks to her heart. Help me to give and receive the pleasures of passion, making sure I always put her first. In Jesus' name I pray. Amen.

VI. DEEPER DISCOVERIES

A. Gems and Minerals in the Song of Songs

1. *Ivory.* This item of wealth and luxury was taken from the tusks of elephants, some of which roamed the upper Euphrates River or were imported from India. The bride compared her husband's body to ivory (5:14), and he described her neck in similar fashion (7:4). Ivory is a symbol of great value and uniqueness.

2. *Marble.* Close-grained crystalline limestone described in the Song was probably white or cream colored and imported from locations near the Gulf of Suez and in southern Greece. It was used for fine statuary, which prompted Shulammite to describe the legs of her beloved as "pillars of marble" (5:15).

3. *Sapphires, jewels.* In their mutual descriptions of each other, the lovers often used extravagant imagery. Sapphires, which are identified by some as lapis lazuli, might have been inlaid on the royal girdle (5:14). His reference to jewels in the description of her thigh (7:1) is linked

by some scholars to movement, literally, "twisting and winding of the upper part of the body by means of the thigh-joint." Beryl, a chrysolite found in ancient Spain, adorned the royal hands (5:14).

4. *Silver, gold.* These precious metals are mentioned together (1:11; 3:10), first spoken by the "daughters of Jerusalem" as Shulammite anticipated the king's gifts of jewelry to her. Later, in the wedding procession, the description of the royal carriage contained costly supporting framework. Gold was also part of her description of the king's hands and feet (a figure of speech for great value and excellence). Silver was mentioned by Shulammite's brothers in describing their protection of her purity. It also spoke of worth.

B. Roles and Responsibilities of the Christian Husband and Wife

The husband's role is head of his wife as Christ is head of the church (Eph. 5:23). This is the husband's biblical assignment or role position. "Head" refers not to man as the source of the woman but to the spiritual leadership that he exercises as "her savior" from the human perspective.

The wife's role is a helper corresponding to her husband (Gen. 2:18). This is the wife's biblical assignment or role position. "Helper" is not a demeaning term but a word that emphasizes differences between the man and the woman. "Corresponding" emphasizes their sameness. The word *helper* is used elsewhere in Scripture of God who condescends to help and serve his people.

The husband's responsibility is to love his wife as Christ loved the church. He loves his wife unconditionally, placing her interests and care above his own in importance. He accomplishes this by:

- Sacrificing for her (Eph. 5:29)—denying himself in order to provide for her
- Nourishing her (Eph. 5:29)—enriching her spiritually by modeling godly living and by sharing and instructing in biblical understanding; seeking to make her a success; providing guidance and encouragement in personal and family affairs
- Modeling trust
- Helping
- Teaching her
- Cherishing her (Eph. 5:29)—treating her with tenderness, care, and romance; protecting her from distress and danger (physically, emotionally, spiritually); examples: compliments, cuddling, flowers, taking her side in an argument, spending time with her just talking after a tough day

- Accepting her (1 Pet 3:7)—caring for her with understanding and honoring her as a partner in Christ and God's daughter!
- Studying her (a lifelong challenge!)
- Developing an awareness of her emotions and moods
- Allowing her the luxury of not doing things the way he would do them
- Having her serve with him in the church

The wife's responsibility is to submit herself to her husband as to the Lord. She places herself under the authority of her husband's leadership, working alongside him to support, encourage, and complete him. She accomplishes this by:

- Yielding to him voluntarily (Eph. 5:22–24; Col. 3:18; 1 Pet. 3:1–6)—acknowledging the position God has given him; supporting and encouraging his efforts; lending cooperation, imagination, and implementation (which includes advising and taking responsibilities); trusting the Lord to guide them both and honor her obedience to the Word.
- Respecting him sincerely (Eph. 5:33)—believing in him; giving him the benefit of the doubt; praising him rather than criticizing him; trusting him to do the right thing.

VII. TEACHING OUTLINE

A. INTRODUCTION: SOME THOUGHTS ABOUT MEN

B. COMMENTARY

1. He Advances in the Praise of His Mate (6:13–7:6)
   a. Praise her publicly.
   b. Praise her physically.
   c. Praise her particularly.
   d. Praise her personally.
2. He Is Aggressive in the Pursuit of His Mate (7:7–9a)
   a. Express a desire for her love.
   b. Expect delight from her love.
3. He Accepts the Passion of His Mate (7:9b–10)
   a. Let there be mutual giving.
   b. Let there be mutual gratification.

C. CONCLUSION: THE HUSBAND OF NOBLE CHARACTER

VIII. ISSUES FOR DISCUSSION

Twelve Ways to Keep Passion Alive in Your Marriage

1. *Work at it.* A lifetime of love and romance takes effort. Few things in life are as complicated as building and maintaining an intimate, passionate relationship. You need to work on it constantly to get through those trying periods that require extra work.

2. *Think team.* When making important decisions, such as whether to work overtime or accept a transfer or promotion, ask yourself, "What will the choice I am making do to the people I love?" Try to make the decision that will have the most positive impact on your marriage and your family.

3. *Be protective.* Guard your marriage and your family from the rest of the world. This might mean refusing to work on certain days or nights. You might turn down relatives and friends who want more of you than you have the time, energy, or inclination to give. You might even have to say no to your children to protect time with your spouse. (The kids won't suffer if this is done occasionally and not constantly).

4. *Accept that good and not perfect is OK when it comes to your mate.* No one is perfect. You married a real person who will make real mistakes. However, never be content with bad. Always aim for great, but settle for good!

5. *Share your thoughts and feelings.* Unless you consistently communicate, signaling to your partner where you are and getting a recognizable message in return, you will lose each other along the road of life. Create or protect communication-generating rituals. No matter how busy you may be, make time for each other. For example, take a night off each week, go for a walk together every few days, go out to breakfast if you can't have dinner alone, or just sit together for fifteen minutes each evening simply talking, without any other distractions.

6. *Manage anger and especially contempt better.* Try to break the cycle in which hostile, cynical, contemptuous attitudes fuel unpleasant emotions, leading to negative behaviors that stress both of you out and create more tension. Recognize that anger signals frustration of some underlying need, and try to figure out what that need might be. Avoid igniting feelings of anger with the judgment that you are being mistreated. Watch your nonverbal signals, such as the tone of your voice, your hand and arm gestures, facial expressions, and body movements. Try to notice subtle signs that anger or irritation is building. If you are harboring these feelings, express them before they build too much and cause an angry outburst.

7. *Declare your devotion to each other again and again.* True long-range intimacy requires repeated affirmations of commitment to your partner.

Remember, love is in what you say and in how you act. Buy flowers. Do the dishes and take out the trash without being asked. Give an unsolicited back rub. Committed couples protect the boundaries around their relationship. Share secrets with each other more than with any circle of friends and relatives.

8. *Give each other permission to change.* Pay attention. If you aren't learning something new about each other every week or two, you simply aren't observing closely enough. You are focusing on other things, not each other. Bored couples fail to update how they view each other. They act as though the roles they assigned and assumed early in the relationship will remain forever the same. Remain constantly in touch with each other's dreams, fears, goals, disappointments, hopes, regrets, wishes, and fantasies. People continue to trust those people who know them best and who accept them.

9. *Have fun together.* Human beings usually fall in love with those who make them laugh, who make them feel good on the inside. They stay in love with those who make them feel safe enough to come out to play. Keep delight a priority. Put your creative energy into making yourselves joyful and producing a relationship that regularly feels like recess.

10. *Make yourself trustworthy.* People come to trust those who affirm them. They learn to distrust those who act as if a relationship were a continual competition over who is right and who gets their way. Always act as if each of you has thoughts, impressions, and preferences that make sense, even if your opinions or needs differ. Realize your partner's perceptions will always contain some truth, and validate that truth before adding your perspectives to the discussion.

11. *Forgive and forget.* Don't be too hard on each other. If your passion and love are to survive, you must learn how to forgive. You and your partner regularly need to wipe the slate clean so anger doesn't build and resentment doesn't fester. Holding on to hurts and hostility will block real intimacy. It will only assure that no matter how hard you work at it, your relationship will not grow. Do what you can to heal the wounds in a relationship, even if you did not cause them. Be compassionate about the fact that neither of you intended to hurt the other as you set out on this journey.

12. *Cherish and applaud.* One of the most fundamental ingredients in the intimacy formula is cherishing each other. You need to celebrate each other's presence. If you don't give your partner admiration, applause, appreciation, acknowledgment, the benefit of the doubt, encouragement, and the message that you are happy to be there with them now, where will they receive those gifts? Be generous. Be gracious.

Song of Songs 7:10–8:4

A Vacation in the Country

Song of Songs
7:10–8:4

Quote

"*A* great marriage is not when the perfect couple comes together. It is when an imperfect couple learns to enjoy their differences."

D a v e   M e u r e r

I N   A   N U T S H E L L

S hulammite provides a pattern of a captivating wife that will speak clearly and deeply to the heart of a man.

A Vacation in the Country

I. INTRODUCTION

25 Essentials of a Fantastic Female

I recently came across some counsel men would like to pass on to women that, at least in our judgment, would go quite a ways in helping you be just the right mate. It is called "25 Essentials for a Fantastic Female."

1. Learn to work the toilet seat. If it's up, put it down. We need it up, you need it down. You don't hear us complaining about you leaving it down.
2. If you won't dress like the Victoria's Secret girls, don't expect us to act like Don Juan or Romeo guys.
3. Don't cut your hair. Ever. Long hair is always more attractive than short hair. One of the big reasons guys fear getting married is that married women always cut their hair, and by then you're stuck with her.
4. Birthdays, valentines, and anniversaries are not quests to see if we can find the perfect present yet again!
5. If you ask a question you don't want an answer to, expect an answer you don't want to hear.
6. Sometimes we're not thinking about you. Just learn to live with it. Don't ask what we're thinking about unless you are prepared to discuss such topics as March Madness, the shotgun formation, and the stupidity of the "prevent defense."
7. Saturday = Sports. It's like the full moon or the changing of the tides. Let it be.
8. Shopping is not a sport, and no, we're never going to think of it that way.
9. When we have to go somewhere, absolutely anything you want to wear is fine.
10. You have enough clothes.
11. You have too many shoes.
12. Crying is definitely blackmail.
13. Ask for what you want. Let's be clear on this one: Subtle hints don't work. Strong hints don't work. Really obvious hints don't work. Just say it!
14. We don't know what day it is. We never will. Mark anniversaries on the calendar.

15. Yes and no are perfectly acceptable answers to almost every question.
16. Come to us with a problem only if you want help solving it. That's what we do.
17. A headache that lasts for seventeen months is a problem. See a doctor.
18. If something we said could be interpreted two ways, and one of the ways makes you mad or sad, we meant the other one.
19. You can either tell us to *do* something or tell us *how* to do something—but not both.
20. Whenever possible, please say whatever you have to say during commercials.
21. All men see in only sixteen colors. Peach is a fruit, not a color.
22. If it itches, it will be scratched.
23. If we ask what's wrong and you say "nothing," we will act like nothing's wrong. We know you are not telling the truth, but it's just not worth the pain.
24. Anything we said six months ago is inadmissible in an argument today. All comments become null and void after seven days.
25. Most guys own three pairs of shoes. What makes you think we'd be any good at choosing which pair, out of thirty, would look good with your dress?

Women may not be very impressed with this list from the men. That is quite understandable. But if we could examine God's perspective on a fabulous female, a picture of his "wonder woman," would you be interested? I believe such a woman is portrayed in Song of Songs 7:10–8:4. She is not characterized by twenty-five peculiar particulars but rather by three overarching attributes that any man would find attractive and irresistible.

II. COMMENTARY

A Vacation in the Country

> **MAIN IDEA:** Shulammite provides a beautiful portrait of a woman who knows how to care for her man.

A She Delivers Her Love Through Personal Invitations (7:10–13)

> **SUPPORTING IDEA:** Sometimes a wife should be the aggressor and take the initiative in romancing her husband.

Solomon, at least at this point in his life, was a one-woman kind of man. Shulammite was a one-man kind of woman. His attention was on her, and her affection was set on him. Kind words of praise and affirmation from her husband had set Shulammite free to respond sensually to her husband. She extended an invitation for a romantic getaway. What were its components?

1. Be specific.

7:10. Shulammite said, **I belong to my lover** ("I am my beloved's," NKJV). She belonged to him and no other. He was the only man in her life. The danger of infidelity was not on her radar screen, and she wisely avoided its snares. A wise husband and a wise wife will covenant never to be alone with a person of the opposite sex other than their spouse. Such a commitment is a sure safeguard against adultery and a pledge of the specific and particular nature of one's love and devotion for his or her mate.

2. Be secure.

Shulammite could also say of her husband, **and his desire is for me.** Solomon had eyes for only one woman, and that woman was his wife. This is how it should be for all men, that our desire is set only for one woman: our wife. A wife who is secure in her relationship with her husband is released to love him without holding anything back. She does not fear that her love will be prostituted or abused.

3. Be spontaneous.

7:11–12. For the first time in the Song, Shulammite took the initiative in requesting a time for romance and lovemaking with her husband. She knew that sex that took place only at home could run the risk of becoming routine. Vacations and special getaways often enhance and rekindle passion in marriage. She invited him—calling him **my lover**—to leave the city and its grind and to go away with her to the country for a time where they could be alone together. Four times she said "let's go": (1) **Let us go to the countryside,** (2) **Let us spend the night in the villages,** (3) **Let us go early to the vineyards,** (4) [Let us] **see if the vines have budded.**

Spring is a universal symbol of love and romance, and its signs should be everywhere in a marriage. There should be a freshness and a sense of anticipation to love. Getting away, if only for a brief time, can invigorate and energize a relationship. Shulammite knew sexual problems could slip into a relationship if it was not properly cared for. As a woman, she was aware of the role she must play to keep their sex life on a high plain. Ginny Graves outlines seven essentials that a woman must give attention to in order to keep the flames of romance burning.

1. *Adjust your hormones.* Sex and hormones are inextricably linked. Hormonal upheaval can strike in a woman's mid- to late 40s, before menopause sets in. "In some women, when levels of sex hormones decrease around menopause, so does sex drive," says Barbara Sherwin, professor of psychology and obstetrics-gynecology at McGill University in Montreal.

2. *Sleep well.* "Sleep deprivation is an underrated cause of decreased sex drive," says Kathleen Blindt Segraves, associate professor of psychiatry at Case Western Reserve University School of Medicine in Cleveland, Ohio. The treatment is easy and inexpensive: seven to nine hours of shut-eye a night.

3. *Exercise wisely.* Most of the news about exercise and sex is good. According to one study, aerobic exercise (an hour a day) has been shown to increase sexual frequency and responsiveness in men, and researchers assume it gives women the same libidinal zing. Extreme exercise, however, may cause a backlash. To reap exercise benefits, be sure to maintain a moderate workout schedule, increase the intensity of your regimen gradually, and consume enough calories to preserve a healthy level of body fat.

4. *Beat depression.* "Depression has a constellation of symptoms, including loss of interest in sex," says Xavier Amador, a New York City psychologist.

5. *Watch those anti-depressants.* "One of the great ironies of anti-depressants is that they can cause sexual dysfunction," says Dr. Andrew Leuchter, director of the Division of Adult Psychiatry at UCLA.

6. *Manage stress.* "Even everyday stressors correlate with reduced sexual desire in men and women," says J. Gayle Beck, professor of psychology at the State University of New York at Buffalo. "Men are more likely to put their feelings aside in the interest of having sex, whereas women will choose not to have a sexual encounter," she says. When stress builds up, people become too distracted to focus on giving and receiving sexual pleasure. "It's no coincidence," says Beck, "that a lot of couples have great sex when they're on vacation." If you suspect that stress is causing low libido, find time to decompress by taking a bath or a long walk early in the evening.

7. *Communicate* (Ginny Graves, "7 Solutions for Sexual Partners," *Readers Digest*, December 1999, pp. 102–06).

4. Be sensual.

7:12. Budding **vines, blossoms** opening, **pomegranates in bloom**, and especially "mandrakes" were all considered aphrodisiacs. Some referred to the mandrake as the "love apple" (Carr, 165). In the midst of these outdoor delicacies, Shulammite said, **There I will give you my love.** "Not just in the country but outside under the sun, moon, and stars, we will find a place just for the two of us and make passionate love."

7:13. Do as verse 13 directs: at the door of your mate, find pleasant fruit or **every delicacy.** Lay your inhibitions aside, and let your imagination run wild. Some will be old (it is good every time without fail), and some should be new (different, previously unexplored). Shulammite said she had all of this **stored up** for her husband.

And men, not only will it be fun; it is also good for you. The British Heart Foundation just released a report that says men who make love three or four times a week are protecting themselves against heart attacks and strokes. Men who have three to four orgasms a week cut in half the risk of having a major heart attack or stroke over the next ten years. Indeed good sex is as good an exercise as jogging or squash (David Derbyshire, "A Little Loving Makes the Heart Last Longer," *Sex and Health*, 29 November 2000). While the research did not look at the impact of sexual activity on women's long-term health, surely the benefits are even better for them!

B She Declares Her Love Through Public Affection (8:1–2)

> **SUPPORTING IDEA:** *Let others know, through appropriate public displays of affection, the love you have for your mate.*

These two verses sound strange to our modern Western ears, but they would have spoken beautifully and affectionately to the heart of Solomon. Indeed, it is the case that kind, loving words are welcomed anytime and anywhere. They are crucial to keeping us well connected. We might be well served to take a little advice from the family dog at this point. "Fido may do a better job of greeting your spouse when he or she comes home than you do," says William Doherty, director of the Marriage and Family Therapy program at the University of Minnesota in St. Paul. The family dog is loyal, enthusiastic, and totally focused on the greeting ritual. But your opening words to your spouse just might be a question about having left the garage door open or remembering to pay a bill. And that attitude makes a difference. Small "couple rituals"—such as a loving greeting—add up in the long run. They help maintain connection between partners and "are the glue we need to help us cling together in times of stress and in seasons of despair," Doherty says. The absence of such intimate rituals may indicate that a marriage is drifting along on "automatic pilot" (Karen S. Peterson, "Take Time to Nurture a Marriage," *USA Today*, 5 July 2000).

Nothing was on autopilot in this marriage. Shulammite made no assumptions, and she left nothing to chance. She wanted her husband and the world to know how she felt. What do we learn from her?

1. Show your loyalty to each other.

8:1. Shulammite said she wished Solomon was her brother so she could shower him publicly with affectionate kisses. In the Ancient Near East, it was considered appropriate only for near relatives to engage in such public displays of love and affection. "The freedom to kiss in public would not apply to her husband" (Garrett, 424). Shulammite regretted this. She wanted everyone to know how she felt about her husband. She would not overturn accepted social expectations and suffer scorn and ridicule. She would not be despised. Her actions may have been curtailed for the moment, but her words trumpeted a message that was music to the ears and heart of her husband.

Pawing one another in public is still in bad taste. Gracious and genuine tokens of our love, loyalty, and affection are always welcomed. They will be well received by our mate, and they will provide testimony of our devotion to each other to others.

A lonely heart, even in marriage, is often a sick heart—and in more ways than one. In an article titled "Lonely Hearts Often Have Sick Hearts," Ronald Kotulak noted:

> Loneliness is bad for the heart in more ways than one, according to new research that shows the physiological toll of psychological isolation. But the research, conducted by a team from the University of Chicago and Ohio State University, also suggests a remedy: Just saying hello or being nice in other small ways can help prevent heart attacks among the lonely. The study found that being lonely is a major risk factor of heart disease, as bad as a high-fat diet, high blood pressure, obesity, smoking, or physical inactivity.
>
> Loneliness tends to raise blood pressure and disrupt sleep, both of which put people at greater risk of heart trouble. Population experts long have known that lonely people tend to be sicker and die younger, but they didn't know why. Women with few social contacts and who feel isolated, for instance, have a greater risk of dying of cancer. Married cancer patients have better outcomes than unmarried cancer patients. But loneliness is not just being alone. It involves feelings of isolation, of disconnectedness, and of not belonging, each of which can occur when a person is in a crowd or alone. Lonely people perceive their world as less reinforcing and more threatening. They may not have a romantic partner or close friends (Ronald Kotulak, "Lonely Hearts Often Have Sick Hearts," *Chicago Tribune*, 8 August 2000).

Demonstrate in clear and unambiguous ways your love and loyalty to each other. Remember, it's good for the heart.

2. Strengthen your desire for each other.

8:2. Shulammite began to play with her husband. She assumed the role of an older sister and told him how she would relate to him. She would lead him and take him into her **mother's house**. The word for **lead** refers to "a superior leading an inferior: a general, his army; a king, his captain; a shepherd, his sheep. . . . She would lead her younger brother to their common home" (Glickman, 90). Shulammite noted it was at home that she received instruction from her mother. In the context she must have meant instruction about matters of sexual intimacy and love.

This is a valuable lesson, especially for those of us who are parents. "The art of preparing for love is best learned at home" (Carr, 167). Dads and moms must take charge at appropriate times and in appropriate ways in teaching their children about the birds and the bees. They cannot leave this vital task in the hands of the schools. They dare not entrust it to a locker room or girl-friend talk. Dads must instruct their sons, and mothers must guide their daughters. This does not mean dads have no part in training their daughters or moms in assisting their sons, but sexual identity often will play a role in who takes the lead with whom.

Shulammite informed Solomon of some things she learned from her mother. **Spiced wine**, special wine, would be on their lover's menu as well as the juice of **pomegranates**. "An ancient Egyptian love poem identifies a wife's breasts with the fruit of the pomegranate" (Carr, 167). Duane Garrett points out that the reference to her "mother's house" could easily be a euphemism for the intimate sexual parts of the woman (Garrett, 425). That the overtones of her words were sensual and erotic are undeniable. The joy of lovemaking they shared did not wane but grew more intensive and creative as their marriage progressed. And much of the credit went to Shulammite.

She Demonstrates Her Love Through Private Consummation (8:3–4)

SUPPORTING IDEA: *Tender actions and good timing are twin essentials for a growing, romantic marriage.*

An article in *Maxim*, a popular men's magazine said, "Monogamy is man's greatest challenge. It takes unshakable commitment, intense emotional maturity, a will of steel in the face of overwhelming temptation. In other words, it ain't gonna happen" (quoted in *Washington Post Online Edition*, 12 November 1999). I don't believe this. In fact, I reject such an argument with every fiber of my being. When a man loves a woman like this Song teaches and when a woman puts her man where her heart is as this Song instructs, the passion, commitment, and devotion they enjoy will produce a glue that will hold them together until death parts them. Solomon and Shulammite again are engaged in the act of lovemaking, but the focus this time is a bit different. It is also very instructive.

1. Tenderness is ensuring.

8:3. His left arm is under my head and his right arm embraces me. Solomon gently and tenderly was holding and caressing his wife. Perhaps they had just finished making love, and they rested in each other's arms in the afterglow of the moment. He did not leap out of bed and run downstairs for a snack. He didn't grab the remote control to get a sports update. She didn't slip out of bed to make a quick phone call, nor did she rush out of the room to attack unfinished chores. They simply lay there loving each other and holding each other. They were tender in their affections, and tenderness speaks to the heart and soul of our mate.

In an article titled "Nourishing Your Love," Marie Pierson advises women on how to touch a man's heart. Her six suggestions:

- Show him admiration and appreciation.
- Nurture his friendship.
- Lower your expectations. (You married a real person!)
- Watch your priorities. (Is he number one after Jesus?)
- Enhance your love life.
- Be forgiving (even as God in Christ has forgiven you; Eph. 4:32).

(Adapted from Pierson, "Nourishing Your Love," *Virtue*)

2. Timing is important.

8:4. For the third time (cf. 2:7; 3:5) the importance of the proper time for lovemaking is addressed. Obviously, God believes timing is important. First, it is the right time for lovemaking—only in marriage between a man and a woman. Second, within marriage, timing and sensitivity to the needs and feelings of our mate is crucial as we build affection and romance in our marriage. Mary Ganske pointed out, "Even the most happily married couples fall into ruts now and then. You know, those times when minor irritations override the love and affection you feel for each other." Drawing upon marriage seminars around the country, she shares five ways to "improve communication, smooth over rough spots and get closer than ever before."

1. *Take a minute to set up your day together.* "We tell couples not to leave home in the morning until they find out at least one thing that's going to happen to their spouse that day," says John Gottman, codirector of The Gottman Institute. Ask your husband what he's doing on his lunch hour or after work. And don't forget to fill him in on your plans. It's also important to make sure that at least once a week, perhaps during dinner, you talk about what really matters. Ask how his relationship with his boss is going or if he's worried about his annual checkup. "You can't get emotionally close if you don't know anything about your partner's inner world," says Dr. Gottman.

2. *Discuss your expectations.* Everyone enters into marriage with preconceived notions of how things should be: We should spend certain holidays with our families, save as much money as possible, go to church every Sunday. The key is to make sure you both know what the other person expects.

3. *Update your dream list.* Sit down together at least once a year to go over your dreams for the future. These may include things you want to have (a

new couch), things you want to do (create a flower garden), and things you want to be (more spiritual, a better listener). Pinpointing your desires not only helps you both grow as people, but it keeps you aligned as a couple. "We are constantly changing," said Sherod Miller, codeveloper of Couple Communication. "Find out if any new dreams have surfaced in him, and be sure to tell him yours. Supporting your partner's goals is one of the best and simplest ways to show you care."

4. *Control the way you argue.* Every happy couple has hot-button issues. Even the most compatible pair yell and scream sometimes. The trick is to contain the disagreements before they spin out of control. "If you handle conflicts poorly—with hostility, nagging, or icy distance—the love and affection you feel for each other will erode over time," says Howard Markman, coauthor of *Fighting for Your Marriage.* Your best bet is to head off fights in the first place by bringing up tough issues before they erupt. If despite your best efforts the conversation turns into a screaming match, call a time-out and agree to revisit the issue when both of you can be civil.

5. *Use praise to change bad habits.* Too often we try to change our partner by railing about what he's doing wrong. "Don't drive so fast!" "Why can't you hang up your clothes?" But highlighting your spouse's flaws is unproductive. "He'll only get defensive and counterattack," says Bernard Guerney Jr., director of the National Institute of Relationship Enhancement. A better approach is to explain what you'd like him to do. Instead of "No one should have to live in such a pigsty," a simple "I'd love it if the bedroom weren't so cluttered" will do. The next step is to heap on praise when he does what you ask.

"As basic as it sounds, people repeat behaviors that make them feel good," says Dr. Guerney. "Just be careful not to temper your approval with digs such as, 'That's a good start' or 'It's about time.' The more positive you are, the more compliant he'll be" (Mary Ganske, "How to Make a Good Marriage Great: Little Habits That Can Make All the Difference," *Woman's Day,* 13 October 2000).

> **MAIN IDEA REVIEW:** *Shulammite provides a beautiful portrait of a woman who knows how to care for her man.*

III. CONCLUSION

Christians' Changing Views About God's Gift of Sex

Some popular pundits say that modern Christian advice concerning sex dates to 1973 and a book by a woman, Marabel Morgan's *The Total Woman.* Actually, advice for Christians concerning sex goes all the way back to the Book of Genesis when before the fall, Adam and Eve "were both naked, and they felt no shame" (Gen. 2:25). The climax of God's counsel is in the Song of Songs. Here we discover that God says sex and romance in marriage are good.

Indeed, they are essential things. It is encouraging to see that more and more Christians "see sex more as a gift to be enjoyed within marriage than as an evil to be endured or avoided," and that "an orthodox view of romance, courtship and sexuality" may be the best road to sexual satisfaction (quote from Robert Michael, John Gagnon, Edward Laumann, and Gina Kolata, *Sex in America: A Definitive Study*).

Solomon worked at doing his part. In these verses we have seen Shulammite doing her part. Why hasn't it always been this way? After all, God's plan for the Christian bedroom has never changed. It is a good thing. It is a great thing. Yes, it is a God thing.

PRACTICAL PRINCIPLES AND APPLICATIONS

- Say the right thing in the right way at the right time.
- Lovemaking does not begin in the bed but in the heart.
- Remember the vulnerability of the male ego.
- Be sensitive to a woman's definition of romance.
- Creativity and sensitivity are twin essentials for a growing and satisfying marriage.

IV. LIFE APPLICATION

Building a Happy Home

Priorities are peculiar. No matter how dogmatic you try to be, you cannot be totally consistent with most of your priorities. But many of life's situations, especially those involving the home, are more permanent and require established priorities. The following are priorities that will enhance your home life and encourage its success.

Persons before things. A common failure, especially of men and of parents, is to give things instead of themselves. This is not real love but a form of bribery. Our priority must be to give ourselves and then our things, whether it is to our marriage partner, children, or elderly parents.

Home before occupation. No man can be described as successful if his home is in shambles because of his commitment to his occupation. Of course, mothers need this admonition, too.

Partner before children. It is possible for either the husband or the wife to devote so much time to the children that the partner is given second place. A failure in this area may manifest itself in disagreements over child rearing in the presence of a child. The husband and wife must consider each other before the children (Titus 2:4). Children learn about love by seeing their parents love each other. Of course, this is what makes divorce so devastating to children. Their whole sense of security rests in their parent's love for each other.

Children must come before friends. As important as friends are, such a lofty statement is never said of them: "Sons are a heritage from the LORD, children a reward from him" (Ps. 127:3).

Partner before self. The husband is to love his wife as Christ loved the church and gave himself for it (Eph. 5:25). In like fashion, the wife is to be in supportive submission to her husband in everything, just like the church is in submission to Christ (Eph. 5:24). To do this there must be the commitment to putting the partner first. This is a fundamental key to marriage.

Spiritual before the material. In 2 Corinthians 4:18 the apostle Paul wrote, "So we fix our eyes not on what is seen, but on what is unseen. For what is seen is temporary, but what is unseen is eternal." While it is necessary for us to spend much of our time on the material aspects of life, it is imperative for us to cultivate the spiritual characteristics of our lives.

The homes that emphasize the unseen things—the permanent attributes—are happier and far more stable than those that emphasize the material. The home that thrives on permanent values stresses the spiritual even if it is invisible (Stan Toussaint, Dallas Seminary).

V. PRAYER

Heavenly Father, thank you for teaching me how to grow and mature in my marriage. I understand now, more than ever, that real love is not so much something you fall into as it is something you grow into. Thank you for giving me some great principles and ideas on how to move forward in my marriage. I readily acknowledge that I need your help every step of the way. Lord Jesus, always be the Lord of our marriage, our family, our home. Amen.

VI. DEEPER DISCOVERIES

The Scriptural View of Marriage

Marriage is ordained of God

- For the welfare and the happiness of mankind (Gen. 2:18).
- Is honorable for all (Heb. 13:4).
- Is not to be forbidden (1 Tim. 4:1–3).
- Physical relationship not to be denied (Heb. 13:4).
- Physical relationship to be enjoyed (Prov. 5:18–19).
- Improper physical relationship is forbidden (Heb. 13:4).

Marriage is blessed by our Lord Jesus Christ

- He endorsed it as a divine institution (Matt. 19:4–6).

- He blessed marriage by his presence at the wedding in Cana (John 2).

Marriage is regulated by God's commandments
- Must be "in the Lord" (1 Cor. 7:39).
- No unequal yokes (2 Cor. 6:14–15).

Mutual responsibilities
- "Submit to one another" (Eph. 5:21).
- "Wives, submit" (Eph. 5:22).
- "Husbands, love" (Eph. 5:25).
- "Do not deprive each other" (1 Cor. 7:5).
- To be permanent (Matt. 19:6).
- Only death should dissolve the marriage relationship. God hates divorce (Mal. 2:16; Matt. 5:32; Mark 10:9; Rom. 7:2).
- Adultery (infidelity) may dissolve the marriage relationship. Opinion is divided, however, on whether the Bible permits the innocent party to remarry.
- Separation is permitted (1 Cor. 7:10–11). Not all are agreed that remarriage is permitted after divorce.
- Reconciliation is always God's desire.

Strengthening the bonds of marriage
- Take Jesus as Savior.
- Take Jesus as the head of the home.

Maintain Christian practices in the home
- Family altar.
- Grace at meals.

Maintain Christian attitudes
- Submitting yourselves (Eph. 5:21).
- Forgiving one another (Eph. 4:32).
- Keep "short accounts" with each other (1 Cor. 13:5).

Maintain proper relationship to the church
- Regular attendance (Heb. 10:25).
- Active participation.

Solving marriage difficulties
- With understanding love (1 Cor. 13). Here sixteen things are said about Christian love.
- With the reading of God's Word, with confession of faults one to another, and with prayer (Col. 3:12–17).

The family council

Why?
- It fosters a sense of security and belongingness.
- It develops responsibility and accountability.
- It provides an environment for creative leadership training.
- It encourages mutual understanding and consideration.
- It facilitates communication.

When?
- A specific time should be appointed, but allow for flexibility.
- Following a meal in a relaxed, informal atmosphere is often best.

What?
- A time for discussion of family problems, issues, interests, and decisions.

What to discuss
- Family spirituality.
- Family recreational program.
- Family vacation.
- Money matters.
- Family worship.
- Work assignments.
- Family problem areas.
- Weekly schedule of activities.

An attempt to find family solutions for family problems

How?
- Begin with the simple problems.
- Expect conflict and disagreement: the idea is not to begin but to end with agreement.
- Consider all the facts and everyone's viewpoints.
- Encourage good listening.
- Avoid meaningless arguments and criticism: focus on problems not people.
- Establish a plan of action: evaluate alternatives.
- Have fun in the process. Be serious but not too serious.

The dynamics of the Christian home

Attitudes
- Respect, honesty, industry, ambition, self-discipline, relaxation, servanthood, etc.
- Relationships.

- A unity of persons—a community of the concerned with a concern for the community.
- A laboratory for the application of biblical truth in a relational setting.
- A training ground for developing human relationships. For example: (1) to the opposite sex, (2) to authority, (3) to the church: local and universal, (4) to oneself, and (5) to other people: saved and unsaved.
- A school for learning love: giving and receiving.
- Convictions.
- A unique style of life—qualitatively different. Known by what it *does* do, not simply by what it does *not* do.
- A unique set of standards.
- A unique concern for the world.
- A unique value system.

VII. TEACHING OUTLINE

A. INTRODUCTION: 25 ESSENTIALS FOR A FANTASTIC FEMALE

B. COMMENTARY

1. She Delivers Her Love Through Personal Invitations (7:10–13)
   a. Be specific.
   b. Be secure.
   c. Be spontaneous.
   d. Be sensual.
2. She Declares Her Love Through Public Affection (8:1–2)
   a. Show your loyalty to each other.
   b. Strengthen your desire for each other.
3. She Demonstrates Her Love Through Private Consummation (8:3–4)
   a. Tenderness is ensuring.
   b. Timing is important.

C. CONCLUSION: CHRISTIANS' CHANGING VIEWS ABOUT GOD'S GIFT OF SEX

VIII. ISSUES FOR DISCUSSION

How to Revive and Rejoice in Relationships (Phil. 2:1–5)

1. Have I made a choice (commitment) to accept this person as he or she is?
2. Do I receive this person as someone valuable in my life?
3. Do I accept personal responsibility for the relationship?
4. Do I rejoice and value the differences (looking for the positive)?
5. Do I determine to communicate by: sharing? listening? talking?
6. Do I assume too much?
7. Am I an encourager?
8. Am I real (honest and willing to admit my own failures)?

Song of Songs 8:5–14

Love Is a Wonderful Thing

I. INTRODUCTION
Love or Infatuation?

II. COMMENTARY
A verse-by-verse explanation of these verses.

III. CONCLUSION
The Measure of True Love

An overview of the principles and applications from these verses.

IV. LIFE APPLICATION
Our Marriage Covenant

Melding these verses to life.

V. PRAYER
Tying these verses to life with God.

VI. DEEPER DISCOVERIES
Historical, geographical, and grammatical enrichment of the commentary.

VII. TEACHING OUTLINE
Suggested step-by-step group study of these verses.

VIII. ISSUES FOR DISCUSSION
Zeroing these verses in on daily life.

Quote

"*A*strong focus on families will be one of the greatest

tools for evangelism and church growth

that we could ever have."

T o m   E l l i f f

Song of Songs
8:5–14

I N   A   N U T S H E L L

*L*ove is the glue that will keep us together, enabling us to honor
our marriage commitment until we are parted by death.

Love Is a Wonderful Thing

I. INTRODUCTION

Love or Infatuation?

 $\mathscr{L}$ ove is a wonderful thing. It can also be a dangerous thing as well as a confusing thing. We often get love confused with infatuation, and the mistake can be disastrous. I came across an article titled "Love or Infatuation?" and printed in Ann Landers' column that contrasts the two. I think you'll find it is right on target.

> Infatuation leaps into bloom. Love usually takes root and grows one day at a time. Infatuation is accompanied by a sense of uncertainty. You are stimulated and thrilled but not really happy. You are miserable when he is absent. You can't wait until you see her again. Love begins with a feeling of security. You are warm with a sense of his nearness, even when he is away. Miles do not separate you. You want her near. But near or far, you know she is yours and you can wait.
>
> Infatuation says, "We must get married right away. I can't risk losing him." Love says, "Don't rush into anything. You are sure of each other. You can plan your future with confidence."
>
> Infatuation has an element of sexual excitement. If you are honest, you will discover it is difficult to enjoy each other unless you will know it will end in intimacy. Love is the maturing of friendship. You must be friends before you can be lovers.
>
> Infatuation lacks confidence. When he's away, you wonder if he's with another girl. When she is away, you wonder if she is with another guy. Sometimes you even check. Love means trust. You may fall into infatuation, but you really never fall in love. Infatuation might lead you to do things for which you might be sorry, but love never will.
>
> Love lifts you up. It makes you look up. It makes you think up. It makes you a better person than you were before.

The Song of Songs teaches us that love is important, so important in fact that it constitutes the final theme of the book. Twelve different aspects of love are addressed. Love truly is, according to God's Word, "a many-splendored thing."

II. COMMENTARY

Love Is a Wonderful Thing

> **MAIN IDEA:** *True love is a multifaceted gift that we choose to give our mate again and again.*

A Love Is Public (8:5a)

> **SUPPORTING IDEA:** *Let others see the love you have for your mate.*

8:5a. It appears that Solomon and Shulammite were riding again in the royal chariot in full public display. She reclined, relaxed and secure and **leaning on her lover**. The phrase **coming up from the desert** (or wilderness) could echo the theme of Israel's forty years of wandering in the wilderness before entering the Promised Land. This couple had passed through those "wilderness periods" in their marriage and safely arrived on the other side. The wilderness also could convey the idea of cursedness (see Jer. 22:6; Joel 2:3). Their love relationship was a redeemed relationship through God's grace. The effects of the Fall and the Genesis curse (Gen. 3:16–24) had been reversed and the disharmony that sin brought into a relationship overcome. This is what God can do when he is Lord of our marriage.

As Frederica Matthews-Green says, "Women need men to call us up toward the highest moral principles; [men] need [women] to call them down to the warmth of human love and respect for gentler sensibilities . . . It's clear that we need each other. You would almost think someone planned it that way" (Matthews-Green, "Men Behaving Justly," *Christianity Today*, 17 November 1997, p. 45). The love that Solomon and Shulammite enjoyed was something that all the world should see and learn from.

B Love Is Private (8:5b)

> **SUPPORTING IDEA:** *Some aspects of love are only for the two of you.*

8:5b. Shulammite again initiated lovemaking (the "I" is feminine). Apparently, they had left the chariot and were now alone. Three times in the Song we have been told not to awaken love until the time is right (2:7; 3:5; 8:4). Well, the time was now right, according to Shulammite. The apricot (or **apple**) **tree** was often associated with sexual activity and romance in the ancient world. "It was the sweetheart tree of the ancient world" (Glickman, 96).

The last part of verse 5 is an example of Hebrew parallelism. **There your mother conceived you, there she who was in labor gave you birth.** Garrett pointed out:

She calls her beloved an apple tree in 2:3 and thus the figure of his mother being "under the apple tree" means that his mother was with his father. Similarly, the place where his mother conceived and gave birth to him refers to the female parts. . . . The woman means she and he are now participating in the same act by which the man himself was given life" (Garrett, 426).

As we have seen throughout the Song of Songs, sex is an important and significant part of a good marriage—and with good reason. Married sex is more satisfying than recreational sex or cohabiting sex for both men and women (Karen S. Petersen, "Quick Lessons for a Long Marriage," *USA Today*, 3 July 2000). Indeed, Linda Waite, coauthor of *The Case for Marriage,* said, "Just being married seems to improve women's satisfaction with sex . . . while marriage works for men sexually by giving them an active and varied sex life."

But we do need to be fair and honest about this area. Sometimes, as we have seen in the Song, the sparks don't fly and the flame is barely at pilot light. Why? The reasons vary. Barbara DeAngelis, author of *How to Make Love All the Time,* warns us of five traps we must avoid.

1. Waiting until late at night to have sex
2. Falling prey to statistics paranoia
3. Stalling until you're in the mood for sex
4. Getting completely out of the habit
5. Using fatigue as a cover-up for other problems

Barbara quickly counters, however, with a fourfold strategy to turn things around.

1. Plan time for sex
2. Plan decompression time after work
3. Give yourself permission to have "quickies"
4. Stop trying to fill a sexual quota; enjoy the sex you do have

(DeAngelis, "Are You Too Tired for Sex?" *Family Circle,* 16 October 1990, pp. 32–37).

This is sound counsel. Coupled with the advice we receive in the Song, we can look forward confidently and expectantly to those private times for love.

 Love Is Personal (8:6)

SUPPORTING IDEA: *Make sure your love reaches the heart of your mate.*

8:6. Shulammite asked her husband to set her as **a seal over** his **heart**. A person's seal was extremely important and personal. In part, it indicated ownership and was placed upon a person's most valued possessions. This wife wanted to know she was her husband's most personal and valuable possession. She wanted to be a seal, but a seal placed in a particular location: upon his heart. In the world of Solomon, it was often customary to wear a signet ring or cylinder seal on a cord or necklace around the neck and near the heart. For Solomon to love his wife in such a way that she felt she was his valued seal located near his heart would speak of unbreakable devotion and commitment.

D Love Is Protective (8:6)

SUPPORTING IDEA: *Love shields and guards the object of its affections from harm or danger.*

8:6. Shulammite also desired to be a permanent possession upon her husband's arm. The arm speaks of strength and security. This woman understood that in true love there was always a feeling of safety. There is rest in the relationship we enjoy with our mate. True love does have a protective attitude. You desire to shield the one you love from any harm, from any injury, from any damage, from anything that will be detrimental in any way.

One key to this protective component of love is knowledge. The better we know our mate, the better equipped we are to give them "protective love."

E Love Is Possessive (8:6)

SUPPORTING IDEA: *There is a healthy jealousy when it comes to marriage.*

8:6. Love is said to be **as strong as death**, **jealousy** as cruel or **unyielding as the grave**. Love is both universal and unavoidable just like death. This is the only occurrence of the word **strong** in the Song. The word means "an irresistible assailant or an immovable defender" (Carr, 170). When love calls, its siren sound is so compelling you cannot resist it. Love "never releases those whom it has once seized" (Garrett, 426).

"Jealousy" may not be the best English translation because of the negative meaning we normally attach to this word. In this context the idea is parallel to the phrase "strong as death" and means a strong emotional attachment to a particular person or thing. This type of love is possessive and exclusive. It swallows men and women once it has gripped them, just as possessively and certainly as does the grave (Garrett, 426). "In godly love a righteous jealousy is as hard or inevitable as the grave" (Patterson, 117). It will not let go.

In football, coaches try to motivate with a saying that goes something like this: "When the going gets tough, the tough get going." That may well be true. However, of one thing I am certain: "When the going gets tough, love keeps going." It refuses to quit, drop out of the race, throw in the towel, or let go of the object of its affection.

Love Is Powerful (8:6)

SUPPORTING IDEA: *No passion can rival that of love.*

8:6. Love **burns like blazing fire, like a mighty flame**. The emphasis here is on the power and intensity of the fire. The last syllable of "flame" in the Hebrew text could refer to the divine name of the Lord, Yahweh. The Jerusalem Bible, American Standard Version (1901), and the NIV (marginal reading) take it this way. If this is correct, God himself is seen as the source of this love. The power of its nature would therefore only be strengthened. The love God kindles in a marriage over which he is Lord is such a fervent and fiery flame that nothing on earth can extinguish it or put it out. Like a raging forest fire, it burns with such intensity that no one can control it. This is a passionate love, a red-hot flame.

Love Is Persevering (8:7a)

SUPPORTING IDEA: *True love never quits; it never gives up.*

8:7a. Marriage is meant to last, and so is love. It is not for a season but for a lifetime. Solomon teaches us that the love God gives cannot be stopped; its flame cannot be put out. Though **many waters** or even floods come against it, it will not be extinguished. It will persevere. "The tenacious staying power of love is set against these tides and perennial rivers which are unable to wash love away or put out its sparks" (Carr, 171). True love—God's kind of love—is persevering.

Love Is Priceless (8:7b)

SUPPORTING IDEA: *True love cannot be purchased. It is a gift freely given.*

8:7b. True love cannot be bought. It has no price tag. It is not for sale. If a person were to give all he owned to try to buy love, he would be despised and scorned, subjected to public ridicule and mockery. "By its very nature love must be given. Sex can be bought, love must be given" (Glickman, 101).

Love Is Pure (8:8–9)

SUPPORTING IDEA: *True love is holy and undefiled, honoring the commands of God.*

8:8–9. Verses 8–12 probably should be understood as a flashback to Shulammite's youth and initial meeting of Solomon. She grew up in a family where her brothers had been tough on her (1:6), but they were also protective. They watched over her and gave attention to her moral development and maturity. Even at a young age when she was a little or **young sister** and **her breasts** had **not yet grown**, they kept an eye out for her as they considered the time when she would give herself to a man in marriage. **If she is a wall** speaks of moral purity and unavailability. If she demonstrated such character, they would honor her as **towers of silver**. She would be given freedom and responsibility.

On the other hand, **if she is a door**, indicating moral vulnerability and weakness, they would **enclose her** and board her up in order to protect her. If she was reckless and irresponsible in her behavior, they would restrict her freedom and opportunities for sexual misbehavior and foolishness. Shulammite's family was wise in their guidance of this young woman. Unfortunately, far too few families today provide this needed guidance. The fallout has been tragic.

Love Is Peaceful (8:10)

SUPPORTING IDEA: *Love fosters calm and tranquility in life's relationships.*

8:10. Shulammite provided a personal word concerning her chaste moral disposition and value to her husband. She had kept herself morally pure for her husband. She was a virgin when they married. Further, she was now a vibrant, sensual, mature woman of God whose breasts were **like towers**. When the time came for marriage, she was ready in every way, and her husband enjoyed the benefits. The text says **in his eyes** she brought **contentment** or "peace." The Hebrew word is *shalom*. It means wholeness, completeness, and wellness in every part of life. Shulammite made her husband complete. She was the "helper suitable just for him" (Gen. 2:18). In her presence he was set at ease. He found peace and favor, pleasure and rejuvenation.

K Love Is Privileged (8:11–12)

SUPPORTING IDEA: *Love is a gift saved for and given to our mate and our mate only.*

8:11–12. The exact meaning of these verses is vague at best. It seems that the main point was a contrast between Solomon's right to administer his possessions as he chose (v. 11) and Shulammite's right to give herself as she determined (v. 12). **Solomon had a vineyard in Baal Hamon** (location unknown). **Tenants** oversaw it, and they were to grow enough from the vineyard to produce **a thousand shekels of silver**. In return they would receive **two hundred** pieces of silver. This constituted a five-to-one profit for Solomon. This was within his rights because the land belonged to him and he had entered into a contract with the tenants of the vineyard.

Shulammite also had her own vineyard—her body (cf. 1:6). She belonged to no one; therefore, she had the right and privilege to give herself and her love to whomever she chose. Solomon's vineyard was a possession and impersonal. Her vineyard was a person and thus intimately personal. Gladly, freely, and willingly she had given herself to Solomon to be his wife. Solomon may have had thousands of possessions, but she came as a gift.

L Love Is Particular (8:13–14)

SUPPORTING IDEA: *Love has a special concern for the one whom it loves.*

8:13–14. We have arrived at the end of our Song and the last two verses. Appropriately, both the husband and the wife speak. Shulammite was in the gardens—she who herself was a garden (cf. 4:12–16). She was a source of perpetual life, joy, excitement, and pleasure to her husband. Friends or companions listened carefully for the voice of this unique and gifted woman. But Solomon wanted to hear her. His request was exclusive and particular. Others may have longed to hear her and see her (cf. 6:13), but she was his and his alone. He asked her to call out to him. She was not a possession but a person. She was not a slave but a partner. The love she gave was freely given.

She responded by inviting him again to go away with her, and she told him to hurry! She told him to be free in his sensual feelings for her **like a gazelle or like a young stag**. She invited him to the **spice-laden mountains**, a reference to her breasts and the pleasures he would find there. Only her lover, her beloved, was welcomed there, and he was always welcomed. They had been married for some time, but the passion and intensity of their love had not waned. This is God's intention. This is God's plan.

MAIN IDEA REVIEW: *True love is a multifaceted gift that we choose to give our mate again and again.*

III. CONCLUSION

The Measure of True Love

The following questions can help you analyze your feelings about a possible love relationship. There are no right or wrong answers. Indicate your answer to each question by checking "Yes," "No," or "?". Use the question mark only when you are certain that you cannot answer "Yes" or "No." The inventory will be more helpful if both you and your fiancé take it and then discuss it.

1. Have the two of your ever worked through a definite disagreement or conflict of interest to the complete satisfaction of both? ❑ Yes ❑ No ❑ ?

2. Do the two of you progress in your conversations to new views and ideas? ❑ Yes ❑ No ❑ ?

3. Do you find yourself storing up experiences and ideas to share with your friend? ❑ Yes ❑ No ❑ ?

4. Are there certain things about your friend that you plan to reform after you are married? ❑ Yes ❑ No ❑ ?

5. Do you find yourself organizing your plans around this person? ❑ Yes ❑ No ❑ ?

6. Are you proud to have other persons for whom you have a high regard to meet your friend? ❑ Yes ❑ No ❑ ?

7. Does the presence or influence of your friend stir intellectual activity or provide inspiration for you? ❑ Yes ❑ No ❑ ?

8. Are the two of you in agreement on your feelings toward and the handling of children? ❑ Yes ❑ No ❑ ?

9. Would you have full confidence in trusting your friend in the presence of another attractive person of your sex for an evening? ❑ Yes ❑ No ❑ ?

10. Do you at times feel uncertain, uneasy, or possessive in your relationship? ❑ Yes ❑ No ❑ ?

11. When outside trouble develops, does it tend to pull you closer together rather than further apart? ❑ Yes ❑ No ❑ ?

12. Have you established sexual standards by open discussion, and cooperatively, so that each feels satisfied with the decision reached? ❑ Yes ❑ No ❑ ?

13. Do you enjoy each other's company when you are together for an evening with no specific activities planned? ❑ Yes ❑ No ❑ ?

14. Do you ever wonder if he or she is sincere in what he or she tells you? ❑ Yes ❑ No ❑ ?

15. Do you feel pangs of jealousy when someone else of your sex pays attention to your friend? ❑ Yes ❑ No ❑ ?

16. Do you find generally that you like the same people? ❑ Yes ❑ No ❑ ?

17. Are there certain things you need to avoid saying or doing lest there be hurt feelings? ❑ Yes ❑ No ❑ ?

18. Can you mention specific things or
    characteristics about your friend that you like? ❑ Yes ❑ No ❑ ?

19. Do you like his or her outlook on life and
    the values that he or she holds? ❑ Yes ❑ No ❑ ?

20. Have you come to understand each other
    mainly through talking or through
    experiences you have had together? ❑ Yes ❑ No ❑ ?

PRACTICAL PRINCIPLES AND APPLICATIONS

- Strong love is rooted in protective, caring relationships.
- Strong love is a result of good personal judgment and decisions.
- Strong love is fashioned in the anvil of adversity.
- Strong love is achieved by choosing to improve yourself rather than focusing on your mate's inadequacies.
- Love deepens only as God's principles are learned and applied.
- God is the author and source of true love.
- Mutual satisfaction is foundational to human love.
- Mutual satisfaction is not only complementary, but it is also exclusive. One man for one woman for a lifetime is the pattern.
- In true love there is rest, joy, and courage.
- Human and spiritual life find their greatest fulfillment in the experience of mutual love.

IV. LIFE APPLICATION

Our Marriage Covenant

BELIEVING that God, in his wisdom and providence, has established marriage as a covenant relationship, a sacred and lifelong promise, reflecting our unconditional love for one another and believing that God intends for the marriage covenant to reflect his promise never to leave us nor forsake us, we, the undersigned, do hereby reaffirm our solemn pledge to fulfill our marriage vows. Furthermore, we pledge to exalt the sacred nature and permanence of the marriage covenant by calling others to honor and fulfill their marriage vows.

IN THE PRESENCE of God and these witnesses, and by a holy covenant, I, (husband's name), joyfully receive you as God's perfect gift for me, to have and to hold from this day forward, for better, for worse, for richer, for poorer, in sickness and in health, to love you, to honor you, to cherish you and protect you, forsaking all others as long as we both shall live.

Husband's Signature _____

IN THE PRESENCE of God and these witnesses, and by a holy covenant, I, (wife's name), joyfully receive you as God's perfect gift for me, to have and to hold from this day forward, for better, for worse, for richer, for poorer, in sickness and in health, to love you, to honor you, to cherish you and protect you, forsaking all others as long as we both shall live.

Wife's Signature _____

Witnessed this _____ *day of* _____, 20 ____

Witness _____

Witness _____

Unless the LORD builds the house,
its builders labor in vain (Ps. 127:1).

V. PRAYER

Dear Father, I want to love my mate like Solomon describes in Song of Songs 8:5–14 and Paul describes in 1 Corinthians 13. I want to love my mate like you love me: unconditionally, no strings attached. Help me to grow in my knowledge of what love is and in my commitment to what I must do. Thank you for the matchless example of your love for me in Christ. I aspire to love my mate and others just like you have loved me. In Jesus' name. Amen.

VI. DEEPER DISCOVERIES

A. Love

The New Testament counterpart to Song of Songs 8:5–14 is found in 1 Corinthians 13. Following an adaption of that text by Howard Hendricks, we can see what real love looks like when lived out in the real world. Note how these "10 Yardsticks for Love" reflect the truths of Song of Songs 8:5–14 and 1 Corinthians 13.

1. *True love involves a responsiveness to the "total self" of the one loved.* You do not fall in love with a body. You fall in love with a person. Indeed, it is better stated: "You grow in love with a person." In a proper love relationship, you enrich the totality of the other person's life.

2. *In true love there is not only a feeling of pleasure but also of respect, even reverence.* Do you ever look at your wife, or your husband, and think, God gave her to me? God hand-tooled him for me?

3. *True love has a quality of self-giving.* God so loved the world that he gave (John 3:16; 1 John 4:9–10). Many people are in love only with themselves. The smallest package in all the world is the person who is all wrapped up with himself. In true love a person thinks more of the happiness of others than he does of himself.

4. *Love embraces a willingness to take responsibility as well as to accept joy.* A person constantly asks himself not what he can get out of a relationship but what he can give to it. For example, marriage is not just a matter of finding the right partner. It's a question of being the right person.

5. *True love is marked by unusual joy while in the company of the other and pain in separation.* Magnetism and companionship develop in love.

6. *There is a mutual enjoyment of each other without the constant need of physical expression.* It is joy simply to be in the presence of the one

you love. Many people have experienced the great satisfaction there is in just being in the same room with that special one.

7. *True love has a protective attitude.* You desire to shield the one you love from any harm, from any injury, from any damage, from anything that will be detrimental in any way. One of the most lethal weapons in a relationship is the little chipping at each other with sarcastic barbs. This is especially hurtful when done in front of others. You develop a person by magnifying his strengths, not his weaknesses. Take pride in each other.

8. *In true love there is a feeling of belongingness.* The person in love always thinks of himself in relationship to the other person, and it's a beautiful way to live. What is he doing? What is she doing? What is he thinking? What is she feeling?

9. *True love has a feeling that you understand each other unusually well.* You feel the same way about important things because there is a fusing of minds. When a couple's communication system is developed, each learns how the other thinks.

10. *Real love matures.* It is dynamic in its growth. Real love, centered in Christ, takes on the characteristics of Christ. It begins to resemble the love Solomon described in Song of Songs 8:5–14 and Paul described in 1 Corinthians 13.

VII. TEACHING OUTLINE

A. INTRODUCTION: LOVE OR INFATUATION?

B. COMMENTARY

1. Love Is Public (8:5a)
2. Love Is Private (8:5b)
3. Love Is Personal (8:6)
4. Love Is Protective (8:6)
5. Love Is Possessive (8:6)
6. Love Is Powerful (8:6)
7. Love Is Persevering (8:7a)
8. Love Is Priceless (8:7b)
9. Love Is Pure (8:8–9)
10. Love Is Peaceful (8:10)
11. Love Is Privileged (8:11–12)
12. Love Is Particular (8:13–14)

C. CONCLUSION: THE MEASURE OF TRUE LOVE

VIII. ISSUES FOR DISCUSSION

1. Have you developed common interests? What do you know about each other's occupation and interests? Try to put yourself mentally into his or her situation to foster mutual understanding.

2. Are you sharpening your sensitivity quotient? Observe your partner for signs of satisfaction, frustration, or weariness and react appropriately.

3. Are you learning to listen? Don't pry open a closed mind, but when he or she talks voluntarily, listen attentively and intelligently.

4. Are you working at making yourself a more interesting and desirable person? Keep mentally and physically fit and fresh, so that you are magnetic to your mate (watch out for those tired late-night conversations).

5. Do you try to avoid the "sore spots" in conversation? Always approach "danger" areas with proper timing and sensitivity. Be emotionally prepared and environmentally aware.

6. Have you learned to accept criticism in a spirit of love and meekness? Try to examine yourself realistically from the viewpoint of your partner.

7. Do you discuss problems with a willingness to settle for limited objectives (not having your way!) if necessary? Remember, your overall relationship is more important than winning a temporary "victory."

8. Do you have a recreational program so you can relax and "let off steam"?

9. As a wife, do you recognize that you need to siphon off tension? Work at being calm and cool headed. As a husband, are you decisive and reassuring in your love?

10. Do you take at least one annual time-out for a husband-wife "retreat" away from home? Evaluate the past and set goals for the future and get away for some time just for the two of you.

Glossary

Song of Songs

Baal Hamon (8:11) lit. "lord of a crowd"; otherwise an unknown location, possibly a reference to a vineyard of which Shulammite was made an overseer (cf. 1:6).

Bath Rabbim (7:4) lit. "daughter of many"; it is an unknown location, possibly parallel to Heshbon, located at the east side of the Dead Sea.

Calamus (4:14) the aromatic peeled and dried rhizome of sweet cane that is the source of a carcinogenic essential oil.

Chrysolite (5:14) greenish mineral that is a complex silicate of magnesium and iron.

Crest of Amana (4:8) location uncertain, probably near the source of the clean waters of the Amana (cf. 2 Kings 5:12).

Damascus (7:4) capital city of Syria, to the northeast of Israel.

Daughters of Jerusalem (1:5; 2:7; 3:5, 10, 11; 5:8, 16; 8:4) group of maidens addressed only by Shulammite in the Song, apparently they are her younger companions. They serve as a chorus group speaking and receiving instruction throughout the Song.

Does (2:7; 3:5) adult female fallow deer.

En Gedi (1:14) fertile area halfway down the western shore of the Dead Sea. David took refuge from Saul in the area.

Fawns (4:5; 7:3) young deer.

Friends (1:4) the onlookers in the Song; see commentary.

Gazelles (2:7,9,17; 3:5; 4:5; 7:3; 8:14) graceful, swift African and Asian antelopes noted for their fertility, agility, and soft lustrous eyes.

Goblet (7:2) bowl-shaped drinking vessel.

Henna (1:14; 4:13) a common Palestinian shrub with fragrant blossoms.

Heshbon (7:4) a Moabite city lying fifty miles east of Jerusalem.

Kedar (1:5) the name refers to the tents of the Bedouin, which were made with black goat hair.

Lattice (2:9) ventilated wall surrounding a garden.

Lebanon (3:9; 4:8,11,15; 5:15; 7:4) mountain range in the northwest part of the land serving as a natural border between Phoenicia and Israel and Syria.

Lilies (2:1,2,16; 4:5; 5:13; 6:2,3; 7:2) a scarlet anemone that grows wild in Palestine.

Mahanaim (6:13) probably refers to two armies or two hosts.

Mandrakes (7:13) Mediterranean herb of the nightshade family with ovate leaves, whitish or purple flowers, and a large forked root traditionally credited with human attributes and thought to promote conception.

Mare (1:9) a mature female horse of breeding age.

Myrrh (1:13; 3:6; 4:6,14; 5:1,5,13) a yellowish-brown to reddish-brown aromatic gum resin with a bitter, slightly pungent taste obtained from trees of east Africa and Arabia.

Mount Carmel (7:5) just south of the modern city Haifa, directly west from the sea of Galilee. Site of Elijah's encounter with 450 prophets of Baal (1 Kings 18).

Mount Gilead (4:1; 6:5) high plateau east of Galilee and Samaria with rugged cliffs as high as thirty-five hundred feet above the floor of the Jordan Valley.

Nard (4:13–14) a fragrant ointment possibly gained from an East Indian aromatic plant of the same name.

Pomegranate (4:3,13; 6:7,11; 7:12; 8:2) a thick-skinned, several-celled reddish berry that is about the size of an orange and has many seeds with pulpy crimson arils of tart flavor.

Pools of Heshbon (7:4) Heshbon was a Moabite city lying fifty miles east of Jerusalem. The reference to pools is likely meant to call up images of calm, still waters.

Ruddy (5:10) red, possibly used to evoke Solomon's Davidic bearing (cf. 1 Samuel 16:12; 17:42).

Rugged Hills (2:17) as the NIV margin indicates, this may be a reference to the "Hills of Bether." Since no geographic location seems to bear this description, many see here a euphemism for the woman's breasts.

Saffron (1:14) the deep orange aromatic pungent dried stigmas of a purple flowered crocus used to color and flavor foods and formerly as a dyestuff and in medicine.

Sachet of Myrrh (1:13) small cloth or pouch of fragrant resinous gum worn next to the body to enhance the smell of one's physical person.

Sapphires (5:14) a gem variety of corundum in transparent or translucent crystals of a color other than red (usually blue or deep purplish blue).

Senir (4:8) Amorite name for Mount Hermon (cf. Deut. 3:9).

Sharon (2:1) coastal plain between Joppa and Mount Carmel, renowned for its fertility and beauty.

Shekels (8:11-12) an ancient coin, a monetary unit.

Stag (2:9,17; 8:14) an adult male red deer.

Tapestry (7:5) a heavy handwoven reversible textile used for hangings, curtains, and upholstery and characterized by complicated pictorial designs.

Tirzah (6:4) an elegant city six miles east of Samaria which became the capital of the northern kingdom after Solomon's death (1 Kings 14:17).

Tower of David (4:4) likely alluded to in Nehemiah 3:25: "projecting from the upper house of the king at the court of the guard."

Verdant (1:16) green with growing plants; figurative of life and growth.

Bibliography

Ecclesiastes

Allen, Diogenes. *Spiritual Theology: The Theology of Yesterday for Spiritual Help Today.* Cambridge: Cowley Publications, 1997.

Allen, Woody. "My Speech to the Graduates." *The New York Times,* 10 August 1979, A25.

Ambrose. "Duties of the Clergy" in *Nicene and Post-Nicene Fathers.* Second Series, vol. 10. Peabody, Mass.: Hendrickson Publishers, 1994.

_____. "Letter LXIII" in *Nicene and Post-Nicene Fathers.* Second Series, vol. 10. Peabody, Mass.: Hendrickson Publishers, 1994.

_____. "On Repentance" in *Nicene and Post-Nicene Fathers.* Second Series, vol. 10. Peabody, Mass.: Hendrickson Publishers, 1994.

Amiel, Barbara. "Saddam Is Not a Human Being." *Macleans,* 4 March 1991, 15.

Anonymous. "Two Epistles Concerning Virginity" in *Ante-Nicene Fathers.* Vol. 8. Peabody, Mass.: Hendrickson Publishers, 1994.

Athanasius. *On the Incarnation.* Crestwood, N.Y.: St. Vladimir's Seminary Press, 1993.

Augustine, Aurelius. "On the Gospel of John" in *Nicene and Post-Nicene Fathers.* First Series, vol. 7. Peabody, Mass.: Hendrickson Publishers, 1994.

_____. "On Marriage and Concupiscence" in *Nicene and Post-Nicene Fathers.* First Series, vol. 7. Peabody, Mass.: Hendrickson Publishers, 1994.

_____. "Sermons on New Testament Lessons" in *Nicene and Post-Nicene Fathers.* First Series, vol. 6. Peabody, Mass.: Hendrickson Publishers, 1994.

_____. *The City of God.* Vol. 18 of the Great Books Edition. Chicago: Encyclopaedia Britannica, 1952.

_____. *The Confessions of St. Augustine.* Edited by Paul M. Bechtel. Chicago: Moody Press, 1981.

Banks, Robert. *The Tyranny of Time.* Downers Grove, Ill.: InterVarsity Press, 1983.

Banks, Robert, and R. Paul Stevens, eds. *The Complete Book of Everyday Christianity.* Downers Grove, Ill.: InterVarsity Press, 1997.

Basil the Great. "Letter CCLXIII" in *Nicene and Post-Nicene Fathers.* Second Series, vol. 8. Peabody, Mass.: Hendrickson Publishers, 1994.

Becker, Ernest. *The Denial of Death*. New York: Simon & Schuster, 1973.

Bellah, Robert N., et al. *Habits of the Heart*. Berkeley: University of California Press, 1985.

Bennett, William J., ed. *The Book of Virtues*. New York: Simon & Schuster, 1993.

Blomberg, Craig L. *Neither Poverty nor Riches*. Grand Rapids: Eerdmans. 1999.

Bloom, Allan. *The Closing of the American Mind*. New York: Simon & Schuster, 1987.

Brander, B. G. *Staring into Chaos: Explorations in the Decline of Western Civilization*. Dallas: Spence Publishing, 1998.

Bridges, Charles. *The Geneva Series of Commentaries: Ecclesiastes*. Carlisle, Penn.: The Banner of Truth Trust, 1961.

Brodie, Fawn M. *Thomas Jefferson: An Intimate Biography*. New York: Bantam Books, 1974.

Brown, Raymond E., Joseph A. Fitzmyer, and Roland E. Murphy, eds. *The Jerome Biblical Commentary*. Englewood Cliffs, N.J.: Prentice-Hall, 1968.

Bunyan, John. *The Pilgrim's Progress*. New York: Signet Classics, 1964.

Burroughs, Jeremiah. *A Treatise of Earthly Mindedness*. Morgan, Pa: Soli Deo Gloria Publications, 1991.

Bush, George. *All the Best: My Life in Letters and Other Writings*. New York: Simon & Schuster, 1999.

Calvin, John. *Institutes of the Christian Religion*. Vol. 1. Translated by Henry Beveridge. Grand Rapids: Eerdmans, 1983.

Carson, D. A. *Exegetical Fallacies*. Grand Rapids: Baker Book House, 1984.

Cassian, John. "The Conferences" in *Nicene and Post-Nicene Fathers*. Second Series, vol. 11. Peabody, Mass.: Hendrickson Publishers, 1994.

Chan, Simon. *Spiritual Theology*. Downers Grove, Ill.: InterVarsity Press, 1998.

Chrysostom. "Concerning the Statues" in *Nicene and Post-Nicene Fathers*. First Series, vol. 9. Peabody, Mass.: Hendrickson Publishers, 1994.

Clement of Rome. "Two Epistles Concerning Virginity" in *Ante-Nicene Fathers*. vol. 8. Peabody, Mass.: Hendrickson Publishers, 1994.

Covey, Stephen R. *The 7 Habits of Highly Effective People*. New York: Simon & Schuster, 1989.

Covey, Sephen R., A. Roger Merrill, and Rebecca R. Merrill. *First Things First*. New York: Simon & Schuster, 1994.

Crenshaw, James L. *Ecclesiastes: A Commentary*. Philadelphia: The Westminster Press, 1987.

Davidson, Robert. *The Daily Study Bible: Ecclesiastes and the Song of Solomon.* Philadelphia: The Westminster Press, 1986.

Defoe, Daniel. *Robinson Crusoe.* New York: Penguin Books, 1970.

Dillard, Annie. *Teaching a Stone to Talk.* New York: Harper Collins Publishers, 1982.

Dostoevsky, Fyodor. *The Brothers Karamazov.* Vol. 52 of the Great Books Edition. Chicago: Encyclopaedia Britannica, 1952.

Drakulić, Slavenka. *Café Europa.* New York: Penguin Books, 1996.

Dreyfous, Leslie. "The Pursuit of Happiness." *The Arizona Republic,* 13 September 1992, A2.

Eaton, Michael A. *Tyndale Old Testament Commentary: Ecclesiastes.* Downers Grove, Ill.: InterVarsity Press, 1983.

Edwards, Jonathan. *The Works of Jonathan Edwards.* 2 vols. Rev. by Edward Hickman. Carlisle, Pa.: The Banner of Truth Trust, 1990.

Elliot, Elisabeth. *Shadow of the Almighty.* New York: Harper & Row Publishers, 1956.

Ellul, Jacques. *Reason for Being.* Translated by Joyce Main Hanks. Grand Rapids: Eerdmans, 1990.

Erickson, Millard J. *Christian Theology.* Grand Rapids: Baker Book House, 1983–85.

Fineman, Howard. "The Virtuecrats." *Newsweek,* 13 June 1994, 31–36.

Flew, Antony. *A Dictionary of Philosophy.* Rev. ed. New York: St. Martin's Press, 1979.

Foster, Richard J. *Celebration of Discipline.* Rev. ed. San Francisco: Harper & Row Publishers, 1988.

Garrett, Duane A. *The New American Commentary: Proverbs, Ecclesiastes and Song of Songs.* Nashville: Broadman Press, 1993.

Goodwin, Doris Kearns. *Lyndon Johnson and the American Dream.* San Francisco: Harper & Row. 1976.

_____. "Commencement Address at Dartmouth College." 14 June 1998, 1–2 (Internet copy).

Gregory of Nazianzen. "On His Father's Silence" in *Nicene and Post-Nicene Fathers.* Second Series, vol. 7. Peabody, Mass.: Hendrickson Publishers, 1994.

Gregory of Nyssa. "On the Making of Man" in *Nicene and Post-Nicene Fathers.* Second Series, vol. 5. Peabody, Mass.: Hendrickson Publishers, 1994.

_____. "On Virginity" in *Nicene and Post-Nicene Fathers.* Second Series, vol. 5. Peabody, Mass.: Hendrickson Publishers, 1994.

Guinness, Os. *The Call.* Nashville: Word Publishing, 1998.

Bibliography

Harris, R. Laird, Gleason L. Archer, and Bruce K. Waltke. *Theological Wordbook of the Old Testament*. Vol. 1. Chicago: Moody Press, 1980.

Hart, B. H. Liddell. *Scipio Africanus: Greater Than Napoleon*. New York: Capo Press, 1926.

Hemingway, Ernest. *The Old Man and the Sea*. New York: Charles Scribner's Sons, 1952.

Henrichsen, Walter A. Various conversations with the author.

Henry, Matthew. *A Commentary of the Whole Bible: Ecclesiastes*. Old Tappan, N.J.: Fleming H. Revell Company, n.d.

Himmelfarb, Gertrude. *The Demoralization of Society: From Victorian Virtues to Modern Values*. New York: Knopf Publishers, 1994.

Homer. *The Iliad*. Vol. 4 of the Great Books Edition. Chicago: Encyclopaedia Britannica, 1952.

———. *The Odyssey*. Vol. 4 of the Great Books Edition. Chicago: Encyclopaedia Britannica, 1952.

Houston, James. *The Heart's Desire*. Colorado Springs: NavPress, 1996.

Jerome. "Letter XLVII to Pammachius" in *Nicene and Post-Nicene Fathers*. Second Series, vol. 6. Peabody, Mass.: Hendrickson Publishers, 1994.

Johnston, Robert K. "Confessions of a Workaholic: A Reappraisal of Qoheleth." *The Catholic Biblical Quarterly* 38 (1976): 14–28.

Kaiser, Walter C., Jr. *Everyman's Bible Commentary: Ecclesiastes*. Chicago: Moody Press, 1979.

Keddie, Gordon J. *Looking for the Good Life*. Phillipsburg, N.J.: Presbyterian and Reformed Publishing Company, 1991.

Kempis, Thomas à. *The Imitation of Christ*. Springdale, Pa.: Whitaker House, 1974.

Keyes, Dick. *True Heroism*. Colorado Springs: NavPress, 1995.

Kidner, Derek. *The Bible Speaks Today: Ecclesiastes*. Downers Grove, Ill.: InterVarsity Press, 1976.

Kierkegaard, Søren. *Purity of Heart Is to Will One Thing*. Translated by Douglas Van Steere. New York: Harper & Row Publishers, 1938.

Kinsley, Michael. "You Must Be Very Busy." *Time*, 20 August 1990, 82.

Kreeft, Peter. *Three Philosophies of Life*. San Francisco: Ignatius Press, 1989.

Kushner, Harold S. *When Bad Things Happen to Good People*. New York: Schocken Books, 1981.

Law, William. *A Serious Call to a Devout and Holy Life*. Edited and abridged by John W. Meister et al. Philadelphia: The Westminster Press, 1955.

Leithart, Peter. *A House for My Name*. Moscow, Idaho: Canon Press, 2000.

Leupold, H. C. *Exposition of Ecclesiastes*. Grand Rapids: Baker Book House, 1952.

Lewis, C. S. *The Problem of Pain*. New York: The Macmillan Co., 1962.

_____. *The Weight of Glory and Other Addresses*. San Francisco: Harper Collins Publishers, 1976.

Lockerbie, D. Bruce. *Dismissing God: Modern Writers' Struggle Against Religion*. Grand Rapids: Baker Books, 1998.

Longman, Tremper, III. *Ecclesiastes*. In The New International Commentary on the Old Testament. Grand Rapids: Eerdmans, 1998.

_____. Personal correspondence with the author. 6 February 2002.

Luther, Martin. *Notes on Ecclesiastes*. Vol. 15. Edited by Jaroslav Pelikan. St. Louis: Concordia Publishing House, 1972.

Marshall, Paul, and Lela Gilbert. *Heaven Is Not My Home*. Nashville: Word Publishing, 1998.

Martin, John A. "Old Testament History II and Poetry Class Notes." Dallas Theological Seminary, Fall 1992.

McCullough, David. *John Adams*. New York: Simon & Schuster, 2001.

McCullough, Donald W. *The Trivialization of God*. Colorado Springs: NavPress, 1995.

Moore, David George. *The Battle for Hell*. Lanham, Md.: University Press of America, 1995.

Moore, T. M. *Ecclesiastes: Ancient Wisdom When All Else Fails*. Downers Grove, Ill.: InterVarsity Press, 2001.

More, Thomas. *Be Merry in God*. Selections compiled by Paul Thigpen. Ann Arbor, Mich.: Servant Publications, 1999.

Morley, Patrick M. *The Man in the Mirror*. Brentwood, Tenn.: Wolegmuth and Hyatt Publishers, 1989.

Morrow, Barry L. *Heaven Observed*. Colorado Springs: NavPress, 2001.

Murphy, Roland. *Word Biblical Commentary: Ecclesiastes*. Dallas: Word Publishers, 1992.

Newbigin, Lesslie. *Proper Confidence: Faith, Doubt, and Certainty in Christian Discipleship*. Grand Rapids: Eerdmans, 1995.

Origen. *De Principis* in *Ante-Nicene Fathers*. Vol. 4. Peabody, Mass.: Hendrickson Publishers, 1994.

Packer, J. I. *A Quest for Godliness: The Puritan Vision of the Christian Life*. Wheaton, Ill.: Crossway Books, 1990.

Pascal, Blaise. *Pensées*. Translated by A. J. Krailsheimer. Baltimore: Penguin Books, 1966.

Bibliography

Pentecost, J. David. "Daniel." *The Bible Knowledge Commentary.* Eds. John F. Walvoord and Roy B. Zuck. Wheaton, Ill.: Victor Books, 1985.

Peterson, Eugene H. *A Long Obedience in the Same Direction.* Downers Grove, Ill.: InterVarsity Press, 1980.

_____. *Answering God.* San Francisco: Harper Collins Publishers, 1989.

_____. *The Contemplative Pastor.* Grand Rapids: Eerdmans, 1989.

Peterson, Jim. *Evangelism for Our Generation.* Colorado Springs: NavPress, 1985.

Piper, John. *Desiring God.* Portland: Multnomah Press, 1986.

Postman, Neil. *Amusing Ourselves to Death.* New York: Penguin Books, 1985.

_____. *Technopoly: The Surrender of Culture to Technology.* New York: Vintage Books, 1993.

Provan, Iain. *The NIV Application Commentary: Ecclesiastes, Song of Solomon.* Grand Rapids: Zondervan, 2001.

Richards, Lawrence O. *Youth Ministry.* Grand Rapids: Zondervan, 1972.

Ryken, Leland. *How to Read the Bible as Literature.* Grand Rapids: Zondervan, 1984.

Ryrie, Charles Caldwell. *Ryrie Study Bible.* Expanded ed. Chicago: Moody Press, 1994.

Sayers, Dorothy L. *Creed or Chaos?* Manchester, N.H.: Sophia Institute Press, 1974.

Seow, Choon-Leong. *The Anchor Bible: Ecclesiastes.* New York: Doubleday, 1997.

Shank, H. Carl. "Qoheleth's World and Life View as Seen in His Recurring Phrases." *Westminster Theological Journal,* 37 (1974): 57–73.

Shelley, Percy Bysshe. *Ozymandias* in *A Treasury of the World's Best Loved Poems.* New York: Avenel Books, 1961.

Sire, James W. *The Universe Next Door.* Rev. ed. Downers Grove, Ill.: InterVarsity Press, 1988.

Sproul, R. C. "Dust to Glory: An Overview of the Bible." Orlando: Ligonier Ministries, 1996.

_____. *The Holiness of God.* Wheaton, Ill.: Tyndale House Publishers, 1987.

Stedman, Ray C. *Solomon's Secret: Enjoying Life, God's Good Gift.* Portland: Multnomah Press, 1985.

Swenson, Richard A. *Margin.* Colorado Springs: NavPress, 1992.

Swindoll, Charles R. *Living on the Ragged Edge.* Waco, Tex.: Word Books, 1985.

Thomas, Gary. "Wise Christians Clip Obituaries." *Christianity Today,* 3 October 1994, 24–27.

Tocqueville, Alexis de. *Democracy in America.* Vol. 1. New York: Vintage Books, 1990

Toland, John. *Hitler: The Pictorial Documentary of His Life.* Garden City, N.Y.: Doubleday, 1978.

Tolstoy, Leo. *The Death of Ivan Ilych and Other Stories.* Translated by David Magarshack. New York: Signet Classics, 1960.

Twiestmeyer, Trent. Quote on postcard shared with the author.

Van Boven, Sarah, and Patricia King. "A Killer's Self-Portrait." *Newsweek,* 11 May 1998, 38.

Webb, Barry G. *Five Festal Garments.* Downers Grove, Ill.: InterVarsity Press, 2000.

Wells, David F. *God in the Wasteland.* Grand Rapids: Eerdmans, 1994.

Whybray, R. N. "Qoheleth, Preacher of Joy." *Journal for the Study of the Old Testament,* 23 (1982): 87–98.

———. *The New Century Bible Commentary: Ecclesiastes.* Grand Rapids: Eerdmans, 1989.

Willard, Dallas. *The Divine Conspiracy.* San Francisco: Harper Collins, 1998.

———. *The Spirit of the Disciplines.* San Francisco: Harper Collins, 1988.

Wilson, Carl W. *Our Dance Has Turned to Death.* Atlanta: Renewal Publishing Company, 1979.

Wilson, Douglas. *Joy at the End of the Tether.* Moscow, Idaho: Canon Press, 1999.

Wilson, Marvin R. *Our Father Abraham.* Grand Rapids: Eerdmans, 1989.

Wolfe, Alan. "White Magic in America: Capitalism, Mormonism, and the Doctrines of Stephen Covey." *The New Republic,* 23 February 1998, 26–34.

Woodbridge, John D., ed. *Renewing Your Mind in a Secular World.* Chicago: Moody Press, 1985.

Wright, Addison G. "The Riddle of the Sphinx: The Structure of the Book of Qoheleth." *The Catholic Biblical Quarterly,* 30 (1968): 313–34.

Wright, J. Robert. Author of forthcoming *Ancient Christian Commentary on Scripture: Proverbs, Ecclesiastes, Song of Solomon.* Downers Grove, Ill.: InterVarsity Press. Phone conversation 12 August 2002.

Wright, J. Stafford. *The Expositor's Bible Commentary: Ecclesiastes.* Vol. 5. Edited by Frank E. Gaebelein. Grand Rapids: Zondervan, 1991.

———. "The Interpretation of Ecclesiastes." *Evangelical Quarterly,* 18 (1946): 18–34.

Wyngaarden, Martin J. "The Interpretation of Ecclesiastes." *The Calvin Forum* (1955): 57–60.

Yankelovich, Daniel. *New Rules: Searching for Self-Fulfillment in a World Turned Upside Down*. New York: Bantam Books, 1981.

Young, Ed. *Been There. Done That. Now What?* Nashville: Broadman & Holman, 1994.

Song of Songs

Ayo, N. *Sacred Marriage: The Wisdom of the Song of Songs*. New York: Continuum, 1997.

Balchin, J. "Song of Songs." *The New Bible Commentary*. 4th ed. Downers Grove, Ill.: InterVarsity, 1994.

Block, A., and C. Bloch. *The Song of Songs: A New Translation*. New York: Random House, 1995.

Carr, G. Lloyd. *The Song of Solomon*. Tyndale Old Testament Commentaries. Downers Grove, Ill.: InterVarsity, 1984.

Deere, Jack S. "Song of Songs." *The Bible Knowledge Commentary*. Eds. John F. Walvoord and Roy B. Zuck. Wheaton, Ill.: Victor, 1985.

Delitzsch, F. *Proverbs, Ecclesiastes, Song of Solomon*. Originally published in 1885. Translated by M. G. Easton. Grand Rapids: Eerdmans, 1975.

Dillow, J. C. *Solomon on Sex*. Nashville: Nelson, 1977.

Dillow, Linda, and Lorraine Pintus. *Intimate Issues*. Colorado Springs: Waterbrook, 1999.

Dorsey, David A. *The Literary Structure of the Old Testament: A Commentary on Genesis—Malachi*. Grand Rapids: Baker, 1999.

_____. "Literary Structuring in the Song of Songs." *JSOT* 46. 1990.

Garrett, D. *Proverbs, Ecclesiastes, Song of Songs*. New American Commentary. Nashville: Broadman & Holman, 1993.

Gledhill, T. *The Message of the Song of Songs*. Bible Speaks Today. Downers Grove, Ill.: InterVarsity, 1994.

Glickman, S. C. *A Song for Lovers*. Downers Grove, Ill.: InterVarsity, 1978.

House, Paul. *Old Testament Theology*. Downers Grove, Ill.: InterVarsity, 1998.

Hubbard, D. *Ecclesiastes, Song of Solomon*. Communicator's Commentary. Dallas: Word, 1991.

Keel, O. *The Song of Songs*. A Continental Commentary. Minneapolis: Fortress, 1994.

Kinlaw, D. F. "Song of Songs." *The Expositor's Bible Commentary*. Vol. 5. Grand Rapids: Zondervan, 1991.

Landy, F. *Paradoxes of Paradise: Identity and Difference in the Song of Songs*. Sheffied: Almond, 1983.

Nelson, Tommy. *The Book of Romance*. Nashville: Nelson, 1998.

Patterson, Paige. *Song of Solomon.* Chicago: Moody, 1986.

Piper, John. *Desiring God: Meditations of a Christian Hedonist.* 2nd ed. Sisters, Oreg.: Multnomah, 1996.

Pope, Marvin H. "A Mare in Pharaoh's Chariotry." *BASOR* 200. 1970.

————. *Song of Songs.* The Anchor Bible, 7C. New York: Doubleday, 1977.

Provan, Iain W. *Ecclesiastes and Song of Songs.* NIV Application Commentary. Grand Rapids: Zondervan, 2001.

Provan, I. "The Terrors of the Night: Love, Sex, and Power in Song of Songs 3." *The Way of Widsom: Essays in Honor of Bruce K. Waltke.* Eds. J. I. Packer and S. K. Soderlund. Grand Rapids: Zondervan, 2000.

Ryken, L., and T. Longman, III, eds. *A Complete Literary Guide to the Bible.* Grand Rapids: Zondervan, 1993.

Shea, W. H. "The Chiastic Structure of the Song of Songs." *ZAW* 92. 1980.

Smalley, Gary, and John Trent. *The Gift of the Blessing.* Nashville: Nelson, 1993.

Snaith, J. G. *Song of Songs.* The New Century Bible Commentary. Grand Rapids: Eerdmans, 1993.

Tanner, J. P. "The History of Interpretation of the Song of Songs." *BibSac* 154. 1997.

Walton, J. H., V. H. Matthews, and M. W. Chavalas. *The Bible Background Commentary: Old Testament.* Downers Grove, Ill.: InterVarsity, 2000.

Webb, B. "The Song of Songs: A Love Poem and as Holy Scripture." *RTR* 49. 1990.

Webb, Barry G. *Five Festal Garments: Christian Reflections on the Song of Songs, Ruth, Lamentations, Ecclesiastes and Esther.* New Studies in Biblical Theology. Downers Grove, Ill.: InterVarsity, 2000.

Wilson, Douglas. *Reforming Marriage.* Moscow, Idaho: Canon Press, 1995.

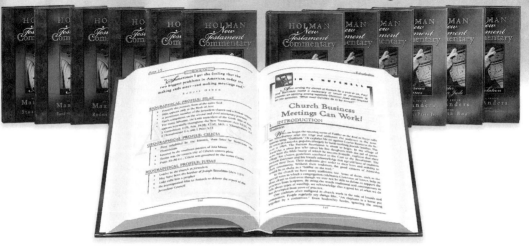